In Fortune's Theater

This innovative cultural history of financial risk-taking in Renaissance Italy argues that a new concept of the future as unknown and unknowable emerged in Italian society between the mid-fifteenth and mid-sixteenth centuries. Exploring the rich interchanges between mercantile and intellectual cultures underpinning this development in four major cities – Florence, Genoa, Venice, and Milan – Nicholas Scott Baker examines how merchants and gamblers, the futurologists of the pre-modern world, understood and experienced their own risk taking and that of others. Drawing on extensive archival research, this study demonstrates that while the Renaissance did not create the modern sense of time, it constructed the foundations on which it could develop. The new conceptions of the past and the future that developed in the Renaissance provided the pattern for the later construction a single narrative beginning in classical antiquity stretching to the now. This book thus makes an important contribution toward laying bare the historical contingency of a sense of time that continues to structure our world in profound ways.

Nicholas Scott Baker is Associate Professor of History at Macquarie University. He is the author of *The Fruit of Liberty: Political Culture in the Florentine Renaissance, 1480–1550* (2013), several articles, and book chapters, and coeditor of two volumes of essays on Italian Renaissance society and culture.

T0384499

In Fortune's Theater

Financial Risk and the Future
in Renaissance Italy

Nicholas Scott Baker

Macquarie University

CAMBRIDGE
UNIVERSITY PRESS

Shaftesbury Road, Cambridge CB2 8EA, United Kingdom

One Liberty Plaza, 20th Floor, New York, NY 10006, USA

477 Williamstown Road, Port Melbourne, VIC 3207, Australia

314–321, 3rd Floor, Plot 3, Splendor Forum, Jasola District Centre, New Delhi – 110025, India

103 Penang Road, #05–06/07, Visioncrest Commercial, Singapore 238467

Cambridge University Press is part of Cambridge University Press & Assessment, a department of the University of Cambridge.

We share the University's mission to contribute to society through the pursuit of education, learning and research at the highest international levels of excellence.

www.cambridge.org
Information on this title: www.cambridge.org/9781108826945

DOI: 10.1017/9781108920674

First published 2021
First paperback edition 2023

A catalogue record for this publication is available from the British Library

ISBN   978-1-108-84388-1   Hardback
ISBN   978-1-108-82694-5   Paperback

Contents

Figures

Preface

I began thinking through some of the ideas that underlie this book in the wake of the economic crisis of 2008 and the global meltdown of speculative financial products and risk systems. That crisis revealed the supposed dichotomy between rational, commercial investment and outright gambling or irrational behavior to be far less distinct than many commentators, policy makers, and regulators had assumed. I am not sure whether it is poignant, bitterly ironic, or something else that I have finished it during another, even more profound and painful period of catastrophe. The timing is purely coincidental, yet the fact that my work on a book about the emergence of an idea of the future-as-unknown has been framed by two worldwide crises resonates deeply and uncomfortably with me.

Completing the final revisions and edits for a book about how people in the past confronted and made sense of the uncertainty and unknowability of the future during the first six months of 2020 has been a surreal experience. The global pandemic and the associated economic collapse have left us all struggling to manage profound uncertainty about the future. It has also cast in relief the continuing complexity and multiplicity of the temporalities in which we live, as well as the foolishness of attempting to draw hard lines between the modern and the premodern. We all know, intellectually, that unexpected and unanticipated events occur, that the future is unknown and frequently unknowable, and yet we also all live our daily lives with an anticipatory sense that tomorrow will be pretty much the same as today until something devastating like our current situation occurs.

Acknowledgments

This book is the culmination of several years' work, which would not have been possible without the assistance, support, and encouragement from many people and institutions. Completing the manuscript of book about financial risk taking and the uncertainty of the future during a time of global pandemic and profound economic recession has made me even more grateful for the help I have received along the way.

The research and writing of the book were made possible by financial support from several different sources. A Research Development Grant from Macquarie University funded the archival trip that prompted a question that set the whole thing in motion. The idyllic year I spent as Jean-François Malle Fellow at Villa I Tatti, the Harvard University Center for Italian Renaissance Studies in Florence, in 2013–14 gave me the time and freedom to develop my early, incoherent thinking into a viable project and to shape a methodology and approach. My initial foray into the Venetian archives in 2015 was made possible by a Gladys Krieble Delmas grant. Most significantly, a Discovery Project grant from the Australian Research Council (DP170101671) provided three years of financial support to complete the research and writing of the manuscript. A Membership in the School of Historical Studies at the Institute for Advanced Study, Princeton, in the first half of 2018 provided the ideal location to complete the initial draft of the manuscript.

Over the years that I have worked on this book I have benefited from the generosity, advice, and constructive critique of friends and scholars around the globe. My colleagues in Modern History at Macquarie University read two chapters in draft versions at our regular work-in-progress group, providing insightful feedback and suggestions on both occasions. The communities of scholars at Villa I Tatti in 2013–14 and the IAS in the northern spring of 2018 provided guidance and companionship at crucial stages along the way. The Early Modern Seminar at IAS workshopped one chapter with me and it is significantly better for that process. I presented papers rehearsing the arguments and ideas presented in the volume at conferences and seminars between

2013 and 2019 in Boston, Denver, Florence, Melbourne, New Orleans, New York, San Diego, Sydney, Toronto, and Vienna. On each occasion, I received perceptive questions and comments from audiences and copresenters alike, for all of which I am grateful. Special mentions to Karl Appuhn, who invited me to share my ideas at NYU's Medieval and Renaissance Center (and who insisted that "finance" had to feature in the book's title); Jeroen Puttevils, who collaborated in organizing several conference panels over many years; and Neslihan Senocak, who invited me to present at Columbia University's Medieval Seminar.

I am particularly indebted to Elena Calvillo, Brian Maxson, Clare Monagle, Sarah Ross, and Jonathan Sachs, who read chapters of the manuscript at various stages and offered thoughtful, crucial advice. I am also very grateful to Cambridge University Press's anonymous readers, who provided generous and constructive criticism. For references, information, and translation advice I am grateful to Davide Baldi, Kate Bentz, John Gagné, and Nerida Newbigin.

Archivists and staff at several archives across Italy facilitated my research throughout the process. I am grateful for the help I received at the Archivio di Stato in Florence, in Genoa, in Milan, and in Venice; the Archivio Storico Civico in Genoa; and the Archivio Storico Civico in Milan. I am also grateful for the assistance I received from libraries around the world, in particular, from Dr. Susanna Pelle at the Biblioteca Nazionale Centrale in Florence, as well as from staff at the Bayerische Staatsbibliothek in Munich, the Biblioteca Berenson in Florence, the Firestone Library at Princeton University, the Getty Research Institute in Los Angeles, and the Historical Studies – Social Science Library at the IAS. In Sydney, the staff of the Inter-Library Loans department at Macquarie University Library worked tirelessly to trace books, chapters, and articles for me. I never cease to be amazed by and grateful for their ability to locate and provide everything I request.

I have rehearsed some of the ideas in this book in less-developed forms in two earlier publications: "Deep Play in Renaissance Italy," in *Rituals of Politics and Culture in Early Modern Europe: Essays in Honour of Edward Muir*, ed. Mark Jurdjevic and Rolf Strøm-Olsen (Toronto: Centre for Reformation and Renaissance Studies, 2016), 259–81; and "Dux ludens: Eleonora de Toledo, Cosimo I de' Medici, and Games of Chance in Ducal Household of Mid-Sixteenth-Century Florence," *European History Quarterly* 46, no. 4 (2016): 595–617.

At Cambridge University Press, Liz Friend-Smith has been an enthusiastic supporter of the project since its very early stages, while Atifa Jiwa and Melissa Ward were always prompt and patient with assistance during the submission and publication processes. For their help with preparing the typescript for publication, I am very grateful to Divya Elavazaghan and copy editor Stephanie Sakson.

I have saved my most important debts to last. Max and Alex have endured my frequent absences, long hours of work, and piles of books and files accumulating on the dining room table with equanimity and even occasional interest. Finally, I am profoundly grateful to Elena, who took a chance on a future with me. Her love, support, and encouragement; her intellectual companionship; and her keen mind and eye have made this book immeasurably better than it otherwise would have been. There is no one with whom I would rather have taken the journey of writing it. Thank you.

Note on the Text

All translations in the text are my own, except where noted.

Different cities in Renaissance Italy had different dates for the beginning of the year. I have standardized all dates in the body of the text to the modern system of 1 January.

Similarly, a wide variety of different currencies circulated in Italy and Europe during the period under examination. They were all based on the Carolingian accounting system of pounds, shillings, and pence, or lire, soldi, and denari in Italian (1 lira = 20 soldi = 240 denari), which served as an artificial money of account. In everyday usage, currencies and denominations varied, and their actual values fluctuated, so consistency is not possible. I have done my best to provide clarity for readers in the footnotes.

Introduction
Histories of the Future

The future began in Italy around the year 1500. Between the last decades
of the fifteenth century and the early decades of the sixteenth century, a
new concept of futurity crystallized in the culture of the Italian city-
states, taking shape in a wide variety of texts and images. Specifically,
Renaissance Italians began to conceive of the future as an unknown and
unknowable time-yet-to-come. What tomorrow or next week, next
month, next year, or even the next one hundred years held was unknown
and, therefore, open to the influence of human agency and random
chance. The unknowability of the future held out the promise of opportunity and potential as well as the risk of loss and disaster. This conception of the future, as both unknown and unknowable, stood in contrast to
the teachings of the Latin Church, in which time-yet-to-come was
revealed in outline, even while it remained obscure in timing.

Of course, it would be absurd to state that the future actually took shape
for the first time in European imaginations in the sixteenth century. Ideas
about time-yet-to-come were at the heart of Christianity. Looking further
back, some mythologies of pre-Christian Europe – Teutonic stories of the
twilight of the gods most famously – had ideas or narratives about the
shape of the future. Throughout the premodern period, moreover, proph-
esies, visions, dreams, and astrological practice all made claims to reveal,
and have knowledge of, time-yet-to-come. Beyond the metaphysical,
Europeans in the centuries prior to 1500 clearly possessed a practical,
prudential sense of the future. They wrote wills and testaments, entered
into contracts and charters, made charitable donations and endowments;
in other words, they planned for the future.[1]

---

[1] On the variety of ways that premodern Europeans interacted with the future, see the
essays collected in Andrea Brady and Emily Butterworth, eds., *The Uses of the Future in
Early Modern Europe* (New York: Routledge, 2010), especially Peter Burke's foreword
(ix–xx) and the editors' introduction (1–18); J. A. Burrow and Ian P. Wei, eds., *Medieval
Futures: Attitudes to the Future in the Middle Ages* (Woodbridge: Boydell Press, 2000),
especially Jean-Claude Schmitt, "Appropriating the Future"; and Brent D. Shaw, "Did
Romans Have a Future?," *Journal of Roman Studies* 109 (2019).

If the turn of the sixteenth century did not witness the discovery of the future, sui generis and for the first time, it did witness a significant transformation in the way that Italians thought about and perceived time-yet-to-come. The eschatological sense of time of the Latin Church encouraged believers to focus on eternity (timelessness) and on the present, at the expense of the future and the past. It conceived of time as cyclical yet also inexorable in its movement toward a preordained end point. The time of ecclesiastical doctrine, of liturgy, and of Scripture was boundless but not endless. The unknown time-yet-to-come of the new futurity instead related to a sense of time as fractured and compartmentalized, consisting of unique and unrepeatable moments. Time in this conception could be bound by human ingenuity or will but had no apparent end point. Each discrete moment would be followed by another.[2] The new idea of the future was a constitutive component of this emergent sense of time.

More significant, the idea that the future was unknown and unknowable was a new concept in European understandings of time, which emerged for the first time in the decades around 1500. The Church taught that the framework of the future was known through revelation. So too, prophesy, visions, and astrology all operated on an understanding that time-yet-to-come was knowable, even if the details remained obscure. The fundamental assumption of all predictive arts is that knowledge of the future is power. They promise that, once known, the future can be altered or at least accommodated. Similarly, the practical, prudential operations of medieval Europeans – in making preparations for the future through a variety of legal forms – were undertaken on the basis of an understanding that time-yet-to-come could be shaped and even constructed. In making wills and testaments, in signing charters and contracts, premodern Europeans operated with a proleptic sense of the future. They anticipated that tomorrow would be just like today, that it would it operate by the same rules, principles, and values as the present. The mundane future might be obscure and contingent, therefore, but it

[2] On medieval Christian notions of time and the emergence of a different conception of time in the fourteenth and fifteenth centuries, see Simona Cohen, *Transformations of Time and Temporality in Medieval and Renaissance Art* (Leiden: Brill, 2014), 39–49; Florence Buttay-Jutier, *Fortuna: Usages politiques d'une allégorie morale à la Renaissance* (Paris: Presses de l'Université Paris-Sorbonne, 2008), 130–38; Jacques Le Goff, *Time, Work, and Culture in the Middle Ages* (Chicago: University of Chicago Press, 1980), 29–42; and Schmitt, "Appropriating the Future." For broader, more theoretical considerations of how human conceptions of time evolve and change, see David Christian, "History and Time," *Australian Journal of History and Politics* 57, no. 3 (2011); Norbert Elias, *Time: An Essay*, trans. Edmund Jephcott (Oxford: Blackwell, 1992); E. R. Leach, *Rethinking Anthropology* (London: Athlone Press, 1966), 124–36.

was knowable, in broad outline at least. Around 1500, by contrast, Renaissance Italians instead began to conceive of the future as unknowable, to consider that tomorrow might in fact be completely different from today and operate by different rules, values, and principles. A key distinction in thinking about the history of the future, then, needs to be made between the future-as-known (in all its various manifestations, from the mundane to the metaphysical) and the future-as-unknown. Jean-Claude Schmitt has recently articulated this as the difference, in the medieval imagination, between *futura* (the plural of the Latin *futurum*) and *avenir* (time-to-come).[3] While the former is known in outline at least, the latter remains entirely obscure. The latter conception, I argue, emerged first around the turn of the sixteenth century in Italy and is the focus of this book.

Since the delineation by Jacques Le Goff between "Church's time" and "merchants' time" – as two distinct temporalities operating in the later Middle Ages – scholars of premodernity have understood that Europeans inhabited a world with complex timing. However, a tendency toward treating these as two fixed, binary opposites has obscured the full complexity of the picture. Some recent studies, in contrast, have emphasized the way that Europeans in the medieval and early modern periods operated with and within multiple temporalities that existed under these two broad categories, including natural rhythms, artificial structures imposed by guilds or other corporate groups, ecclesiastical and secular ritual calendars, and categories such as old and new.[4]

The emergence of the future as unknown time-yet-to-come added another temporality to the already complex notions of time within which Renaissance Italians operated. It did not result in the displacement of the eschatological future of Christianity. Neither did the conception of time as compartmentalized and subject to human will extinguish the theological understanding of time as a fluid sweep from Creation toward the Last Judgment. Instead of one temporality replacing another, they intertwined and coexisted. The new concept of the future, as it emerged in

---

[3] Schmitt, "Appropriating the Future," 6.
[4] See the very different but equally enlightening arguments of Matthew Champion, *The Fullness of Time: Temporalities in the Fifteenth-Century Low Countries* (Chicago: University of Chicago Press, 2017), esp. 1–63; Alexander Nagel and Christopher S. Wood, *Anachronic Renaissance* (New York: Zone Books, 2010), esp. 7–19. Several of the contributions to Merry E. Wiesner-Hanks, ed., *Gendered Temporalities in the Early Modern World* (Amsterdam: Amsterdam University Press, 2018), highlight the multiplicity of premodern conceptions of time. See those by Alisha Rankin and Elizabeth Cohen in particular. See also the much briefer speculations and critique of binary rigidity in Nick Wilding, "Galileo and the Stain of Time," *California Italian Studies* 2, no. 1 (2011).

Renaissance Italy, constituted a significant addition to this plurality, while also laying the foundations for the modern sense of time and timing. The future began in Italy around 1500 because, around the turn of the sixteenth century, Italians began to imagine time-yet-to-come in a way that appears more familiar to twenty-first-century conceptions than the soteriological, divinatory, or anticipatory notions of the Middle Ages.

The choice of 1500 as the keystone in my argument, the date around which change coalesced, may appear somewhat arbitrary. I should emphasize that I am in no way suggesting an abrupt shift, akin to turning on the lights in a darkened room. Italians did not wake up in 1501 with a fully formed conception of time-yet-to-come as unknown and unknowable. As I hope will become clear, the transformation in ideas about futurity occurred over several decades, hesitatingly, and via complex paths. The place of 1500 in this process emerged from the archival data and sources themselves as my research proceeded. Ideas and images of the future began to shift in the second half of the fifteenth century and, as will be analyzed in much greater detail through the text, began to crystallize in the decades immediately on either side of the turn of the century through the convergence of three factors in particular – the European encounter with the Americas, the onset of the Italian Wars, and impact of Epicurean physics – in conjunction with longer-term shifts in mercantile culture. *Around 1500* is a shorthand way of expressing a complex process of extended change that bridged the late fifteenth and early sixteenth centuries.[5]

In this book, I present the first extended analysis of how Renaissance Italians thought about the future, and how their ideas about time-yet-to-come changed between the fifteenth and sixteenth centuries.[6] In so

[5] Given my focus on futurity, it is worth noting that 1500 also enjoyed a particular prominence in millennial anticipation in the European imagination and that a culture of vernacular prophecy flourished in Italy in these same decades: see Ottavia Niccoli, *Prophecy and People in Renaissance Italy*, trans. Lydia G. Cochrane (Princeton, NJ: Princeton University Press, 1990). The coincidence of this with the development of the new futurity endorses the emphasis on the years around 1500 as a point in time in which Italians were particularly concerned with and sensitive to temporality.
[6] Schmitt, "Appropriating the Future," identifies a "breaking point" in the way that Europeans thought about the future in the sixteenth century but does not offer an explanation for this occurrence. Maia Wellington Gahtan, "Notions of Past and Future in Italian Renaissance Arts and Letters," in *Symbols of Time in the History of Art*, ed. Christian Heck and Kristen Lippencot (Turnhout: Brepols, 2002), suggests that some different ideas about the future were emerging in the sixteenth century. Jessyn Kelly has analyzed the visualization of chance and future contingency in Northern Renaissance art and culture, "Renaissance Futures: Chance, Prediction, and Play in Northern European Visual Culture" (PhD dissertation, University of California, Berkeley, 2011), while J. K. Barret has explored articulations of the future as uncertain in English Renaissance

doing, my argument reveals the ways in which some of the long-standing historiographical narratives of the Renaissance – about secularization and the origins of modernity in Europe – are more complex than either their telling or their refutation would suggest. Just as historians now reject simplistic linear chronologies, which posit the Renaissance as a signifi-cant break from the medieval past, so too narratives that emphasize only continuity between the Middle Ages and the Renaissance should be resisted. Continuing either of these dichotomous viewpoints is neither productive nor helpful for historical understanding.[7]

As with 1500, my use of *Renaissance* requires some explanation. Long a significant way station in traditional narratives of western European history, the concept has in recent decades come under scrutiny and deserved criticism. I am using the concept here quite deliberately because of both these factors, not in spite of them. The idea of the Renaissance is profoundly entangled with European notions of tempor-ality, particularly with ideas about progress and modernity.[8] I use it in an attempt to reappropriate it from these earlier ideas, as well as from more recent arguments that it is nothing but a hollow label, and to suggest how it might profitably fit into a different understanding of the history of European temporalities.

In Italy, at least, the label *Renaissance* can justifiably and appropriately be used to discuss the convergence and interconnections between a cultural movement, a political moment, and a commercial flourishing, born of the particular historico-cultural, geopolitical, and economic natures of the peninsula, which unfolded roughly from the mid-fourteenth to the late sixteenth century. Inspired by the material rem-nants of antiquity that surrounded them, artists and intellectuals looked to the classical past for models and inspiration for the amelioration of contemporary society and culture. In search of legitimacy, the governors of the Italian city-states similarly turned to antiquity for justifications and defenses of their existence in a Europe of emperors, popes, and emergent national monarchies. The cultural movement benefited the aspirations of these Italian rulers but should never be reduced simply to a material

---

literature, *Untold Futures: Time and Literary Culture in Renaissance England* (Ithaca, NY: Cornell University Press, 2016). The approaches and methods of these last two scholars, while different from my own, offer arguments that complement the one I offer here by highlighting the particular sensitivity to time and futurity that emerged during the Renaissance.

[7] Stefan Hanß, "The Fetish of Accuracy: Perspectives on Early Modern Time(s)," *Past and Present*, no. 243 (2019), offers a similar critique.

[8] I discuss this in more detail in the Conclusion. See also Nicholas Scott Baker, "A Twenty-First Century Renaissance," *I Tatti Studies: Essays in the Renaissance* 22, no. 2 (2019).

expression of political forces. The convergence on the peninsula of a rich commercial network that connected Italy and Europe to the rest of the Afro-Eurasian land mass in these centuries made possible, at least in part, both the autonomy of the city-states and the productivity of their authors and artists. From the second half of the sixteenth century, the establishment of an uneasy Spanish hegemony following the end of the Italian Wars, the creation of the Tridentine Church, and the gradual eclipse of the importance of the Mediterranean for European commerce by the Atlantic ended the political moment of the Renaissance and curtailed the connections and wealth that had helped to fuel its artistic productivity. The cultural movement, however, had an enduring influence, and developed into new forms across Europe and eventually European colonies in the Americas and Asia.

In my analysis, the Renaissance emerges as a period in Italy's history when time mattered, when a greater consciousness and concern about the passing of time manifested in the Italian imagination. The idea that the Renaissance witnessed the construction of a new idea of the past is long established and, indeed, central to the entire concept of cultural rebirth associated with the period. I argue in the following chapters that the Renaissance also experienced the invention of a new idea of the future. As I demonstrate, the awareness of time and the development of a new concept of time-yet-to-come manifested itself in a variety of ways that problematize and complicate any straightforward attempts to categorize the period.

In particular, while the Renaissance did not produce the modern European sense of temporality in a dramatic rupture from the medieval, it certainly prepared the ground for the hardening of categories such as progress, linearity, and civilization that would eventually characterize the perception of such a break. The story of how that particular modernism developed and how it became co-opted into European projects of empire-building and Enlightenment is not the work of this book. My intention instead is to demonstrate how multiple notions of time and temporality cohered in fifteenth- and sixteenth-century Italian culture, some of which – the unknown time-yet-to-come in particular – laid foundations that made possible the eventual development of modernist European time. Futile debates about whether the Renaissance was modern or not miss the true complexity of the period.

Futurity had posed an intellectual and theological problem for western European Christianity throughout the Middle Ages. The New Testament clearly asserted that the form of the future was known – in the second coming of Christ and the resurrection of the dead – and the Latin Church taught that these statements were unassailable truths.

However, Aristotle, the second pillar of medieval intellectual life, had written that any statement about time yet-to-come was contingent, in that neither the truth nor the falsity of the claim could be proven until the future event actually occurred. As a result of this contradiction, the question of future contingency became an important one for scholastic debate and discussion.

No consensus or satisfactory solution to the myriad of subsequent, related problems emerged between the twelfth and fifteenth centuries. The two most consistent strands of thought both emphasized the ultimate knowability and truth of the future. The first argued that because God existed in eternity (and so outside time), everything occurred simultaneously in the present for him, but added that because divine foreknowledge involved simple, subsequent necessity and not coercion, it did not trouble contingency. This line of argumentation asserted that even if no choice actually existed, human beings chose freely because God exercised neither force nor constraint on their actions. The second line of thinking argued that God knows equally well what he does know and also what he does not know. It held that because knowing and not-knowing are identical for God, future contingency was not affected by divine foreknowledge. By this logic, a claim about tomorrow can be contingent because God can know equally that it is true and that it is not true; only time will reveal to humanity which is the case.[9] At the end of the fourteenth century, therefore, the fundamental Christian conception of the future held that the time-yet-to-come was known to God even if it remained largely obscure to humanity. Moreover, the soteriology of the Latin Church encouraged believers to focus not on questions about the future but rather on the present and on the eternity that awaited them.

Outside scholastic theological debates, in both the learned and popular cultures of early Renaissance Italy, considerations of the problem of future contingency were largely framed through the figure of *fortuna*. The preference of Renaissance authors and artists to use *fortuna* as the vehicle for considering the nature of time-yet-to-come reflects the fact that the allegorical was a central mode of thought in the intellectual and cultural life of Italy between the fourteenth and seventeenth centuries. As Ernst Cassirer pointed out, several decades ago, the use of allegory in Renaissance thought was not merely a rhetorical choice or an aesthetic preference for embodied forms to clothe abstract concepts but rather a

---

[9] Calvin Normore, "Future Contingents," in *The Cambridge History of Later Medieval Philosophy: From the Rediscovery of Aristotle to the Disintegration of Scholasticism, 1100–1600*, ed. Norma Kretzmann et al. (Cambridge: Cambridge University Press, 1982). See also Champion, *The Fullness of Time*, 69–75.

key structure in the way that ideas were processed and considered.[10] It was the principal vehicle used by Renaissance authors and artists for the communication of complex ideas in a manner that was simultaneously intellectually sophisticated, subtle, and playful. Allegorical form worked on multiple levels in fifteenth- and sixteenth-century Italian culture, engaging a deep heritage of classical and Christian ideas and conveying this efficiently and effectively in a single figure. Allegory bridged the space between the cultural memory of the viewer, reader, or listener and the creativity of the author or artist.[11] *Fortuna* cast in the form of the homonymous Roman deity provided the perfect figure for discussing and imagining the passage of time, particularly the appearance of chance and unexpected events, that is to say, the contingency of the future.

In Christian Europe, the classical goddess Fortuna – with her sphere, rudder, and cornucopia – transformed into a regal woman presiding over a relentlessly turning wheel.[12] Conceived as an agent of Providence, she became the moral educator of humanity. The inevitable rise and decline of all upon her wheel reminded mortals of the fleeting nature of earthly success in comparison with the eternal rewards promised by Christian theology. In this way the figure of *fortuna* explained the role of chance and the unexpected in a universe governed by divine omniscience, and also acted as a caution against trusting too much in the prudential sense of the future that tomorrow would be identical to today, providing an understanding for why it might be different than anticipated.

The contingency of future events could thus be explained and integrated within the eschatological time of the Church via the figure of *fortuna*, understood as servant of divine will. Providence and *fortuna* constituted the principal vocabulary of futurity in the late fourteenth and early fifteenth centuries, and the two terms operated independently yet inseparably. The former described the consistent unfolding of time toward its predetermined, if obscure end. The latter provided an explanation for the irruption of the unanticipated and seemingly random in this inexorable sweep, in a manner that did not contradict divine foreknowledge of the future.

---

[10] Ernst Cassirer, *The Individual and the Cosmos in Renaissance Philosophy*, trans. Mario Domandi (Oxford: Basil Blackwell, 1963), 74.

[11] Lina Bolzoni, *The Gallery of Memory: Literary and Iconographic Models in the Age of the Printing Press*, trans. Jeremy Parzen (Toronto: University of Toronto Press, 2001).

[12] Throughout the book, I will distinguish the more general, allegorical figure of *fortuna* from the clearly embodied Roman deity, Fortuna. While the former encompasses the latter, as the following chapters will demonstrate, the meanings attached to the figure of *fortuna* extended beyond the literary invocation and imagination of the goddess.

In this book, I examine how these two key terms for understanding the future were disentangled and how the figure of *fortuna* came to bear new meanings, over the course of several decades between the mid-fifteenth and mid-sixteenth centuries. Uncovering how the figure of *fortuna* increasingly lost its connection with a Christian ethical-instructional impetus, I trace the paths by which new guises, new significations, and new associations cohered around it in the cultural spaces where religion, morality, wealth, commerce, and time converged. These were never broad, smooth avenues but rather circuitous, often hesitant, and dog-legged crosscuts. I have not uncovered a linear progression from one temporality to another. Instead, my analysis reveals the messy, compli-cated ways in which the concept of the future, as unknown time yet-to-come, emerged, as one more temporality experienced in sixteenth-century Italy. As a result of these processes, the figure of *fortuna* ceased to work as an allegory that made sense of the contingency of future events in a divinely governed universe and instead began to emphasize and embody the very uncertainty and unknowability of tomorrow.

The prominence of the figure of *fortuna* in Renaissance thought – so extensive that one recent study labeled it a "banality" – has resulted in a rich literature on its form and appearance. These studies have principally considered its usage as a metaphor or allegory for the instability of human experience. Two significant contributions advanced this idea to argue that it represented or captured the more ephemeral concept of the spirit or creative energy of the Renaissance, while a handful of analyses have suggested that as a representation of variability it served principally as a political allegory.[13] An acknowledgment of the passage of time and,

[13] For interpretations of *fortuna* as a Renaissance allegory for human experience, mostly focused on the term's appearance in literary and philosophical works, see Vincenzo Cioffari, "The Function of Fortune in Dante, Boccaccio and Machiavelli," *Italica* 24, no. 1 (1947); Roberto Esposito, "Fortuna e politica all'origine della filosofia italiana," *California Italian Studies* 2, no. 1 (2011); Thomas Flanagan, "The Concept of *Fortuna* in Machiavelli," in *The Political Calculus: Essays on Machiavelli's Philosophy*, ed. Anthony Parel (Toronto: University of Toronto Press, 1972); Iiro Kajanto, "Fortuna in the Works of Poggio Bracciolini," *Arctos: Acta philologica fennica* 20 (1986); Frederick Kiefer, "The Conflation of Fortuna and Occasio in Renaissance Thought and Iconography," *The Journal of Medieval and Renaissance Studies* 9, no. 1 (1979); Cary J. Nederman, "Amazing Grace: Fortune, God, and Free Will in Machiavelli's Thought," *Journal of the History of Ideas* 60, no. 4 (1999); Achille Olivieri, "'Dio' e 'fortuna' nelle *Lettere storiche* di Luigi da Porto," *Studi veneziani* 13 (1971); Howard R. Patch, *The Goddess Fortuna in Mediaeval Literature* (London: Frank Cass & Co, 1967); Mario Santoro, *Fortuna, ragione e prudenza nella civiltà letteraria del Cinquecento* (2nd ed.) (Naples: Liguori, 1978); and Francesco Tateo, "L'Alberti fra il Petrarca e il Pontano: La metafora della fortuna," *Albertiana* 10 (2007). The classic work on *fortuna* as expressing the spirit and energy of the Renaissance is Aby Warburg's 1907 essay on Francesco Sassetti, reprinted in Aby Warburg, *The Renewal of Pagan Antiquity: Contributions to the Cultural History of the European*

especially, of the unexpected turn of events in human experience underlies all these interpretations. However, only one previous study has
explicitly recognized that *fortuna* served principally as an allegory of time
during the Renaissance. While a handful of other scholars have considered the significant connection between the figure of *fortuna* and
conceptions of time, they directed their focus elsewhere.[14]

In this book, building most obviously on the considerations of these
latter scholars, I argue that the figure of *fortuna* served principally as an
allegory for the contingent nature of the future and that the meanings of
this allegory changed significantly between the late fourteenth and mid-
sixteenth centuries. In doing so, however, I have eschewed a systematic
genealogy of the appearance of *fortuna* in words and images in
Renaissance Italian culture. Not only would such a labor be prohibitively
extensive and frankly dull for the reader, it would also needlessly repeat
an existing body scholarship.

Beyond the literature on *fortuna* in the Renaissance, I also build on the
growing body of scholarship on the history of temporality. Time lies at
the center of the disciplinary practice of history. It is the defining dimension on which historical analysis rests. For this reason, it remains a
slippery and elusive concept to subject to analysis itself. The analytic
nomenclature for talking about time in historical practice and the relationships between past, present, and future in historical scholarship tend
to fold back on themselves. In the face of these challenges, the collected
essays of the German historian Reinhart Koselleck offer a useful analytical framework for thinking about time in history. In particular, his work
provides a conceptual language for thinking about the history of the
future. Koselleck proposed that *experience* and *expectation* constitute a
pair of meta-historical epistemological categories, which are inseparable

Renaissance, ed. Julia Bloomfield et al., trans. Caroline Beamish, David Britt, and Carol
Lanham (Los Angeles: Getty Research Institute for the History of Art and the
Humanities, 1999), 222–62; but Kiefer also expresses the sentiment. For
interpretations of *fortuna* as a political allegory in the Renaissance, see Buttay-Jutier,
Fortuna; Giuliano Procacci, "La 'fortuna' nella realtà politica del primo
Cinquecento," *Belfagor* 6 (1951); and Edgar Wind, "Platonic Tyranny and the
Renaissance Fortuna: On Ficino's Reading of Laws IV, 709 A-712A," in *De artibus
opuscula XL: Essays in Honour of Erwin Panofsky*, ed. Millard Meiss (New York: New York
University Press, 1961). Buttay-Jutier identifies *fortuna* as "une banalité" in the
Renaissance imagination.
[14] Rudolf Wittkower, "Chance, Time and Virtue," *Journal of the Warburg Institute* 1, no. 4
(1938); Kiefer, "The Conflation of Fortuna and Occasio"; and Buttay-Jutier, *Fortuna*,
130–38, recognize the connections between time and *fortuna* but their analytic focus lies
elsewhere. Cohen, *Transformations of Time*, 199–243, analyzes the iconographical
conflation of *fortuna* and *kairos* identified by Kiefer in greater length and detail, but her
analytic focus lies on time in general rather than on time-yet-to-come.

(in that they cannot exist or be analyzed independent of one another), fundamental to human life, and essential for historical analysis.[15] They embody past and future, respectively, and make these temporalities manifest in the present. The manifestation of these two categories, Koselleck suggested, is both temporal and spatial. Experience exists as a totality, a space that contains all past time in a single moment. Expectation, however, is a horizon, beyond which lie new experiences as yet unseen and of unknown possible durations. Once the horizon of expectation is breached, it recedes into the distance again.

One of Koselleck's key arguments was that the future (by which he meant *avenir* not *futura*) is an invention of modernity.[16] In premodern Europe, he claimed, the distance between the space of experience and the horizon of expectation was short. Before the eighteenth century, the great majority of Europeans based expectation solely on experience. Tomorrow would be just like yesterday. The future, then, was entirely predictable. Time passed slowly. Even for the educated elite, the eschatological future of Christianity posed a firm limit on the horizon of expectation. The revealed time-yet-to-come of the New Testament was imminent, known, and based on experience. Biblical texts were history, even as they discussed events yet to occur. According to Koselleck's narrative, this providential future became increasingly redundant between the late fifteenth and late seventeenth centuries. However, the horizon of expectation did not recede too far into the distance because early modern Europeans still assumed that the future was predictable and subject to a restricted range of experience.

Koselleck argued that beginning in the later eighteenth century, however, the distance between the space of experience and the horizon of expectation increased, while the passage of time started to accelerate, as the horizon was breached with increasing rapidity through techno-industrial development. European thinkers and authors, most notably Kant, articulated an idea of progress. They rejected the notion that things would always stay the same, and promoted an expectation of

[15] Reinhart Koselleck, *Futures Past: On the Semantics of Historical Time*, trans. Keith Tribe, (Cambridge, MA: MIT Press, 1985), 267–88. I am grateful to Jonathan Sachs, who told me to read Koselleck and lent me his battered copy before I acquired my own. Despite the many valid critiques of Koselleck (see my own a little further on), he remains unavoidable. For example, all of the contributors to the recent "Viewpoints: Temporalities" forum in *Past and Present*, no. 243 (2019), engage with his ideas in some way.
[16] In addition to the essay cited immediately above, see also Koselleck, *Futures Past*, 3–20, and Koselleck, *The Practice of Conceptual History: Timing History, Spacing Concepts*, trans. Todd Samuel Presner and Kerstin Behnke (Stanford, CA: Stanford Universtiy Press, 2002), 100–114.

improvement and amelioration, an expectation that the future could not and should not correspond to the past. This conception of the future as unknown, unknowable, and fundamentally different from past experience because of techno-industrial progress, Koselleck concluded, is a defining feature of modernity (*Neuzeit*).

As a conceptual historian, Koselleck was more interested in categories of analysis and the development of a vocabulary for thinking through the problems of historical practice than in the fine-grained description of past societies and cultures. As a result, his broad brushstroke depiction of medieval temporal stasis can easily be dismissed.[17] However, taken as a framework for further analysis, which can proceed via a closer, more historically accurate picture of premodern Europe, Koselleck's categories provide an effective scaffold, even while his chronology and the linearity of his vision of time can be challenged. The relationship between experience and expectation that he proposes, and the ways that this relationship structured European conceptions of the passing of time and of the future, provide perceptive insight. In particular, the transition from ideas of the future as known or at least knowable to notions of the future as unknown and unknowable was clearly an important moment in the history of temporalities in Europe and a key element in the construction of European modernity.

The evidence presented in this book obviously supports a different timing than that proposed by Koselleck, as it demonstrates that the distance between the space of experience and the horizon of expectation grew significantly in the decades on either side of 1500, some three hundred years before he placed this transition. Nevertheless, I do not advocate pushing Koselleck's thesis further back in time, in a manner akin to the use of Jürgen Habermas's concept of the public sphere in much recent early modern scholarship.[18]

In the first place, the evidence does not suggest the articulation of an idea of progress in sixteenth-century Italy, a key component to Koselleck's analysis. Moreover, my own argument rejects the notion

---

[17] Champion, *The Fullness of Time*, 7, for example, gives Koselleck short shrift, dismissing his analysis in a single paragraph. Peter Burke offers a more nuanced critique in the foreword to Brady and Butterworth, *The Uses of the Future*. From the other side of Koselleck's chronological divide, see also the thoughtful, critical engagement of A. R. P. Fryxell, "Time and the Modern: Current Trends in the History of Modern Temporalities," *Past and Present*, no. 243 (2019).

[18] For a succinct and useful summary of the reception and use of Habermas's ideas in early modern scholarship, see Massimo Rospocher, "Beyond the Public Sphere: A Historiographical Transition," in *Beyond the Public Sphere: Opinions, Publics, Spaces in Early Modern Europe*, ed. Massimo Rospocher (Bologna: Il Mulino; Berlin: Duncker & Humblot, 2012).

underlying Koselleck's thesis of a simple, linear temporality operating from the medieval to the modern. As outlined above, I instead argue that Renaissance Italians inhabited a world of multiple temporalities. The increasing distance between the space of experience and the horizon of expectation – the emergence of a concept of the future as unknown time-yet-to-come – created another, new temporality that coexisted with others. This thesis neither replaces Koselleck's nor insists on its displacement to an earlier period, but rather demonstrates that the transition from the future-as-revealed to the future-as-unknown was not a simple, linear progression. It also suggests that this occurred at different rates in different temporalities within and across Europe.

Koselleck considered the sixteenth century to be a transitional moment in European conceptions of the future, but for him it represented the replacement of the Church's revealed, providential future by an equally predictable, limited set of expectations based on experience. Several other scholars have identified the decades around 1500 as a key moment in the history of European temporality. Roberto Quinones argued that time was a "great discovery" of the Renaissance, in the sense that authors from the fourteenth to sixteenth centuries expressed a consciousness of time and timing that they identified as lacking in their predecessors. Time became commodified, rendered precious, and, therefore, something that Renaissance authors struggled to seize and use effectively.[19] Other studies have suggested, in a variety of ways, that significant changes occurred in relation to Europeans' conception of time during the period: through the acceptance of deep time in a more pervasive recognition of the idea that the Earth was older than Christian theology claimed, or through an increasing, if melancholic, fascination with the destructive power of the passage of time and the profound tension between mutability and order.[20] Simona Cohen and Maia Gahtan have demonstrated the ways in which these

[19] Ricardo J. Quinones, *The Renaissance Discovery of Time* (Cambridge, MA: Harvard University Press, 1972). Jacques Le Goff made a similar point, very briefly, in Le Goff, *Time, Work, and Culture*, 51–52. Quinones has recently revisited this argument in a different context: Ricardo J. Quinones, *North/South: The Great European Divide* (Toronto: University of Toronto Press, 2016), 53–65.
[20] On Renaissance ideas about the age of the planet (and what we would now call deep time), see William J. Connell, "The Eternity of the World and Renaissance Historical Thought," *California Italian Studies* 2, no. 1 (2011), and Ivano Dal Prete, "'Being the World Eternal ...': The Age of the Earth in Renaissance Italy," *Isis* 105, no. 2 (2014). On the destructive/creative power of time, see Simona Cohen, "The Early Renaissance Personifications of Time and Changing Concepts of Temporality," *Renaissance Studies* 14, no. 3 (2000), and David A. Roberts, "Mystery to Mathematics Flown: Time and Reality in the Renaissance," *The Centennial Review* 19, no. 3 (1975).

various ideas about time, and others, appeared in Renaissance artworks, independent of texts.[21]

With the partial exception of Cohen, however, all these studies treat time in the Renaissance imagination as unitary or no more than binary – Quinones refers to Le Goff's distinction between ecclesiastical and mercantile time – and, in particular, as universal, rather than as distinctly European. The contribution of Alexander Nagel and Christopher Wood on the anachronic nature of Renaissance artworks presents an important shift, then, in its emphasis on the plurality of temporalities inhabited by Italians in the fifteenth and sixteenth centuries. Indeed, they argued that what defined the Renaissance, as a distinct period, was a new, increasing consciousness of, and concern about, the temporal instability of artworks.[22]

In presenting my argument, I consider both meanings attached to ideas about the future and experiences of time-yet-to-come in the sixteenth century. Chapters 1–4 examine the experiences of the new futurity in sixteenth-century Italy in its most prevalent and accessible forms: commerce and gambling. Chapters 5–8 analyze the transformation of the meaning of the figure of *fortuna* across a variety of texts and images produced between the late fourteenth and late sixteenth centuries. This format eschews the traditional approach of similar cultural intellectual histories, which tend to move from meaning to experience, from the realm of ideas to that of practices.[23]

Structuring the book in this way underlines a key claim of my argument: that changes to Italian (and European) notions of time did not occur through a sudden rupture between the medieval and the modern, through the revelation of a eureka moment. Rather, the embodied, relational practices and experiences of temporalities facilitated an increasing receptivity to new ideas about time's passing and the shape of time-yet-to-come. The slow germination of the concept of the unknown and unknowable future lay in the everyday exchanges of commerce and gambling. The quotidian culture of financial risk taking common to Italian cities provided a long familiarity with uncertainty and speculation. Between the fourteenth and sixteenth centuries, Italians not only thought and imagined their way to a new futurity; they also and particularly played and transacted it. If anything, the experience of the

---

[21] Cohen, *Transformations of Time*, esp. 115–304; Gahtan, "Notions of Past and Future."
[22] Nagel and Wood, *Anachronic Renaissance*.
[23] I am grateful to the anonymous reader for Cambridge who suggested rearranging the book's chapters, which proved a liberating recommendation. The order I have settled on is slightly different to that entertained by the reader.

unknown time-yet-to-come preceded and facilitated the articulation of
its meaning.

In pursuing an analytical structure that considers both meaning and
experience, I am following loosely in the methodological footsteps of two
recent works that have presented models for this type of interlinked
analysis: Craig Koslofsky's study of the night and nocturnalization in
early modern Europe, and Sandra Cavallo and Tessa Storey's mono-
graph on late Renaissance ideas and practices of hygiene and preventative
medicine.[24] Koslofsky presents a method for combining an intellectual
history of ideas with a cultural-anthropological analysis of everyday life to
examine how complex ideas and thought processes interacted, in a
reciprocal way, with daily life. Cavallo and Storey provide methodological road maps for navigating the circular reinforcement of values
between learned writings and daily life by combining analysis of intellectual treatises and popular publications with analysis of personal correspondence to examine the mutual influences between the two realms.

I have based my analysis on archives, images, and printed sources
drawn principally but not exclusively from four city-states: Florence,
Genoa, Milan, and Venice. These four locales were significant cultural,
economic, and political centers during the Renaissance, constituting
what Fernand Braudel identified as the "Mediterranean quadrilateral":
key nodes for the circulation and exchange of goods and ideas across not
only the Italian peninsula but the surrounding region.[25] The new concept of the future emerged first, most clearly, and coherently in the
mercantile-humanist culture of these cities, a union of a commercial,
speculative, quantifying mentality with an admiration for classical motifs
and allegorical forms.

As a result of the vagaries of archival survival and other methodological
choices discussed in individual chapters, I have not treated the four cities
as equal case studies. Rather, the book presents a series of comparative
analyses of sources, visual and textual, well known and obscure, together
with archival evidence drawing from each of the four cities as well as
occasionally from other parts of the peninsula. If Florence has a particular prominence in the analysis, this is due both to the depth of its archives
and to the density of exchanges, both financial and intellectual, that
occurred in what is still a relatively small city. The layering of these

---

[24] Craig Koslofsky, *Evening's Empire: A History of the Night in Early Modern Europe*
(Cambridge: Cambridge University Press, 2011); Sandra Cavallo and Tessa Storey,
Healthy Living in Late Renaissance Italy (Oxford: Oxford University Press, 2013).
[25] Fernand Braudel, *The Mediterranean and the Mediterranean World in the Age of Philip II*,
trans. Siân Reynolds, 2 vols. (New York: Harper and Row, 1973), 387–94.

different sources presents an examination of how the new concept of the future took shape and cohered across the late fifteenth and sixteenth centuries.

The book opens by examining how the unknowability of the future was experienced and tamed by Renaissance professionals in futurity: merchants, who practiced long-distance trade and pursued financial speculation, and gamblers, who chased more immediate but no less risky speculative gains. These two groups had lengthy, professional experience with uncertainty and shared some continuities of experience with pre-1500 forebears. Chapter 1 examines a group of texts about play and games of chance produced in the sixteenth century, when the new conception of the future had already cohered. It considers how a small group of authors used their long familiarity with gambling to present themselves as experts in this new futurity and demonstrates how, in doing so, they went much further than their contemporaries in embracing it. Chapter 2 considers a variety of sources, particularly sixteenth-century legislation and legal proceedings, to examine how Italians from across all social strata experienced the unknown future in gambling and games of chance, and to reveal how deep-seated cultural values about character and status helped to make sense of and structure the unknowability of time-yet-to-come revealed in the roll of dice and the turn of cards. Chapter 3 analyzes mercantile correspondence from sixteenth-century Florence, Genoa, and Venice to reveal the interconnections between ideas about the future and the central problem of premodern commerce, the cultivation of trust over long distances and with strangers. In turn, Chapter 4 examines the rich vocabulary of futurity in this same correspondence, tracing the way merchants thought about time and operated within multiple temporalities, the new future of unknown time-yet-to-come nesting within a providential vision of the passage of time.

Chapters 5–8 trace the ways in which the new unknown future cohered in texts and images from the late fourteenth century up to its full development in the early sixteenth century. Chapter 5 examines the figure of *fortuna* and its relationship to concepts of time and futurity in the works of three early Renaissance humanists associated with the papal *curia* and Florence – Petrarch, Leon Battista Alberti, and Poggio Bracciolini – and one born in Venice but more commonly connected with France, where she lived most of her life, Christine de Pizan. It traces the continuing cultural force of a moral allegory that originated in Boethius's *Consolation of Philosophy*. Chapter 6 maps the beginning of a process of the disentanglement of the figure of *fortuna* and Providence and the early emergence of new meanings and associations for the former through the writing of three Florentine merchants whose careers span the late four-teenth to late fifteenth centuries: Buonaccorso Pitti, Giovanni Rucellai, and Francesco Sassetti. Chapter 7 examines how the new allegorical meanings attached to the figure of *fortuna* appeared in visual culture from the late fifteenth to the late sixteenth century as a new iconography took shape, analyzing a range of works by artists associated principally with Florence and Venice, including Giorgio Vasari, Alessandro Allori, Paolo Veronese, and Giuseppe Porta. Chapter 8, the longest chapter, considers the catalyzing impact of the Italian Wars and the rediscovery of Epicurean physics (via Lucretius's *De rerum natura*), set against the ongoing revelations of the age of encounters, on the transformation of the figure of *fortuna* and its disconnection from Providence in texts produced by participant-observers in the chaos and dramatic changes of the last decades of the fifteenth century and the first decades of the sixteenth in Florence, Milan, Naples, and the Veneto, including Laura Cereta, Giovanni Pontano, Niccolò Machiavelli, and Luigi da Porto, the original author of the story that became *Romeo and Juliet*.

In *Fortune's Theater* demonstrates that Renaissance Italians began to experience the future as unknown time-yet-to-come and gave meaning to that experience between the middle of the fifteenth century and end of the sixteenth century. The book suggests that this process never followed a simple, linear progression from an older, medieval sense of eschato-logical time toward a more modern, secular temporality. Rather, the cumulative analysis of the eight chapters establishes that Renaissance Italians continued to inhabit and think with multiple temporalities through the sixteenth century. The book thus reveals a new, complex understanding of the significance of time to the society and culture of Renaissance Italy. Time was not simply binary, as many scholars have argued, and a new consciousness of the future was an equally defining feature of the Renaissance as a new relationship with the past. The increasing richness of time in the sixteenth century, the new concept of the unknown time-yet-to-come, and the myriad of ways that its experi-ence shaped daily life as well as high culture reveal what is distinctive and defining about the period that historians call the Renaissance in Italy: an increased sensitivity to the multiplicity of time, an increased importance given to the passage of time, and an increased awareness of the potential gains of time's passing. The changes traced in this book also laid the foundations for the development of nineteenth-century European tem-poralities. While not yet modern, time in Renaissance Italy was definably different from that of the Middle Ages.

1   Experts in Futurity

Around the mid-sixteenth century, the Milanese physician and mathematician Girolamo Cardano observed that gambling was superior to strategic games such as chess for alleviating anxiety because "it has the expectation of *fortuna.*"[1] Games of chance, he suggested, offered a distraction from the everyday, an irruption of the random and capricious into an otherwise ordered existence. By surrendering to the moment before the dice rolled to a halt or the cards were revealed – the moment when the future remained unknown yet ripe with potential – one could enter a brief window of disruptive possibility in the mundane. In several works during his prolific writing career, Cardano presented himself as an expert in futurity and probability: someone who understood the taking of risks on future outcomes. This claim to expertise rested on his knowledge and experience of games of chance. While young and poor, he confidently – although not without twinges of conscience – earned money by gambling. In later life, he would think and write profoundly about his experiences of risk taking and of the unknowable time-yet-to-come in the form of games of chance. In this regard, he was not an isolated figure but one of many Italians who experienced a new idea of the future, and the taking of risks on future outcomes, in the form of gambling in the sixteenth century. While most of this community did not leave any record of their understandings and experiences, a few – like Cardano – did.

Italians had played games of chance since antiquity. Theological condemnations notwithstanding, wagering on dice was a common pastime in medieval communes on the peninsula. While there was nothing new about gambling, in the middle decades of the sixteenth century something of a minor industry in writing about play and games evolved. What prompted this development was the crystallization of a new understanding of the future in Italian society and culture: a vision of the future as

---

[1] Girolamo Cardano, *Liber de ludo aleae*, ed. Massimo Tamborini (Milan: FrancoAngeli, 2006), 56.

18

unknown, unknowable time-yet-to-come. This conception was familiar to gamblers, who understood the anxiety of waiting for the dice to fall or an opponent to show their hand. In this historical moment, experienced gamers such as Cardano recognized an opportunity to present themselves as experts in futurity, confident in their ability to explain the experience of navigating the confrontation with the unknown to the bewildered and perplexed.

This chapter does not present a systematic genealogy of sixteenth-century texts about play and games of chance. Rather, by using a complementary analysis of a variety of sources, both textual and visual, I trace how cultural connections between the future, gambling, and notions of status and social credit cohered in this new genre. While forming part of an identifiable trend, the texts are stylistically various; and although they address an audience of the educated and sociopolitical elite, the background of their creators was heterogeneous. Some belonged to the nobility, but others had decidedly more humble upbringings, so historical analysis should not simply assume an exclusive, restrictive reading of their works. The attitudes and expectations they express probably enjoyed broader and deeper social resonance than the works themselves. The relationship of gambling with notions of honor, status, and credit that cohered in these texts was shared across all strata of Italian society in the sixteenth century, as is discussed at greater length in Chapter 2.

The texts on gambling and associated images reveal the sometimes contradictory, cross-cutting currents that underlay expectations and values about gaming. When confronting the problematic and ambiguous nature of the pursuit, for example, sixteenth-century literary authors generally avoided outright condemnation. Instead of complete disapprobation, they tended to focus on the relative appropriateness of games of chance: discussing rules for when, where, why, and with whom one should play, and examining how to balance the risks of loss, fraud, or violence against the potential benefits, both immaterial and financial. These texts reveal the way notions of honor, status, and credit framed and helped Renaissance Italians make sense of the future as unknown time-yet-to-come. In particular, the authors examined here presented gambling as a sentimental education for life, which equipped players with the necessary emotional skills to navigate the agonistic nature of daily interactions. In this chapter, I argue that these authors used their familiarity with games of chance in order to present themselves as experts in futurity, as skilled navigators of the stormy waters of anxiety provoked by confrontation with the unknown future, not only at the gaming table but in everyday living.

Cardano and the other authors examined here wrote toward the end of the process that transformed how Italians articulated ideas about the future. They positioned themselves in these works as guides for others still seeking to make sense of a world in which time-yet-to-come no longer seemed certain or even knowable. Quotidian life, they suggested, was more like a game of dice or a hand of cards than their readers might like to imagine; outcomes were random and determined by chance. In so doing, these self-appointed experts articulated a vision of the future that appears quite familiar to twenty-first-century eyes.

Cardano, physician, astrologer, mathematician, and inveterate gambler, is one of the most revealing authors for analyzing the meanings attached to games of chance and the future in the sixteenth century. By his own reckoning, the Milanese-born polymath gambled and also staked money on games of chess for some forty years. In his autobiography – *De propria vita liber* (*Book of My Life*, written 1575) – he berated himself for the habit, confessing by way of mitigation: "Nor is any excuse left to me for this fact, except the trivial: the poverty of my birth, having some skill of this sort, and not being entirely foolish."[2] Regardless, Cardano laid claim to an expertise in futurity in works that ranged across several genres. He first did so in the *Practica arithmeticae et mensurandi singularis* (*Practice of Mathematics and Individual Measurements*, 1539), in which he tackled the well-known points problem, also called the interrupted game problem.[3] In its classic formulation, two players each stake one ducat on winning three games of chess (i.e., the first to win three games wins the other's coin), but they have to cease playing before resolving the bet, with the first player having won two games and the second none. The problem is, how much of the second player's ducat had the first won?[4]

---

[2] Girolamo Cardano, *De propria vita liber* (Paris: Iacobus Villery, 1643), 62.

[3] On Cardano and the points problem, see Ivo Schneider, "The Market Place and Games of Chance in the Fifteenth and Sixteenth Centuries," in *Mathematics from Manuscript to Print, 1300–1600*, ed. Cynthia Hay (Oxford: Oxford University Press, 1988), and Edith Dudley Sylla, "Business Ethics, Commercial Mathematics, and the Origins of Mathematical Probability," *History of Political Economy* 35, annual supplement (1952).

[4] The ducat (*ducato*) was a gold coin, first minted in Venice in 1285 as the equivalent of the Florentine florin (*fiorino*). By the mid-fifteenth century, the latter had been substituted by the ducat as the principal currency for long-distance commerce in the Mediterranean. Without getting lost in the thickets of the relative and fluctuating value of Italian currencies, the reader can best gain a sense of the value of this wager from knowing that in Florence, at the time Cardano was writing, one ducat could pay the wages of an unskilled laborer for fourteen days: Richard A. Goldthwaite, *The Economy of Renaissance Florence* (Baltimore, MD: Johns Hopkins University Press, 2009), 612–13. On the relationship between the florin and the ducat in the middle sixteenth century, see Richard A. Goldthwaite, "Il sistema monetario fino al 1600: Pratica, politica, problematica," in *Studi sulla moneta fiorentina (Secoli XIII–XVI)* (Florence: Olschki,

The famous fifteenth-century mathematician Fra Luca Pacioli argued in favor of a proportional division of rewards, awarding the first player two-thirds of his opponent's ducat. This is a solution based in the everyday practices of the late medieval commercial world, a solution oriented toward the past and the arithmetical division of profits: it awarded the first player on the basis of what he had achieved. In a chapter pointedly titled "On the Errors of Fra Luca," Cardano rejected this as absurd because it failed to reward the first player sufficiently. He pointed out that if the players agree to play for nineteen games and cease playing with a score of 18:9, by Pacioli's reasoning the first player still receives just two-thirds of his opponent's stake despite needing only one more win to claim the entire ducat, while the second requires ten more victories. Cardano proposed that the problem of points did not actually have a unique solution, but rather that the division needed to be tailored according to each specific situation.[5]

This tailoring, Cardano explained, should focus on the exposure to risk each player would take in continuing to play. He highlighted the somewhat counterintuitive fact that the risk from each subsequent game is higher for the first person, who is winning, than for the second, who has little to lose by further play at this point. In other words, Cardano's solution was future oriented. Cardano looked at the problem in terms of what each player still needed to do in order to win the bet. According to Cardano, even a simple wager such as this involved a particular experience of the future, as unknown and unknowable, open to speculation, and requiring a particular expertise to navigate successfully.

Despite his claim to such expertise and his personal success at gaming, Cardano considered gambling a vice best avoided. In his treatise on probability in games of chance, De ludo aleae (On Games of Chance, ca. 1564), he stressed that "the greatest utility of games of chance is never to play."[6] Other commentators were more sanguine. In his fantastical dialogue Le carte parlanti (The Talking Cards, 1543), the satirist Pietro Aretino raised the question of morality but passed over it quickly. Early in the text – in which the noted card painter Federico Padovano

---

1994), 63–64, 99–100. The correct answer, to the classical formulation of the problem, is that the first player has won three-quarters of his opponent's ducat.
5   Girolamo Cardano, Practica arithmetice et mensurandi singularis (Milan: Iohannes Antonins Castellioneus, 1539), 572–73. The pagination cited here is that handwritten in ink on the copy scanned and uploaded by the Wellcome Trust available on Internet Archive, which has no printed pagination. The relevant extract from this chapter, along with another earlier in the work, is available, transcribed, and translated into English by Richard J. Pulskamp for his Sources in the History of Probability and Statistics web page: www.cs .xu.edu/math/Sources/Cardano/cardan_pratica.pdf (accessed August 2020).
6   Cardano, Ludo aleae, 50.

discusses gaming with the eponymous, animated deck of cards –
Padovano suggests that playing cards had a diabolical origin. The
Cards retort that, in fact, Palamedes invented them during the siege of
Troy, prompting the card painter to muse, with typically Aretinesque
humor, that a Greek creator was possibly worse than an infernal one. Still
doubtful, Padovano observes that because of his profession, the priest to
whom he confesses has accused him of facilitating and promoting blasphemy, theft, fraud, and deception, all the usual litany of vices associated
with gambling. The Cards counter that commerce is responsible for just
as many problems. A merchant who loses everything when a ship sinks
simply looks for the next opportunity. A gambler, they conclude, does
exactly the same. However, playing cards also provides pleasure, while
trade does not. "It is better to remain Ser Brullo playing, than Don
Falcuccio speculating," the Cards claim, referring to proverbial figures
of wasteful inconstancy and gullible failure, respectively, "because cards,
in ruining the one, at least appeared pleasing to him sometimes, but
commerce in breaking the other never looked upon him pleasantly."[7]
    Given the deliberately provocative and contrary nature of the text, the
judgment of the Cards is hardly surprising. However, Aretino's treatment of the vices associated with gambling in the dialogue is more
complicated than a simple comparison between play and equally
irrational financial speculation. The great irony and conceit of *Le carte
parlanti* is that it takes an inanimate object (a deck of playing cards) to
make the case that gambling is sinful only when, and if, human nature
makes it so, because the game itself is played with nonsentient constructs
of paint and paper. The Cards in the text assert that they are able to
express so many emotions because they have absorbed them from human
hands. Likewise, they observe, the game itself can only ever reflect the
sentiments and attitudes of the players.[8] Gambling leads to vice and sin
only if the players lose control of themselves.
    Writing within courtly milieux, both Baldassare Castiglione and
Torquato Tasso gave the question of whether gambling should be lauded
or condemned short shrift. In the dialogue *Il Gonzaga secondo ovvero del
giuoco* (*The Second Gonzaga or Concerning Games*, 1582), Tasso had the

---

[7] Pietro Aretino, *Le carte parlanti*, ed. Giovanni Casalegno and Gabriella Giaccone
(Palermo: Sellerio, 1992), 43–48. The quoted text is on page 47. On Federico
Padovano, to whom Aretino addressed no fewer than eight letters, see Nicola Antonio
De Giorgio, "Un 'padovano' cartaro accusato di frode," in *Il giuoco al tempo di
Caravaggio: Dipinti, giochi, testimonianze dalla fine del '500 ai primi del '700*, ed. Pierluigi
Carofano (Pontadera: Bandecchi & Vivaldi, 2013).
[8] On this point, see Gabriella Giaccone, "La scrittura come gioco: Da Aretino a Calvino,"
Critica letteraria 17, no. 65 (1989): esp. 777–78.

ɛponymous protagonist, Giulio Cesare Gonzaga, include the issue of whether games are worthy of praise or not among the topics that Annibale Pocaterra should discuss. The third participant in the debate, Margarita Bentivoglio, requests that the question of praiseworthiness be discussed first. However, Pocaterra begins instead by defining what a game is, and the topic of morality never reappears.[9] Castiglione gave the matter even less attention in *Il cortegiano* (*The Book of the Courtier*, 1529). Asked whether gambling is an acceptable activity for the ideal courtier, Federigo Fregoso responds in the affirmative, "except for those who do so too assiduously ... or truly for no other reason than to win money."[10] Both authors acknowledged the potentially illicit nature of gambling, thereby avoiding appearing overly dismissive of its problematic status, but they also moved swiftly on to discussing games' potential benefits. These texts, more so than those by Aretino and Cardano, voiced an attitude shaped by aristocratic sociability.

Francesco Berni, writing in a similar context, also heaped more praise than blame on gambling. The doubled meaning of his *Capitolo della primiera* (1526), alluding to both sex and card playing, however, underlined the potentially transgressive and illicit nature of both activities.[11] In the conclusion of the poem, Berni recognized the possible harmful effects of play – in the dual sense of his subject – when he observed that if he had done and said all that he could for *primiera* (a type of proto-poker), "I would not have done what I should have"; that is, he would have failed in his duties and obligations as he would have impoverished himself.[12] The poet here displays the sensibility that one scholar had recently identified as "patrimonial rationality" in attitudes toward wealth and expenditure. In the sixteenth century, Renaissance Italians from higher socioeconomic estates began to judge economic behavior in terms of its appropriateness relative to social obligations and relationships, rather than according to moral principles.[13] Gambling and sensuality were not immoral in and of

[9] Torquato Tasso, *Dialoghi: Edizione critica*, ed. Ezio Raimondi (Florence: Sansoni, 1958), 461.
[10] Baldassare Castiglione, *Il libro del Cortegiano*, ed. Amedeo Quondam and Nicola Longo (Cernusco: Garzanti, 1998), 2.31, 166.
[11] The theme of card playing and transgressive sexuality appeared in sixteenth-century Italian artworks also; see Antonella Fenech Kroke, "Ludic Intermingling/Ludic Discrimination: Women's Card Playing and Visual Proscriptions in Early Modern Europe," in *Playthings in Early Modernity: Party Games, Word Games, Mind Games*, ed. Allison Levy (Kalamazoo: Medieval Institute Publications, Western Michigan University, 2017).
[12] Francesco Berni, *Rime*, ed. Danilo Romei (Milan: Mursia, 1985), 64. On *primiera*, see David Parlett, *A History of Card Games* (Oxford: Oxford University Press, 1991), 90–92.
[13] Elizabeth W. Mellyn, *Mad Tuscans and Their Families: A History of Mental Disorder in Early Modern Italy* (Philadeliphia: University of Pennsylvania Press, 2014), 10; see also

themselves, but could become problematic if they led to wasteful consumption of time and money.

While these literary commentators diverged on the morality of gambling, they all broadly concurred on the benefit and utility of games of chance: by providing a confrontation with the unknown future, they served as a proving ground for character. The deliberate, conscious taking of risks on uncertain future outcomes by gambling both developed and revealed a player's mettle and temperament. Games of chance provided a space within which *virtus* (the quintessentially Roman trait combining physical and moral courage, and conveying a sense of force and vigor, revived and praised by Renaissance authors), fortitude, and other praiseworthy traits could be rehearsed for the challenges of life. All the authors defined gambling positively by focusing on the immaterial stakes of the game.[14] Moreover, each of these commentators emphasized that a financial imperative deserved no consideration and, indeed, that the ideal gambler was free from avarice. The real reward earned from confronting the unknown time-yet-to-come, according to these experts in futurity, was not monetary but social.

Castiglione, through Federico Fregoso, stipulated that gambling was appropriate provided that monetary gain was not the motivation. Players prompted by avarice, he observed, demonstrated great displeasure at losing, implying that the ideal courtier of the dialogue's imagination would lose without demurral.[15] Tasso, similarly, denounced avaricious players – who revealed themselves by playing cautiously – as the antithesis of the ideal, "liberal player," whom the protagonists of *Il Gonzaga secondo* sought to delineate. The participants in the dialogue carefully considered the role of money in games. Giulio Cesare Gonzaga suggests that victories earned by *ingegno* (skill or ingenuity) rather than chance were more satisfying and that such triumphs do not result in gaining money "or something that can be measured by money." Annibale Pocaterra concurs to an extent, but argues that a monetary or material prize clearly makes a victory more valuable. When Margarita Bentivoglio condemns this attitude as avaricious, Pocaterra continues by explaining

94–127 (chapter 10) for an extended analysis of the concept and its operation in sixteenth-century Florence.

[14] This is also the central claim, although made in various ways, by the three significant twentieth-century sociological theorists of play: J. Huizinga, *Homo Ludens: A Study of the Play-Element in Culture* (London: Routledge, 1949; reprint, 1999), esp. 49–63; Erving Goffman, *Interaction Ritual: Essays on Face-to-Face Behavior* (Harmondsworth: Penguin, 1967), 149–270; Clifford Geertz, *The Interpretation of Cultures: Selected Essays* (New York: Basic Books, 1973), 412–53.

[15] Castiglione, *Cortegiano*, 2.31, 166.

that it would be so only if the winner desired the money for itself. The ideal player, by contrast, simply desired victory, which brought honor. The utility of financial reward was pleasant side effect.[16] Of course, the potential for material benefit distinguishes gambling. Its purposive nature separates it from other games pursued simply for pleasure.[17] Aretino did not shy away from this reality. "Playing for nothing is the action of a nobody," the Cards declaim at one point. In the text, Aretino did not value the possible financial gain of gambling any more than Castiglione or Tasso, but he made explicit what they merely implied. Rather than stressing the need to avoid avarice while playing, Aretino asserted that gamblers had to be prepared to lose and to do so gracefully when it happened, in order to demonstrate their lack of greed. The Cards continue, "it is necessary to place on the table as much money as one can lose without caring." Discussing Ferrante Sanseverino, prince of Salerno, one of Aretino's patrons, and the dedicatee of the *Le carte parlanti*, the Cards observe: "Instead of the horrified visage and beastly language that play usually puts on the face and in the mouth of those who lose, [Sanseverino] deports himself with a playful visage and graceful words" when confronting a loss.[18] The necessity of losing well constitutes a constant theme in the work. Aretino praised the prodigal generosity of Pope Leo X at the gaming table, and noted that the much-feared *condottiere* Girolamo Accorsi – whose very glance made men tremble – showed neither anger nor dismay at losing a wager.[19]

Given his self-confessed mercenary motivations, Cardano displayed a more ambiguous attitude toward playing for financial gain. He made no clear-cut statement on money, but suggested that a desire for material gain was problematic and compounded the negative aspects of gambling. A game of chance is torture, the Milanese physician observed, "if the stakes are not small." A player who focuses on the money won or lost can quickly become irrational or enraged, he warned.[20] Berni's *Capitolo della primiera* also shows a certain complexity as it praises only one particular card game, and that with a sense of doubled meaning. Berni did, however, condemn all other games as diversions played by "nobodies and

[16] Tasso, *Dialoghi*, 478–79.
[17] See Alessandro Arcangeli, *Recreation in the Renaissance: Attitudes towards Leisure and Pastimes in European Culture, c. 1425–1675* (Basingstoke: Palgrave, 2003), 3.
[18] Aretino, *Le carte parlanti*, 292–93.
[19] Ibid., 168, 360. See further, similar examples at pp. 171, 172, 178, 197, 241–42, 273 (the comedic anecdote of a baker, who staked a tooth on a game, and his opponent who insisted on collecting), and 323.
[20] Cardano, *Ludo aleae*, 50. Aretino also compared gambling to torture, for those who seek financial gain from it: Aretino, *Carte parlanti*, 245.

fools" in search of a quick profit, implying a rejection of financial motivation. *Primiera*, he suggested, was a game of subtleties and strategies. Moreover, he claimed that he would happily lose his eyes playing it, but would fall to blasphemy should he lose as little as three *baiocchi* playing backgammon.[21] Within the narrow focus of the poem, then, Berni praised the playing of *primiera* heedlessly but adjudged other games as so worthless that monetary losses become problematic. The overall tone suggests that such games are only ever played for monetary gain, whereas the delight of *primiera* lies in the contest.

Although they broadly agreed on the beneficial nature of gambling, each of the authors took varying approaches and emphasized differing aspects. For Cardano, games of chance provided an overt test of character. The confrontation with the unknown future in a game of chance unmasked the true nature of its players because "the game is, in fact, a rack: anger, greed, and honesty or dishonesty are found out in play." Gambling, the physician continued, served as "a trial of self-control, for when you have been defeated by anger, by honest men and finally by the game itself."[22] Beyond any financial stake, reputation and status were all chanced, as the roll of the dice or turn of the cards revealed one's real character. What mattered above all else was how one behaved when confronted by the anxiety of the unknown future outcome and, particularly, how one behaved when the game ended in loss and defeat. Although never stated, the concept of *virtus* lay implicit at the heart of Cardano's judgment: the courage and vigor that enabled one to endure adversity and to triumph morally, if not in actuality. For the Milanese physician, the ideal player would rise from a fair game in defeat with neither rancor nor resentment.

The nuances of Cardano's understandings about how gambling crystallized one's character appear in an anecdote recounted in his autobiography. Once, while in Venice in early September, the physician lost all his money, together with some rings and clothing while gambling for two days in the house of a Venetian senator. Sometime during the second day, Cardano realized they were playing with marked cards. Outraged, he wounded his cheating opponent in the face with a dagger. He did not explain what occurred next with complete clarity, but – being locked in the house – the two men returned to the game and the physician proceeded to win back not only his losses but also all the Venetian's money. Deciding to make good on his victory, Cardano magnanimously

---

[21] Berni, *Rime*, 63–64. A *baiocco* was a small Roman coin, worth less than one one-hundredth of a ducat.

[22] Cardano, *Ludo aleae*, 50.

returned some of the latter, in order to make amends for the wound, and managed to force an exit. In his haste to flee the city – as he had offered violence to a member of the Senate – he slipped and fell into a canal only to be rescued by a passing boat, which contained none other than his injured opponent. The senator, far from seeking vengeance, dressed the physician in dry clothes and traveled with him as far as Padua.[23]

This story – included in a chapter that recounts a series of misadventures that could have resulted in death, disfigurement, or disgrace – resists simple analysis, but it suggests that both Cardano and the unnamed Venetian nobleman survived with their honor intact. While the physician clearly lost his temper, he made no apologies for his actions in the text because the game had been rigged. As he had stressed, in *De ludo aleae*, in the passage quoted above, only a fair contest with an honest opponent represented a true test of character.[24] Confronted by fraud or cheating, anger was acceptable and reasonable. Moreover, Cardano revealed the real strength of his character, as well as his indifference to financial gain, when he returned part of his winnings. In so doing, he demonstrated that his wrath had not arisen in response to the material loss but rather to the dishonesty by which it had been accomplished. The distinction is a subtle one, but the unspoken message is that had he lost fairly, the physician would have accepted defeat and its cost with equanimity. The Venetian senator, after failing the test of the card game, the duress of which led him to cheat, regained face by aiding Cardano's escape rather than seeking revenge either directly through violence or indirectly via the law.

Like Cardano, Aretino identified gambling as character revealing. He too emphasized the ways that the confrontation with the unknown future in games of chance could shape and build character, in particular because they served as a rehearsal for life. The text of *Le carte parlanti* presents these as interrelated concepts. At the very beginning of the dialogue, the Cards articulate one of the central themes of the text: the correlation between card games and warfare, and the way in which the former prepares players for the latter. Playing at cards, they claim,

---

[23] Cardano, *Propria vita*, 111–13; Cardano, *The Book of My Life*, trans. Jean Stoner (New York: New York Review of Books, 2002), 92–93. Cardano arranged his autobiography thematically rather than chronologically, and frequently did not identify the year in which the events he recorded occurred.

[24] David Bellhouse, "Decoding Cardano's *Liber de Ludo Aleae*," *Historia Mathematica* 32 (2005), discusses the centrality of ideas about fairness and justice in Cardano's approach to probability in gambling. These ideas, in turn, related to the association of economics with justice in Aristotelian philosophy; see further discussion in Chapter 6.

helps to preserve the spirits of soldiers "ever vigilant and ever ardent." When Padovano suggests that physical or martial exercise would be better, the Cards respond that such sports are better suited to those who prefer "the jousts of love" to actual combat. They constitute appropriate training for lovers, not for soldiers. Such sports, the Cards assert, focus on agility and aesthetics, but those who value "attention, wisdom, judgment, and the test of knowing" should favor cards. This is because gambling has two purposes: "the first teaches how to handle the prosperity of victory, while the other counsels how to tolerate the misery of defeat." The same courage and heart "that one displays in obtaining victories and receiving defeats" on the battlefield "is required for the joys and calamities that one receives in our combats."[25] Aretino, then, stressed the manner in which the emotions provoked by gambling provided a sentimental education for life, and for warfare in particular. Playing at cards enabled one to learn how to control the anxiety and anticipation provoked by a confrontation with the unknown time-yet-to-come, as well as the joy or despair that occasioned its resolution in either victory or defeat.

The resonance between Aretino's opinion, despite its sharp-tongued humor, and that of the other commentators analyzed here suggests that it should not be dismissed as entirely satirical. Beneath its comedic surface, the text resonated with moral and philosophical ideas about the necessity to meet both prosperity and adversity with equanimity that dated back to late antiquity, as well as with the late fifteenth-century revival of Epicurean ideas about the necessity for adaptability in the face of the infinite instability and variability of life.[26] Aretino's dialogue, for all its deliberately provocative and disruptive humor, placed a clear value on the ability to face the uncertainties of the future with forbearance. When the text turns to consider the relative merits of various contemporary rulers in sixteenth-century Italy, this skill emerges as an essential attribute for success.

The Cards commence by praising Emperor Charles V. It would be a mistake, they suggest, to think that the emperor played cards because he had the leisure to do so. His melancholic temperament knew no such freedom. Instead, the Cards claim: "He consents to our game in order to keep the virtues of his heroic spirit exercised." In playing at cards, Charles rehearsed for military enterprises and demonstrated the necessary attributes of a great commander. Referring to the emperor's ill-fated expedition to North Africa in 1541, the Cards observe: "The determined

---

face, the strong color, and the sure glance that Augustus kept in the difficulties of Algiers, he similarly bears in the misfortunes of play." In victory and defeat, at the card table as on the battlefield, Charles V never forgot himself, never lost control, never appeared less than his status required. This, Aretino maintained, is the true meaning of the double-headed Habsburg eagle: "the supreme prudence that he adopts in both happiness and difficulties."[27] The text is, of course, satirical and provocative. However, the significance of its meaning transcends Aretino's humor. *Le carte parlanti* is funny only because the reader recognized the truth that the ability to confront the unknown future and the variability of life with equanimity was valuable and laudable.

In Aretino's dialogue, gambling provided a space to forge and hone the essential attributes and emotions for success, in preparation for the uncertainty and variability of human existence. The ideal gambler depicted in the pages of *Le carte parlanti* played neither for material gain nor for simple diversion, but in order to train him- or herself – Aretino praises a small number of women in the text, including Eleonora de Toledo, duchess of Florence, and Margaret of Austria, duchess of Parma – in self-control, equanimity, and fortitude.[28] This assessment accorded with contemporary practice, through which noblewomen such as Eleonora used games of chance to demonstrate their honor, character, and *virtus* in a manner identical to their male peers.[29] The shared confrontation with the unknown future at the card table cautions against too readily assuming that men and women encountered time differently in Renaissance Italy. Women certainly had profoundly different experiences of embodied temporality than men, through menstruation, pregnancy, and childbirth, and gendered imaginings also shaped the figure of *fortuna*. The new futurity that emerged in the sixteenth century, however, does not appear to have been limited to male experience and understandings.[30]

---

[27] Aretino, *Carte parlanti*, 171.
[28] On this point, see Giaccone, "La scrittura come gioco," and Gabriella Giaccone, "Le *Carte parlanti* di Pietro Aretino," *Lettere italiane* 61, no. 2 (1989).
[29] See Nicholas Scott Baker, "Dux ludens: Eleonora de Toledo, Cosimo I de' Medici, and Games of Chance in the Ducal Household of Mid-Sixteenth-Century Florence," *European History Quarterly* 46, no. 4 (2016), and further discussion in Chapter 2.
[30] For critiques of the notion of discreet and distinct gendered temporalities in early modern Europe, see Merry E. Wiesner-Hanks, ed., *Gendered Temporalities in the Early Modern World* (Amsterdam: Amsterdam University Press, 2018), esp. 14. The contributions by Elisha Rankin and by Holly Barbaccia, Bethany Packard, and Jane Wanninger specifically address embodied temporality. The gendering of the figure of *fortuna* appears throughout the current book; in particular, see Chapters 5 and 7 as well as discussion of Tasso's *Gonzaga secondo* below.

The idea of play as a space for rehearsing the essential emotions and attributes for life occurs also in Tasso's *Gonzaga secondo*, where it becomes a point of debate between the dialogue's protagonists. Annibale Pocaterra initially defines a game as "a contest of *fortuna* and skill between two or more." This provokes an extended debate between him, Giulio Cesare Gonzaga, and Margarita Bentivoglio about the extent to which life itself is, therefore, a game, and whether games are actual contests or simply imitations of contests in life (such as battles or duels). This discussion ends with general agreement that play is an imitation and that the greater the mirroring, the more pleasing the game. The pleasure of play derives from its mimetic nature.[31] In Tasso's assessment, play, including games of chance, was largely a contest that imitated life. This mimesis constituted the essential nature of play and the source of the enjoyment derived from it. In short, the poet suggested that games imitate the agonistic aspects of human existence. Playing constituted a rehearsal for conflict.

As the dialogue continues, the protagonists expound on the nature of the pleasure derived from play. Pocaterra suggests that both players and spectators share in it equally, in both private and public games, and that it ultimately resides in victory. On further reflection, prompted by Gonzaga asking whether enjoyment can be found elsewhere or only in winning, Pocaterra suggests that every game consists of a series of small contests and small triumphs, each with its own pleasure, even while the final outcome remains uncertain. He further explains that this pleasure can blend elements of disquiet or even fear, stressing: "this is what we really mean, when we speak of the enjoyment of play, which is not simple pleasure, since it is mixed with other emotions," such as the hope of winning, the fear of losing, the thrill of victory, the bitterness of defeat. Pocaterra adds that the skill (*ingegno*) of the player works to moderate the emotional highs and lows, and so contributes toward victory.[32] Although less explicit than Aretino, Tasso just as clearly proposed that playing games, including gambling, provided a sentimental education for life. Playing, he suggested, equipped one with the fortitude to confront and deal with the uncertainty of the unknown future. It prepared players for the contests of the everyday and the ability to recognize and take advantage of opportunities as they arose.

Beyond the pages of these texts, the courtly milieux within which Tasso, Aretino, and Castiglione moved recognized and placed a value on the mimetic nature of gambling to demonstrate mastery in the

[31] Tasso, *Dialoghi*, 462–70.   [32] Ibid., 474–76.

contests of power that characterized Renaissance courts. At the Medici court in Florence both Cosimo I and Eleonora de Toledo used games of chance as a vehicle to demonstrate self-control, fortitude, and *virtus*. The ducal couple gambled regularly for high stakes, and the correspondence of their secretaries recorded their winnings and losses, their gaming partners, and the hours they played, circulating the details through the household. On 2 September 1545, for example, Giovanni Francesco Lottini reported to the ducal maiordomo, Pierfrancesco Riccio: "Yesterday, a most excellent game of *primiera* was played by the Lady duchess, so much so that messer Lorenzo Pucci recovered in one day some seven hundred scudi that he had lost in four."[33] In the autumn of 1549, Cristiano Pagni recounted that Eleonora had lost a staggering 3,000 scudi in three days of gambling, but added that she and Cosimo had "played the most beautiful game."[34] What mattered was neither victory nor defeat, but the way the games were played. They were "beautiful" and "excellent" because the players were demonstrably unconcerned by material gain. They played for high stakes and the winnings and loses were spectacular and faced with equanimity and forbearance. In losing well, the ducal couple made manifest their suitability as governors by their ability to confront uncertainty and the tribulations of life.[35]

The value placed on gambling, and losing well, could at times prove a challenge requiring delicate handling. In November 1515, the adolescent Federico Gonzaga, son of the marquis of Mantua, Francesco, and Isabella d'Este, was a guest of Francis I, king of France, in his recently acquired Milanese territory. One afternoon at Vigevano, the monarch invited Gonzaga and others to play *flusso* (a type of proto-blackjack). Stazio Gadio, Gonzaga's secretary and maiordomo, reported to the marquis that the youth "not possessing the means to risk five or six-hundred scudi in a hand, extricated himself gracefully and returned home." Francis demanded to know where Gonzaga had gone but was apparently satisfied to learn that he was playing *palla* (either football or more probably *pallacorda*, an early form of royal tennis). As Charles du Solier, admiral of France and governor of Turin, won 1,500 scudi in the

---

[33] ASF, MDP 1170A: Fasciolo 1, 83r: Giovanni Francesco Lottini, at Poggio a Caiano, to Pierfracesco Riccio, in Florence, 2 September 1545: "ieri se fece dalla Sig[no]ra duchessa una bravissima primiera, tanto che m[esser] lore[n]zo pucci si riscattò in un dì de sette cento scudi che egli haveva perso in quattro." The *scudo* was a gold coin of a slightly higher value than the ducat.

[34] ASF, MDP 1175: Insert 6, doc. 38: Cristiano Pagni, at Poggio a Caiano, to Pierfrancesco Riccio, in Florence, 11 September 1549: "Si fanno bellisimi giochio."

[35] For more detailed analysis, see Baker, "Dux ludens."

ensuing game – and Gadio observed that he and Gonzaga had only 200 scudi on hand – the young nobleman's handling of the potentially perilous situation was particularly admirable.[36] The unspoken threats of the situation extended beyond Gonzaga losing the small sum that he had. Playing would have risked his status and reputation, should he have appeared reluctant to gamble due to his penurious situation or, worse, if he had displayed distress or anger at playing and losing. On this occasion, rather than take the chance, he prudently chose to withdraw with his honor intact.

The centrality of play, and its risk-taking confrontation with the unknown time-yet-to-come, to aristocratic self-presentation in sixteenth-century Italy manifests with startling clarity in Parmigianino's *Portrait of Lorenzo Cibo* (Figure 1.1), dating from the mid-1520s.[37] The painting depicts its subject as self-assured and resplendent in a slashed pink doublet, gilt-edged shirt, red hat with feather, and black mantle. According to Giorgio Vasari, it celebrated Cibo's role as captain of the guard for his cousin, Pope Clement VII in 1527. The painting may, instead, commemorate his appointment as governor and castellan of Spoleto in 1524.[38] In either case, Cibo commissioned it to record a significant and public office in papal service. In the three-quarter-length portrait, he stands gently contrapposto against the backdrop of a balustrade and leafy trellis, confronting the viewer with a confident gaze. His right hand rests on the cross-guard of a massive two-handed sword, the weight of which is supported by a very young, blonde page. Cibo's left hand clutches a shorter blade at his side, the jutting handle accentuating and mimicking the red, gilt-decorated codpiece behind it. In the foreground, immediately below this hand, a backgammon board sits on a ledge or table, one die and two counters visible.

The deliberate inclusion of this ludic diversion in an otherwise martial image highlights the constitutive role of play in sixteenth-century Italian

---

[36] Stazio Gadio, in Vigevano, to Francesco Gonzaga, 3 November 1515, printed in Raffaele Tamalio, *Federico Gonzaga alla corte di Francesco I di Francia nel carteggio privato con Mantova (1515–1517)* (Paris: Honoré Champion, 1994), 100. I am grateful to John Gagné for this reference. On *flusso*, see Parlett, *History of Card Games*, 90–92.

[37] On the portrait, see Mario Di Giampaolo and Elisabetta Fadda, *Parmigianino: Catalogo completo dei dipinti* (Santarcangelo di Romagna: Idea Libri, 2003), 71–74, cat. 20; David Ekserdjian, *Parmigianino* (New Haven, CT: Yale University Press, 2006), 132–34; and Vittorio Sgarbi, *Parmigianino* (Milan: Rizzoli/Skira, 2003), 191–92, cat. 17.

[38] On the dates of Cibo's various papal appointments, see Ekserdjian, *Parmigianino*, 132. The recent scholarship on the portrait, cited above, follows Sydney J. Freedberg, *Parmigianino: His Works in Painting* (Cambridge, MA: Harvard University Press, 1950), 108, in dating it to around 1525, which would make it a commemoration of the earlier office. Cibo was the son of Maddelena di Lorenzo de' Medici and Francesco Cibo (the illegitimate son of Pope Innocent VIII).

Figure 1.1 Parmigianino, *Portrait of Lorenzo Cibo* (ca. 1525), oil on panel, 126.5 x 104.5 cm, Copenhagen: Statens Museum for Kunst.
Credit: Statens Museum for Kunst, Copenhagen, Denmark/Bridgeman Images.

court culture. It neither detracted from nor contrasted with the depiction of Cibo as courtier and military commander, but rather underlined and testified to his suitability for both roles. It suggested that his confidence extended to the confrontation with the uncertainty of the unknown future – both in play and in combat – and that he was capable of self-control and, therefore, worthy of the offices that he held.

Figure 1.2 Unknown artist, *The Chess Players* (late sixteenth century), oil on canvas, 82.3 x 106.3 cm, Berlin: Gemäldegalerie, Staatliche Museen zu Berlin.
Credit: bpk/Gemäldegalerie, SMB, Eigentum des Kaiser Friedrich Museumsvereins/Jörg P. Anders.

The Parmigianino portrait does not explicitly depict gambling, but the evidence of Cardano's autobiography demonstrates that strategic games – like backgammon – were frequently the object of bets, something confirmed in *The Chess Players* (Figure 1.2), painted in the second half of century. This image further emphasizes the place of gambling in the social imaginary of Renaissance Italy's higher social status groups. Sometimes attributed to Ludovico Carracci, but probably the work of an as-yet-unidentified northern Italian painter, the image depicts two men sitting in profile to the viewer, absorbed in a game of chess.[39]

---

[39] On the painting and the debate over its attribution, see the catalogue entry by Gail Feigenbaum in Andrea Emiliani, ed., *Ludovico Carracci* (Bologna: Nuova Alfa, 1993), 35–36, cat. 16, and Alessandro Brogi, *Ludovico Carracci (1555–1619)*, 2 vols. (Ozzano dell'Emilia: Tipoarte, 2001), 1: 258–59, cat. R21. In the early twentieth century, the painting was attributed to an unknown Venetian painter. Feigenbaum identifies it as by Carracci, while Brogi returns to the earlier attribution and considers it the work of an unidentified Veneto-Lombardian artist.

A small dog sits by the man on the left-hand side of painting. The subjects are clearly not as high-ranking as Cibo. Their appearance is simple and sober, far removed from his martial, courtly persona. However, their clothing is elegant in an understated manner; an Anatolian carpet covers the table on which they are playing; and the wall behind them bears rich damasked decoration. All these elements indicate the game is occurring not in a tavern but in a more up-market locale. In the foreground, near the center of the image, two coins sit on the table beside the chess board: the stakes of the game. The painting could almost be a visual representation of the scenario in the points problem. Like the portrait of Cibo, the image captures the connections between play, gambling on the unknown future, and ideas about honor and status. The bet between the two men is not shameful but central to the image. The players demonstrate their worth and character in a contest of skill and luck. The clearly visible financial stake is a cipher for all that they are risking in the game, the immaterial as well as the material.

Given the object of their various writings, and their shared understanding that gambling provided a test of character and rehearsal for life, Aretino, Cardano, and Tasso all directly engaged with the problem of the future as unknown time-yet-to-come. Like so many authors and artists in Renaissance Italy, all three authors used the figure of *fortuna* to discuss the unknowable, variable, yet still measurable, nature of the future.

Strikingly, they stripped away any of the moral or allegorical attachments with which their fifteenth-century forebears and many sixteenth-century contemporaries imbued the figure.[40] In presenting themselves as experts in the new futurity, these authors removed the mask of *fortuna* and denuded the figure of meaning, revealing it simply as a convenient label referring to the unknown time-yet-to-come, an elegant term to clothe the fact that in human perception the future is opaque. They used *fortuna* simply as a convenient and readily comprehensible shorthand for the endless variability of human experience in the face of the unanticipated, the unexpected, the uncertain. In this sense, a modern, secular notion of the future – removed from ideas of Providence or fate – first manifested itself on the gaming table. No wonder, then, that the first experiments in the mathematics of probability, in probability based on frequency not experience, developed in writing about gambling: first by Cardano, then by Galileo Galilei, and finally by Pascal and others in the seventeenth century.[41] Expertise in futurity could be acquired in games of chance.

---

[40] See Chapters 5–8 below.
[41] See Lorraine Daston, *Classical Probability in the Enlightenment* (Princeton, NJ: Princeton University Press, 1988), chapter 1.

Tasso introduced the figure of *fortuna* and the unknown future in an indirect manner. When Gonzaga and Pocaterra agree that a man may lose to a woman in any game in order either to earn her favor or to avoid a too-earnest and manly contest, Bentivoglio immediately objects. She observes that such behavior is duplicitous rather than courteous. She counters that a man could instead earn praise by losing to a woman in a true contest; however, she suggests that "women cannot compete with men in either skill (*ingegno*) or *fortuna*." Gonzaga disputes that women cannot match male skill but concedes that "to me it seems that women more often have to concede to men due to *fortuna* than to ability." To this, Bentivoglio laments: "It is an unfortunate thing, then, to be born a woman; because even if Fortuna is depicted as female and a goddess, she shows herself less favorable to her own sex than to men."[42]

The suggestion here, that *fortuna* favors men over women, invokes a gender dynamic that accompanied some of the imagining of the new concept of the future: time-yet-to-come as variable, mutable, and feminine, so requiring masculine *virtus* to tame it. Women, Gonzaga suggests, lack the foresight and fortitude to confront the future and adapt to its protean nature. The evidence of Tasso's own dialogue – with its ready references to court ladies playing *primiera* – and of a wealth of other sources, both textual and visual, suggests that this sentiment needs to be read as idealizing and within the rich admixture of cultural memory and heritage engaged by the figure of *fortuna*, rather than as reflecting social realities concerning female gambling or even female experiences of the confrontation with the future in games of chance.[43]

Despite lamenting the misfortunes of her sex, Bentivoglio shifts quickly to expressing skepticism toward the entire figure of *fortuna*. She muses whether it is nothing but "an empty name without subject," observing that certain theologians dispute its existence. At Gonzaga's urging, Pocaterra then offers a definition of *fortuna* as a chance event, something that occurs as a result of human action but contrary to human intentions. Tasso, at this point, appears to develop Aristotle's explanation of causality: connecting the unexpected to a mismatch between outcome and intention but also defining human agency as the crucial element in distinguishing *fortuna* from simple chance. Gonzaga suggests that this definition is too narrow to explain the role of *fortuna* in games because in play human intention becomes less relevant. When gambling, he explains, one attempts to achieve an end that is both uncertain and dependent on external causes rather than on skill. In a game of *primiera*,

---

[42] Tasso, *Dialoghi*, 484–85.   [43] See Chapters 2 and 7 below for further discussion.

for example, a player cannot intend to win, because winning depends on getting certain cards, which cannot be predicted, and so remains always unsure.[44] Gonzaga suggests, however, that players can acquire certain aptitudes that assist in games of chance despite their unpredictability, just as a sailor can learn to observe nature and so forecast storms. Gamblers can consider how much money they have and how much the other players possess; they can remember the cards that have been played in order to identify which remain in the deck; and they can study their opponents and, therefore, know which of them have difficulty concealing emotions.[45] The skills acquired at games of chance provide a basis for expertise in futurity.

At this point, the dialogue starts to circle around to the initial definition of what a game is and why playing is beneficial. As contests that imitate life, games require both skill and luck. Playing teaches one to become adaptable, to change with circumstances, and to develop abilities and attributes that help in confronting the unknowability of the future. An echo of Epicurean thought, perhaps, resonates here, in the emphasis on the necessity of adaptability in the face of the randomness of life.[46]

In *De ludo aleae*, Cardano offered practical suggestions to those who wished to gamble, despite his admonition to avoid it. In addition to suggestions on where to play, with whom, and how to identify and avoid cheats and frauds, Cardano also discussed the role of *fortuna* in games of chance and the extent to which skill could influence the outcome. He thought carefully but not always consistently about the subject, although the apparent contradictions in his musings may be attributable to the hasty way in which he composed the entire text, leaving errors and inconsistencies uncorrected. The most coherent definition that he offered identified *fortuna* as "a disposition of affairs suitable or adverse to the will and intention of man; so that no matter how you carry it out, the matter turns out either well or badly, either agrees with human plans or does not."[47] Similar to Tasso, the defining element is human intention through which *fortuna*, the unknown time-yet-to-come, becomes commensurable to human experience. Quite simply, Cardano suggests that humanity makes sense of the apparent arbitrariness of life, and of games

---

[44] Tasso, *Dialoghi*, 485–90.   [45] Ibid., 492–93. A point comparable to Cardano's.
[46] See Chapter 8 on the influence of Epicurus on Renaissance Italian ideas about the future.
[47] Cardano, *Ludo aleae*, 83. I have adapted and slightly altered the translation by Sydney Henry Gould printed in Oystein Ore, *Cardano: The Gambling Scholar* (Princeton, NJ: Princeton University Press, 1953), 227.

of chance, by measuring outcomes against expectations and purposes. The future either happens the way one hoped and planned or does not. In this sense, Cardano used the figure of *fortuna* as a shorthand for the unexpected and the variable nature of life. In an earlier observation about the outcome of card games, he stripped this meaning of any particular moral sense beyond human expectations. Cards "are reckoned good or bad according to the judgment of men, since they themselves signify nothing." No external or metaphysical force – "the conjunction of the stars or some fashioning and order of the universe" – intervenes, he concludes, and the effect is as random as the patterns of clouds or beans thrown on the ground.[48] The meaning of future outcomes is entirely attributable to human interpretation and judgment. *Fortuna* is good or bad depending on whether one wins or loses any given hand in a card game or roll of the die.

With perceptive insight into human psychology, however, Cardano recognized the power of the anxiety provoked by the unknowability of the future. He observed that self-consciousness about the arbitrariness of the outcome could affect a gambler's chances of winning. Players who threw the dice timidly, he suggested, regularly lost because they began to think that *fortuna* was against them: "because *fortuna* is opposed the die falls badly, and because the die falls badly he is defeated; and because he is defeated he throws the die timidly."[49] Keeping in mind Cardano's definition that *fortuna* is nothing more than a label for giving meaning to future outcomes by measuring them against human intentions, the physician here suggests that disquiet about losing could become a self-fulfilling prophecy, endowing the randomness of events with a sense of foreboding and even malice that they do not actually possess.

Aretino offered a similar assessment about the way in which people imbued the unknown future with meaning according to their own hopes and fears. He was equally dismissive of claims about a metaphysical force determining the outcome of games of chance. When they reach the Wheel of Fortune, while describing the trumps in a deck of *tarocchi*, the Cards assert: "although it is believed that she dominates everything, among us she had no true cause." They further suggest that the placement of the Wheel, in tenth position, lower than the Devil, Death, the World, and Justice, underlines the ineffectuality of Fortuna in human life.[50] Padovano then observes, "I do not think that *fortuna* is anything

---

[48] Cardano, *Ludo aleae*, 75. Cardano's identification of cards as neutral vessels of human emotion recalls the defining and central satirical observation of Aretino's *Carte parlanti*.
[49] Ibid., 76.
[50] Aretino, *Carte parlanti*, 61. In Renaissance Italy, *tarocchi* (tarot) was a trick-taking card game. The association of the tarot deck with fortune-telling and the occult dates only from the nineteenth century: Timothy B. Husband, *The World in Play: Luxury Cards,*

other than what we ourselves choose." The Cards concur with this opinion. Aretino did acknowledge, through the voice of Cards, the opinions of many ancient and contemporary authors that Fortuna had actual power and moral force, but the dialogue clearly judges this to be nothing more than a fantasy conjured by human minds. Padovano offers the final and definitive assessment: "It is very true that when we meet any unfortunate outcome, that human ignorance from which our every failure proceeds, in order to excuse itself, attributes this to her; who is but the veil of human incapability."[51]

Like Cardano, then, Aretino identifies *fortuna* as little more than a mask – "we wear her guise," the Cards assert – that lends shape to the unknown future, a label that gives meaning to the mutability of human existence.[52] This assessment lies at the heart of *Le carte parlanti*, in which Aretino sought to demonstrate the absurdity of casting moral judgments on gambling and of excusing human failings with notions such as *fortuna* and fate.[53] Aretino's perfect gambler – as discussed above – possessed equanimity and prudence. To such a player, games of chance offered little harm because the only evils present were those that the human actors brought to the table themselves: irrationality, anger, fear, weakness. The objects of play were inanimate. The game itself was neutral. Rather than accepting the blame, however, a poor player would attribute losses and defeats to *fortuna*.

The ideal gambler, instead of fearing the unknown outcome, recognized that the true pleasure of games of chance lay in embracing the uncertainty of the outcome. When Padovano asks why the pleasure of sitting down to a game is greater than the enjoyment of actually playing it, the Cards reply: "Cards promise happiness to all those who take them up, moreover the pleasure of holding them in one's hand would never diminish if one never began to play."[54] The real joy lay in anticipation, in surrendering to the unknowability of the future, to its infinite potentialities, which offered both a disruption in the everyday of today and a distraction from mundane anxieties about tomorrow.

Cardano and Tasso agreed with Aretino on this point. The Milanese physician wrote that "during times of grave anxieties and grief, [gambling] seems not only permissible, but even expedient." He went on to

---

1430–1540 (New York: Metropolian Museum of Art, 2015), 76–78; Parlett, *History of Card Games*, 238-47.
[51] Aretino, *Carte parlanti*, 67-68.   [52] Ibid., 74–75.
[53] On this point, see Giaccone, "Le *Carte parlanti*"; Christopher Cairns, *Pietro Aretino and the Republic of Venice: Researches on Aretino and His Circle in Venice* (Florence: Olschki, 1985), 211.
[54] Aretino, *Carte parlanti*, 334.

suggest that those who were ill and those condemned to death could also find solace in games of chance.[55] Those confronted by the cruelty of life and the obscurity of the future, Cardano implied, could take comfort in the way that gambling compressed the unknown time-yet-to-come into a defined, finite moment. Dice and card games offered swift resolution to the anxiety of waiting for the future to reveal itself and a quick end to the more profound disturbance of the new conception of that future as unknowable and unknown. For this reason, the "expectation of *fortuna*" that constituted the essence of gambling made it superior to other diversions in times of difficulty.[56] Tasso offered a more nuanced and more equivocal endorsement. However, Pocaterra's evocation of the complex sentiments provoked by play – including both joy and sadness, hope and fear – highlights the central importance of uncertainty in enjoyment: "this is what is properly called the delight of gamblers, which is not a simple pleasure, since it is mixed with other sensations."[57] The rabbi, scholar, and frequent gambler Leon Modena identified in himself a prompting that mirrors these literary assessments. His autobiography maps a pattern by which he turned to gambling in moments of grief or crisis, such as the loss of his eldest son in 1617: "Following the death of the apple of my eye and root of my heart, I returned out of great anxiety to the enemy that always drove me out of the world – namely, playing games of chance."[58]

Gambling, in the assessment of authors such as Cardano, offered a vision of life as sixteenth-century Italians most deeply did not want it to be: a world in which random chance, rather than fate or Providence, determined the outcome of events.[59] These writers unfurled a disquieting vision of life as uncertain and unstable, of the future as always unknown and unknowable. The one line of comfort, however, that they offered was their expertise in this futurity, as guides who could furnish the reader with the facility to navigate the obscure waters of time-yet-to-come. As the rest of this book demonstrates, Cardano, Aretino, Tasso, and the others were outliers in the middle decades of the sixteenth century. The stark vision of a single, remarkably modern-seeming conception of the future was not one shared widely across the Italian culture

---

[55] Cardano, *Ludo aleae*, 48. I have again adapted Gould's translation from Ore, *Cardano*, 185–86.

[56] Cardano, *Ludo aleae*, 56.   [57] Tasso, *Dialoghi*, 476.

[58] Leon Modena, *The Autobiography of a Seventeenth-Century Venetian Rabbi: Leon Modena's Life of Judah*, trans. Mark R. Cohen (Princeton, NJ: Princeton University Press, 1988), 113; see also 103, 155–56, 159; and Howard E. Adelman, "Leon Modena: The Autobiography and the Man," in *The Autobiography of a Seventeenth-Century Venetian Rabbi: Leon Modena's Life of Judah*, ed. Mark R. Cohen (Princeton, NJ: Princeton University Press, 1989), 43.

[59] I am, of course, paraphrasing Geertz, *Interpretation of Cultures*, 444, here.

and society. However, the confidence with which they embraced it underscores the familiarity gamblers felt in confronting the unknown and the uncertain.

Games of chance provided the most immediately accessible and widespread vehicle for Italians encounter the future in its new form as unknown time-yet-to-come, a field open to human endeavor and intention, a time in which money could be won or lost through speculation. Games of dice and cards compressed the experience of the future into a definable form, and their very structure demonstrated the way in which time consisted as a series of discrete, unrepeatable moments, as each roll or hand proved unpredictable and unique. Through this experience, gambling helped to give sense and structure to this new futurity. The authors examined in this chapter guided their readers through this process. The game provided a space in which character could be created, demonstrated, and maintained. It provided a sentimental education in essential skills for managing the intense, face-to-face, status-conscious society of the peninsula: self-control in the face of adversity and uncertainty, the harnessing of anxiety and disquiet, magnanimity in defeat and victory. Through games of chance, Renaissance Italians could play their culture by playing the future as unknown.

2   The Future in Play

On 18 February 1522, the tireless Venetian diarist Marin Sanudo recorded the appearance of lotteries in the city during Carnival that year. At the Rialto, he noted, "a new means of making money has emerged, by placing a small sum on *fortuna*."[1] The widespread use of the lottery constituted an innovation in games of chance in sixteenth-century Italy. Although the earliest examples date to the mid-fifteenth century, they truly became popular and frequent only in the following century, adding to the myriad of ways in which Renaissance Italians gambled. From simple bets on almost any sort of future outcome (the sex of an unborn child, the identity of the next pope, whether a prince might die) to structured card or dice games and organized lotteries, gambling was ubiquitous across virtually all strata of society, from poor widows to ruling dynasts. It represented the most common and most mundane field in which Italians encountered the future as unknown time-yet-to-come in the sixteenth century, time open to speculation in which random chance and some human agency could determine outcomes. Gambling compressed into a defined window an experience of the future as unknowable yet also accessible. Games of chance as well as betting practices offered the lure of opportunity – for increased wealth, for increased status, to demonstrate skill or daring – if only it could be seized or won.

Gambling then provided the most likely experience through which Italians from all walks of life could or might think about the nature of time and the future. The act of throwing dice, playing a hand of cards, or buying a lottery ticket compressed the anxiety and expectation of waiting for the unknown time-yet-to-come to reveal itself in a controlled fashion into a moment, a few minutes, or a few days. Wagering and games of chance gave material form to the experience, making it both accessible and unavoidable. This chapter considers the experiences of the future as

---

[1] Marino Sanuto, *I diarii di Marino Sanuto*, 58 vols. (Bologna: Forni, 1970), 32: col. 467.

unknown time-yet-to-come through the medium of games of chance in everyday life, in contrast to the more literary evidence considered in Chapter 1. It examines the experience to which the authors examined in the previous chapter attempted to give meaning, the realm in which they had earned their expertise. It reveals how the experience and understanding of the future, in the form of gambling, were deeply entwined with and structured by significant and profoundly rooted sociocultural forces in Renaissance Italian life. The unknown, unknowable nature of the future was ordered, made sense of, and tamed by notions of honor and status, by ideas about social credit that the financial debts engendered by gambling made manifest. The nature of the evidence available might make this sense of the future appear particularly aristocratic, but the conditioning forces of honor, status, and credit operated across all strata in sixteenth-century Italian society, suggesting that this experience was not restricted to sociopolitical elites, despite the vagaries of documentary survival.

While financial gain constituted an important part of the attraction that games of chance held, the significance of gambling always lay beyond diversion and material stakes.[2] In games of chance, Renaissance Italians played with the idea of the future as unknown time-yet-to-come, pursuing the opportunity and potential that it offered to speculate both financially and socially. In a status-conscious society concerned with maintaining honor and managing appearances, in which *credit* could refer both to financial well-being and to honor, the lines between what was staked on the roll of the dice or the turn of the cards blurred with particular ease. All levels of society, all professions, all people, even the apparently dishonorable, thought of themselves as having something to lose beyond their financial stake.[3] Gamblers in Renaissance Italy, as well as seeking profits, sought to demonstrate themselves to be men and women of *action*. Seizing the opportunity offered by the compressed moment of the unknown future that existed in games of chance, they could exhibit and gain – but also lose – face and status among their peers.[4]

---

[2] This is the central claim, although made in various ways, by the three significant twentieth-century sociological theorists of play: J. Huizinga, *Homo Ludens: A Study of the Play-Element in Culture* (London: Routledge, 1949; reprint, 1999), esp. 49–63; Erving Goffman, *Interaction Ritual: Essays on Face-to-Face Behavior* (Harmondsworth: Penguin, 1967), 149–270; Clifford Geertz, *The Interpretation of Cultures: Selected Essays* (New York: Basic Books, 1973), 412–53.
[3] On the importance of honor even among the apparently dishonorable in sixteenth-century Italy, see, for example, Elizabeth S. Cohen, "Honor and Gender in the Streets of Early Modern Rome," *Journal of Interdisciplinary History* 22, no. 4 (1992).
[4] On *action*, see Goffman, *Interaction Ritual*, esp. 185.

In playing with the future, Renaissance Italians expressed a sense of the unknown time-yet-to-come inscribed in terms of honor and status. Futurity, gambling, and notions of social credit existed in a triangular, reinforcing relationship. The act of gambling compressed the unknown future into a moment, while also serving as a proving ground for character, which was, in turn, tested by the unknowability of the future. The chapter undertakes a comparative analysis of legislation on gambling in Florence, Genoa, Milan, and Venice from the late Middle Ages to the sixteenth century, in order to reveal the connections between games of chance and ideas about character in the Renaissance social imaginary. It also examines the enforcement of these laws and the activities of gamblers to demonstrate how the structuring forces of face, honor, and status operated for both women and men across all social strata.

As well as risking both social and financial credit, playing of games of chance carried metaphysical risks and more mundane disapprobation in Renaissance Italy. Gambling remained an ambiguous and conflicted pursuit. Identified as sinful by theologians, condemned as a vice by philosophers, it occupied a legal limbo between toleration and proscription. Yet games of chance were also widely popular and potentially enriching, not only for individuals but also for governments that could regulate their practice. In this regard, the experience of gambling in the sixteenth century exhibited both continuities and also some significant differences compared with preceding centuries.

Much of the ambiguity about the place of games of chance in late medieval Italy originated in their conflicting and complicated legal status, pulled in antithetical directions by Roman and Germanic law, and subject to a shifting debate within canon law. No coherence existed in regulatory attitudes toward gambling. The contradictions and ambiguities of legislation, from the late middle ages into the sixteenth century, revealed something of the cross-cutting currents present in Italian society toward games of chance and ideas about the future. In particular, they reveal how underlying assumptions about status and honor structured proscriptive approaches to games of chance.

These contradictions existed from the communal era. During the thirteenth and fourteenth centuries, Italian cities had generally tolerated gambling as a licit but illegal pastime, subjecting it to specific limitations. Dante's ready use of the aftermath of a dice game as a metaphor to describe the manner in which the throng of the souls of those who died by violence and repented too late surrounded the Pilgrim in Purgatory testifies to the broad acceptance of games of chance: "The crowd leaves with the winner: some in front, / some tugging at him from behind, the rest / close to his side beg to be recognized."[5] Most cities instituted the principle of Germanic law that identified an agreement to gamble, whatever its morality, as a binding contract. Unlike Roman legal practice, therefore, a loser could not sue to recover losses. However, the majority of communes restricted the playing of games of chance to specific prescribed places and times. Usually, authorities tolerated gambling – although not necessarily without financial penalties for those apprehended doing so – during the twelve days of Christmas and other locally determined feasts and festivals.

Almost uniformly, communal legislation permitted the playing of games of chance in public spaces only. In Florence, for example, frequently mentioned locations included the Piazza Santa Trinita, the Ponte Vecchio, the Ponte della Carraia, and even the cloisters of Santa Maria Novella. A Venetian legend ascribing freedom to gamble between the columns of Saint Mark and Saint Theodore in the Piazzetta San Marco reflected this governmental preference for such games to occur in easily surveilled and policed locales. In actuality, a law of 1329 permitted gambling (for limited stakes) in the Loggia dei Mercanti at the Rialto. By contrast, gambling in taverns, private homes, and at night – in places and times that favored concealment – remained forbidden and attracted harsher penalties. Some communes, particularly in Tuscany (but not Florence), instituted an office of professional gambler in the city, usually referred to as a *baratteria*, charged with managing gambling in permitted spaces, policing the behavior of players, and enforcing restrictions against games being played elsewhere.[6]

Overall, civic laws concerning gambling in the late medieval period tended toward attempting to control the antisocial behaviors it might prompt, rather than regulating the practice itself. The governors of Italian communes did not concern themselves with the speculative

[5] Dante Alighieri, *Purgatorio*, 6: 4–6. The translation is from Dante Alighieri, *The Divine Comedy, vol. 2: Purgatory*, trans. Mark Musa (New York: Penguin, 1985), 57.
[6] Giovanni Ceccarelli, *Il gioco e il peccato: Economia e rischio nel Tardo Medioevo* (Bologna: Il Mulino, 2003), 65–109; Giampaolo Dossena et al., *Fanti e denari: Sei secoli di giochi d'azzardo* (Venice: Arsenale, 1989), 185–201; Gherado Ortalli, "The Origins of the Gambler-State: Licenses and Excises for Gaming Activities in the XIII and XIV Centuries (and the Case of Vicenza)," *Ludica* 3 (1997); Gherado Ortalli, "Lo stato e il giocatore: Lunga storia di un rapporto difficile," in *Il gioco pubblico in Italia: Storia, cultura e mercato*, ed. Giuseppe Imbucci (Venice: Marsilio, 1999); Ilaria Taddei, "Gioco d'azzardo, ribaldi e baratteria nelle città della Toscana tardo-medievale," *Quaderni storici* n.s. 92/a. 31, no. 2 (1996); Ludovico Zdekauer, *Il gioco d'azzardo nel Medioevo italiano* (Florence: Salimbeni, 1993), esp. 25–62, 116–17; Andrea Zorzi, "Battagliole e giochi d'azzardo a Firenze nel tardo Medioevo: Due pratiche sociali tra disciplinamento e repressione," in *Gioco e giustizia nell'Italia di Comune*, ed. Gherado Ortalli (Treviso: Fondazione Benetton; Rome: Viella, 1993).

nature of games of chance, with the fact that their resolution depended on unknowable outcomes. Laws concerning gambling did not focus on the mechanics and metaphysics of the act itself. Instead, they targeted the collateral vices most readily associated with the practice – fraud, violence, and blasphemy. These were crimes prompted by the sins of aversion – pride, anger, greed, envy – and so related to ideas about status and reputation, and also transgressions that threatened to unravel the social fabric. Although not explicitly stating so, communal legislation recognized that the act of gambling invoked questions of honor and sought to militate against the potential for such intrigues to erupt in antisocial and violent behavior.

Canon law, by contrast, not only concerned itself with the collateral effects of gambling but also specifically targeted its speculative, future-oriented nature. In penitential thought gambling remained not only immoral, un-Christian behavior, but also a sin. As well as provoking avarice, anger, and cursing, the act of gambling itself was blasphemous. Gambling was the inversion of prayer. A gambler either trusted to chance over Providence – thereby denying divine will and omnipotence or demonstrating pride akin to Lucifer's – or abused the act of prayer – by seeking material gain determined luck and claiming victory as a sign of providential favor.[7] While the position of canon law was fundamentally straightforward, it developed complexities and subtleties as gambling became entangled in the scholastic discussion about economics and speculative, commercial risk taking that developed in the later thirteenth century.[8] With regard to games of chance, a significant debate developed between the thirteenth and sixteenth centuries over the status of winnings.

Initially, penitential thought associated such financial gain with theft or usury: illegal earnings derived from an illicit act, which required

---

[7] Ceccarelli, *Il gioco e il peccato*, 47–64; Bernardette Patton, *Preaching Friars and Civic Ethos: Siena, 1380–1480* (London: Centre for Medieval Studies, Queen Mary and Westfield College, University of London, 1992), 315–16; Rhiannon Purdie, "Dice Games and the Blasphemy of Prediction," in *Medieval Futures: Attitudes to the Future in the Middle Ages*, ed. J. A. Burrow and Ian P. Wei (Woodbridge: Boydell Press, 2000); Zorzi, "Battagliole e giochi d'azzardo," 96. Two Bible verses in particular underlay this understanding: Numbers 33:54: "And you shall divide it among you by lot. To the more you shall give a larger part, and to the fewer a lesser. To every one as the lot shall fall, so shall the inheritance be given"; and Proverbs 16:33: "Lots are cast into the lap, but they are disposed of by the Lord" (Douay-Rheims translation). The Church interpreted these verses to indicate that the outcome of seemingly chance events (the casting of lots) was ordained by divine will.

[8] See Joel Kaye, *Economy and Nature in the Fourteenth Century: Money, Market Exchange, and the Emergence of Scientific Thought* (Cambridge: Cambridge University Press, 1998), and Chapter 6 below.

restitution before absolution could be granted. Moreover, the profits derived from such acts could not be distributed to charity as a penance because the winner did not have legal, legitimate possession of the money in question and so had no right to give it away. When it came to gambling, however, canon law added an additional complication because it tended to identify both the winner and loser as sinners, and so posited charitable dispersion as an effective punishment for all parties. This complicated the penitential association between gambling and theft because almsgiving implied that a legitimate transfer of property had occurred.[9] While neither a theologian nor a lawyer, Francesco Petrarch captured this sentiment effectively in his popular, mid-fourteenth-century guide to living *De remediis utriusque fortunae* (*Remedies for Fortune Fair and Foul*), observing that in gambling, "what you win is not yours, and what you lose ceases to be yours, although it does not really belong to anyone else."[10]

This complexity caused continuing debate about the status of winnings. A significant shift in thinking began with Thomas Aquinas, who stated that local, civil statute or custom could supersede the Roman law prohibition on gambling. This observation made it possible to untangle the legal status of games of chance from the sin of blasphemy, and to develop arguments that gaming winnings constituted a legitimate transfer of property, although the Dominican never took this step himself. Instead, as with the debates about speculative commercial activities, the Friars Minor took the lead in developments during the thirteenth and fourteenth centuries. Discussion about gambling occurred within the larger shift in thinking about commerce and value.

Franciscan economic thinkers revived both the Aristotelian concept of the economy as functioning via geometrical exchange and the arithmetical model preferred by earlier Christian thinkers. Because a geometrical, proportional vision of exchange recognized and rewarded risk, it enabled Peter John Olivi and others to identify the decision to gamble as a legitimate economic act. Gamblers entered into a contract for a particular type of exchange, one in which the outcome was conditional on a dice roll. As a result, some Franciscan writers began to classify winnings from games of chance no longer with theft or usury but instead with earnings from prostitution: legitimate profits made from an illicit activity bound

---

[9] Ceccarelli, *Il gioco e il peccato*, 65–109.
[10] Francesco Petrarca, *Petrarch's Remedies for Fortune Fair and Foul*, ed. Conrad H. Rawski (Bloomington: Indiana University Press, 1991), 1.27, 82. Petrarch did, however, counsel restitution of winnings, with interest. On Petrarch and *De remediis*, see Chapter 5 below.

by contractual obligation. Money won by gambling became property legitimately transferred and so not subject to restitution. Because the act itself remained a sin, donation of at least part of the winnings to charity was encouraged to help mitigate against the inevitable spiritual penalties.[11]

This shift in Franciscan economic and penitential thinking did not translate into a uniform acceptance of gambling as a legitimate contract, even within the Order of Friars Minor. Indeed, contemporaneously with these developments, other Franciscan commentators – such as Duns Scotus and Ricardo di Mediavilla – continued to condemn the practice as an illegitimate transfer that required restitution, even while accepting the broader approbation of commercial risk taking and profit making. The key distinction such thinkers made centered on the concept of utility. The labor of a merchant, they argued, produced not only personal wealth but also broader social benefits. The idle speculation of the gambler, by contrast, produced nothing and was instead wasteful.[12]

Ecclesiastical condemnation of gambling in fact gained traction across Italy in the fifteenth century. Led by charismatic, popular preachers from the Observant wings of the three main mendicant orders – such as Bernardino of Siena – religious hostility toward games became increasingly vocal and influential. It formed part of a broader campaign against immorality and illicit behavior that also targeted sodomy, blasphemy, and prostitution. These orators opposed not only gambling, although it received particular criticism, but also table games (such as early versions of backgammon), chess, and even organized festivities such as horse races, bullfights, and tournaments. In contrast to the preceding centuries, preachers no longer simply urged secular authorities to control play; they now called for its complete suppression and staged public conversion events at which dice, cards, and board games could be burned.[13] In the *Quadragesimale de evangelio aeterno*, for example, Bernardino of Siena

---

[11] Ceccarelli, *Il gioco e il peccato*, 181–255; Kaye, *Economy and Nature*, 79–162; Germano Maifreda, *From Oikonomia to Political Economy: Constructing Economic Knowledge from the Renaissance to the Scientific Revolution*, trans. Loretta Valtz Mannucci (Farnham: Ashgate, 2012), 43–72. See also further discussion in Chapter 6 below.

[12] Ceccarelli, *Il gioco e il peccato*, 257–327; Kaye, *Economy and Nature*, 116–62.

[13] Ceccarelli, *Il gioco e il peccato*, 329–427; Patton, *Preaching Friars*, esp. 313–17; Alessandra Rizzi, "Il gioco fra norma laica e proibizione religiosa: L'azione dei predicatori fra Tre e Quattrocento," in *Gioco e giustizia nell'Italia di Comune*, ed. Gherado Ortalli (Treviso: Fondazione Benetton; Rome: Viella, 1993); Alessandra Rizzi, "Gioco, disciplinamento, predicazione," *Ludica* 7 (2001). But note that Patton (pp. 310–13) identifies a clear distinction between Observant and Conventual mendicant attitudes toward play and recreation in this period. While the former condemned all play as spiritually harmful, the latter showed acceptance for harmless recreation, condemning only antisocial and sinful activities such as gambling.

called on civic governors "to forbid games, punish playing, dismiss the
baratterie, condemn dice and other gaming equipment, and those in possession of them."[14] In particular, preachers condemned the contradictions
of existing laws, calling for an end to limited toleration of gambling.
The practical effects of such preaching, however, tended to be limited
and short-lived. New statutes banning gambling, many of which bore the
names or cited the influence of specific preachers, always proved more
aspirational than effective. Games of chance remained an endemic feature of urban life in Italy through the fifteenth and sixteenth centuries.
Civic authorities found it more financially beneficial, as well as more
conducive to social harmony, to avoid complete repression in favor of
continuing the limited toleration of earlier centuries.[15] In early fifteenth-
century Florence, for example, convicted gamblers paid what amounted
to a tax on their activities: ten lire for players – with increasing increments
for recidivists – and twenty-five to fifty lire for those who hosted games or
provided the dice and cards for play.[16] Venetian legislation from
1455 ordered the confiscation of the stakes by the Avogadori di Comun
(State Attorneys) and fines of 100 ducats, as well as six months' imprisonment and public shaming. As magistrates retained discretion in the
imposition of punishment, in normal practice they enforced only the
financial penalties.[17]

By the sixteenth century, then, the contradictions and ambiguities of
gambling in Italian law remained unresolved. If anything, the contrac-
tualist position of the Franciscan economic thinkers added to the compli-
cations. This stance reached its logical conclusion and definitive
expression in the work of two Dominican legal commentators: John
Mair, who taught at the University of Paris, and his most prominent
student, Dominigo de Soto. Both argued that any agreement to gamble –
in which both parties shared the risk equally – constituted an aleatory
contract under natural law and became a licit, legitimate economic
exchange, even while remaining morally dubious and potentially sinful.[18]

[14] Quoted in Rizzi, "Il gioco fra norma laica e proibizione," 163, n. 58.
[15] Dossena et al., *Fanti e denari*, 185–201; Rizzi, "Il gioco fra norma laica e proibizione,"
esp. 180–82; Zorzi, "Battagliole e giochi d'azzardo," esp. 93–105.
[16] Zorzi, "Battagliole e giochi d'azzardo," 104. The fines cited here date to the first third of
the fifteenth century, when the nominal daily wage of an unskilled laborer was ten soldi
(half of one lira): see Richard A. Goldthwaite, *The Economy of Renaissance Florence*
(Baltimore, MD: Johns Hopkins University Press, 2009), 612–13. Between 1400 and
1425, the value of the florin rose from seventy-five to eighty soldi.
[17] Dossena et al., *Fanti e denari*, 189.
[18] Ceccarelli, *Il gioco e il peccato*, 329–47; Giovanni Ceccarelli, "Gambling and Economic
Thought in the Late Middle Ages," *Ludica* 12 (2006); James Franklin, *The Science of
Conjecture: Evidence and Probability before Pascal* (Baltimore, MD: Johns Hopkins

The notion of gambling as an aleatory contract complemented the emergent idea of the future as unknown time-yet-to-come that provided a potentially profitable space for human agency. It gave legitimacy to gambling as a form of speculation on this unknowable moment that was, perhaps, less tainted by sin than a purely providential sense of temporality would suggest. The continual issuance of new legislation and proclamations concerning games of chance across the sixteenth century testifies both to the ongoing concern of civic authorities to regulate risk-taking behavior in this new ethical landscape and to the ultimate ineffectuality of such attempts.

In 1539, the Venetian Council of Ten transferred surveillance and regulation of gambling from the Avogadori di Comun to the newly created Esecutori contro la bestemmia (Executors against Blasphemy). This shift in jurisdiction – from the broad remit of the State Attorneys to a magistracy specifically enjoined to monitor and discipline morality – represented a deliberate choice by the governors of Venice, in the face of arguments for the contractual legitimacy of games of chance, to emphasize the still problematic ethical status of gambling. It suggests that the blasphemous nature of the act itself continued to make it subject to proscription and regulation. Later laws, in 1586 and 1591, in fact declaimed that games of chance were an offense against divine majesty.[19] The language of the legislation authorizing the transfer of jurisdiction, however, emphasized the older tradition of concern focused on the collateral vices rather than on the act of gambling itself. The office of the Esecutori existed, the law stated, to ensure the hope of obtaining "the protection and grace of Divine Majesty toward our state," and justified the new competency because "beyond the blasphemies uttered, many other enormous and detestable sins" accompanied games of chance.[20]

The legislative approach in Venice, however, remained riven with contradictions, not least because the government had been operating public lotteries to help fund the cost of ongoing military campaigns since the middle of the previous decade.[21] The initial decree of

University Press, 2001), 286; Ivo Schneider, "The Market Place and Games of Chance in the Fifteenth and Sixteenth Centuries," in *Mathematics from Manuscript to Print, 1300–1600*, ed. Cynthia Hay (Oxford: Oxford University Press, 1988), 226.
[19] ASV, Esecutori 54, Tomo primo, 21r, 22v.
[20] ASV, Esecutori 54, Tomo primo, 15r: "onde si può sperar' prottetione et gratia dalla Divina Maestà verso il stato nostro"; "oltre le Biasteme commessi molti altri enormi et detestandi peccati accompagnati dal gioco." The office of the Esecutori was created by the Council of Ten in 1537 and remained subject to the latter's control. On concerns about morality and gambling in sixteenth-century Venice, see also Dossena et al., *Fanti e denari*, 191.
[21] Dossena et al., *Fanti e denari*, 123–24, 191. On lotteries in Renaissance Italy, see more below.

30 April 1539 prohibited games of chance in "houses or *ridotti* and in any other place either on land or in a boat or other ship of this City," on pain of fines of 100 ducats and a ban on holding office for two years (for nobles) or exile from the Venetian dominion for two years and identical financial penalties (for non-nobles), and the same punishment for hosts of gaming parties. It also, however, included specific exemptions. The legislation permitted groups of noblemen and *cittadini* of no more than six "relatives, friends, and companions" to play card and table games "in their private homes." Dice games remained forbidden; a daily limit of one ducat per person could be staked; and gambling had to cease after the first hour of the night from March to September and the third hour of the night between October and February. The law cautioned that these concessions did not permit regular gaming but only "on those occasions when, finding themselves together, as usually occurs, they wish to settle themselves to playing and not otherwise."[22]

As the magistrates enacting and enforcing the 1539 decree were themselves nobles, the legislation represented the desires, values, and expectations of Venice's governors, in both its restrictions and its exceptions. In attempting to ban and regulate gambling in the city, the Council of Ten expressed the continuing concern of urban government to militate against antisocial behavior that threatened peace and stability. But the legislation also recognized and legitimized the place of gambling in the sociability of Venice's socioeconomic elite castes: the office-holding nobility and the *cittadini*, who enjoyed a privileged status between the former and the mass of the city's population. This implied recognition of the way that games of chance – as a form of speculation on an unknown future outcome – became a principle vehicle for the manifestation of honor and status across the Italian peninsula in the sixteenth century. The unknown time-yet-to-come became an ideal temporal space in which to demonstrate one's social credit and standing.[23]

[22] ASV, Esecutori 54, Tomo primo 15v–18r: "Quelli veramente che se reducesse ad'alcuna di dette case over redutti et in ogni altro loco cosi in terra come in barca over altri legni in questa Città e tutto il Dogado et per xxv miglia oltra per zuogar' et zuogasse contra la forma del presente ordine" (15v); "Sia veramente permesso alli Zentil'homeni et Cittadini Nostri et cadauno altro nelle private case loro con li habitanti possendo etiam intervenir' di fora via da quattro cinque summura sei persone de parenti amici et compagni " (16v); "non se intenda per quelli che volesserò tener reduto ordinario et quotidiano ma per quelli solamente che qualche volta attrovandose insieme come suol accader' volessero redursi a zuogar' et non altramente" (17v).
[23] On the connections between gambling and social status in Venice, see also Jonathan Walker, "Gambling and Venetian Noblemen, c. 1500–1700," *Past and Present*, no. 162 (1999).

Limitations to the number of players permitted, as well as the concern about *ridotti* – locations dedicated to gambling, identified as a principal object at issue in the 1539 and subsequent laws – represented concerns that gathering to gamble could conceal conspiracies or forbidden political caucusing.[24] In addition to forbidding *ridotti*, the law also explicitly banned gaming "in vaults or any other secret and occluded locale."[25] The limited permission given nobles and *cittadini* to play games of chance, however, clearly testified to the sociocultural value of such future-oriented speculation for elite status and credibility. The regular appearance of legislation forbidding the establishment and frequenting of *ridotti* throughout the century – in 1567, 1575, 1586, 1591, and 1598 – further suggests that the potential rewards of gambling, both financial and social, outweighed concerns about conspiracy for the majority of Venice's office-holding class.[26]

Concern about the financial implications of gambling appeared less frequently and less insistently. The decree of 1539 had observed that, as well as occasioning sin, games of chances provoked "the manifest ruin of faculties and people," while the law of 1586 made reference to the damage and offense that it caused families and private interests. The legislation of 1591 was the most explicit, noting that *ridotti* existed "either for the most avaricious cupidity of those who host them or for the great gain extracted from them." It continued that the principal drivers of their survival, in any case, "are the gamblers of the greatest sums of money, who impoverish and ruin families."[27] Such language reveals anxieties about the harm that excessive losses could wreak on patrimonies. It appears to operate in accordance with the emergent "patrimonial rationality" in sixteenth-century attitudes toward wealth and expenditure.[28]

---

[24] The term *ridotto* probably derived from the verb *ridurre* (to reduce, restrict, enclose) and carried connotations of secrecy; see ibid., 32–34. On the Venetian government's profound suspicion of secret alliances or factions within the office-holding class, as well as its attempts at the surveillance and control of political communication, see most recently Filippo De Vivo, *Information and Communication in Venice: Rethinking Early Modern Politics* (Oxford: Oxford University Press, 2007).

[25] ASV, Esecutori 54, Tomo primo, 16v: "non si possi zuogar in Volte over in alcun loco secreto et occulto nè in Venetia nè fuora."

[26] ASV, Esecutori 54, Tomo primo, 18v–24v.

[27] Ibid., 15r: "manifesta rovina delle facoltà et delle persone"; 21r; 22r–v: "che quello che li genera e nutrisce o per lo più l'avarissima cupidità di quelli che li tengono [o] per il molto guadagno che ne cavano et che quelli che più li fomentano sono li giocatori di grossissime summe di denari, che impoveriscono et rovinano le fameglie."

[28] Elizabeth W. Mellyn, *Mad Tuscans and Their Families: A History of Mental Disorder in Early Modern Italy* (Philadelphia: University of Pennsylvania Press, 2014), 10. See also Chapter 1 above.

Here again, the Venetian decrees reveal more about elite expectations and values than about ethical concerns. Strikingly, only the 1598 legislation mandated (partial) restitution of monies lost from gambling, with the losing player receiving half to three-quarters of the confiscated winnings from games in which less than 100 ducats had been staked.[29] This combination of two contrary penitential attitudes appearing only at the very end of the century suggests some continuing resistance to the argument that gambling represented a binding, legitimate aleatory contract. The silence of earlier legislation on such questions, however, as well as the opening of a state-operated *ridotto* at the Palazzo Dandolo a San Moise in 1638, indicates that such concern was short lived and never a driving factor for Venice's governors.

The distinction that Venetian legislation made between card and dice games, permitting the former in restricted elite gatherings, speaks also to ideas about status connected with certain games. A dice game called *zara* (hazard), played with three dice between two opponents, had been the most popular game in the late middle ages. Not only was this the game specifically referred to by Dante in *Purgatorio*; it also appears frequently in paintings of the crucifixion in the figures of gambling soldiers at the foot of the cross. Girolamo Cardano assumed his readers' familiarity with it, making it the basis of his attempt at formulating a mathematical theory of probability in *De ludo aleae*.[30] Its quick action, low requirements, and raucous nature suited the public spaces in which most gambling occurred.[31] It also, doubtless, lent the game a lower-class, popular tone antithetical to the restrained sociability to which the Venetian decrees aspired in their exceptions. Card games, by contrast, required more expensive materials and encouraged a more sedate and decorous atmosphere of play. Playing cards had appeared in Europe – via the Islamic world – in the last decades of the fourteenth century, and through the early modern period their use became an increasingly aristocratic recreation.[32]

---

[29] ASV, Esecutori 54, Tomo primo, 24r. An informer, if there had been one, would receive one-quarter of the sum that otherwise went to the loser. The remaining quarter went to the coffers of the Esecutori. In cases in which over 100 scudi had been lost, the Esecutori were to distribute any remaining sum, after their own cut and that owed an informer, to pious causes. The 1539 decree had made provision for an informer, who had also gambled and lost, to the restitution of their losses.

[30] See Chapter 1 above.

[31] On the origins, nature, and rules of *zara*, see Elizabeth Lapina, "Gambling and Gaming in the Holy Land: Chess, Dice and Other Games in the Sources of the Crusades," *Crusades* 12 (2013); Purdie, "Dice Games," esp. 170–71; Zdekauer, *Il gioco d'azzardo*, 23.

[32] On the association between card playing, court culture, and aristocratic sociability, see Nicholas Scott Baker, "Dux ludens: Eleonora de Toledo, Cosimo I de' Medici, and Games of Chance in the Ducal Household of Mid-Sixteenth-Century Florence,"

A similar distinction appeared in a Genoese decree publicized in February 1584, which banned gambling in private homes with the exception of three card games: *primiera*, *truco*, and *pichetto* (a type of poker and two trick-taking games, respectively). The legislation permitted a more generous limit than the Venetian law, allowing wagers up to twenty-five scudi, and as much as 300 scudi could be expended in total in a game.[33] While not stating so explicitly, the exception for card games and the large sums involved clearly denote that the Procuratori of Genoa – whose office was charged with policing and reforming the morals and behavior of the city – had the city's nobility in mind.[34] Like the Esecutori in Venice, they sought to balance outright repression of gambling with allowances for aristocratic sociability. Increasingly in the sixteenth century, legislation in Italian cities sought to control who could gamble, forbidding lower socioeconomic estates from the pastime but indulging the elite. In all cases, of course, this represented self-indulgence, or at least indulgence of one's peers, on the part of those crafting the laws.

As in the republics of Venice and Genoa, laws issued in grand-ducal Florence in the later sixteenth century also made allowances for noble gambling. Legislation issued in May 1579 by the Otto di Guardia e Balìa, the chief criminal and security magistracy of the city, banning "games of any sort" in private homes, "*logge*, shops, and gardens," included an exception for "men of good condition" who gathered to entertain themselves as a distraction from "familiar cares and labors, and for a real contest of *fortuna* and skill" by playing games. A later amendment sought to restrict this freedom, provoked by paternalist concern that it had become a cover for "men of not very good condition" to stage games of chance which attracted "many artisans and poor men, with great damage to their families, and to the entire city [*universale*], by the committing of dishonest sins, deceits, frauds, and financial deceptions offensive to

---

European History Quarterly 46, no. 4 (2016), and Paul R. Keenan, "Card-Playing and Gambling in Eighteenth-Century Russia," *European History Quarterly* 42, no. 3 (2012). On the transmission of playing cards from the Islamic world, most probably via Mamluk Egypt, to Europe, see David Parlett, *A History of Card Games* (Oxford: Oxford University Press, 1991), 35–41.

[33] Giulio Pallavicino, *Inventione di Giulio Pallavicino di scriver tutte le cose accadute alli tempi suoi (1583–1589)*, ed. Edoardo Grendi (Genoa: Sagep Editore, 1975), 36. The *grida* that Pallavicino cites does not appear to be preserved. Certainly it is not collected in the *busta* (file) of sixteenth-century *gride* (proclamations), ASG, Archivio secreto 1016, which has significant chronological gaps including all of the 1580s. On *primiera*, *truco*, and *pichetto*, see Parlett, *History of Card Games*, 90–92, 169–73, and 175–78, respectively.

[34] On the jurisdiction and purpose of the Procuratori, see ASG, Manoscritti, Leges 1528–1600, 9r, 11r.

Divine Majesty."[35] In this case, the decree made a clear and explicit value
judgment about who could gamble based on social status and financial wherewithal. In so doing, it unconsciously echoed the assessment of Eleonora de
Toledo, duchess of Florence and mother of Grand Duke Francesco de'
Medici, in whose name the law was promulgated. In September 1544,
Eleonora – for whom games of chance served as a frequent source of recreation – berated the court pages for wasting money gambling after observing the
disrepair of their clothing.[36] In the minds of the Florentine elite, aristocratic
gambling was legitimate entertainment and a worthy form of diversion, but for
the lower orders of society it was ruinous, criminal, and sinful.

From the mid-sixteenth century, the Florentine government issued a
range of laws that attempted to control who could gamble and to mitigate
the potential financial damage that risk-taking ludic behavior could cause.
This legislation initially focused not on structured games of chance – for
which the fifteenth-century penalties and proscriptions still applied – but
on the more protean habits of betting.[37] Renaissance Italians displayed a
willingness to wager on almost every event or incident that had an uncertain outcome. Like playing with dice, such practices were more fluid and
open to broader social participation than playing with cards. Of particular
concern was *maschio o femmina*, the notorious game of soliciting bets on
the sex and even birth date of an unborn child.[38] The practice appears to
have been widely popular but also especially ripe for deception and
cheating, making it the source of frequent legal complaints. In 1547, for
example, the widow Monna Tita petitioned the Florentine mercantile
court for redress, claiming that she had been cheated in such a bet by
Giovanni da San Miniato, who had staked cloth he claimed to be worth
nine scudi that he knew to be worth much less.[39]

[35] Lorenzo Cantini, ed., *Legislazione Toscana*, 32 vols. (Florence: Pietro Fantosini e Figlio,
1800–1808), 9: 162–64. Cantini prints the amendment, not the original legislation. The
quoted text is at 163.
[36] ASF, MDP 1171: 274. On Eleonora's gambling habits, see Baker, "Dux ludens"; Bruce
Edelstein, "The Camera Verde: A Public Center for the Duchess of Florence in the
Palazzo Vecchio," *Mélanges de l'Ecole française de Rome: Italie et Méditerranée* 115,
no. 1 (2003).
[37] Legislation and penalties from 1473 were reissued in 1565: Cantini, *Legislazione
Toscana*, 5: 240–42. Later laws did ban card games (vol. 13, 192) and dice games
(vol. 14, 79).
[38] On *maschio o femmina*, see Paul Renucci, "Fille ou garçon? Un singulier jeu de hasard
florentin du XVIe siècle," *Revue des etudes italiennes* 24 (1978); Giorgio Roberti, *I giochi a
Roma di strada e d'osteria: Dalla "Passatella" alla "Morra," dalla "Ruzzica" alla
"Zecchinetta," più di 400 modi per divertirsi ricostruiscono il vivace e popolare spaccato della
Roma d'una volta* (Rome: Newton Compton, 1995), 379–81.
[39] ASF, Mercanzia 11516, unfoliated: two separate, but largely identical, supplications on
behalf of Mona Tita de' Pellicioni, undated but last quarter of 1547. Giovanni had
further gone on to have Mona Tita attest to a receipt stating that she owed him 18 scudi

A Florentine statute issued on 6 June 1550 aimed to limit the ability of women to play *maschio o femmina*. The law did not target morality – although it did note that gambling offended against "the solemnity required by the obligations of being women" – but rather the financial "disorders and damage" caused by women "imprudently dissipating their possessions and those of their husbands." The law stated that any bets made by a married woman without her husband's permission "would be invalid and of no value."[40] A further decree, dated 19 February 1564, forbade men under the age of twenty from playing the game. It also attempted to regulate the practice more stringently by attempting to prevent the most obvious fraudulent acts, such as soliciting bets from the unwary on a child already born or substituting a baby of one sex for the other in order to cheat.[41] The Genoese government, citing fraud and extortionate practices, by contrast, banned betting on pregnancies "in any manner" in February 1587.[42]

The focus of these statutes on the financial implications of gambling reveals again the guiding mentality of patrimonial rationality, the concern to secure and protect family wealth against the unwitting depredations of those incapable of the self-control that the patriarchal, gerontocratic civic culture of Renaissance Italy idealized: women, boys, and the artisanal and laboring classes. In itself, this further reveals the way that these Florentine laws, and those of Venice and Genoa, operated on the basis of underlying, cross-cutting concerns about honor, status, and credit, and the way that these forces structured and made sense of the future as unknown time-yet-to-come in games of chance.

Legislation concerning gambling in Milan provides a contrast with the laws already examined. The language and structure of Milanese decrees retained a basic similarity from the late fifteenth century despite alterations in regime. Almost uniformly, they prefaced provisions against games of chance with measures against blasphemy, privileging the latter.[43] Superficially, then, like the Venetian legislation, these

---

for three pieces of cloth, worth six scudi each, that he had sold to her, to disguise the gambling involved. See also the case of unpaid debts from *maschio o femmina* at ASF, OGBP 2215: docs. 8, 128, and 212. All undated but ca. late 1547.

[40] Cantini, *Legislazione Toscana*, 2: 171.

[41] Ibid., 5: 64–66; Renucci, "Fille ou garçon?," 164–67.

[42] Pallavicino, *Inventione*, 165. As above, the *grida* that Pallavicino cites is not preserved in ASG, Archivio secreto 1016.

[43] See, for example, ASCM, RLD 15, 107r–108v (24 January 1492), 228r–v (28 March 1494); RLD 18, 147v–149r (19 February 1517), 287r–289r (1 April 1523); RLD 21, 16r–18r (2 April 1538), 134v–139r (31 March 1541), 170v–174r (1 April 1544); ASM, Registri 27, 205r–207r (10 January 1534); Registri 28, 4v–6v (20 January 1537), 25v–27v (3 April 1538).

prohibitions suggest that theological concerns about the nature and morality of gambling represented the primary motivation for the governors of the duchy. A law of February 1517, issued in the name of Francis I of France in his short-lived capacity as duke of Milan, observed that games of chance incited "not only the aforesaid vice of blasphemy and the displeasure of God and his saints but also many other scandals, evils, and other behaviors of the worst kind."[44] By the mid-century this had become simplified to the formula that "gambling is an inciter of blasphemy."[45] Partly because of this stated religious concern, and also partly because the nature of ducal (as opposed to republican) government required at least the outward image of equality before law, the Milanese decrees made no exceptions for aristocratic pursuits, in their written form. The 1517 provision of Francis I ordered that "no person of whatever status or grade he may be, or wish to be, should dare or presume to hold a *baratteria* in his own house or a rented property, or to play or to let play at any game of *zara* or other prohibited game." Again, by mid-century the language had simplified. A decree of 1541 issued by the Spanish governor commanded the punishment of "all those who hold public *baratteria* in their homes or in other places to play at *zara* or other, similar prohibited games and all those who play at the said games."[46]

Beneath this superficial condemnation, however, the same forces that conditioned tolerance of noble gaming in Florence, Genoa, and Venice operated in Milan. Gambling was a regular, much-loved pursuit at the Sforza court, and Francis I also encouraged and played games of chance.[47] The centrality of the pastime to aristocratic culture and identity in the city from the fifteenth century is revealed in the decoration of a ground-floor room in the palazzo Borromeo with a fresco of a game of *tarocchi* (Figure 2.1). Three women and two men, all elegantly and fashionably attired, play cards at a clothed table set in a garden or other

---

[44] ASCM RLD 18, 148v: "inductivi non solum del predicto vitio de la biastema et dispretio de Dio et soi sancti sed etiam de molti altri scandali malefitij et altri pravissimi costumi."
[45] ASCM RLD 21, 136r: "Et perché il gioco è dela biestemma incitativo." See also 173v; ASM Registri 28, 5v, 26v.
[46] ASCM RLD 18, 148v: "non sia persona alchuna de qual stato e grado esser voglia se sia qual ardischa nè presuma tenere barataria in casa sua o che tenga ad pigone nè giochare nè lassar giochare ad giocho alchuno de zarro o altri giochi prohibiti"; 21, 136r: "tutti coloro li quali teneno Barattaria publica nele loro case o in altro loco per gioccare a zarra o altri giochi simili prohibiti et tutto colori che giocherano alli detti giocchi."
[47] Sandra Bandera, ed., *I tarocchi: Il caso e la fortuna* (Milan: Electa/Ministero per i Beni e le Attività Culturale, 1999), 17; Raffaele Tamalio, *Federico Gonzaga alla corte di Francesco I di Francia nel carteggio privato con Mantova (1515–1517)* (Paris: Honoré Champion, 1994), 100.

Figure 2.1 Unknown artist, *A Game of Tarocchi* (ca. 1450–75), fresco,
Milan: Palazzo Borromeo.
Credit: Palazzo Borromeo, Milan © 2020. Photo Scala, Florence.

outdoor space. Possibly commissioned by Vitaliano Borromeo, count of
Arona and treasurer to Duke Filippo Maria Visconti, the image celebrates games of chance as a suitable, even idealized activity for the elite of
the city, housed in the family palace of the one of the most prominent and
powerful lineages of the new courtly nobility.[48] Slippages in the language
of the decrees further reveal the extent to which they tolerated and
excused aristocratic gambling, while condemning the same behavior in
lower status groups.

The Milanese legislation uniformly specify *baratterie* as the source of
the problem, invoking associations of undifferentiated public gambling,
infamy, and shame. The holders of *baratterie* in late medieval Italy had to
perform unpleasant or dishonorable tasks – such as public cleaning,

---

[48] On the debate over the authorship and dating of the frescos, see Bandera, *I tarocchi*,
120–21. On the origins and rise to prominence of the Borromeo, see Hermann
Kellenbenz, "I Borromeo e le grandi casate mercantili milanesi," in *San Carlo e il suo
tempo: Atti del convegno internazionale* (Rome: Edizioni di storia e letteratura, 1984), esp.
807–9.

spying, and executions – in exchange for the licenses granted them to gamble.[49] The decree of February 1517 further qualified the matter in observing that "various and diverse persons" congregate at such locales, revealing an underlying concern with who was actually gambling and with controlling the behavior of the lower orders of society.[50] Notably, in addition to specifying *baratterie*, all the Milanese laws name *zara* as the principal game played before referring generically to "other prohibited games." As noted above, this dice game had particular associations with raucous, lower-class, and public gambling, far removed from the genteel pleasures illustrated in the Borromeo fresco. While exceptions for noble gambling remain unstated in the Milanese sources, the context and circumstances of their creation, including the domination of public administration in the duchy by the city's nobility, suggests that as in Florence, Genoa, and Venice, the actual target of these decrees was gaming by the lower estates of society and not by the elite themselves.[51]

The fundamental basis for all these laws was a conception of who could play with the future through games of chance, safely and reasonably. If gambling always involved the risk not only of material loss but also of loss of face and social standing, then the authors of these sixteenth-century decrees reveal a basic belief that only those who had something to lose, and so something to prove, possessed the social wherewithal and personal self-control actually to gamble.[52] Staking money and reputation on an unknown future outcome determined by the random turning of cards required sufficient levels of both to begin with, at least in the imagination and understanding of the mature men who wrote the laws considered here. They were, in this regard, imagining themselves: the aristocratic, mercantile elites of the Italian cities, the possessors of credit (both social and financial) and *virtus*.

The fact that these paternalistic governors felt the need continually to reissue and restate bans on other members of society gambling – in Florence alone over a dozen decrees concerning games of chance and betting appeared between 1537 and the end of the century – reveals that the excluded (aristocratic women and adolescent males, the laboring and

---

[49] See Taddei, "Gioco d'azzardo."
[50] ASCM RLD 18, 148v: "ove concore varie e diverse persone ad giochare." See also 15, 108r.
[51] On the Milanese patriciate's monopoly on the highest offices in the duchy, see Stefano D'Amico, *Spanish Milan: A City within the Empire, 1535–1706* (New York: Palgrave Macmillan, 2012), 37; Domenico Sella and Carlo Capra, *Il Ducato di Milano dal 1535 al 1796* (Turin: Unione Tipografico-Editrice Torinese, 1984), 37–39.
[52] On the immaterial and social stakes of gambling, see Huizinga, *Homo Ludens*, esp. 49–63; Goffman, *Interaction Ritual*, 149–270; Geertz, *Interpretation of Cultures*, 412–53.

artisanal classes) did not share this restricted vision of the possession of honor and credit, but felt themselves equally equipped to risk immaterial but significant stakes in a game of chance. Prosecution of crimes, of course, reflects the selective choices made by those in power about whom to target. Given the underlying mentality of Renaissance Italian legislation concerning gambling – which permitted gaming by sociopolitical elites – the relative scarcity of noble surnames from the one surviving sixteenth-century volume of condemnations by the Esecutori in Venice is not surprising. Read another way, however, the source reveals the penetration of gambling across gender and social divides.

The majority of the men convicted for gambling and related offenses did not possess family names but only patronyms or were identified by a trade or origin, such as "Polo di Maffei da Venezia, called Poleto, and Piero di Antonio, called Passalaqua, pourer or bearer of wine," or "Piero Bergamesco, Domenego di Antonio, wool comber, and Francesco cloth weaver."[53] While women appear less frequently than men, when they do show up in the records they do so most often not simply as players but rather as entrepreneurs of chance, convicted for operating *ridotti*, such as Zanetta di Barbara, identified as a prostitute of Dalmatian origin, or Andriana, "the wife of Diego Barbier."[54] A comparison might be made to Maria d'Antonio da Rabatta, who explained in a supplication to Cosimo I de' Medici of Florence that she could not yet pay the 100 scudi she owed Carlo di Ser Bastiano da Firenzuola for a game of *maschio o femmina* because "other people are in debt to me to the sum of 200 scudi for similar bets."[55]

These traces demonstrate the extent to which women, frequently of lower socioeconomic status, operated comfortably in the economic culture of gaming in Renaissance Italy, using it to make a living as well as to demonstrate their credit, both financial and social. Among the nobility, the well-known gambling habits of Eleonora de Toledo, duchess of Florence, mentioned by the Venetian ambassador and the satirist Pietro Aretino; the unproblematic, passing acknowledgment of women playing *primiera* at the court of Ferrara in Torquato Tasso's dialogue on play; and the visual evidence of the Borromeo fresco and other paintings

[53] ASV, Esecutori 61, Raspa Seconda 1540–1570, 51r: "polo di Maphei da venetia detto poleto, Piero de Antonio detto passalaqua travasador, sive portador de vin"; Notario di sentenze e termination 1590–1614, 7r: "Piero Bergamesco, Domenego q[uondam] Antonio Pettenador da lana et Franc[esc]o tesser da panni."
[54] Ibid., Raspa Seconda, 90v; Notario di sentenze, 9v. See also Raspa Seconda, 51r; Notario di sentenze, 26r, 30r.
[55] ASF, OGBP 2215, doc. 128: "alcune altre persone mi sono debitore per simili scommesse per la somma di [scudi] 200." See also docs. 8 and 212.

from the sixteenth century depicting women and men gaming together indicated the extent to which upper-class women also regularly partici- pated in games of chance. The experience of a confrontation with the future as unknown, unknowable time-yet-to-come that they offered was neither gendered nor exclusive to men. Moreover, as I have argued elsewhere, women benefited equally with men from the character- affirming aspects of facing the unknown future in this way.[56]
While they were clearly observed in breach more often than not, the ideas articulated in these various laws reveal something of the underlying sentiments and values that structured the way Renaissance Italians engaged with the new conception of the future. The confrontation with the unknown time-yet-to-come that occurred in the compressed moment of a game of cards or dice required an ability to master the emotions of hope and fear in the face of uncertainty. The immaterial loss that players risked never actually became manifest, because no matter what the hazard, no one ascended or descended the social hierarchy on the out- come.[57] What mattered, what was at stake, was the ability to harness the emotional consequences of the risk and to display a suitable level of indifference to them. Renaissance Italian society valued the maintenance of face, of social appearances.
At the heart of success in this intensely face-to-face society lay the ability to navigate multiple, potentially conflicting, relationships and networks.[58] The maintenance of honor, credit, and social standing as well as opportunities for political advancement, for valuable patronage, and for favors and obligations all depended on the skillful negotiation of the intersections of one's own emotions and expectations with those of others. This agonistic sense of social life as a continual contest of face and standing framed the future as a time of potential reward and loss.[59]

---

[56] On Eleonora and women demonstrating honor, character, and *virtù* by gambling, see Baker, "Dux ludens." For women playing *primiera* at the Estense court, see Torquato Tasso, *Dialoghi: Edizione critica*, ed. Ezio Raimondi (Florence: Sansoni, 1958), 487. On sixteenth-century frescos depicting aristocratic groups of women and men playing cards, see Antonella Fenech Kroke, "Ludic Intermingling/Ludic Discrimination: Women's Card Playing and Visual Proscriptions in Early Modern Europe," in *Playthings in Early Modernity: Party Games, Word Games, Mind Games*, ed. Allison Levy (Kalamazoo: Medieval Institute Publications, Western Michigan University, 2017), esp. 63–65.
[57] Geertz, *Interpretation of Cultures*, 443–44.
[58] On this vision of Italian Renaissance society, see, in particular, John Jefferies Martin, *Myths of Renaissance Individualism* (Houndmills: Palgrave Macmillan, 2004); Ronald F. Weissman, "The Importance of Being Ambiguous: Social Relations, Individualism, and Identity in Renaissance Florence," in *Urban Life in the Renaissance*, ed. Susan Zimmerman and Ronald F. Weissman (Newark: University of Delaware Press, 1989).
[59] Huizinga identified *agon* (contest) as the constitutive heart of play and the crucial element in the role of play in forming any culture or society. He further suggested that

Figure 2.2 Caravaggio, *The Cardsharps* (ca. 1595), oil on canvas,
94.2 x 130.9 cm, Fort Worth: Kimbell Art Museum.
Credit: Kimbell Art Museum, Fort Worth, Texas, USA/Bridgeman Images.

Taking a chance on an unknown outcome necessitated removing oneself
from the security of predictable expectations and risking the consequences of losing face by managing anxiety and anticipation poorly.
The unknown time-yet-to-come was the field of contest for everyday
honor, the assessment by one's peers of how well one managed and
met expectations. The governors of Italian cities who wrote laws concerning gambling recognized this and attempted to restrict access to
those they conceived as worthy, as possessing the requisite abilities in
the first place.

By way of comparison with such statutes, Caravaggio's famous depiction of gambling, *The Cardsharps* (Figure 2.2), presents an alternative
perspective on the same concerns that reflects the attitude of the ruled,
rather than the rulers.[60] The painting presents a moment of high tension.

cultures that favored mutually destructive contests, including games of chance, value
competition, daring, honor, group esteem, and liberality over utility, caution, and
calculation: Huizinga, *Homo Ludens*, 53–63.
[60] On the painting, see Maurizio Marini, *Caravaggio "pictor praestantissimus": L'iter artistico
completo di uno dei massimi rivoluzionari dell'arte di tutti i tempi* (Rome: Newton and

Two young men, scarcely more than boys, play at cards, accompanied by a third, clearly older, man. The youth on the left-hand side of the image, facing the viewer, absorbed in his own hand, fails to notice that he is being cheated. The older man, looking over the dupe's shoulder, silently gestures to his accomplice. The latter carefully extracts a card from a concealed pocket (little more than a slash in the top layer of the fabric) in the back of his doublet, clearly visible to the viewer. While the young man on the left-hand side is dressed in a rich but sober style, suggesting an aristocratic background, his two deceivers are decidedly more down-at-heel. The loud, contrasting colors and patterns of their clothing, its general grubbiness, and obvious need of repair, suggest a lower social status. They are clearly not the working poor, but rather bravos of the type common to any European city in the late sixteenth-century: grifters and brawlers, aspiring to a life of gentlemanly leisure that they cannot quite afford.

The painting reveals two conflicting notions of what mattered in sixteenth-century Italian society, about how character and reputation should be judged: the poise of self-control in the face of the unknown, or the cunning determination to outwit any opponent in order to win. While the young man on the left might share the mentality and beliefs of the sixteenth-century legislators, his deceivers subscribe to a less-aristocratic vision, one in which the unknown future is too important to be left to chance, in which economic survival depends on rigging the odds. They subscribe to the code of what one scholar has recently described as *virtù*-ous behavior: actions that spanned a spectrum from amoral, rational calculation to outright deception and even criminality in order to succeed, both financially and socially.[61] Just as for the authors of Renaissance laws concerning gambling, so for Caravaggio and his card-sharps ideas about reputation and character structured and tamed the confrontation with the future in games of chance. However, they had different ideas of what was at stake, what constituted acceptable behavior, and how honor and face might be assessed by peers.

The painting also subjects the viewer to a test of character. To make the image work, Caravaggio had to make the fraud visible, and in doing so he forces the viewer to choose, imaginatively at least, whether to intervene to warn the dupe or to laugh at him with his deceivers. The viewer of the painting has to ally with one concept of what matters or the

Compton, 2001), 401–4, no. 19; Sebastian Schütze, *Caravaggio: The Complete Works* (Cologne: Taschen, 2009), 248–49, cat. 8.
[61] Guido Ruggiero, "Getting a Head in the Renaissance: Mementos of Lost Love in Boccaccio and Beyond," *Renaissance Quarterly* 67, no. 4 (2014).

other. In either case, the outcome of the story remains unknown. Unlike historical, mythological, or scriptural subjects, genre paintings like this presented unique and unfamiliar narratives that left the viewer in the dark as to the denouement of the scene depicted.[62] In this way, as well as a reflection on lower-class attitudes toward the future, Caravaggio's *Cardsharps* presents a visualization of the unknowability of time-yet-to-come.

Caravaggio's painting is art, a fiction that plays with its own deceptiveness. In making the invisible (the fraud) visible, he unveiled the deceit of the image itself. Its trompe l'oeil realism suggests a slice of actuality, but the fact that the entire moment is visible reminds the viewer that it is only art.[63] The criminal and civil archives of sixteenth-century Italian cities and other sources, however, reveal traces of similarly *virtù*-ous behaviour and nonaristocratic attitudes toward the character-revealing nature of the unknown future in relation to games of chance. The actions of Giovanni da San Miniato, who deceived the widow Monna Tita in a game of *maschio o femmina*, present a clear, real-life example of such an understanding of character and financial risk taking.[64]

Condemnations by the Esecutori in Venice reveal multiple convictions for playing with marked cards or false dice. Another particularly common fraud practiced in the lagoon city was pretending to be a foreigner, such as Piero da Verona called Captain Moreto, condemned for "faking his mother-tongue, and falsifying his nationality and habits" in order to deceive actual unwary visitors into playing with him.[65] When Francesco Vettori mentioned gambling in his *Viaggio in Alemagna* (*Journey to Germany*), which recounted his 1507–8 embassy to Emperor Maximilian I on behalf of the Florentine republic, he generally did so in connection with cheating. His experiences crossed social boundaries, from a Mantuan gentleman and a page from the Gonzaga court who deceived a canon from Trent into playing with false dice to the Milanese

---

[62] Jessen Kelly, "Renaissance Futures: Chance, Prediction, and Play in Northern European Visual Culture" (PhD dissertation, University of California, Berkeley, 2011), 103–4.

[63] Elizabeth Cropper, "The Petrifying Art: Marino's Poetry and Caravaggio," *Metropolitan Museum Journal* 26 (1991): 199. On the affinities between the painting and *commedia dell'arte*, which depended on a similar play between apparent authenticity and acknowledged deceptiveness, see Marini, *Caravaggio*, 401–4, no. 19; Francesco Porzio, *Caravaggio e il comico: Alle origini del naturalismo* (Milan: Skira, 2017), 37–40; Schütze, *Caravaggio*, 248–49, cat. 8; John T. Spike, *Caravaggio*, 2nd revised ed. (New York: Abbeville Press, 2010), 37–43.

[64] ASF, Mercanzia 11516, unfoliated. See note 39 above.

[65] ASV, Esecutori 61: condemnations for cheating and/or using marked cards and weighted dice at Raspa Seconda, 13r, 22v, 23v, 79r, 97r; condemnations for pretending to be foreigner to facilitate cheating at 24r, 35r, 40r, 42r, 64v. The quoted text and case of Piero da Verona is at 24r.

cardsharp Franceschino, whom Vettori encountered in Memmingen, who was in turn tricked by a servant of the Venetian ambassador named Polo.[66] In all these examples, the cheats and fraudsters felt the need to rig the odds in their favor and did so based on a conviction that cunning and wit were worthy characteristics and that a reputation for success mattered for survival. In its own way, Monna Tita's pursuit of Giovanni through the civil legal system also presents an example of the ways that the conditioning forces of character and reputation operated well below the aristocratic estates of the legislators discussed above, but did so in a different register. Monna Tita could not afford to remain indifferent to her loss. The financial stakes were too high. Instead, she saw value in publicizing Giovanni's deception. It might be all very well and *virtù*-ous to cheat when one could but being publicly revealed as a fraud or a liar was a loss of face among the poor, as it was for the nobility. Shame lay in being caught in a lie or a deceit, not in perpetrating it in the first place.[67] Those lower down the socioeconomic scale, whether as victims or perpetrators of fraudulent practices, could not afford to lose. The legislators themselves were also not indifferent to the financial consequences of gambling. The concerns about protecting patrician patrimonies and preventing the financial immiseration of the already economically vulnerable expressed in the sixteenth-century decrees were genuine. Indeed, the blurring of financial and social credit in Italian Renaissance society meant that monetary anxieties entangled inextricably with notions of face and character. The ability to pay one's debts was as crucial to social status and honor as managing appearances in a society that faced chronic problems of liquidity.[68] On 16 September 1570, the podestà of Milan issued a public proclamation concerning Geronimo Pozzobonelli, a scion of an old patrician family of the city. The *grida* identified Pozzobonelli as a "gambler at illicit games" and banned anyone from playing, or even entering into any sort of contract, with him. His "closest male relatives" had requested the interdict because Pozzobonelli's gaming had led to him "heedlessly dispersing his patrimony."[69] His reckless behavior

[66] Francesco Vettori, *Viaggio in Alemagna* (Florence, 1837), 22–25, 163–67.
[67] Edward Muir, "The Double Binds of Manly Revenge in Renaissance Italy," in *Gender Rhetorics: Postures of Dominance and Submission in History*, ed. Richard C. Trexler (Binghamton, NY: Center for Medieval and Early Renaissance Studies, 1994), 78–81.
[68] On the connections between social status and debt, see David Herlihy and Christiane Klapisch-Zuber, *Tuscans and Their Families: A Study of the Florentine Catasto of 1427*, trans. David Herlihy and Christiane Klapisch-Zuber (New Haven, CT: Yale University Press, 1985), 104–5.
[69] ASM, Governatore degli statuti, Gride e citazioni 78, unfoliated grida concerning Messer Hieronimo Pozzobonello, 16 September 1570: "Essendo statto [sic] notificato al s[igno]r vicario del podestà de M[i]l[an]o per tre prossimi agnati … qualmente il detto

threatened not only his personal finances and reputation, but also the honor and respectability of his entire lineage.

The interplay between honor and finance revealed itself in legal disputes over the payment of gambling debts in sixteenth-century Florence. In 1571, the brothers Leonardo and Antonio di Francesco Salvetti attempted to claim a debt of 400 scudi from the estate of Roberto Strozzi, which they claimed had been amassed by Strozzi's son Michele in 1559 betting *maschio o femmina*. As Michele had subsequently fled Florence, his father had reached an accord with his scapegrace offspring's creditors in January 1563, agreeing to make payment within eight years. After Strozzi's death in 1571, however, his other sons and legal heirs, Federico and Giovanni, attempted to shirk this obligation. They initially tried moving the dispute to the arch-episcopal tribunal, because Michele was a priest. Next, they alleged that the Salvetti could prove a debt of only forty scudi in cash as most of the wagers had staked material goods, the value of which was now unclear. The Strozzi brothers challenged Leonardo and Antonio to produce evidence of the worth of the goods gambled, from their own account books, in order to have the matter settled.[70]

The dispute between the Salvetti and Strozzi brothers reveals several layers of interaction between social and financial credit. In the first place, Leonardo and Antonio expected that family had an obligation, both financial and social, to meet the debts of kin. Roberto Strozzi had clearly agreed and felt honor-bound to pay his son's gambling arrears. Not only did he agree to satisfy the creditors; his testament also charged his heirs to observe the arrangement. The social credit and standing of the family name intertwined with keeping the family accounts in financial credit. Federico and Giovanni, however, while observing their father's wishes, erred on the side of caution with regard to the financial obligations of Michele. They agreed to pay the debts of their brother but only so far as the Salvetti could prove them to exist. They would honor the family name and keep it in credit but also restrict the diminishment of the patrimony to a minimum. In challenging the Salvetti, the Strozzi brothers required them to demonstrate that they too were men of honor, that they had not inflated Michele's obligations, and that their claims were true and verifiable.

m[es]s[e]r Hier[oni]mo è pub[li]co giocatore de' giochi reprobati e che in ciò inconsideratemente dispensa le sue facultà." The *grida* also noted that Pozzobonelli was forbidden from administering his own estate.

[70] ASF, OGBP 2255, docs. 125 and 331. See the similar interplay of honor and credit in the dispute between Neri di Neri Pepi and Bernardo Carnesecchi: ASF, OGBP 2255, docs. 221 and 222.

The intricate connections between financial credit and social status prompted much of the concern manifested around the sudden popularity of lotteries in sixteenth-century Italy. Anxiety focused on the way they promised precipitous wealth. After recording what was apparently the first lottery in Venice, on 8 March 1522, Marin Sanudo reported the rapid inflation of both prices and prizes, from twenty soldi in that initial drawing up to one ducat each per ticket and including silver jewelry valued at two hundred ducats.[71] The Venetian government soon involved itself in the practice, licensing operators and offering annuities drawing on public revenues, public offices, and even government-owned property as prizes in state-run lotteries to raise money for the fisc. Sanudo began compiling lists of winners, all the while expressing unease at the enthusiasm with which his compatriots embraced the innovation.

While he never stated so explicitly, much of Sanudo's concern appears motivated by fears about how the sudden wealth bestowed on winners could disrupt established social hierarchies and norms. These unspoken anxieties seem to lie behind his observation that "Many women have put money on the said lottery; such that all run to place a little in order to have a lot, because they see that with one *ducato* they could gain up to one hundred."[72] This brief observation carries a multiplicity of significances. It provides further evidence of how the experience of a confrontation with the unknown future that gambling offered was not a gendered one, but something shared by all individuals. However, it also demonstrates how unsettling this commonality could be. A patrician by birth and a member of the Great Council, Sanudo shared the paternalistic mentality of the legislators examined earlier in this chapter. Women, in his estimation, lacked the necessary self-control to play games of chance, and the ease with which they could participate in lotteries challenged his sense of social and gender hierarchies.

The randomness of the process, the way the lottery reduced a financial transaction to pure chance with no space for skill or recognition of social worth to influence the outcome, disturbed Sanudo and other observers. The diarist emphasized this fickleness in his initial record, noting that playing the lottery involved speculating a small sum "to *fortuna*" in the hope of earning a greater one.[73] Hopeful entrants also sometimes

---

[71] Sanuto, *I diarii*, 32: col. 467–68. On the emergence of lotteries in sixteenth-century Italy, see Dossena et al., *Fanti e denari*, 122–54, and Evelyn Welch, "Lotteries in Early Modern Italy," *Past and Present*, no. 199 (2008). For comparison, on lotteries in the Low Countries in the fifteenth and sixteenth centuries, see Jeroen Puttevils, "Invoking *fortuna* and Speculating on the Future: Lotteries in the Fifteenth- and Sixteenth-Century Low Countries," *Quaderni storici* 52, no. 3 (2017).
[72] Sanuto, *I diarii*, 32: col. 501.   [73] Ibid., 32: col. 467.

acknowledged this. While most participants recorded their name on their ticket, some instead scrawled short verses or invocations, such as Soranza Soranzo, whose winning slip on 10 April 1522 read: *"bondì, bon anno, questa ventura non sia invano* (good day, good year, may this *ventura* not be in vain)."* A close synonym to *fortuna, ventura* bore a sense of a lucky outcome or profitable speculation. More circumspectly, one successful ticket from February that year, urged, "God send me *ventura*."[74] As a form of gambling, the lottery enacted the idea of the future as unknown yet accessible time-yet-to-come in a material way. The outcome of each drawing, determined by chance alone, was unpredictable and uncontrollable. This was precisely what made it both exciting for participants and a cause for concern for disapproving observers such as the Venetian diarist. Lotteries undermined the careful edifice of sixteenth-century Italian governors' attitudes toward gambling – the balancing of aristocratic sociability with paternalistic concern – that had attempted to control who could play.

The satirist Pietro Aretino was, unsurprisingly, less restrained than Sanudo in his scathing condemnation of the practice, styled in the form of a letter addressed to Giovanni Manetti, an early entrepreneur of the lottery. Despite his own relatively humble origins, Aretino identified the threat that the promise of sudden wealth posed to social hierarchies as well as to the financial well-being of those foolish enough to participate, and he abhorred the randomness of the process. The lottery, he wrote, was not the invention of Manetti (despite what some might say) but rather the creation of "chance, [who is] an ass, and hope, [who is] a cow." Like gypsies at a country fair, their intention was solely to drain the purses of anyone whom they could lay their hands on. Reflecting on the potential cost of lotteries' popularity and accessibility, he speculated: "How many serving women throw away their salaries? how many concubines put up all they have earned from screwing? how many families pawn their holiday shoes to this end?"[75] Aretino's actual concern was less the real chance of destitution than the idea that the unworthy, those lacking in status, were free to speculate on the lottery, and (even worse) that they might dramatically improve their social standing if they won. His letter mocks the pretensions and ambitions of gamblers of low

---

[74] Ibid., 33: col. 144; 32: col. 502, respectively. On the meanings and use of *ventura*, see Chapter 4. Jeroen Puttevils examines the use of verse and invocations in sixteenth-century Low Country lotteries in Puttevils, "Invoking *fortuna*," 714–18.

[75] Pietro Aretino, *Del primo libro dele lettere di M. Pietro Aretino* (Paris (?): Matteo il Maestro (?), 1609), 213r–214v. I have adapted and altered the translation offered in *Aretino: Selected Letters*, trans. George Bull (Harmondsworth: Penguin, 1976), 133–35.

socioeconomic status, presenting them as incapable of managing either the anticipation or the reality of wealth.

That both Aretino and Sanudo felt the need to criticize the opportunity lotteries offered to women, servants, artisans, and laborers to speculate on the future speaks to the pervasiveness of gambling in sixteenth-century Italy as well as to the deeply rooted social prejudices and concerns associated with it. Games of chance and wagers presented the experience of a confrontation with time-yet-to-come as unknown and unknowable to a broad cross-section of Italian society from the late Middle Ages. It constituted the principal way that women and men from all walks of life could become familiar with the idea that pragmatic or providential approaches to the future might be insufficient because chance and sometimes skill (whether at games or at cheating) could affect what happened next, that the future might be uncertain, and outcomes unexpected.

A similar motivation and understanding drove sixteenth-century Italian legislation targeting games of chance that attempted, unsuccessfully, to control who could and could not gamble. Because gambling always risked more than the material sum staked, because it always chanced status and reputation, legislators distinguished between those whom they considered in possession of the requisite financial and social capital necessary to play and those whom they judged lacking in both. However, restricted or prohibited groups – women, youths, the artisanal and laboring classes – continued to gamble regardless. They did so not only because of the potential financial rewards but also because they possessed their own understandings of what mattered socially, of what one stood to lose in taking a risk on an unknown future outcome. In either case, Renaissance Italians from all walks of life used notions of reputation and character to structure and tame the disquieting and exciting potential of the future as unknown time-yet-to-come.

3   Trust in the Future

On 31 August 1573, the Genoese merchant Antonio di Giovanni Brignole wrote to his compatriots Battista and Antonio di Negro in Lyon. Earlier in the month, Brignole reminded his correspondents they had received a letter of credit from Niccolò and Giulio Cibo in Florence for the benefit of Brignole and his company. Once the Di Negro had played the sum on the exchange market, the letter continued, they should remit it back to the Cibo or to Brignole himself, if there were no impediment, "according to whatever you judge will be to our greater profit, and we need not remind you to trust well, because the risk of debtors remains yours alone."[1] This brief epistle encapsulates much of the texture of Italian mercantile culture in the later sixteenth century. Antonio Brignole operated in Genoa at a remove – geographically and temporally – from much of the commercial undertaking that underwrote his wealth. He relied on a network of agents and partners across the greater Mediterranean world – such as the Cibo in the cloth manufacturing hub of Florence and the Di Negro in the financial markets at Lyon – and speculated on the outcome of their actions. His apparently disingenuous aside, that he would not warn the Di Negro to use caution when deciding in whom to place their faith, worked to highlight and emphasize, both in the sixteenth century and for twenty-first-century historians, the critical role that trust played in premodern commerce.

In the previous two chapters, I argued that gambling provided the most common and immediately accessible experience of the future as unknown time-yet-to-come for Italians in the late Middle Ages and the

---

[1] ASCG, BS 104, 60v, to Battista and Antonio di Negro, in Lyon, 31 August 1574: "quando non trovaste scontro remetete in fir[enze] a detti nostri Cibo o a noi in Ag[ostin]o de Ciamb...i secondo giudicarette più nostro utt[il]e e non vi raccomandando al ben fidare havendo a restar il risico de' debb[itor]i sopra di voi." Between 1528 and 1576, the Brignole were inscribed in the *albergo* Cicala, and so used Cicala as their surname during that period. For the sake of specificity and to avoid confusion, I have identified all Genoese merchants discussed in this chapter and the next by family name rather than by the name of their respective *alberghi*.

Renaissance. As the concept of this new futurity crystallized in the early decades of the sixteenth century, Cardano and a few other authors took advantage of their familiarity with games of chance to offer themselves as experts in confronting and navigating the anxieties and opportunities attendant on this experience. Another group within Italian society, however, could also lay claim to similarly lengthy familiarity and expertise: merchants, in particular the pan-European, transcontinental merchants and bankers who brought wealth and commodities, both exotic and mundane, to the peninsula. Through the everyday hustle and grind of commercial activity they confronted the unknowability of the future and attempted to mitigate against it. This chapter, and the one following, examine mercantile correspondence from Florence, Genoa, and Venice together with documentation concerning commercial disputes from Florence and Milan to consider experiences of the future as unknown time-yet-to-come through the lens of commercial activities, and the meanings attached to them.[2] The two chapters focus particularly on representative examples drawn from each city: Antonio Brignole and Francesco di Negro from Genoa, the Botti family firm and the bank operated by the heirs of Luigi Capponi in Florence, and two Venetians working in the Levant, Andrea Berengo and Giovanni Alvise Tagliapietra.

Like gambling, long-distance commerce in the sixteenth century shared continuities with preceding centuries. Italian merchants had confronted the uncertainty of the future long before the concept of the unknown and unknowable time-yet-to-come started to cohere in the wider culture of the peninsula in the second half of the fifteenth century. Since at least the ninth century, the intensity of commerce on the peninsula had begun to revive through the use of techniques learned from Muslim and Jewish merchants operating in North Africa and the Levant. By the thirteenth century, the mercantile republics of Venice and Genoa had started to dominate long-distance maritime trade in the Mediterranean, importing in-demand luxury items from Asia and

---

[2] While archives in Florence, Genoa, and Venice preserve a wealth of commercial and mercantile papers, including account books and correspondence, such traces remain elusive in Milanese archives. Patrizia Mainoni has suggested that many of the leading families of the merchant nobility of the city may have destroyed such records at the end of the sixteenth century when the College of Jurists ruled that commerce was incompatible with patrician status: Patrizia Mainoni, "L'attività mercantile e le casate milanesi nel secondo Quattrocento," in *Milano nell'età di Ludovico il Moro: Atti del convegno internazionale 28 febbraio–4 marzo 1983* (Milan: Comune di Milano/Archivio Storico Civico e Biblioteca Trivulziana, 1983), 583. On the ban on commercial activity, see Stefano D'Amico, *Spanish Milan: A City within the Empire, 1535–1706* (New York: Palgrave Macmillan, 2012), 40.

Africa and exporting a growing range of manufactured goods.[3] Because of the time and distance involved in such commerce, Italian merchants had a long familiarity with confronting the unknown future before 1500. However, the world that sixteenth-century Italian merchants inhabited was materially and experientially different to that of their forebears: a world that had become dramatically and unexpectedly larger after 1492. The European encounter with the Americas and the gradual realization of just how distant the New World was from Asia transformed the potential marketplace for Mediterranean-based traders into a truly global one. It introduced new commodities and dramatically altered the supply and demand for familiar ones, most notably, precious metals and enslaved peoples. Significantly, it also impacted notions of temporality and futurity.

The Italian peninsula quickly became a central clearing house for information on the New World, eagerly consuming and producing representations and knowledge about the continents beyond the Atlantic. This placed Italy at the forefront of the age of encounters in a virtual fashion, despite the relatively minor physical presence of Italians in the projects of conquest and colonialization.[4] The existence of the Americas, outside European Christian understandings of sacred history and the classical past, absent from their previously reliable authorities for knowledge of the natural world, challenged their confident assumptions about how history and geography aligned.[5] Prior to the 1510s, Italians (and Western Europeans generally) had understood that their past lay to the east, that their origins resided in Asia. There sacred and human history had begun in the now lost Garden of Eden. There too the human incarnation of God was born and died, profoundly altering the course of both and transforming Jerusalem into the geographic and temporal center of the world.

---

[3] Luciano Pezzolo, "The *via italiana* to Capitalism," in *The Cambridge History of Capitalism*, ed. Larry Neal and Jeffrey G. Williamson (Cambridge: Cambridge University Press, 2014), 269–72.

[4] Elizabeth Horodowich and Lia Markey, "Italy's Virtual Discovery: An Introduction," in *The New World in Early Modern Italy*, ed. Elizabeth Horodowich and Lia Markey (Cambridge: Cambridge University Press, 2017).

[5] See Anne Dunlop, "On the Origins of European Painting Materials, Real and Imagined," in *The Matter of Art: Materials, Practices, Cultural Logics, c. 1250–1750*, ed. Christy Anderson, Anne Dunlop, and Pamela H. Smith (Manchester: Manchester University Press, 2014), and Alexander Nagel, "Some Discoveries of 1492: Eastern Antiquities and Renaissance Europe" (Groningen: Gerson Lectures Foundation, 2013). Compare with Giancarlo Casale, "Did Alexander the Great Discover America? Debating Space and Time in Renaissance Istanbul," *Renaissance Quarterly* 72, no. 3 (2019), for analysis of the analogous impact on Ottoman understandings of the alignment between history and geography.

The realization that the world was, in fact, significantly larger, that the peoples of the Americas lay outside the unfolding of sacred history as European Christians understood it, undermined their understanding of both the past and the future. If the Americans had lived outside the course of both human and sacred history – which their absence from the authorities of Christianity and classical antiquity suggested – then they might also lie outside the soteriology of the Church, untouched (perhaps) by Original Sin, and with no need for the penitential cycle offered by its priests.[6] Not only did their past look completely different to that of Europeans, but their notion of the future did too.

The encounter with the Americas represented part of a profound rupture around the turn of the sixteenth century in how Europeans thought about time. But its impact was gradual, not sudden. This chapter reveals a transitional period between the late medieval entanglement of trust and faith, of commerce and Christianity (in which credit referred equally to both), and the eighteenth century when credit could refer only to commercial trust and not to religious belief.[7] The emergence of the new concept of unknown time-yet-to-come was crucial to the evolution of the latter world. In this chapter, I argue that the problem of trust in premodern commerce was fundamentally a problem of futurity. Trust relies on the anticipation of future actions. People are trustworthy when they behave in a manner that conforms with expectations. Relationships of trust constituted one principal way through which Renaissance Italian merchants encountered and so thought about time-yet-to-come as unknowable, as they weighed the costs and benefits of placing their faith in others. In order to do so, commercial operators developed a series of behaviors and mechanisms to hedge against future contingency: maintaining reputations and relationships, sharing news, keeping documentation that could be produced at a later date. Such actions were one way in which merchants constructed themselves as experts in the new futurity.

The economy that sixteenth-century Italian merchants inhabited was variegated and diversified. While differences existed between the cities of Florence, Genoa, Venice, and Milan, they all relied, to varying extents, on three economic pillars: long-distance trade, manufacturing, and

---

[6] Lee Palmer Wandel, *The Reformation: Towards a New History* (Cambridge: Cambridge University Press, 2011), chapter 2.

[7] On credit in eighteenth-century mercantile culture, see J. G. A. Pocock, *Virtue, Commerce, and History: Essays on Political Thought and History, Chiefly in the Eighteenth Century* (Cambridge: Cambridge University Press, 2002), 91–102, who observes, "Far more than the practice of trade and profit, even at their most speculative, the growth of public credit obliged capitalist society to develop as an ideology something society had never possessed before, the image of a secular and historical future" (99).

finance. The dramatic expansion of European horizons after the 1490s – not only from the encounter with the Americas but also from the maritime intrusion into the Indian Ocean initiated by the Portuguese – altered the shape and form of these enterprises but not their fundamental substance. These four cities remained the dominant commercial and economic centers on the Italian peninsula throughout the sixteenth century, as they had been from the 1300s. Over the past thirty years, scholarship on the economic history of Renaissance Italy has overturned older theses of crisis or decline in the period. Instead, a historiographical picture has emerged of a vibrant, innovative, and highly adaptable economy that enabled Italian merchants and bankers to retain an important position in transcontinental commerce and finance across Europe from the late fourteenth to the early seventeenth centuries.[8]

A more significant change had occurred earlier. From the fourteenth century, a new type of sedentary merchant began gradually to replace the roaming operator of earlier centuries, a transition requiring an increased reliance on others. While the latter had traveled widely and undertaken transactions personally, the former, following an apprenticeship that might involve travel, most often settled in single place and operated via a network of partners, factors, and agents. Because transcontinental trade – importation, exportation, reexportation, and speculative finance – constituted a significant portion of the Italian economy in the sixteenth century, these correspondents were frequently far distant and beyond surveillance. As a result, interpersonal trust became fundamental to the operation of the Renaissance economy.[9] The arrangement and execution

---

[8] For an excellent recent synthesis and survey of the state of the field, and additional bibliography, see Judith C. Brown, "Economies," in *The Cambridge Companion to the Italian Renaissance*, ed. Michael Wyatt (Cambridge: Cambridge University Press, 2014). See also Stephan R. Epstein, "L'economia italiana nel quadro europeo," in *Commercio e cultura mercantile*, ed. Franco Franceschi, Richard A. Goldthwaite, and Reinhold C. Mueller (Treviso: Fondazione Cassamarca/Angelo Colla Editore, 2007), who contrasts the Italian economy against European developments and argues that the peninsula's apparent decline was only relative and not absolute. For more detailed and specific recent studies of the four cities, start with Giorgio Doria, "Conoscenza del mercato e sistema informativo: Il know-how dei mercanti-finanzieri genovesi nei secoli XVI–XVII," in *La repubblica internazionale del denaro tra XV e XVII secolo*, ed. Aldo de Maddalena and Hermann Kellenbenz (Bologna: Il Mulino, 1986); Richard A. Goldthwaite, *The Economy of Renaissance Florence* (Baltimore, MD: Johns Hopkins University Press, 2009); Luciano Pezzolo, "The Venetian Economy," in *A Companion to Venetian History, 1400–1797*, ed. Eric R. Dursteler (Leiden: Brill, 2013); Giovanna Tonelli, "The Economy in the 16th and 17th Centuries," in *A Companion to Late Medieval and Early Modern Milan: The Distinctive Features of an Italian State*, ed. Andrea Gamberini (Leiden: Brill, 2015).

[9] On the centrality of trust to premodern commerce, in Italy and beyond, see Sebouh Aslanian, "Social Capital, 'Trust' and the Role of Networks in Julfan Trade: Informal and Semi-Formal Institutions at Work," *Journal of Global History* 1 (2006); Ricardo

of any transaction was impossible without it. While many continuities marked the period between the late Middle Ages and the Renaissance, from the sixteenth century the potential scope of Italian trade had increased dramatically as a global economy took shape. As the scale of commerce expanded with European horizons, the risks associated with it increased correspondingly, as did the need for trust. Investing money to transport pepper by sea directly from South India, for example, posed greater risks and required greater trust than chancing the same sum to ship it from Aleppo or Alexandria.

Not surprisingly, concerns about the reliability and credibility of agents and partners, and the associated risks of trusting such individuals, permeated mercantile correspondence. Antonio Brignole continually reminded his agents and partners to "trust well," that is, to be sure of the reliability of third parties with whom they had dealings. At times, he offered more precise and detailed instructions. On 28 August 1573, he instructed Simone Lomellino, his longtime contact in Sicily: "you should pay great attention to whom you trust; if you can contract with known foreigners, whom you judge to be reliable, then you should not concern yourself with trusting anyone of our nation, except those of our color and someone whom we can keep content."[10] The reference to "our color" most likely refers to other families, like the Brignole, considered *nobili nuovi* in Genoa. During the summer of 1573 the ongoing conflict between the Vecchi and Nuovi in the Ligurian city, which would culminate in the crisis and constitutional reforms of 1575, was particularly acute.[11]

Court, *"Januensis ergo mercator:* Trust and Enforcement in the Business Correspondence of the Brignole Family," *The Sixteenth Century Journal* 35, no. 4 (2004); Ricardo Court, "The Language of Trust: Sixteenth-Century Genoese Commercial Correspondence," *The UCLA Historical Journal* 20 (2004); Steven A. Epstein, "Secrecy and Genoese Commercial Practices," *Journal of Medieval History* 20 (1994); Avner Greif, "Reputation and Coalitions in Medieval Trade: Evidence on the Maghribi Traders," *The Journal of Economic History* 49, no. 4 (1989); Avner Greif, "The Maghribi Traders: A Reappraisal," *The Economic History Review* 65, no. 2 (2012); Sebastian R. Prange, "'Trust in God, but tie your camel first': The Economic Organization of the Trans-Saharan Slave Trade between the Fourteenth and Nineteenth Centuries," *Journal of Global History* 1, no. 2 (2006).

[10] ASCG BS 103, 41r–v: to Simone Lomellino, in Messina, 28 August 1573: "avertiate molto a cui fidare e potendo contrare con forastieri conosciuti sicuri a giuditio vostro non vi curate de fidare alla nation nostra salvo se fussi del nostro collore e persona da poter quietare." For the more general admonitions about trust, see, for example, 43v, 48v, 120v, 125r; BS 104: 60v, 80r.

[11] Claudio Costantini, *La Repubblica di Genova nell'età moderna* (Turin: Unione Tipografico-Editrice Torinese, 1978), 103–5. In late medieval and Renaissance Genoa, *"colore"* was used to refer to the various, institutionalized partisan groupings active in communal politics; see Serena Ferente, "Parties, Quotas, and Elections in Late

Giovanbattista di Simone Botti – who operated several interlinked merchant-banking concerns across Italy, France, Spain, and the Atlantic world with four of his brothers – wrote an aggrieved letter to the Giunti and Antinori company in Valladolid in 1554 concerning the delayed transfer of several thousand ducats: "because of the great faith that I had in you, I thought that you would pay immediately."[12] Andrea Berengo, a factor working in Aleppo for several different Venetian merchants, cast the importance of trust into relief, when he observed, concerning a still-absent cargo: "I do not know what more to say, no less than I know in whom we could have greater faith."[13] Unstated in the letter is Berengo's confidence in the agents and shippers responsible for the transaction. He had found the most reliable partners that he could. In these and other letters, Italian merchants gave voice to the constant necessity of trust, the filament that bound together the trading networks crisscrossing the Mediterranean and, increasingly in the sixteenth century, the globe, which brought wealth to the peninsula.

At its base, the problem of trust was fundamentally a problem of time, specifically the challenge posed to merchants by the unknowability of time-yet-to-come. A letter with instructions or requests sent today could only arrive at an unknown future date. Merchants could not know when, or even if, an agent would receive a letter. Hence every piece of commercial correspondence began with a ritual recitation of letters most recently received and dispatched. They could not know when their instructions might be acted on. They could not know if the market conditions that existed at the moment of writing the letter would still persist when the requested trade or exchange was executed. As a result, sixteenth-century merchants relied on institutional mechanisms and modes of behavior to mitigate against the unknowability of the future, to guard against breaches of trust, and to maintain honesty and fairness in trade. When relationships broke down these structures could be cast in sharp relief.

Supplications to Duke Cosimo I de' Medici of Florence and to the Imperial governors of Milan reveal the limits and frailties of trust in the premodern marketplace. A dispute from April 1552, for example, reveals the multiple ties of dependence required for even straightforward commercial transactions. The Livornese shipping agent Salvatore Quaratesi petitioned the Medici prince concerning a case involving himself, the

Medieval Genoa," in *Cultures of Voting in Pre-Modern Europe*, ed. Serena Ferente, Lovro Kunčević, and Miles Pattenden (London: Routledge, 2018).
[12] ASF LCF 723, 47v: to the Giunti and Antinori, in Valladolid, 20 March 1554: "per la gran fede avevo in voi pensavo l'avessi a pag[a]re subito."
[13] Ugo Tucci, ed. *Lettres d'un marchand vénitian Andrea Berengo (1553–1556)* (Paris: S.E.V.P.E.N., 1957), 63, letter 53.

company of Luigi and Piero Capponi in Florence, and the company of
Forese Foresi and Prospero Minerbetti in Palermo. Quaratesi claimed to
have sent a shipment of textiles, on the orders of the Capponi, to Sicily. It
had not arrived, however, because the Ottoman admiral and governor of
Tripoli, Turgut Reis (Dragut), had seized the ship carrying it. The
Capponi appeared to have cast doubt on whether the cloth had actually
been sent. Foresi and Minerbetti, accepting the story of the captured
vessel, instead alleged that Quaratesi had failed to insure the cargo. In
response, the shipping agent maintained that he had simply followed the
instructions of his clients, as their correspondence would demonstrate,
and was, therefore, the victim of circumstances beyond his control.[14]
The competing claims and counterclaims reveal the multiple relationships of trust operating in any exchange, all of which depended on future
actions conforming with expectations. Foresi and Minerbetti trusted the
Capponi to supply promised goods. They and the Capponi trusted
Quaratesi to ship the order to Sicily and to do so with all necessary care.
Quaratesi trusted that he would receive fair treatment and recompense
from both other parties, regardless of the outcome of the transaction.
Quite where the relationship broke down and who was guilty of
what remains unclear, but the collapse of faith resonates through the
supplications, revealing, in relief, its absolute centrality to commercial
relationships.

An example from Milan underlines the hazards that distance and
limited oversight placed on commercial relationships. In 1585, Ippolito
Affaitati petitioned Sancho de Guevera y Padilla, governor of the city for
Philip II of Spain, for protection from a suit brought by the heirs of
Geronimo del Conte concerning unpaid debts, which amounted to
around 4,000 scudi. The suit alleged that until 1564, Del Conte had
transferred monies to a company managed by Affaitati and Piero Ducco,
in Antwerp, for investment in merchandise or exchange rate speculation
"to the greater profit of the said late Geronimo." In 1578, having
received no return on his capital, Del Conte dispatched an agent to the
Low Countries to demand the accounts of any transactions and the
restitution of all sums owing. When Affaitati refused to meet these
requests, Del Conte began legal proceedings. The council of Brabant
had decided in favor of the latter's suit, but by the summer of 1585 the
debt, including an estimated return of 6 percent per annum on the
invested capital, still remained unpaid. Affaitati sought to have the original sentence overruled in Milan, claiming that it was invalid because

[14] ASF Mercanzia 11517, unfoliated: supplications from Salvatore Quaratesi (1 and 5 April 1552) and from Forese Foresi and Prospero Minerbetti (11 April 1552).

Antwerp had been in rebellion against the Spanish crown at the time, and also that he had a royal letter granting a stay of execution. The heirs of Del Conte, asserting that they had receipts and correspondence to prove their claim, countered by appealing for the finding to be upheld.[15] In this case, the distance between Italy and the Low Countries had left Del Conte with no choice but to trust that his requests would be fulfilled honestly. As Affaitati did not dispute the essence of the matter, in seems clearer in this case than in the previous one that this faith had been breached by the Antwerp-based company, but why and precisely how remains unknown.

These two examples, as well as the many other similar ones in the Florentine and Milanese archives, underline the limitations and challenges that had confronted Italian merchants since at least the late fourteenth century because of the interpersonal nature of premodern commerce. A significant proportion of transactions occurred at a considerable remove, both geographically and temporally, from the principal, leaving the merchant to rely on agents or partners to execute commissions faithfully, to pay profits, or to cover debts accordingly. The ability to undertake such operations and to surveil their execution was hampered by the limitations of communication. Economic operators had to rely on correspondence, which could take days, weeks, or (in the case of agents working in south Asia or the Americas) months to reach the desired recipient. Even local transactions were not immune to breaches of trust. In 1547, Cosimo de' Pazzi and Piero Ugolini in Florence disputed whether a debt owed by the former to the latter had been paid or not, each claiming to possess written evidence to support his assertion.[16]

At the most immediate level, the petitions all reveal the reliance on mercantile law and institutions for the enforcement of contracts and commercial obligations. While addressing their claims to a presiding ruler, the suppliants did not request summary justice but rather attempted to provide a narrative for a case under consideration by the commercial court in each respective city.[17] Significantly, the petitioners

---

[15] ASM Famiglie 1, Fasciolo Affaitati, unfoliated: supplication from Ippolito Affaitati, 1585: "Espongono che sino del anno 1564 detto q[uon]dam Geronimo sborsò a detto Hippolito, et Pietro Ducco – et compagni in Anversa in mercantie, overo sopra cambij a maggior utile del detto q[uon]dam Geronimo."

[16] ASF Mercanzia 11516, unfoliated: undated supplication from Cosimo de' Pazzi and accompanying memorandum from ser Zanobi Buoni, chancellor of the Mercanzia, last quarter of 1547.

[17] On the nature of such supplications, see James E. Shaw, "Market Ethics and Credit Practices in Sixteenth-Century Tuscany," *Renaissance Studies* 27, no. 2 (2013).

tended to present their narratives in as neutral a tone as possible. While clearly partial and concerned to favor their own account, accentuating both their own good faith and the failings of others, the supplications avoided denunciations of guilt or direct accusations of wrong-doing in favor of constructing a purportedly objective account. This suggests that the recourse to legal institutions was part of a negotiating process to conclude a dispute. By crafting their supplications in this manner, petitioners could leave open the option for face-saving compromises with or without the assistance of the formal apparatus of the law. In this way, the parties could potentially revive or repair their relationship at a later date. A complete rupture in any commercial relationship would close off future profits as well as those at immediate stake in the case at hand.[18]

On 2 February 1555, Simone di Simone Botti – one Giovanbattista's brothers and partners – wrote to Tommaso Guadagni, whose company in Lyon had managed Botti's investments in French royal finance. Botti observed that Guadagni had recently refounded this company under a new name, possibly because of an earlier failure. The middle years of the sixteenth century witnessed many commercial collapses in Lyon, as well as elsewhere in Europe. Botti thanked Guadagni for his offer of continued services and concluded that "whenever the occasion arises to avail myself of them, I shall do so with that trust that I always had in the past."[19] Regardless of earlier circumstances, the Florentine merchant assured his compatriot of a continuing relationship and future opportunities. The case involving Salvatore Quaratesi remains opaque, in a large part because – apart from Foresi and Minerbetti suggesting that the shipping agent had failed to insure the cargo – none of the protagonists made outright accusations of fraud or dishonesty. In so doing, they all left open the possibility of a negotiated settlement and future, mutually beneficial, transactions.

The supplications also reveal the significant reliance on written records as an institutionalized means of facing the challenge of the unknown future. Salvatore Quaratesi pointed to the correspondence between himself and the Capponi as evidence of his good faith and the reliable execution of their instructions. The heirs of Geronimo del Conte,

---

[18] On the preference to maintain relationships, and the benefits of doing so, see Ricardo Court, "De fatigationibus: What a Merchant's Errant Son Can Teach Us about the Dynamics of Trust," in *Il registro di lettere di Giovanni Francesco di Negro (1563–1565): Regole e prospettive di un mondo non clamoroso*, ed. Grazia Biorci and Ricardo Court (Novi Ligure: Città del silenzio, 2014).

[19] ASF LCF 743, 20r: to Tommaso Guadagni, in Lyon, 2 February 1555: "sempre che me ne verrà occasione servirmene lo farò con quella fiducia che sempre ho fatto per il passato."

likewise, claimed to have correspondence and receipts that would prove their claims, while Ippolito Affaitati countered with a royal letter granting him immunity from the original sentence in Antwerp. Cosimo de' Pazzi asserted that he possessed receipts from Piero Ugolini, which demonstrated that the debt had been paid. The latter's representatives responded by pointing to account books that recorded the sum as still outstanding. All these claims and counterclaims demonstrate the way in which Renaissance merchants relied on a myriad of written materials to provide a prophylactic against bad faith, misunderstanding, and breaches of trust in the future, as well as to keep track of transactions, instructions, profits, and losses. Writing constituted a major part of any merchant's daily activity. Although such documents had neither a notary's seal nor signature, by the sixteenth century they possessed legal validity in Italian courts of law, and so could be presented as evidence in any proceeding.[20] They could be produced at a future date and utilized for financial redress, thus providing a crucial instrument of mitigation against the hazards of the unknown time-yet-to-come.

Correspondence served an additional role in the creation and maintenance of networks of trust in premodern commerce: the circulation of crucial information. In light of the long distances that could separate merchants from their agents or partners, frequent letter writing could help maintain relationships, keeping the bonds between individuals close and so minimizing the chances of betrayal or indifference. Correspondence bridged time as well as space. The letter that a merchant wrote today would arrive at its destination on some future date. The act of writing it, therefore, required the anticipation of time-yet-to-come. The letter itself once received, in turn, made the past present for its reader. Correspondence created a sense of immediacy that was both spatial and temporal.

Several studies have highlighted the particular importance of this spatial and temporal immediacy for merchant diasporas, relatively closed networks, or coalitions of merchants from a common religious and ethnic group. The circulation of correspondence among members helped to sustain a shared identity and to strengthen the integrity of the network as a whole. One scholar has argued that sixteenth-century Genoese merchants displayed traits similar to a diaspora in their dispersal across the

[20] Frederic C. Lane, *Andrea Barbarigo, Merchant of Venice, 1418–1449* (New York: Octagon Books, 1967), 98; Francesca Trivellato, *The Familiarity of Strangers: The Sephardic Diaspora, Livorno, and Cross-Cultural Trade in the Early Modern Period* (New Haven, CT: Yale University Press, 2009), 168.

Mediterranean and into northern Europe and the Americas.[21] The argument could be extended to other Italian cities in the same period. Certainly, the merchants considered in this chapter – Florentine, Genoese, and Venetian – demonstrated a marked preference for dealing with compatriots, although this was never exclusive. Other Florentines predominated among the correspondents of the Botti company of Florence, whose operations stretched to locations as far south as Messina, as far west as the Canary Islands, as far east as Pera (in modern-day Istanbul), and as far north as Antwerp. Of the twenty-two family names that appear among the recipients in a single volume of *copialettere* (covering May 1539 to July 1540), eighteen are identifiably Florentine and another (Puccini) was clearly Tuscan. The final three names have an uncertain geographic origin but are probably all Italian.[22] A rubric compiled by Antonio Brignole in 1552 also revealed a majority of the named correspondents to be civic compatriots, although by a less dramatic margin: seven of eleven individually identified recipients possess names of certain Genoese origin. Another is Florentine (Quaratesi), a second could be from Abruzzo or Rome (Chiavarini), while the other two (Nazelli and Ferrero) are of uncertain origin. The Brignole index, however, also includes broader, nonspecific categories of correspondents such as "letters to diverse [recipients] for Spain" or "letters for the fair," presumably Besançon.[23]

Within a network of correspondents who shared a common home and diaspora-like traits, or within a more diverse group, mercantile correspondence helped to cultivate and maintain trust, and to mitigate against the risks of long-distance trade and speculative finance in the premodern era.[24] Beyond serving as a record of account that could be produced in

[21] Sebouh Aslanian, "'The Salt in a Merchant's Letter': The Culture of Julfan Correspondence in the Indian Ocean and the Mediterranean," *Journal of World History* 19, no. 2 (2008); Doria, "Conoscenza del mercato"; Greif, "The Maghribi Traders." On the civic (as opposed to Italian) identities of Italian merchants nations operating across Europe, see also Giovanni Petti Balbi, "Le *nationes* italiane all'estero," in *Commercio e cultura mercantile*, ed. Franco Franceschi, Richard A. Goldthwaite, and Reinhold C. Mueller (Treviso: Fondazione Cassamarca/Angelo Colla Editore, 2007).
[22] ASF LCF 713. The three uncertain names are written as Pionbini (there is a Pisan family da Piombo), Del Castiglio (which could also be Spanish, del Castillo), and Feruffino.
[23] ASCG BS 102, indice.
[24] Francesca Trivellato, while analyzing the Sephardic diaspora in Livorno, resists too ready conclusions based on shared ethnic and religious identities as the basis of commercial trust, instead highlighting the way that correspondence helped merchants to develop cross-cultural networks: Trivellato, *The Familiarity of Strangers*, 177–93. On this point, see also Gagan D. S. Sood, "'Correspondence is equal to half a meeting': The Composition and Comprehension of Letters in Eighteenth-Century Islamic Eurasia," *Journal of the Economic and Social History of the Orient* 50, nos. 2–3 (2007).

court, it did so principally through the circulation of information. Merchants exchanged news about prices and commodities, about colleagues, insurers, ship owners, and captains, but also about political and military affairs that could disrupt or affect trade.[25] Prices in premodern Europe remained fairly inelastic, due to technological and communication limitations, so merchants paid close attention to any activity or event which might exert pressure on commodity markets.

In a contested space like the sixteenth-century Mediterranean, rumors and news of impending conflict were prevalent but often vague. Much of the information that merchants conveyed was speculative and anticipatory. They looked ahead and considered, based on available knowledge, what might happen in the future, whether in several months or in just a few weeks. In January 1541, Francesco Leone, a Florentine merchant banker residing in Venice, warned a colleague in Lyon that shipping spices from the Ottoman empire would be increasingly difficult during the summer because "the sea will be full of the armadas of various princes and so merchants' ships will run a greater risk." To make such a perilous journey worthwhile, he instructed that it should go ahead only if no less than three-quarters of the asking price were met in cash.[26] On other occasions, merchants reacted to more specific and immediate threats. Antonio Brignole wrote to Simone Lomellini, in Sicily, in May 1572 concerning reports that the vice-regal court in Naples was impounding shipping to serve in an armada; presumably for Don Juan of Austria's pursuit of Uluç Ali, the admiral of the Ottoman fleet who had led the Turkish retreat from their defeat at Lepanto the previous year. Brignole worried about whether it would be possible to get a ship to Messina in order to load the olive oil that Lomellino had acquired, whether the oil could be stored without damage during the hot summer months, and, if it could, whether it might not be better to wait until September, when the campaigning season was over and "here and on the riviera at that time, there will be need of the said oil," resulting in greater profits.[27]

The networks of Italian merchants in the sixteenth century, however, extended beyond the Mediterranean, and so news from much further

---

[25] On mercantile correspondence and the circulation of information, see Mario Infelise, "La circolazione dell'informazione commerciale," in Franceschi et al., eds., *Commercio e cultura mercantile.*

[26] ASF LCF 2927, 188r–v: to Salviati, in Lyon, 29 January 1541: "se questa state manderei la nave che disegniate sapiate che gli è bene avere avertenza che il mare sarà pieno d'armate di diversi principi e che le nave de' mercanti coreranno magior risico."

[27] ASCG BS 102, 39r–40r: to Simone Lomellino, in Monteleone or Messina, 23 May 1572. The quoted text is at 40r: "qui e in riviera in tempo che sarà il bisogno de' detti ollei."

afield could affect prices and prospects on the peninsula. In the summer
of 1539, Simone Botti reported rumors that the Portuguese had suffered
a defeat in Asia and, therefore, that the pepper fleet would not arrive that
year.[28] In August and September 1573, Brignole paid close attention to
reports of the Dutch Revolt, which left him without "much good hope"
regarding the sale of silks there.[29] In August 1581, Filippo Sassetti
reported from Lisbon that the convoy from India had not yet arrived,
prompting great anxiety for himself and other merchants expecting
goods, and exerting pressure on the prices for spices and sugar.[30] Once
he had transferred to the subcontinent, Sassetti supplied detailed reports
on political and military events in Asia in addition to mercantile information for his correspondents in Florence, all of which served commercial purposes as well as ethnographic interest. In one letter dating
probably from December 1585, for example, he provided a disquisition
on the differences between the pepper shipped by the Portuguese from
southwest India and the superior product sourced by Muslim merchants
from Aceh.[31]

While merchants did exchange news about military and political events
for the purposes of general interest, their principal concern remained
how these reports might affect the price and availability of specific
commodities. News about the markets for goods in various locales constituted the most essential component of mercantile correspondence,
after issuing or responding to instructions. The nature of the long-
distance commerce practiced by Italian merchants in the sixteenth century meant that communicating precise details required proficiency in a
wide range of currencies, weights, and values in order to understand
pricing and maximize the opportunity for profit. Even on a local scale,
municipal ordinances and the diversity of coinage circulating in premodern cities necessitated knowledge and expertise on the part of retail-
ers.[32] Since the thirteenth century, scholastic economic thought had
charged merchants with a crucial role as arbiters of value in the provision
of necessary goods. Their own profession further required that they be

[28] ASF LCF 713, 19r.
[29] ASCG BS 103, 41r, 125r. The quoted text is from the latter folio: "a detta impieta de
    sete di quale non havemo molto bona speranza"
[30] Filippo Sassetti, Lettere edite e inedite di Filippo Sassetti, ed. Ettore Marcucci (Florence:
    Felice le Monnier, 1855), 171, 174.
[31] Ibid., 311–12; see also 299–303, 325–34, 341–51, 364–71.
[32] On prices and value on a local level in Renaissance Italy, see Guido Guerzoni, "The
    Social World of Price Formation: Prices and Consumption in Sixteenth-Century
    Ferrara," and Evelyn Welch, "Making Money: Pricing and Payments in Renaissance
    Italy," in The Material Renaissance, ed. Michelle O'Malley and Evelyn Welch
    (Manchester: Manchester University Press, 2007).

experts in prices, calculating when to buy, and when to sell. The act of providing information on commodities and costs, however, also required a level of expertise in futurity, because it was, in itself, a form of speculation on how markets might move in weeks or months ahead.

Such speculation could at times demonstrate a high level of precision. In September 1573, Antonio Brignole instructed Simone Lomellino: "if the price of silk should fall, when it reaches eighteen to eighteen and half [scudi?] you should certainly not fail to invest in it all that will be advanced to you there."[33] Understanding prices also required understanding exchange rates and the value of money in various locales. Giovanbattista Botti, writing to the Rucellai company in Rome in July and August 1552 concerning the reinvestment of profits made from exchange speculation at the fair of Medina de Rioseco (one of the Iberian centers for the redistribution of American silver), provided precise and detailed instructions about what was to occur. If they could get 502 maravedis per ducat in Seville, then the Rucellai should remit the sum to Giovanbattista's brother, Iacopo, there. If not, then it should be returned to the Affaitati at 500 maravedis per ducat for reinvestment at Medina de Rioseco. If neither price could be obtained in either location, then the sum should be sent to the Guadagni for speculation at the August fair in Lyon, "for the price will run the market."[34] Frequently, however, correspondence about prices concerned not specific details but basic information that would enable more precise assessments to be made. In January 1556, Andrea Berengo discussed the disjuncture in price between commodities in Venice and what he could purchase in the Levant with one of his many correspondents: "I see the prices offered there for spices, which are certainly low and yet little is sold; and also here the same occurs; silk is up in the air and there is little of it, there it has bottomed out and there is a great deal; spices are up in the air and at much greater prices than I told you in other letters."[35]

Finally, merchants also shared information about the professionals with whom they dealt: other merchants, ship captains, and owners. Several scholars have highlighted the crucial role that reputation played in premodern commerce across the Afro-Eurasian land mass. It operated, some have argued, as a mechanism or even an institution that

---

[33] ASCG BS 103, 43v: to Simone Lomellino, in Messina, 2 September 1573: "se sete abassare di pretio che quando venissero a [unclear currency] 18 in 18 ½ le bene non mancherette de impietare in esse tutto quello vi avanzera per voi."

[34] ASF, LCF 723, 3r: Giovanbattista Botti, in Florence (?), to Rucellai, in Rome, 30 July and 6 August 1552: "per el pregio corerà la piaza." The silver maravedi was the Spanish money of account in the sixteenth century, valued at one-thirty-fourth of a silver reale.

[35] Tucci, *Lettres d'un marchand*, 222, letter 191.

helped to create and preserve mercantile networks, enabling the operation of trust between distant partners and even strangers.[36] By maintaining a good reputation – as honest and trustworthy, but also as an astute and successful operator – an individual merchant maximized the potential for profits and commercial success. The long-term benefits of trustworthy and reliable behavior outweighed the short-term gains that might be obtained by deception or fraud. By cultivating the trust of others, a merchant cultivated wealth, now and in the future.

As a result, sixteenth-century Italian merchants took pains to present themselves as careful, trusting, and trustworthy. In a 1554 supplication to Cosimo I de' Medici, concerning a case against Stefano Cotoni of Messina and a merchant captain, Piero di Radaglia, for a debt of 200 scudi, Tommaso Cavalcanti and Giovanni Giraldi presented themselves as "prudent and virtuous merchants."[37] On 30 September 1562, Giovanbattista Botti wrote to Agostino del Marino, in Seville, invoking the "honor and good reputation [fama]" of his recently deceased brother, Iacopo, in order to urge immediate payment of any outstanding debts he had left.[38] Not only was Iacopo's posthumous name and standing put at risk by delay, but the credit of the surviving brothers would also suffer if Del Marino did not make the remittances. The relatives of Zuan Maria Ventura, a young Venetian sent to Istanbul to pursue commercial opportunities, reminded him to consider his name and reputation so that he could return to Venice with honor.[39]

The Genoese merchant Francesco di Negro, understanding the necessity of a good reputation in commerce, devoted much ink and anguish to the delinquent behavior of his son, Geronimo. Having performed poorly in a previous posting to the exchange fair at Besançon, Geronimo was dispatched by his father to Messina to continue an apprenticeship in business. However, he proved resistant both to paternal instructions and to the guiding hand of his cousin, Niccolò di Negro. What Geronimo did that so distressed and infuriated his father – beyond refusing the return to Messina from Palermo, where he had established himself – is not clear. Francesco used the evocative, but elusive, phrase la

[36] See Aslanian, "Social Capital," esp. 390–93; Epstein, "Secrecy"; Greif, "Reputation and Coalitions"; Prange, "'Trust in God.'"
[37] ASF, Mercanzia 11517, unfoliated: supplication from Tommaso Calvalcanti and Giovanni Giraldi, undated but ca. June 1554: "quelli prudenti et virtuoso mercatanti,"
[38] ASF LCF 716, 5r: to Agostino del Marino, in Seville, 30 September 1562: "Poi avete avertire al onore e buona fama a lasciato la b[uona] m[emoria] di mio fr[ate]llo che in groria sia in pagare subito chi arà avere sanza dilazione né gavilazione alchuna." Marino was the husband of Iacopo's daughter Maddalena.
[39] Ugo Tucci, "La formazione dell'uomo d'affari," in Franceschi et al., eds., Commercio e cultura mercantile, 495.

carogna (the carcass) to discuss the state of his son's life and manner of living.[40] Clearly, however, Francesco fretted about the potential damage to his own reputation and the family name, as well as to Geronimo's future prospects. In May 1564, Francesco informed Niccolò that he was considering returning his son to Besançon and the supervision of his uncles, but did not want to tell him so outright: "I am writing him that it is not important to me that he stay there more than anywhere else, except regarding my honor, which, I judge, necessitates having someone to whom he can be entrusted."[41]

Merchants wrote concerning not only their own reputations or those of family members but also those of associates. In September 1540, Francesco Leone informed a compatriot in Florence, with dismay, about the costs of the damage caused to grain being shipped by one Bernardi (apparently the owner of the vessel): "if I ever afflict myself with him again, may I lose everything because he is, in effect, a man without discernment."[42] By openly sharing his disdain, Leone consciously chose to damage the reputation of Bernardi within the merchant banker's commercial network.

In the sixteenth century, commercial trust was not confined simply to human relationships, and for all their hard-headed speculation, Italian merchants did not think about the future in purely secular terms. Indeed, when discussing trust in commercial transactions, they implicitly, yet persistently, reminded themselves and their correspondents of Christian belief and religious obligations. Since at least the thirteenth century, commerce and Christianity had been deeply entwined in Italy. The enduring of these bonds into the 1500s constituted a principal continuity between medieval and Renaissance commerce. In particular, the centrality of trust to the operation of the premodern economy bound the two together. The language of trust was the language of faith. Italian does not distinguish between the two terms in the same way that English does. Religious belief, Christian morality, personal reputation, and commercial relationships all worked with the same lexicon of *fidare* (to trust, to have faith) and *credere* (to believe).[43] Credit had a dual meaning of

[40] See Court, "De fatigationibus," for a detailed analysis of this correspondence and the relationship between father and son.
[41] Grazia Biorci and Ricardo Court, *Il registro di lettere di Giovanni Francesco di Negro (1563–1565): Regole e prospettive di un mondo non clamoroso* (Novi Ligure: Città di silenzio, 2014), 153.
[42] ASF LCF 2927, 95r–v: to [Da] Sommaia, in Florence, 25 September 1540: "se mai più mi travaglio con esso poss'io perdere ogni cosa perché in efetto è omo senza ragione."
[43] Giacomo Todeschini has produced some of the most insightful and sensitive analysis of the intricate links between Christian theology and commerce, in both language and

both personal and financial worth. One could acquire credit with God, with business partners, or with one's bankers. When Simone Botti expressed his continuing confidence in Tommaso Guadagni, he wrote of his *fiducia* (trust) in the Lyon-based merchant banker. When his brother, Giovanbattista, sought to shame the Giunti and Antinori firm regarding an unexecuted transaction, he emphasized *la gran fede* (the great faith) that he had had in them. Antonio Brignole, in his repeated adjurations to his partners and agents to trust well, advised them to *ben fidare*.[44] Trust in God was the one fail-safe investment that every merchant could make, and they invoked it at the beginning of every account book, ledger, and letter book: "In the name of omnipotent God and of his most glorious mother, my lady, Holy Mary, and of messer Saint John the Baptist, our advocate, and of all the court of Paradise, amen."[45]

The correspondence considered in this chapter reveals the persistence of a religious, soteriological vision of the future in the mercantile culture of the sixteenth century, alongside the emergence of the new concept of time-yet-to-come as unknown and unknowable. The letters reveal that commercial operators in Renaissance Italy thought about temporality and futurity in complex ways. They were comfortable with multiple, even conflicting, explanations for the passage of time and the unfolding of events, and inhabited a mental world in which different temporalities and conceptions of time coexisted and overlapped. Even as they had recourse to human institutions and relationships to mitigate against the proximate causes of bad luck and commercial damages in the near future (such as piracy, weather, and bad faith), Renaissance Italian merchants also relied

practice in late medieval Europe. See especially Giacomo Todeschini, *Ricchezza francescana: Dalla povertà volontaria alla società di mercato* (Bologna: Il Mulino, 2004), 159–72. See also Court, "De fatigationibus," esp. 55–56; Angela Orlandi, "Note su affari e devozione nei documenti di alcuni mercanti fiorentini (1450–1550)," *Storia economica* 13, no. 3 (2010); Giacomo Todeschini, "Theological Roots of the Medieval/Modern Merchants' Self-Representation," in *The Self-Perception of Early Modern Capitalists*, ed. Margaret C. Jacob and Catherine Secretan (New York: Palgrave Macmillian, 2008). John F. Padgett and Paul D. McLean, "Economic Credit in Renaissance Florence," *The Journal of Modern History* 83, no. 1 (2011), examines the relationship between personal (honor) and financial credit in fifteenth-century Florence, at 31–34 especially; but their focus on quantitative data obscures the religious imperatives of the language of credit in Renaissance Italy. The qualitative analysis of the phenomenon at 37–39 mentions religious imperatives but does not explore them.
[44] See notes 19, 12, and 10 above, respectively.
[45] ASF LCF 712, 1r: "Al nome sia del onipotente iddio et della sua groliossima madre madonna santa maria e di messer santo giovanni batista nostro avochato e di tutta la chorte del paradiso amen." "Messer" was the honorific title used by lawyers and knights in late medieval and early modern Italy. It was also frequently used (as it is here) in addressing male saints and sometimes even God.

on their relationship with the divine to administer their ultimate accounting of profit or loss, in both their professional and personal lives.

These institutional and sociocultural mechanisms, however, could only mitigate against the challenges of the unknown future: the problem of trust and the limitations of communication in premodern commerce. They could never eliminate them completely. In July 1574, Antonio Brignole laconically summed up the essence of the problem that faced Italian merchants: "in trusting, one runs risks."[46] The practice of commerce in premodern Europe required trust in others. This, in turn, left merchants open to potential damages, financial as well as reputational, from trusting poorly. The outcome of any venture – for a myriad of reasons – remained unknown at its outset. Merchants confronted the unknowability of time-yet-to-come on a daily basis. Commercial enterprise had always been speculative; the merchants of sixteenth-century Italy were not new in this regard. However, they confronted, thought about, and attempted to give meaning to the unknown time-yet-to-come in a world that had become dramatically and unexpectedly larger, proving that the unanticipated could disrupt even the most sure knowledge, and in a society and culture possessed with new conceptions of the future and temporality. In the assessment of risks, prices, and values, successful merchants demonstrated themselves experts in this new futurity.

---

[46] ASCG BS 104, 7v: to Niccolò and Giulio Cibo, in Florence, 9 July 1574: "nel fidare si corre risico."

4   The Mercantile Vocabulary of Futurity in Sixteenth-Century Italy

On 4 March 1575, Antonio Brignole wrote to Niccolò and Giulio Cibo, his long-term associates in Florence. Brignole confirmed that he would relay to his agent at the exchange fair of Besançon that the Cibo "do not wish to continue any more in that business in order not to make a further test of *fortuna*."[1] This brief statement from one merchant to another encapsulated the central challenge of the profession, the speculation on unknown future outcomes that lay at the heart of commerce. In the premodern world, the technological and logistical limitations of communication heightened the unknowability of time-yet-to-come. Renaissance Italian merchants and financiers confronted problems of asymmetry in information about the present and the future as a matter of course. The ability to know the date of the arrival of the spice caravan from Mecca in Aleppo, the possibility of storms in the Adriatic Sea, the likelihood of an agent in Lyon acting dishonestly, or the chance that the price of raw Spanish wool would fall before a shipment arrived in Livorno remained strictly limited and often utterly impossible. Even when news did arrive, it was likely out of date. Merchants like Brignole and the Cibo, then, had to grapple with the unknown and unknowable future on a daily basis. As discussed in Chapter 3, they relied on trust and a variety of structures to maintain relationships in order to operate in this world.

Brignole used the figure of *fortuna* in this particular letter to refer to the unknown future, to both the hazards and the potential of financial speculation. However, this was just one term in the broad vocabulary merchants in the sixteenth century used to talk about temporality, particularly time-yet-to-come, and the risks associated with the passage of time. They did so reflexively and un-self-consciously as part of the grammar of their profession. Due to the inherent uncertainty of

---

[1] ASCG, BS 104: 175r: Antonio Brignole, to Niccolò and Giulio Cibo, in Florence, 4 March 1575: "si recapiteranno sotto nostri nomi conforme al desiderio vostro aff[erman]do non voler più continuar' tal negozio per non far più prova della fortuna." Giulio Cibo was the husband of Brignole's sister, whose name I have not uncovered.

premodern commerce, Renaissance merchants had to become experts not only in prices and values but also in futurity. They developed a sophisticated type of probabilistic reasoning – based on past experience and subjective impressions rather than on statistics or estimations of frequency – to calculate and weigh the potential profits and losses of any particular venture. So in the early months of 1575, Niccolò and Giulio Cibo clearly estimated that the risks of further speculation on exchange rates outweighed uncertain gains.

This chapter analyzes the vocabulary of futurity used by sixteenth-century Italian merchants. It does so using the same archival sources as the previous chapter: commercial correspondence from Florence, Genoa, and Venice, with particular emphasis on the same representatives examples. It demonstrates the flexible and varied lexicon that merchants used to describe the unknown future and to give meaning to the opportunities and risks that speculation on it offered. They thought in detail and often with great precision about the passage of time, placing a price on the unknown yet accessible time yet-to-come, weighing the probabilities of particular occurrences. Through their correspondence, through this rich vocabulary and careful parsing of possibilities, sixteenth-century merchants presented themselves as professionals in futurity. They presented themselves as experts in the recognition of the opportunities that could arise from chance and the unknowability of the future: identifying, pricing, and even selling risk as a commodity.

Like the authors considered in Chapter 1, merchants acquired this expertise through long familiarity and occupational necessity. Unlike Cardano and the others, however, they did not communicate this expertise outside professional circles. The mercantile vocabulary structured a closed conversation about futurity. Notably, merchants never articulated a stark, singular vision of the future events determined entirely by chance analogous to that presented by the gambling experts. Mastery of the new concept of time yet-to-come did not result in these commercial operators breaking completely with earlier soteriological and anticipatory temporalities. Instead, the richness of their lexicon of futurity matched the complexity of their visions of the future.

As noted in the Introduction, the figure of *fortuna* served as the principle vehicle for discussing and imagining the problem of future contingency in Renaissance Italy, outside theological considerations. Merchants, however, used the word and its associated meanings sparingly. Part of the explanation for the relative absence of the term from mercantile correspondence lies in the fact that they possessed a rich, varied vocabulary for discussing the passage of time, owing no doubt to their deep and intimate familiarity with uncertainty and risk taking.

Furthermore, when merchants did use the word, especially in northern Italy, they frequently assigned to it the older meaning of a storm at sea, reflecting the predominance of maritime commerce in the peninsula's economy. Antonio Brignole, for example, on 9 July 1574, observed that Gian Andrea Doria had arrived in Porto Venere from Spain "having run a strong *fortuna*."[2] Merchants from Florence – perhaps unsurprisingly given the density of humanist and literary exchanges in the city – used the term more readily and did so to speak about the unknowability of the future more frequently than those from Genoa and Venice. Matteo Botti, writing to his brother Iacopo, in Cadiz, in June 1524, and noting the dangers caused by the ongoing conflict between Emperor Charles V and Francis I of France, reminded him of the need to insure cargoes of sugar shipped from Spain to Italy, "so that we do not have to throw ourselves on *fortuna*."[3] The language is particularly evocative of instability – given the common image of Fortuna balanced atop a sphere – as well as the hazards to commerce posed by the unknown future.

In 1584, the Capponi bank recorded a transaction that involved sending thirty-three pieces of light silk cloth (*ermisino*) to Francesco Cambi. The profits were to be divided, with Cambi receiving half and the Capponi's portion to be shared with Filippo Velluti and Alamanno Alamanni, "who are obliged to run the same *fortuna* as us, and to bear the good or bad that will come from this enterprise."[4] The bank's use of *fortuna* here to refer to the risks of commercial speculation on unknown outcomes – indeed, the phrase would translate most readily as "run the same risk" – encapsulates precisely the sense of the future as unknown time-yet-to-come subject to the vicissitudes and uncertainties of human experience. Simone Botti employed it in 1555 in an identical fashion. Reacting to rumors that the French monarchy was considering a plan to default on one-third of the debt owed to each individual creditor, Simone sent precise instructions to his brother, Giovanbattista, in Lyon. These detailed the action that the Guadagni bank – which handled the brothers' investments in French royal finances – should take. Hoping to minimize his losses, Simone requested that the Guadagni sell 1,000 scudi of his

---

[2] ASCG BS 104, 38r: to Federico de' Ricci, in Florence, 9 July 1574: "Il s[igno]r Gio: and[re]a con la gallera se intende che venendo di spagna e giontò in portovenere però haver corso gagliarda fortuna doverà esser qui domani."

[3] ASF LCF 711, 8r: to Iacopo Botti, in Cadiz, 23 June 1524: "che tutto quello ai per nostro conto a manddare bixongnia tu facci conto di mandarlo sichurato di chostà sino che queste guerre durano che non fa per noi gittarci alla fortuna."

[4] ASF LCF 1089, 11r: "della qual nostra metà ne assegnamo un quarto a filippo Velluti e un quarto a Alamanno di Vinc[enz]o Alam[ann]i li quali si oblig[hi]no di correre con noi la med[esi]ma fortuna e di star' a tutto il bene o male che procederà da tale incetta."

investment in the crown's debt at the best available rate, before the government acted, and then withdraw the remaining 1,000 scudi as soon as possible following any default, if it occurred: "beg them not to lack in serving me, since for such a sum I do not wish to run this *fortuna*." Simone did not wish to take the chance that rumor would prove false, deciding to act first and take a small loss in the hurried sale rather than lose more in any default.[5]

Filippo Sassetti, who worked in Lisbon as an agent for other Florentine merchants before relocating to southwest India pursuing wealth in the pepper trade, reflected something of a long-established tradition that personified Fortuna and endowed her with cruel intent, when he discussed his motivation for traveling to Asia. Writing to Baccio Valori, in December 1581, Sassetti stated that he hoped for greater success in India than he had enjoyed on the Iberian peninsula, and desired that his move would "blunt the ill-will of *fortuna*."[6] The Florentine merchant had traveled first to Madrid and then to Lisbon, hoping to restore his family's finances, but had found his ambitions frustrated. The Venetian Nadal Venier similarly evoked this vision when he spoke of wishing "to break this harsh wheel of *fortuna*," which had left him without friends and money in Zadar but hopeful of opportunities while the Dalmatian coast remained free of plague and warfare with the Ottoman empire.[7]

If *fortuna* remained relatively rare in mercantile correspondence, other words that gave meaning to the unknown time-yet-to-come appeared more frequently. The word *ventura* appeared far more often than *fortuna* itself, occasionally also in the verb form *avventurare*. It possessed and possesses a complex, multiple meaning referring to chance, destiny (or at least an end point), and good fortune. In the letters of sixteenth-century Italian merchants, it appears, most commonly, to imply an amalgam of these meanings: a speculative, hopefully profitable venture, which often might best be translated as *opportunity*. While *fortuna* was more common in the epistles of Florentine merchants, Venetian merchants appeared particularly to favor *ventura*.

Andrea Berengo, a factor working in Aleppo for a number of Venetian patrician merchants, used the term constantly to express his hopes for

[5] ASF LCF 743, 24v: to Giovanbattista Botti, in Lyon, 15 March 1555: "pregarli che non manchino di servirmi che per a tanta somma nè voglo correr' questa fortuna."
[6] Filippo Sassetti, *Lettere edite e inedite di Filippo Sassetti*, ed. Ettore Marcucci (Florence: Felice le Monnier, 1855), 186.
[7] ASV, MCNA 18/19, unfoliated: Nadal Venier, in Zadar, to Pasquale Padovani, in Venice, 27 January 1527: "spero purch'el paese stia sano e senza guere de' turchi spezar' questa dura rota de fortuna."

future commercial success. Writing to one of his principal employers, Zuan Giustinian, on 8 October 1555, Berengo requested that, if possible, Giustinian send some dark green textiles and pink *arquimie* cloth together with the planned scarlet fabrics, "because if it is as good as I hope, it will not lack *ventura*."[8] Berengo's ambitions were often ill-founded because he arrived in Aleppo during the middle of a Venetian boycott of the local spice dealers – in protest at increased export duties – which had disrupted and distorted the markets for every other product. However, he maintained a hopeful attitude in his correspondence, always promising his employers better opportunities in the near future. To Lodovico de Niccolò, in November 1555, he wrote that little Persian silk was available and that he expected high prices due to the spice boycott, which left Venetian merchants in Aleppo competing for the other products available, driving up demand. He added, however, "Patience, everything has its *ventura*."[9]

Giovan Alvise Tagliapietra, another Venetian working in the Levant as an agent in the same period, used the term in an identical fashion to express hopes for future, profitable opportunities. Venetian merchants operating in the Ottoman Empire preferred to barter Italian textiles for spices, Persian silks, and other Asian products rather than buying and selling with cash.[10] This caused factors like Berengo and Tagliapietra constant difficulties because the Ottoman traders with whom they dealt preferred silver, and the local market was probably saturated with European cloth, making pure barter transactions difficult. In August 1550, Tagliapietra informed Lorenzo Aliprando that he was in desperate straits because he needed cash to sweeten any purchase but had not been able to conclude any sales for currency. Moreover, the merchants who did make deals for cash "show little *ventura*, all the more so for the low prices."[11] In March 1551, Tagliapietra wrote to Antonio Alberti that he had sold most of Alberti's textiles and was awaiting the arrival

[8] Ugo Tucci, ed. *Lettres d'un marchand vénitian Andrea Berengo (1553–1556)*, (Paris: S.E.V.P.E.N., 1957), 31, letter 9.
[9] Ibid., 122, letter 106. On the Venetian boycott, which began in July 1555, see Ugo Tucci's introduction, 19–20.
[10] See James D. Tracy, "Syria's Arab Traders as Seen by Andrea Berengo, 1555–1556," *Oriens* 37 (2009): 166–69; Tucci, *Lettres d'un marchand*, 15–18.
[11] ASV MCNA 20, unfoliated copialettere of Giovan Alvise Tagliapietra: to Lorenzo Aliprando, 19 August 1550: "trovarmi disperatto a non potter' finir' qual cosa a contt[ant]i che quando ni avesse da compagniar' dila roba averia fatto qualche mercado ancora che questi che se fano mostrano poca ventt[ur]a e tantto meno per li precii bassi."

of silks and spices, "and I will invest your money in whichever promises greater *ventura*."[12]

Although most common in Venetian mercantile correspondence, *ventura* also appeared regularly in the letters of merchants from other cities. Antonio Brignole wrote to Simone Lomellini, in September 1572, concerning the tin that the latter had sent to Palermo in search of a market, as he could not sell it in Messina. Brignole reported that it had been received but not yet sold. However, he continued, the recipients "strongly hoped that they would not miss their *ventura*."[13] Here, as in the Venetian usage, *ventura* expresses a currently unrealized, and so aspirational, profit from an enterprise whose outcome remains unknown. Reflecting the complexity of the word's meaning, Filippo Sassetti used it, in June 1581, when discussing the prices and availability of various products in Lisbon. "If for *ventura* more than usual arrive this year like last year," he wrote to Francesco Valori, regarding cloves, "or 2000 cantars as usual, it would be no great thing since one could acquire [them] at little more than 100 florins a cantar of the same weight, at which price one could invest some thousands of ducats in it."[14] In this letter, *ventura* appears initially as simple chance, an unknown future event the causation of which is unclear. However, it also clearly carries the sense of profitable opportunity, because as a merchant Sassetti would have understood that the arrival of spices and other American and Asian goods in Lisbon was due not to luck but to transactions that had occurred elsewhere in the world. What might appear as chance on the docks of the river Tagus was actually the realization of a profitable opportunity on the other side of the globe.

Merchants also expressed the anticipation and expectation of financial opportunities using the term *occasione*. Unlike *ventura*, they used this exclusively to discuss the passage of time and potential of the unknown future on a human scale. God might send *ventura*, but it appeared he was never invoked to send *occasione*. Merchants from Florence, Genoa, and Venice all used the word equally. While it translates directly and simply as opportunity, it also sometimes possesses a meaning more akin to its

---

[12] ASV MCNA 20, unfoliated copialettere of Giovan Alvise Tagliapietra: to Antonio Alberto, 11 March 1551: "son restato per aspetar' vengi dele sede over spe[zi]e et in quello che prometerà magior' ventura inves[tir]ò li dan[ar]i vostri."
[13] ASCG BS 102, 219r: to Simone Lomellino, in Messina, 26 September 1572: "a p[aler]mo harette poi m[anda]to il resto delli stagni poichè costì non vi era speranza di venderli e di quelli havevano già rice[vu]to non havevano però venduto cosa alcuna speravavano bene non li dovessi mancar' loro ventura."
[14] Sassetti, *Lettere*, 159. The cantar was the unit of weight by which spices were sold in Portugal. Sassetti describes a cantar of cloves as 167 pounds, presumably by Florentine measure.

English cognate, "occasion." Its regular appearance in commercial cor-respondence is particularly striking in relation to the new concept of the future as unknown time-yet-to-come. As is discussed in detail in Chapter 7, an important part of this development involved the conflation of the figure of *fortuna* with that of *kairos* or *occasio*, opportunity. The letters considered in this chapter did not evoke the *fortuna-kairos* imagery that developed around the turn of the sixteenth century. However, Renaissance Italian merchants inhabited the same world as the artists and authors who created it. They were not, or at least not all, hard-headed proto-capitalists with little time or interest in culture. Many enjoyed and indulged in the literary and visual arts as well as the pursuit of commerce. Giorgio Vasari identified Matteo and Simone Botti as particular friends to artists in the city of Florence.[15] They invested in a significant collection of art, which included Raphael's *Donna velata*, and commissioned Vasari himself to paint an altarpiece for the family chapel in Santa Maria del Carmine. Matteo's personal library, moreover, con-tained works by Boccaccio, Erasmus, and Machiavelli, including *The Prince* and the *Discorsi*.[16] Filippo Sassetti openly preferred a life dedicated to letters over the commercial career that family circumstances forced him to pursue. He studied at the university of Pisa, became a member of the Accademia degli Alterati in 1575, and peppered his correspondence with allusions to contemporary and classical texts.[17] Although direct causation remains elusive, the overlapping worlds of commerce and culture, and the long familiarity of merchants with the problems of future speculation, suggest that their usage may have influenced the develop-ment of the *fortuna-kairos* figure. Certainly, the frequent use of *occasione* by merchants reflected a conception of time as fractured into graspable moments, and the future as pregnant with potential to be seized and turned to material benefit.

Antonio Brignole particularly favored the word. It punctuated his correspondence with regularity. In April 1572, he sent instructions his brother Teramo and Antonio Pallavicino, who operated a branch of the family business in Seville, concerning the disbursement of 5,000 scudi. The sum should be invested in either Spanish wool or cochineal from the

---

[15] Paola Barocchi, "Sulla collezione Botti," *Prospettiva*, no. 93/94: 128, n. 8.
[16] These, together with other books, including an Italian-language Bible, were surrendered to the inquisitor at Santa Croce in 1559: ASF, LCF 742, 30r. On the Botti's cultural pursuits, see also Barocchi, "Sulla collezione Botti"; Françoise Point-Waquet, "Les Botti: Fortunes et culture d'une famille florentine (1550–1621)," *Mélanges de l'Ecole française de Rome: Moyen-Age, Temps modernes* 90, no. 2 (1978).
[17] On Sassetti, see, in particular, Marica Milanesi, *Filippo Sassetti* (Florence: La Nuova Italia Editrice, 1973).

Americas if the prices were right. In short, Teramo and Pallavicino should "dispose of it all according to what seems to you to promise us more profit by investing in merchandise or remitting it as soon as possible to our procurator, depending on what *occassioni* occur."[18] In late September 1573, writing to Felice del Beccuto and Guglielmo Giuliani, in Pisa, Brignole stated that "when *occasioni* for investment, which seem interesting to your Cibo of Florence, present themselves, we will not miss them, pausing only to consider if it offers a pleasing *occasione* with hope of profits."[19] While unclear, it seems likely from this letter and others that the Cibo referred to are the same Niccolò and Giulio Cibo, with whom the Brignole had extensive dealings.

On 12 December 1555, Andrea Berengo wrote to Zuan Contarini, in Nicosia, Cyprus, concerning 350 ducats that Berengo had sent for the purchase of Venetian silks: "But if up to now there has been no *occasione* to invest the said money, send it back here in many good silver coins, so that the damage may be repaired, and there will also be some little profit from it."[20] This construction, in particular, highlights the use of *occasione* to refer to moments for profit that had to be seized or missed. If Contarini had not realized an opportunity for investment in Cyprus, then the damage from that failure – that is, the unrealized profits – could be best repaired by sending the sum back to Berengo in cash, which he could use to purchase other goods in Aleppo.

The Florentine bank that operated under the name of the heirs of Luigi Capponi invested much of its operations in insurance brokering. The maritime insurance market in sixteenth-century Florence was one of the most long-established and competitive on the peninsula. Brokers, like the Capponi bank, shared the risk of a contract between several

---

[18] ASCG BS 102, 2r: to Teramo Brignole and Antonio Pallavicino, in Seville, 1 April 1572: "E di tutti disponerette secondo a voi parrà più nostro utt[il]e con impietarli in merce o con remetterli in la più prossima al nostro procuratore secondo le occasioni che occoriranno." In the nonstandardized Italian of the sixteenth century, there were various spellings of *occasione*, most commonly *ocaxione* and *ocasione*. In the body of the text I have standardized the spelling to modern Italian for the purposes of analytic clarity.

[19] ASCG BS 103, 134r: to Felice del Beccuto and Guglielmo Giuliani, in Pisa, 25 September 1573: "e quando si rapresenteranno occasione de impiete che a vostri cibo de firenze paia de interesarnelli non li mancheremo resta solamenti aspetar si offerisca occassione gratta con speranza de guadagno."

[20] Tucci, *Lettres d'un marchand*, 155, Letter 35. Berengo literally instructed Contarini to send *mocenigi* and *marcelli*, which were silver coins first minted in the 1470s. The *mocenigo* was a *lira di piccoli* worth 20 *soldi di piccoli* and the *marcello* was worth half as much; see Ugo Tucci, "Monete e banche nel secolo del ducato d'oro," in *Storia di Venezia dalle origini alla caduta della Serenissima*, ed. Alberto Tenenti and Ugo Tucci (Rome: Istituto della Enciclopedia Italiana fondata da Giovanni Treccani, 1996), 771–73.

underwriters, for whom the investment was a speculative one: they received a percentage of the premium but bore a proportionate risk of any claim.[21] On 3 May 1586, for example, the bank wrote to Niccolò Lomellino, in Genoa, informing him of the various credits to his account for the vessels that he had co-insured at rates between 5.5 and 9.5 percent, concluding: "when the *occasione* to insure other risks for you presents itself to us, it will be done and you will know everything."[22]

In December 1539, responding to Battista Puccini's offer to serve as an agent in Rome, Simone Botti wrote, "we have faith in you, such that what should happen with regard to merchandise will be well handled, and therefore when the *occasione* arises, we will trust you as much in our own affairs as in those of our friends."[23] In all these examples, and many others, Italian merchants gave meaning to the unknown time-yet-to-come as a series of opportunities, to the passage of time as a concatenation of moments, each potentially offering profits. Assessing each of these and determining which was an *occasione* worth seizing required skill, knowledge, and experience. Commerce was an exercise in the anticipation and evaluation of the unknown and yet-to-come. It required an expertise in futurity.

While sixteenth-century Italian merchants used *ventura* and *occasione* to express the positive potential of the future, they used *rischio* and *periculo* to refer to the dangers of speculating on unknown outcomes. The word *rischio* first appeared in Italian commercial texts in the mid-twelfth century, in its cognate Latin form *resicum*, most likely as a borrowing from the Arabic *rizq*. While in the Quran, *rizq* meant a material benefit or gift from God, by the High Middle Ages it appeared to have a acquired a more specifically economic sense, in usage at least. Via the circulation of ideas and goods in the medieval Mediterranean, it entered Italian mercantile vocabulary to refer to the unknown outcome

---

[21] On the operation of the Florentine maritime insurance market, see Giovanni Ceccarelli, *Un mercato del rischio: Assicurare e farsi assicurare nella Firenze rinascimentale* (Venice: Marsilio, 2012). Other markets in Europe operated in a similar manner; see, for example, Jeroen Puttevils and Marc Deloof, "Marketing and Pricing Risk in Marine Insurance in Sixteenth-Century Antwerp," *The Journal of Economic History* 77, no. 3 (2017).

[22] ASF LCF 1053, 323v: to Niccolò Lomellino, in Genoa, 3 May 1586: "quando ci verrà occasione di assicurarvi altri risichi lo far e tutto il saprete."

[23] ASF LCF 713, 114v: to Battista Puccini, in Rome, 6 December 1539: "avamo desidero avere costì qualche persona che aprezassi la merchantia come mi persuado siate per fare noi dil che sino a ora male l'aviamo costà trovato ma aviamo fede in voi chè in quello accadrà per essa sta bene trattata e però quando verrà l'occasione prederemo di voi fiducia tanto di cose nostre quanto di amici nostri." I have translated *essa* as referring to *la merchantia*, which seems the most logical option, but it could also refer to *fede*, that is, that our faith will not be misplaced, whatever happens.

of a commercial venture, often in tandem with *periculum* (danger) and *fortuna*. Indeed a Pisan text from 1260 used *resicum* and *fortunam* as synonyms, while mid-fourteenth-century marine insurance contracts promised protection against every *"resicum, periculum* and *fortunam* of God, man, or the sea."[24] By the sixteenth century, merchants used it as an antonym for *ventura* and *occasione*. *Rischio* referred to the potential hazards of any venture and translates directly as its English cognate, risk. It was not, however, precisely synonymous with *periculo* (danger), which derived from the Latin *periculum*. *Rischio* retained a sense of the unknown and speculative about it. *Periculo*, by contrast, referred to more defined, certain, and known hazards in any investment.

The word *rischio* peppered the correspondence of merchants across the Italian peninsula, a constant element in the calculation of the profitability and viability of any investment or speculation. In July 1564, writing to Pietro de Franchi de Rovo, in Messina, Francesco di Negro noted that the price of Sicilian silk had fallen and that he hoped it would reach a point at which Rovo could execute his commission to purchase. Di Negro added, however, that he did not want to increase the commission and buy more, "judging it an error to undertake enterprises with a seemingly great *rischio* of losing."[25] In October the same year, he instructed Geronimo Olignano to sell the remaining oil in Ventimiglia, "in order to relieve me of the *rischio* and labor and shrinkage" that would result from transporting it to Genoa.[26] In both instances, Di Negro used *rischio* to indicate the potential, unknown, future dangers of commercial

---

[24] The transmission and adaptation of *rizq* to *resicum* remains unclear and the scholarship is largely speculative. See Alain J. Lemaître, "Une nouvelle approche," in *Pour une histoire culturelle du risque: Genèse, évolution, actualité du concept dans les sociétés occidentales*, ed. Emmanuelle Collas-Heddeland et al. (Strasbourg: Éditions Histoire et Anthropologie, 2004); Constant J. Mews and Ibrahim Abraham, "Usury and Just Compensation: Religious and Financial Ethics in Historical Perspective," *Journal of Business Ethics* 72, no. 1 (2007): 4; Sylvain Piron, "L'apparition du resicum en Méditerranée occidentale aux XIIème–XIIIème siècles," in Collas-Heddeland, et al., eds., *Pour une histoire culturelle du risque*. On the ambiguity of *resicum* and *rischio* in fourteenth century texts, see Florence Edler de Roover, "Early Examples of Marine Insurance," *The Journal of Economic History* 5, no. 2 (1945): 180–82; the quote from the 1350 insurance contract is cited at 183.

[25] Grazia Biorci and Ricardo Court, *Il registro di lettere di Giovanni Francesco di Negro (1563–1565): Regole e prospettive di un mondo non clamoroso* (Novi Ligure: Città di silenzio, 2014), 159. As with *occasione*, sixteenth-century Italian spelled *rischio* in a variety of ways – including *risico, rixego*, and *rixico*. I have similarly standardized the spelling in the body of the text for the purposes of analytic clarity.

[26] Ibid., 181. Di Negro wrote *"rixico et fatica et reduro."* Shrinkage seems the best translation of the ultimate word, which – derived presumably from *ridurre* – implies a reduction or loss.

enterprise, both financial and material: overinvesting in one commodity and the inherent hazards of coastal shipping in the Mediterranean. Risk was also clearly at the forefront of Antonio Brignole's mind in every transaction; the word appears frequently in his correspondence. In January 1573, for example, he warned Giulio Cibo and Giovanbattista Usodimare, in Palermo, not to underwrite the insurance of the ship owned by a certain Calisano, "when it returns loaded with grain, because we understand it is not a vessel for running *rischio*, and with other ships you should proceed always with due consideration."[27] In December 1555, Andrea Berengo advised Antonio Bragadin that, given the poor market in Aleppo and Tripoli, "it is less harmful to you to keep your capital at home, than to send it forth with such *rischio* and without profit."[28] Giovan Alvise Tagliapietra, in April 1551, used the term more precisely to refer to unknown and potential hazards. He informed Lorenzo Aliprando that at least one of the bales of goods sent from Venice had received water damage. He advised employing one messer Minio in Tripoli to check the merchandise before consigning it to muleteers (presumably to carry it to Aleppo), "since if you were to do otherwise you could run some *rischio* in not knowing who had caused the harm, either those in Tripoli or the muleteers."[29] In other words, Aliprando needed to inform himself of the state of merchandise before it left Tripoli, so that he could pursue the appropriate people for compensation. In December 1539, Matteo Botti wrote an admonitory letter to his brother, Iacopo, in Cadiz, regarding the latter's speculative financial dealings. In particular, Matteo was concerned about Iacopo's dealings with members of the Spanish nobility, "with whom there is not little *periculo* and not much profit for the *rischio* one runs there."[30] This particular letter neatly demonstrates the distinction between *periculo*, in this case the known dangers of lending money to nobles in a foreign

[27] ASCG BS 102, 84r: to Giulio (?) Cibo and Giovanbattista (?) Usodimare, in Palermo, 23 January 1573: "non vogliamo pigliate sopra la nave di calisano quando sarà di ritorno carricca de' grani intendendo non esser' vassello da correrli risico e con altri vasselli anderette sempr' con la debita consideratione."

[28] Tucci, *Lettres d'un marchand*, 164, letter 42.

[29] ASV MCNA 20, unfoliated copialettere of Giovan Alvise Tagliapietra, to Lorenzo Aliprando, 2 April 1551: "potrete servir' al mag[nifi]co messer minio a trip[ol]i quello sarà dentro dele bale acio che delli la roba se posi trovar' et ecian poterlla consegnar' alli mucari, che se altramente farete potrete corer' qualche risego ne non si saperà cui abii fato el malle o quelli de trip[ol]i overo li mucari."

[30] ASF LCF 713, 117v: to Iacopo Botti, in Cadiz, 10 December 1539: "e similmente s[igno]ri ne' quali non vi è poco pericolo e con non molto profitto al ristio che vi si corre." On Iacopo Botti's financial dealing with members of the Spanish nobility, see Enrique Otte, "Los Botti y los Lugos," *Coloquio de Historia canario-americana*, 3rd colloquim, vol. 1 (1980); Point-Waquet, "Les Botti," 693.

kingdom, and *rischio*, the speculative, financial chance taken with capital that might have been invested elsewhere.

This last example, from Matteo Botti, also demonstrates the way in which Italian merchants in the sixteenth century had begun to think about *rischio* – about the potential dangers of speculation on unknown future outcomes – as something that could be calculated, commodified, and valued. The unknown time-yet-to-come could be sliced, weighed, and apportioned. The future had a price.

In pricing time-yet-to-come, these merchants were not thinking about risk in terms of frequency, in the statistical fashion of modern-day actuaries. They did, however, clearly consider the problems of the unknown future in a probabilistic fashion, assessing potential hazards such as storms, warfare, piracy, fraud, and cheating, according to professional experience and information about the likelihood for such events to occur.[31] They also clearly assessed this probability in terms of prices and values. Matteo Botti, in the letter cited immediately above, adjured his brother to weigh risks against profits and consider whether the latter were sufficient reward for the former. Iacopo was undertaking risks at too low a price; he had undervalued the negative potential of the unknown future.

Antonio Brignole, in a more mundane and straightforward example, instructed Simone Lomellino that, when shipping silk from Sicily to Genoa or Livorno, he should use multiple ships or galleys, "dividing the *rischio* as much as possible."[32] Risk had become something that could

---

[31] In this way, they thought probabilistically in the sense distinguished by Ian Hacking as pre-seventeenth century: to indicate an opinion certified by authority rather than by specific evidence. Sixteenth-century merchants did not possess precise data on the frequency of risks, but their collective and personal experience provided a source of authority to identify the probability of a particular opinion being correct: Ian Hacking, *The Emergence of Probability: A Philosophical Study of Early Ideas about Probability, Induction and Statistical Inference*, 2nd ed. (New York: Cambridge University Press, 2006), 18–30. Giovanni Ceccarelli, in "The Price for Risk-Taking: Marine Insurance and Probability Calculus in the Late Middle Ages," *Journal Electronique d'Histoire des Probabilités et de la Statistique/Electronic Journal for History of Probability and Statistics* 3, no. 1 (2007), and *Un mercato del rischio*, has argued convincingly that Italian merchants thought probabilistically about risk before the seventeenth century. James Franklin, *The Science of Conjecture: Evidence and Probability before Pascal* (Baltimore, MD: Johns Hopkins University Press, 2001), esp. 275–76, presents the contrary case. The evidence of mercantile correspondence, I suggest, clearly supports Ceccarelli's conclusions. See also Edith Dudley Sylla, "Business Ethics, Commercial Mathematics, and the Origins of Mathematical Probability," *History of Political Economy* 35, annual supplement (1952), and Lorraine Daston, *Classical Probability in the Enlightenment* (Princeton, NJ: Princeton University Press, 1988), 116–24.

[32] ASCG BS 103, 43v: to Simone Lomellino, in Messina, 2 September 1573: "mandandole poi con gallere o con più nave qui a noi e in li[vor]no al quarantesi a nostro or[di]ne

be measured and partitioned. Lorenzo Aliprando, one of the Venetian merchants who worked with Giovan Alvise Tagliapietra, even put a precise price on it. The latter, in October 1550, informed Aliprando how the camlet he had purchased was loaded on two different galleys, "for the other [letters] you wrote me ordered me not to put at *rischio* more than 1000 ducats per ship."[33] Filippo Sassetti, similarly but from the opposite perspective, informed Francesco Valori on 7 August 1581 of his anxious wait for the arrival of the Portuguese fleet from India, which was later than the three previous years: "I am in torment about it, because I have 600 ducats of *rischio* on three of them."[34] Brignole, Aliprando, and Sassetti all calculated the price of risk, the price of an unknown future danger, according the value of goods exposed to it. By the end of the century, however, in the maritime insurance market, *rischio* had become a commodity itself.

The Capponi, in dealing in maritime insurance, apportioned the potential dangers of the unknown time-yet-to-come into tranches and assigned them to the bank's clients. They sold risk as a commodity, for financial speculation and investment. "We have assigned you one-hundred and fifty scudi of *rischio* for your underwriting account," the bank informed Geronimo Franchi, in December 1584, "from Livorno to Messina, on the ship owned by Marolino di Giovanni the Ragusan, insured by the Ugolini in Venice at 4.5 percent."[35] The minutes of the bank's correspondence are filled with hundreds of similar letters asking clients to take note of the *rischio* assigned them or informing clients of new transactions undertaken in their names. These minutes demonstrate the existence of an ever-increasing appetite for financial speculation on unknown future outcomes.

A mature and well-populated market for risk existed in late sixteenth-century Italy. Some of the bank's clients invested heavily in insurance. Niccolò Lomellini of Genoa, in the spring of 1586, exposed himself to thousands of lire worth of risk, insuring vessels sailing across the western

---

repartendo il risico più che sarà possibile." This is the same Quaratesi who features above in Chapter 3 at note 14 in dispute with the Capponi.

[33] ASV MCNA 20, unfoliated copialettere of Giovan Alvise Tagliapietra, to Lorenzo Aliprando, 14 October 1550: "per le alttre me scrivette mi cometeti che non abia a corere a risigo più de' d[ucati] 1000 per nave."

[34] Sassetti, *Lettere*, 171.

[35] ASF LCF 1053, 11v: to Geronimo Franchi, in Genoa, 15 December 1584: "Vi habb[iam]o assegniato di risico per il vostro conto di sicurtà [scudi] cento cinquanta da L[ivor]no a messina sopra la nave p[atro]ne marolino di Gio[vanni] Raugeo assicurati alli ugolini alla Ven[ezi]a a 4 1/2 per cento." Keeping in mind that the underwriter made no upfront outlay, maritime insurance offered a short-term, high-risk, but low-cost form of investment; see Ceccarelli, *Un mercato del rischio*, esp. 203–32, and, by way of comparison, Puttevils and Deloof, "Marketing and Pricing Risk."

Mediterranean in exchange for returns between 5.5 and 9.5 percent of his portion of the insured total. He clearly had an appetite for more: as the bank noted, they would assign more *rischio* to him when it became available.[36] At times, demand exceeded supply. More often than they no doubt would have liked, the bank had to explain that commissions had not yet been filled. On other, more specific occasions, it had to decline exotic or particular requests that fell beyond its remit. While the Capponi would arrange insurance on shipping between Cadiz and Livorno, for example, they did not offer contracts on the river transport of the same goods from Seville to Cadiz in the first place.[37] To Giovanni Enriques, in Rome, the bank had to confess that it could not offer him premiums on the Portuguese convoy from southwest India to Lisbon in 1586 because the request was an unusual one for the Florentine insurance market and they could not find anyone "who wants to run such a *rischio*, particularly in the manner proposed to us by your friend in Lisbon."[38]

In assessing the potential opportunities and risks of future outcomes, the grammar of sixteenth-century Italian merchants included more than the lexicon of *fortuna, ventura, occasione,* and *rischio.* Their correspondence also demonstrates a finely tuned awareness to the passage of time, to its measurable actuality, and to the value that could be derived from speculation on its passing. Mercantile expertise in prices and values, and the knowledge that these changed over time, provided the foundation for this acute temporal sense. In 1564, Francesco di Negro had to deal with a suit brought by one Agostino Porro for a debt owed by Di Negro's now-dead father-in-law, Paolo di Negro, to Porro's father, Giovanbattista, dating back to 1552. Porro was pursuing Di Negro's brother-in-law and business partner, Niccolò (Paolo's son), whose residence in Sicily left Di Negro to handle the matter. Writing to Giovanbattista Olignano about it, Di Negro cast doubt on the claim because he could find no mention of it in Paolo's account books, and his father-in-law had generally paid all his creditors. If the debt were genuine and had not been paid, Di Negro still felt it was unreasonable to demand "something which might be damaging to the heir, because many times things are better at one time than they are at another."[39]

[36] ASF LCF 1053, 323v: Heirs of Luigi Capponi to Niccolò Lomellino, in Genoa, 3 May 1586.

[37] See, for example, ASF LCF 1053, 258r, 259r.

[38] ASF LCF 1053, 394r: Heirs of Luigi Capponi, to Giovanni Enriques, in Rome, 9 August 1586: "come cosa insolita in questa piazza non se'l può far altro che ne duole per non potervi servi come desiderate non sendoci chi voglia correr' tal risico maggiormente sotto la forma denotatoci dal vostro amico di lisbona."

[39] Biorci and Court, *Il registro di lettere,* 183.

Awareness of the changing value of commodities and currencies with the passage of time lent merchants an acute urgency about the importance of not wasting time or missing opportunities, not for reasons of eternal salvation but for the material rewards of everyday life. The ticking of the mechanical clock – the passing of days, weeks, months, and seasons – echoed in the marketplace, in the perception of these merchants. The passage of time, the passing of one unique, unrepeatable moment to the next, could be counted and measured in money made or lost, in opportunities taken or missed.

Feeling a tightness of liquidity in late August 1573, Antonio Brignole urged Simone Lomellino, with the assistance of one Paolo Vincenzo, to take payments from debtors "with particular care in order to finish as soon as possible." If Lomellino and Vincenzo recognized a notable danger, presumably of default, in any, he adjured: "do not lose time in getting out, by taking it [the debt] in silk or by acting to defend yourself covertly and tenaciously as best you can."[40] Andrea Berengo, in November 1555, wrote to Florio Mattina, in Cyprus, seeking advice and instructions on what transactions he wanted Berengo to execute. He urged Mattina to tell him what he wished, "because one never regains lost time."[41] The same reason doubtless motivated Giovan Alvise Tagliapietra to reassure Michele Padovani, on 2 June 1550, that he would sell or exchange Padovani's silk textiles "as quickly as will be possible and with the greatest profit that one can."[42]

In the spring of 1528, Matteo Botti expressed disquiet at the lack of alacrity displayed by Iacopo Miniati in dispatching the company's textiles from Ancona: "we beseech you again for their expedition since we are losing much time, which is no little thing by every account."[43] Delayed arrival of merchandise in Ancona – a major port in the Adriatic for exchanges with the Ottoman Empire – proved a source of frustration for Francesco Leone several years later. In April 1540, Leone informed

---

[40] ASCG BS 103, 41v; to Simone Lomellino, in Messina, 28 August 1573: "si pigli essi debbitori particular' cura per venirne a fine quanto pr[i]ma e se in alcuni di essi conoscerette periculo nottabile non perderete tempo in uscirne con piglarne sete o farvi a cautelare sordo che meglio potrette."
[41] Tucci, *Lettres d'un marchand*, 130, letter 11.
[42] ASV MCNA 20, unfoliated copialettere of Giovan Alvise Tagliapietra, to Michiel di Padovani, 2 June 1550: "non mancherà di darli fine al più presto sarà il possibile et con quel magior utile si potrà." See also the similar sentiment expressed in a letter of the same date to Augustin Pelicer.
[43] ASF LCF 712, 16v: to Iacopo Miniati, in Ancona, 25 May 1512: "di nuovo vi preghiamo per la loro speditione chè perdiamo di molto tempo quale per ogni conto non inporta pocho."

his agent in Pera that Venetian authorities in Zadar had seized the ship bearing their goods from Constantinople to Ancona, including 126 cases of dried fruit, on suspicion of carrying contraband. Leone objected to the Signoria in Venice that the ship and its merchandise were Florentine, and therefore not subject to Venetian jurisdiction. The government, however, remained reluctant to release the vessel, and suggested bringing it to the lagoon city instead. The Florentine banker observed that "considering the great damage to the merchandise of letting time be lost and, moreover, that in truth the stuff would perhaps sell better here than in Ancona," it might be preferable to agree to divert the ship to Venice.[44]

The commodification of the passage of time and the conception of the future as unknown, actual, and subject to human will and intention – expressed in the vocabulary of ventura, fortuna, occasione, and rischio – did not mean, however, that the merchants of sixteenth-century Italy possessed only a secular, rational vision of time and the universe, any more than their fourteenth- or fifteenth-century forebears had done.[45] On this point, they clearly diverge in their self-presentation as experts in futurity from the writers about gaming, such as Girolamo Cardano. The emergence of the new conception of the future, as unknown and unknowable time-yet-to-come, did not follow a linear progression, and did not involve the displacement of a soteriological temporality with a more modern, secular conception of time. The hard-headed merchants who calculated risks and values inhabited a world of multiple temporalities, slipping comfortably and easily from one conception of the future to another, even in the space of a line or two in the same letter. As discussed in Chapter 3, references to God, in particular to a providential understanding of the passage of time that imbued divinity with

---

[44] ASF LCF 2927, 11r: to Da Sommaia, in Pera, 29 April 1540: "considerando il dan[n]o grande di lassare perdere tempo alla mercanzia e in oltre che'n vero le robe si venderan[n]o forse meglio in q[uest]a terra che in ancona."

[45] Christian Bec, in two studies that examined Florentine merchants' vocabulary in the fifteenth century and extrapolated the analysis to the sixteenth century, also, in contrast, argued that they possessed a rational, calculating mentality divorced from a medieval, providential tradition: Christian Bec, "Au début du XVe siècle: Mentalité et vocabulaire des marchands florentins," Annales. Histoire, Sciences Sociales 22, no. 6 (1967); Christian Bec, "Fortuna, ratio et prudentia au début du Cinquecento," Les Langues Neo-Latines, no. 181 (1967). Achille Olivieri has similarly argued that the transition from the fifteenth to the sixteenth centuries in Italy was accompanied by a shift from a medieval to a more modern, rational, proto-capitalist mentality; see Achille Olivieri, "Jeu et capitalisme a Venise (1530–1560)," in Les jeux à la Renaissance, ed. Philippe Ariès and Jean-Claude Margolin (Paris: Librarie Philosophique J. Vrin, 1982); Achille Olivieri, "Giuoco, gerarchie e immaginario tra Quattro e Cinquecento," in Rituale, cerimoniale, etichetta, ed. Sergio Bertelli and Giuliano Crifò (Milan: Bompiani, 1985).

omniscience, were threaded through mercantile correspondence in the sixteenth century. While cumulatively the lexicon of the future as unknown time-yet-to-come outweighed these acknowledgments of Providence, mentions of God were more prevalent than any one of the terms *fortuna*, *ventura*, and *occasione* individually. Indeed, *ventura* most commonly appeared in both Venetian and Florentine correspondence in combination with an appeal to divinity. Andrea Berengo, Giovan Alvise Tagliapietra, Filippo Sassetti, Matteo Botti, and Francesco Leone all, with varying frequency, utilized some version of the phrase "may God send *ventura*" in their correspondence. For Berengo it served as a constant invocation, appearing in almost every letter in his extant correspondence. On 22 January 1556, for example, he informed Zuan Contarini that while he had bartered seventy-one pieces of Venetian silk for twenty-three bales of Ottoman leather, he had not managed to make deals for the rest of Contarini's textiles. "But," he concluded, "I will not fail to do the best that will be possible, should the Lord God send *ventura* for it."[46] Others used it more sparingly. Francesco Leone informed his agent in Pera that he would sell the latest shipment of goods from Constantinople for the best possible profit, "and daily you will know what happens, should God send the *ventura* that we desire for it."[47]

The extent to which this choice of words reflected either sincere religious faith or a routine and empty rhetorical acknowledgment of Christian belief is discussed further below. My emphasis here lies on the manner in which the phrase combined, effortlessly and without apparent contradiction in the minds of those who used it, two conceptions of the future – one providential, the other the unknown time-yet-to-come – and two temporalities, in a union that appears inconsistent to twenty-first-century eyes. It invoked the divine, as the ultimate source of all human affairs and future events, in an prayer-like formula that requested intercession and aid in commercial affairs. However, it asked for an opportunity (*ventura*) rather than profit or a specific outcome. That is, the merchants who wrote the phrase requested an opportunity, which they could seize and hopefully turn to profit, reflecting not the eternity of a divinely ordained universe and future but the uncertainty of time yet-to-come, open to human hands and will.

---

[46] Tucci, *Lettres d'un marchand*, 204, letter 180. See other examples, passim.
[47] ASF LCF 2927, 22v: to Da Sommaia, in Pera, 21 May 1540: "domani il tutto si trarà di doghana e si procurerà di far' fine del tutto con quello vantaggio che sarà possibile come se il tutto a me a tenessi e giornalmente saperete quello seguirà chè iddio ne mandi quella ventura se ne desidera."

In a letter to Antonio di Manieri, written in November 1555, Berengo penned a more expansive sentiment that offers further insight into the adaptive way in which Renaissance Italian merchants moved between temporalities. Reflecting on the death of colleagues, he observed that while saddened he did not know what comfort or wisdom he could offer, except that "one should seek to live and do so with the grace of God, and then leave the rest to *fortuna* [*lassar operar alla fortuna*]."[48] Berengo appears to suggest that while divinity was the ultimate arbiter of human life and so living well as a Christian – which would seem to be the intent of living with the grace of God – was important on the scale of eternity, when it came to everyday life and the here-and-now, a different causation and temporality were at work. On this scale, the future is unknown, the human experience diverse and unexpected, and one can do no more than accept the randomness of life. Read in this light, the invocation that God send *ventura* represents an appeal for a divine finger on the scale of human existence, permitting the arrival of a potentially beneficial moment, an opportunity that the merchant could, with skill and knowledge, turn into greater profits.

This pairing of Providence and *ventura* also underlines the way in which sixteenth-century Italian merchants inhabited multiple temporalities simultaneously. Beyond the almost formulaic invocation for divine intercession to provide profitable future opportunities, acknowledgment of divine omniscience and omnipotence appeared constantly in mercantile correspondence. In particular, merchants frequently expressed, in complex ways, a comprehension of the universe as divinely ordained and of human plans as an only partial prophylactic against the unknown and unexpected. On 6 May 1575, Antonio Brignole gave detailed instructions to Lorenzo Scavino for the transportation of nine bales of silk and four barrels of Spanish reales from Lerici to Lucca by sea and then by mule, for consignment to Pietro Menocchi and Giusfredo Cenami. Brignole concluded, "about the shipping we will not tell you anything else, trusting greatly in your prudence and vigilance, so that with divine favor we are certain of every excellent outcome, may Our Lord bear you and bring you back safely."[49] The letter expressed Brignole's faith in Scavino's good sense and acumen to make the necessary arrangements to militate against the proximate causes of danger on such a short, coastal

---

[48] Tucci, *Lettres d'un marchand*, 103, letter 94.
[49] ASCG BS 104, 196v: to Lorenzo Scavino, in Lerici, 6 May 1575: "circa la navigatione vi nè diremo altro riposando tanto nella prudenza e vigilanza vostra chè col divino favore siamo certi di ogni ottimo recato che nostro si[gno]r vi conduchi e riduchi a salvam[en]to."

voyage – bad weather, shallow or dangerous waters, piracy – as well as an acknowledgment that God would be the ultimate arbiter of the transaction's success or failure.

An entreaty for divine assistance with the passage of goods, particularly the risky sea voyages of the sixteenth-century global economy, was the most common invocation of God after the appeal for *ventura*. Andrea Berengo, in October 1550, informed Antonio Bragadin that he had acquired a quantity of raw Persian silk, which he would transport via Tripoli and Cyprus to Venice, adding, "I pray that eternal God sends it safely."[50] Francesco Farre, in Milan, in 1511, wrote to Battista Farre, in Venice: "I wait with great desire for the sixteen bales of cotton, may God send them safely, because I hope to sell them quickly and for a good profit."[51] Francesco Leone tracked the location and course of ships bearing his merchandise throughout his correspondence, frequently adding, "God send it safely."[52] While this reads almost like a textual genuflection, an automatic, almost superstitious, acknowledgment of divine omnipotence and avoidance of hubris, Leone clearly did not write unthinkingly. In October 1540, discussing the ship owned by Bernardi (who cost Leone money due to damaged merchandise), among others, the banker wrote, "may God send them safely, according to the merits of their owners," an obvious expression of his residual anger with the earlier recklessness.[53] Reminding Geronimo Franchi of his obligations to pay up should a ship he had underwritten suffer loss or harm, the Capponi bank added, "may it please God that everything goes safely and without damage."[54] Most significantly, in these examples and many other analogous letters, merchants paired appeals to divine protection and assurance with mundane, human intervention and actions. Brignole expressed faith in Scavino's "prudence and vigilance" for the safe transportation of valuable merchandise. The Capponi bank dealt in maritime insurance, the ultimate human protection against the unknown future.

---

[50] Tucci, *Lettres d'un marchand*, 29, letter 6.
[51] ASV, MiscGreg 12 bis 1, unfoliated: Francesco Farre, in Milan, to Battista Farre, in Venice, 18 July 1511: "Aspeto con gran desiderio li colli 16 cottoni che dio li manda a bon salva perché spero ne farne [*sic*] presto fine et con buono guadagno."
[52] See, for example, ASF LCF 2927, 11v, 18v, 28r, 28v, 31r, 33r, 80v, 95r, 174v, 209r.
[53] ASF LCF 2927, 101v: to Da Sommaia, in Pera, 7 October 1540: "Iddio le mandi a salvamento secondo che il patrone d'esse merita." On the incident with Bernardi, see Chapter 3 above.
[54] ASF LCF 1053, 5r: to Geronimo de' Franchi, in Genova, 7 December 1584: "ritendendovi per anc[o]ra l'obligo vostro per le sicurtà che si corre risico e di altri danni a perdite che si avessino a pag[a]re che a dio piaccia che tutto vadia a salvam[en]to e senza danno."

As discussed in Chapter 3, merchants operated through a variety of sociocultural and institutional mechanisms to mitigate the risks and perils of long-distance trade in the premodern world, so such precautions should be read even into those letters, such as Berengo's or Leone's, which make no overt mention of them. Italian merchants in the sixteenth century comfortably inhabited a universe structured by multiple temporalities and conflicting visions of the future. They shifted fluidly and easily from speculating on the profits to be made from unknown future outcomes that relied on their own skill and expertise to undertaking actions to protect their risk taking from proximate dangers (through insurance and trust) to appealing to God to protect their speculation and endeavors in an acknowledgment of his omniscience and a vision of the future as preordained regardless of human intention and will.

Assessing belief and faith in the past, and indeed in the present, is a fraught exercise. The stock nature of the phrases considered in the preceding paragraphs – that God send *ventura* or guide a ship to safety – and their prevalence might suggest that they were little more than rhetorical formulae. In this perspective, such invocations might represent nothing more than a studied acknowledgment of sociocultural niceties, a sort of politeness. They might, then, be read as little more than medieval holdovers, indicating not the existence of multiple temporalities but rather a lingering, hollow gesture toward a conception of time that no longer had much real power over the mind of such worldly, calculating individuals. However, other evidence suggests that historians should consider these statements more sincerely as expressions of faith and, therefore, as indicative of the complex temporality of the sixteenth century, of the way that the new understanding of the future layered on other perceptions and coexisted with them rather than replacing or effacing them. Merchants did not simply deploy rhetorical formulae to refer to divinity, but also made much more specific appeals for intervention and assistance or acknowledgments of divine omnipotence.

On 18 November 1555, Berengo wrote, "I pray the Lord God that he will extend his hand for the benefit of this poor merchandise and make sure that we are not throwing away money, which I fear."[55] Giovan Alvise Tagliapietra, in a variation of the invocation that God send *ventura*, worried in a letter to Lorenzo Aliprando about insufficient funds: "I have no hope unless God sends me something better to sell."[56] In October

---

[55] Tucci, *Lettres d'un marchand*, 119, letter 103.
[56] ASV MCNA 20, unfoliated copialettere of Giovan Alvise Tagliapietra: to Lorenzo Aliprando, 11 March 1551: "mi trovo desperato nè tengo speranza se idio qual cosa de meglio non manda di vender."

1574, Antonio Brignole wrote to Niccolò and Giulio Cibo concerning losses suffered by a consortium of prominent Florentine families – the Ricci, the Carnesecchi, and the Strozzi – in a transaction at the fair of Besançon in August. He informed the Cibo that Antonio di Negro no longer wished to undertake transactions at the fair under his name, "having recognized that the Lord God did not send that tribulation without reason, it is necessary that we understand, with good heart, that everything comes from his hand."[57] In these examples, as in others similar to them, merchants demonstrate an active faith, rather than an insincere genuflection at belief. Underlying all of them is an understanding of time operating on a universal scale. If they do not make explicit references to eternity or salvation, they clearly make assumptions about the unknown future being a realm in which divinity operated. Time-yet-to-come unfolded from divine Providence, so submission to, and acceptance of, divine will was essential to human experience, and intercession for divine aid was as prudent and rational as taking out insurance.

One final example emphasizes and highlights the multiple temporalities of sixteenth-century commerce in a particularly effective way. It also echoes the consolatory letter written by Andrea Berengo, discussed above, in which the Venetian encouraged a friend to live with God's grace, and so follow the precepts of being a good Christian, but to leave the rest to *fortuna*. That letter represented an implicit acknowledgment of the need to protect one's soul, for the sake of eternity, but also to accept the instability of human existence and unknowable nature of time-yet-to-come. In the middle of 1539, a firm operated by Benedetto and Francesco Gondi in Valencia had collapsed with large, outstanding debts, including money owed to Iacopo Botti in Seville. In a letter that he apparently did not send, Matteo Botti chastized his brother and, observing an abundance of bad news in Florence also, offered the following sentiment: "here and there we must live with little hope of good, in any case everything is in the name of God. I will not recall you to greater prudence because that is not enough, instead I recommend you to good *fortuna*, who I pray puts you on her good road, of which we have much need, by every account."[58] Like the letter from Berengo, Matteo's

---

[57] ASCG BS 104, 154v: to Niccolò and Giulio Cibo, in Florence, 29 October 1574: "se il nostro Antonio non cambia pensiero non vole esser' più nom[ina]to per le fiere havendo conosciuto che non senza occ[asio]ne il S[igno]r Iddio ne ha mandato quella tribulatione quale bisogna aceriamo in bon grado venendo tutto da man' sua."
[58] ASF LCF 713, 80v: to Iacopo Botti, in Seville, 30 August 1539: "perché alle cose che vanno attorno mi pare che anche queste di qua da poco fondarcisi di modo che qua e costà aviamo da vivere con poca speranza di bene, sia tutto nel nome di dio a ogni modo, non vi ricordo più la prudentia perché la non basta ma vi rachom[an]do alla bona fortuna

somewhat tortured thoughts offer an insight into the layers of temporality in which he lived. Everything in human existence is subject to divine will – "in the name of God" – but also, clearly, humanity acts independently and the future is unknown, so good luck is as important as prudence and divine grace.

Sixteenth-century Italian merchants possessed a complex, nonreductive sense of causality and the passage of time. They confronted the unknown, unknowable future on a daily basis and appeared comfortable with multiple, even conflicting explanations for the unfolding of events. The nature of their profession required them to accept that the future was unknown and, therefore, open to speculation, and also to attempt to pierce that veil of unknowability and make predictions about what would happen in a given time and place. A profound tension lay at the heart of Renaissance commerce: acceptance and denial of the unknowability of time-yet-to-come in one and the same moment. This tension rested on the human scale of the new conception of the future. The future was unknown rather than being ordained, and actual rather than being a distraction from the salvation and eternity promised by religion. Because it existed on a human scale, the opportunities offered by its unknowability could be seized and turned to profit by the merchant who was smart enough, quick enough, or lucky enough. The practice of commerce in sixteenth-century Italy consisted in the assertion of a particular expertise in futurity, a skill in prices, values, and risks, all expressed in a shared, richly textured vocabulary

Medieval commerce had always involved a practice of speculation. However, commercial mathematics and practice through the fifteenth century had rested on solutions to problems of distribution that looked to the past and experience. Its basis was a contractual arrangement for the fair distribution of profits and losses between business partners, in which the rewards of trade were distributed in a proportional manner according to what had been achieved and determined by the original contract.[59] The emergence in the sixteenth century of a market in which risk itself existed as a commodity suggests that a shift had occurred in commercial thinking. The business model of the Capponi bank and other insurance brokers, as well as of the clients (almost uniformly other merchants) who

al quale prego che vi metta per la sua bona strada che n'aviamo molto di bix[ogn]o per tutti e conti." The minute is annotated in the margin: "non si mandò però si cancella."
[59] Sylla, "Business Ethics." See, for example, Ginori Conti, ed., *Il libro segreto della ragione di Piero Benini e comp* (Florence: Olschki, 1937), 37, 41, and Ugolino di Niccolò Martelli, *Ricordanze dal 1433 al 1483*, ed. Fulvio Pezzarossa (Rome: Edizioni di Storia e Letteratura, 1989), 214–16, 253–56, 261.

used their services as a form of investment, rested on calculations about what might happen and how the future could be measured and priced.

During the sixteenth century, Italian merchants confronted the unknown time-yet-to-come on a daily basis. They made sense of it and explained it through a vocabulary, which they deployed reflexively. This lexicon helped them to process a sentimental education necessary for functioning in an economy and society based on trust: the need to manage the anxieties and expectations of taking risks on unknown future outcomes. However, it offered little practical guidance for how calculate and weigh the competing risks of any such speculation. They also, therefore, developed increasingly sophisticated mechanisms to mitigate against the perils of speculating on the future, as well as to commodify those same risks and very unknowability of time-yet-to-come. Yet they did so with a mentality that still acknowledged the ultimate sovereignty of Providence in determining the outcome of any future speculation. Merchants offer a clear historical insight into the simultaneous operation of multiple temporalities in sixteenth-century Italy, into the way that the new conception of the future operated in everyday life.

5   The Renaissance Afterlife of Boethius's Moral
     Allegory of *Fortuna*

The fourteenth-century Florentine merchant-adventurer Buonaccorso
Pitti displayed a particular fascination with the unexpected and the
unanticipated in the course of life. As a merchant and frequent gambler,
his interest was professional and purposive, but his swashbuckling and
self-aggrandizing *Cronica* also records other more personal anecdotes,
such as the time he survived a lightning strike or the occasion he fell from
a staircase in Milan. Sometime in the 1420s, toward the end of his life,
Pitti wrote a poem about the role of chance and the unexpected in human
affairs, which he imagined – as so many had done in the centuries since
antiquity – embodied in the form of the Roman goddess, Fortuna. In
four stanzas he presented himself as an advocate for the deity against
those who condemned her as the cause of their miseries. Fortuna, Pitti
declared, is changeable but neither random nor blind. Instead, she
"follows her course as the moon does." Like the moon, she plays a role
as part of creation and operates only in accordance with divine will:
"Fortuna is good and bad, / as Providence commands her." Therefore,
Pitti observes, those who suffer misfortune in this life should blame
themselves and not the goddess because their griefs result from their
own sins and mistakes. "My song," he concluded, "if you should find
yourself where there is / any who speaks ill of Fortuna, / tell him that it
avails little / to curse her and quarrel with her, / since she is blessed and
does not bow / to anyone who feels bad for his own folly."[1]
    Pitti's verse reflects the way in which, during the late Middle Ages and
early Renaissance, European Christians thought about the future on a
universal scale and in a soteriological sense. The future was obscure but
known by revelation. Individuals moved inexorably toward death. Time
moved relentlessly toward the Apocalypse and the Last Judgment.
Humanity, therefore, existed in an eternal present, in which past and
future were less-than-distinct categories of time because, while linear,

[1] Antonio Lanza, ed., *Lirici toscani del Quattrocento*, 2 vols. (Rome: Bulzoni, 1975), 278–79.

112

time was also ultimately cyclical. In the medieval European imagination, time existed in tension with the vision of eternity and eventually folded back on itself into the eternal.[2] Describing the end of time in the mid-fourteenth century, the poet Francesco Petrarch wrote, in the *Triumph of Eternity*, "All that presses upon and encumbers our soul: 'before, now, yesterday, tomorrow, morning, and evening' / will pass at once like shadows; / no more will 'used to be' 'will be' nor 'was' have a place, / but 'is' alone and immediate, and 'now' and 'today' / and eternity alone, together and whole."[3]

The beginning of time was the end of time: God and the Word. Augustine concluded, in Book 11 of the *Confessions*, that time was a distraction, a distention of eternity: "I recollect myself and follow the One. I forget what is past, and instead of being distracted, I reach out, not for what is in the future and so transitory, but for those things that are before me.... I became alienated as I entered into time, not knowing the order in which it passes, and my thoughts, the innermost parts of my soul, are ripped apart by turbulent vicissitudes, until I flow back together toward you [God]."[4] Nothing was actually random, nothing happened simply by chance. Providence, the foreknowing and protective sight of God, lay behind the apparently inexplicable and the seemingly chance occurrence.

Pitti's verse also makes clear that when Italian Christians thought about the experience of the passage of time in the early fifteenth century, and in particular when they considered the future, they principally articulated and imagined it through two concepts: Providence and *fortuna*.[5] These constituted the principal lexicon by which authors made

---

[2] See Simona Cohen, *Transformations of Time and Temporality in Medieval and Renaissance Art* (Leiden: Brill, 2014), 39–49; Jean-Claude Schmitt, "Appropriating the Future," in *Medieval Futures: Attitudes to the Future in the Middle Ages*, ed. J. A. Burrow and Ian P. Wei (Woodbridge: Boydell Press, 2000).

[3] Francesco Petrarca, *Rime, trionfi e poesie latine*, ed. F. Neri et al. (Milan: Riccardo Ricciardi, 1951), 556, lines 64–69; see also p. 555, lines 25–33: "Qual meraviglia ebb'io quando ristare / vidi in un punto quel che mai non stette [i.e., time] / ma discorrendo suol tutto cangiare! / E le tre parti sue [past, present, future] vidi ristrette ad una sola, e quella una esser ferma / sì che, come solea, più non s'affrette; / e quasi in terra d'erbe ignuda ed erma , / nè 'né 'fia' nè 'fu' nè 'mai' nè 'innanzi' o "ndietro' / che umana vita fanno varia e 'nferma."

[4] Augustine, *Confessions*, ed. Carolyn J.-B. Hammond (Cambridge, MA: Harvard University Press, 2016), book 11, chapter 29, esp. 254. On the influence and significance of Augustine for later medieval conceptions of time, see Sven Stelling-Michaud, "Quelques aspects du problème du temps au moyen âge," *Schweizer Beiträge zur allgemeinen Geschichte/Études suisses d'histoire générale/Studi svizzeri di storia generale* 17 (1959).

[5] On the central and constitutive role of allegory – such as *fortuna* – in Renaissance thought and imagination, see Ernst Cassirer, *The Individual and the Cosmos in Renaissance*

sense of and gave meaning to the murky unknowability of time-yet-to-come. In Pitti's verse the two concepts appear tightly intertwined, separate but aligned forces in human experience. Most significantly, in the poem, Fortuna is clearly subordinate to Providence. In this regard, the Florentine merchant was representative of early Renaissance thought.

In the first four chapters, I examined specific experiences of futurity in the sixteenth century. My focus was on how Italian merchants and gamblers navigated the brave new world in which the concept of the future as unknown time-yet-to-come had already cohered and taken shape. In particular, I explored how continuities in experience with earlier centuries and long familiarity with uncertainty allowed members of these two professions to assert some expertise in futurity. This chapter, and the three following, examine how that world came to be, by tracing the emergence of the concept of unknown time-yet-to-come in Italian culture.

This concept cohered in a culture pervaded by the particular risk-taking mentality shaped by the realms of commerce and the ubiquity of games of chance. Without claiming direct causality, it remains important to recall the deep-seated familiarity with uncertainty and the problems of future contingency that colored the quotidian hustle of markets and dice games in this society as this new idea took shape. The scholars, artists, and thinkers of the early Renaissance shared both an intellectual and a physical habitat with merchants and gamblers. Libraries and studios were closer to the benches of bankers than the historiographical separation between socioeconomic and cultural-intellectual interpretations of the period might suggest. As I will argue in Chapter 6, in fact, the earliest articulations of this new futurity appeared in literary-mercantile writings in the fifteenth century.

This chapter traces the arc of ideas about the unexpected in human life in fifteenth-century Italy, demonstrating how what I identify as Boethius's moral allegory of *fortuna* underwent subtle changes in the work of four early humanists.[6] While all the authors kept intact the Christian imperative of this allegory, their formulations began a process

Philosophy, trans. Mario Domandi (Oxford: Basil Blackwell, 1963), esp. 73–74, who observes that "allegory is no mere external appendage, no casual cloak; instead it becomes the vehicle of thought itself," and Lina Bolzoni, *The Gallery of Memory: Literary and Iconographic Models in the Age of the Printing Press*, trans. Jeremy Parzen (Toronto: University of Toronto Press, 2001), esp. 179–82.

6 One of the four, Christine de Pizan was by strict definition not a humanist, but she clearly prized education in the humanities, possessed proficiency in Latin, and was familiar with the works of Petrarch at least. Through her husband, Etienne du Castel, she had some distant connection with Coluccio Salutati and others of the first generation of Italian humanists; see Sarah Gwyneth Ross, *The Birth of Feminism: Woman as Intellect in Renaissance Italy and England* (Cambridge, MA: Harvard University Press, 2009), 19–23.

of disentangling the twinned figures of *fortuna* and Providence at its center, thus laying the foundation for the emergence of a new sense of futurity. The chapter proceeds by examining several works produced between the late fourteenth and late fifteenth centuries. Rather than a comprehensive systematic and chronological genealogy of ideas, the chapter presents a cumulative portrait by analyzing how particular concepts cohered and took shape in the early humanist culture of Quattrocento Italy.

Medieval and Renaissance Italy inherited the figure of *fortuna* from ancient Rome, where it had a dual existence as both a deity and a literary construct. While the genesis of the cult of Fortuna, the bringer of good luck – whose name derived from *ferre*, to bear – remains obscure, it clearly developed indigenously on the Italian peninsula if not in Rome itself, rather than owing anything to the Greek concept of *tyche*.[7] With the advent of Christianity, Fortuna disappeared as a deity, along with the rest of pantheon of Rome. Both Lactantius and Augustine argued that the powers attributed to the goddess consisted in nothing more than a mistaken understanding of the true cause of the apparently inexplicable. They differed, however, over the true explanation. Lactantius proposed an argument that ascribed misfortunes to the operation of the devil, while Augustine favored the notion of Providence. For the North African bishop, chance events had their origin in the hidden workings (*causae latentes*) of God.[8]

Because *fortuna* had existed in Roman antiquity as a literary figure, markedly distinct from religious beliefs and practices, the idea did not disappear entirely from the western European imagination at the same time as the popular cult of the goddess. Whereas the deity had a clear, uniform identity as the bearer of good luck, in literature multiple meanings adhered to the word. It could refer to status, position, or circumstance. It could appear simply to indicate chance or the incalculable element in human affairs, but with no sense of causal force, such as in the writings of Cicero, Sallust, and Livy. In this sense, *fortuna* often bore an antithetical sense to *virtus*, that defining Roman masculine trait combining physical and moral courage and conveying a sense of force and

<hr>

[7] On the Roman cult, see Florence Buttay-Jutier, *Fortuna: Usages politiques d'une allégorie morale à la Renaissance* (Paris: Presses de l'Université Paris-Sorbonne, 2008), 35, 43–44; Iiro Kajanto, "Fortuna," in *Aufstieg und Niedergang der römischen Welt: Geschichte und Kultur Roms im Spiegel der neueren Forschung*, ed. Hildegard Temporini and Wolfgang Haase (Berlin: Walter de Gruyter, 1981), 503–21.
[8] On early Christian attitudes to the cult of Fortuna, see Jerold C. Frakes, *The Fate of Fortune in the Early Middle Ages: The Boethian Tradition* (Leiden: Brill, 1988), 20–25; Kajanto, "Fortuna," 553–57.

vigor. *Fortuna* could also be used as a synonym for *felicitas* and a sense of good luck – an attitude shared between literature and religion – sometimes in conjunction with *virtus*, a peculiarly Latin sense that, for example, a successful general needed luck as well as skill. More rarely, the concept could indicate an attribute of an individual or people, a guardian spirit like the *Fortuna populi Romani* of the popular cult. The most enduring literary manifestation of *fortuna* was that most removed from Roman religion: the depiction of *fortuna* as blind, fickle, and malicious, an understanding heavily influenced by the Greek *tyche*. This conception of *fortuna* as a capricious, causal power in human affairs appeared as early as the third and second century BCE in the poetry of Ennius and Pacuvius. References recur throughout the canon of Roman writing – in Cicero, Horace, Ovid, and Tacitus, for example – generally becoming more prominent and more prevalent in the Principate. In the works of Apuleius (second century CE) and Ammianus Marcellinus (fourth century CE), it had become the predominant, almost unequivocal, depiction of *fortuna*.[9] This image proved so influential that it colored early Christian attitudes and understanding, to the exclusion of the actual cultic practices that such authors thought they were condemning. Augustine, for example, pointed out that if Fortuna were truly blind she could not reward her worshippers.

Beyond the confusion of the Church Fathers, the rich, multivalent Roman literary tradition of *fortuna* bequeathed a compelling poetic device to the literature of medieval Christian Europe. The most influential intervention, in the long term, came in Boethius's *Consolation of Philosophy*, which placed the figure within a Christian framework.[10] The intertwining of *fortuna* and Providence presented in this text created a powerful moral allegory that endured into the fifteenth century and beyond, which underlies all the texts and images considered in this chapter. The Master of Offices for Theoderic at Ravenna, Marcus Manlius Torquatus Boethius, fell from grace, apparently in a court intrigue. Imprisoned in 524 CE, he was eventually executed. The Roman aristocrat gave form to the acceptance of his fall and impending death in the *Consolation*: imagining the personification of Philosophy visiting him, in his imprisonment, and guiding him from despair to acceptance.

---

[9] On *fortuna* in Roman literature, see Frakes, *The Fate of Fortune*, 13–20; Kajanto, "Fortuna," 532–53.

[10] See Buttay-Jutier, *Fortuna*, 60–66; Frakes, *The Fate of Fortune*. Broader, but with a far less critical framework, is Howard R. Patch's *The Goddess Fortuna in Mediaeval Literature* (London: Frank Cass, 1967).

Fortuna features as a key, albeit absent, protagonist in the *Consolation*. The first two books of the text present a systematic deconstruction of her role in human life. Although clearly not divine and ultimately subject to Providence, Fortuna here appears as a powerful presence in worldly affairs, bestowing or removing wealth, power, and status. She is a personification of chance and disruption, constant only in her inconstancy and fickleness: "This power that I wield comes naturally to me; this is my perennial sport. I turn my wheel on its whirling course, and take delight in switching the base to the summit, and the summit to the base."[11] As a result, Philosophy argues in the text, the worldly goods that Fortuna bestows are worthless, only ever transitory, and no basis for happiness. In the concluding chapter to Book Two, Philosophy articulates a Christianized vision of the role of Fortuna in human life, suggesting that the adversity suffered by those she has turned against provides a moral education, making humanity realize that the true source of happiness and worth does not lie in earthly success or material possessions: "good Fortune with her enticements diverts men from the path of the true good, whereas adverse Fortune often yanks them back with her hook to embrace true goods."[12]

Aligning with Augustine's conception of the eternal present – "What is now patently clear is that neither future nor past events exist"[13] – Boethius used the image of Fortuna not to evoke the future but to discuss the experience of the present, as a way of explaining sudden changes in state. The moralized, presentist allegory of *fortuna* that he articulated had an enduring legacy in western Europe, reemerging in the late Middle Ages. Dante invoked it in the *Inferno*: Virgil explains the role of Fortuna in human life, while he and the Pilgrim pass through the fourth circle of Hell. Confronted by the souls of the miserly and the prodigal heaving weights – representing the wealth they had either coveted or wasted in life – at one another for eternity, the Roman poet adjures: "You see, my son, the short-lived mockery / of all the wealth that is in Fortune's keep, / … for all the gold that is or ever was / beneath the moon won't buy a moment's rest / for even one among these weary souls." When the Pilgrim queries what this means, Virgil explains that Fortuna is the divinely appointed "guide and general ministress" of worldly possessions, distributing them according to her whim. Dante's vision is far more material and embodied than that of Boethius. In *Inferno*, Fortuna

---

[11] Boethius, *The Consolation of Philosophy*, trans. P. G. Walsh (Oxford: Oxford University Press, 1999), book 2, chapter 2, 22.
[12] Ibid., book 2, chapter 8, 38. See also Frakes, *The Fate of Fortune*, 63.
[13] Augustine, *Confessions*, book 11, chapter 20, 230.

is angelic: "with all God's joyful first-created creatures / she turns her sphere and, blest, turns it with joy."[14] *Fortuna* served as a moral allegory, teaching the mutability and transitory nature of earthly goods. It referred to the future only tangentially as it reminded humanity of the need to prepare for eternity, for the only future that mattered: the Last Judgment.

The iconography of the figure of *fortuna* that developed in the Middle Ages expressed the same moral, allegorical message as Boethius and Dante. The imagery, which appeared particularly in northern Europe, centered on the wheel. A sphere had served as one of defining visual attributes of *fortuna* in antiquity and this appears to been reduced to two dimensions in the Middle Ages, possibly in connection the centrality of the circular in other medieval visualizations of time.[15] By the beginning of the fifteenth century, the iconography had become fairly standardized: a female figure – often queenly in appearance, sometimes particolored – turns or presides over the turning of a wheel on which human figures rise and fall.[16] These figures are usually depicted in increasing and declining degrees of wealth, power, and status, such as in a mid-thirteenth-century manuscript of the *Carmina Burana* (Figure 5.1). "I will rule," asserts the ascending figure on the left-hand side of the image. "I rule," proclaims the crowned figure at the summit. "I used to rule," laments the one falling on the right-hand side, whose crown tumbles from his head. "I am without power," bewails the fourth figure, who lies prostrate, crushed beneath the wheel, arms flailing. The image served to emphasize the perpetual instability of human life and the fleeting nature of earthly rewards as the human figures rose and fell under the impetus of the relentless, unstoppable turning of the wheel.

The image also visually expressed some of the ambivalence and tensions in medieval conceptions of time. Like the Boethian moral allegory of *fortuna*, it rested on the dichotomy articulated by Augustine between time and eternity: the multiplicity of the former set against the unity of the latter. The turning of the wheel illustrated the vanity of prizing human accomplishments and earthly success in the face of the potential

---

[14] Dante, *Inferno*, 7: 61–96. The translation is Mark Musa's: Dante Alighieri, *The Divine Comedy, vol. 1: Inferno*, trans. Mark Musa (New York: Penguin, 2003), 131–32.

[15] On the centrality of the circular in late medieval imaginings of time, see Matthew Champion, *The Fullness of Time: Temporalities in the Fifteenth-Century Low Countries* (Chicago: University of Chicago Press, 2017), 164.

[16] See Buttay-Jutier, *Fortuna*, 66–86; Cohen, *Transformations of Time*, 53–79; Frederick Kiefer, "The Conflation of Fortuna and Occasio in Renaissance Thought and Iconography," *The Journal of Medieval and Renaissance Studies* 9, no. 1 (1979): 2; Jessen Kelly, "Renaissance Futures: Chance, Prediction, and Play in Northern European Visual Culture" (PhD dissertation, University of California, Berkeley, 2011), 23–26.

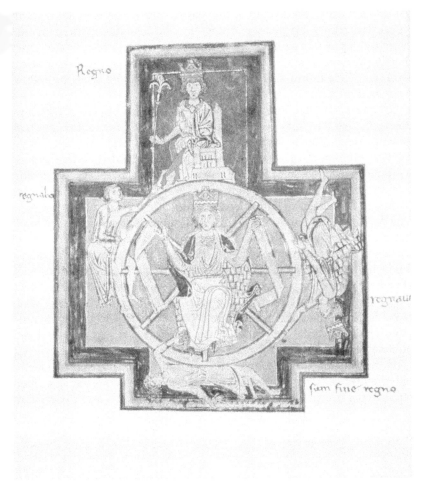

Figure 5.1 Unknown artist, *Wheel of Fortuna* from *Carmina Burana*
(ca. 1230), watercolor on parchment, Munich:
Bayerische Staatsbibliothek.
Credit: Lebrecht History/Bridgeman Images.

rewards of eternity. Like the eternal present of Augustine, there is really
no past or future on the wheel of *fortuna* but simply the experience of the
now. The wheel turns but it is static; its movement leads nowhere. The
rotation of the wheel also captured the lack of abstraction in medieval
thought about time, which itself is connected to the eternal present. Time
was experienced and understood in terms of motion, in the passage of the

planets and stars, the turning of the seasons, the rhythms of the natural world, the rising and setting of the sun, the repetitive pattern of the canonical hours, the turning of a wheel. Time was concrete, in the sense that it provided a measure for things as they happened, rather than abstract.[17] The future, like the past, did not exist. The wheel turned in an eternal present.

Of course, in their lived experience, ordinary European Christians during the Middle Ages perceived the passage of time and distinguished between past, present, and future. Years passed. Children were born, grew to adulthood, aged, and died. The physical landscape changed as old buildings collapsed or burned down and new construction occurred, as arable land expanded and contracted. Merchants drew up short-term contracts that specified future dates at which profits would be shared. The wealthy made provisions for charitable donations to occur after their death. The faithful of all social strata drew up testaments, and made whatever arrangements they could afford for the health of their souls following their inevitable passing. People prepared for the future.[18] However, they did so with a proleptic sense of time, anticipating that tomorrow would be essentially the same as today and yesterday. The same values would adhere, the same rules of behavior would apply, the same practices would be followed. An underlying repetitiveness, then, underlay even the pragmatic perception of the passage of the time.[19] By the mid-fourteenth century, the introduction of mechanical clocks into the town squares of Italy had initiated a process of abstracting time, removing it from diurnal rhythms and monastic hours.[20] Far from

---

[17] See Cohen, *Transformations of Time*, 39–49, and Champion, *The Fullness of Time*, esp. chapter 2. See also Norbert Elias's more conceptual *Time: An Essay*, trans. Edmund Jephcott (Oxford: Blackwell, 1992), for a broad-stroke sociological argument connecting increasing social complexity to increasingly complex ideas about timing.

[18] On this pragmatic and practical sense of the future, see the contributions by Paul Brand, Elizabeth Brown, and Marcus Bull in J. A. Burrow and Ian P. Wei, eds., *Medieval Futures: Attitudes to the Future in the Middle Ages* (Woodbridge: Boydell Press, 2000).

[19] Seeta Chaganti has recently argued that the apparent cyclical and repetitive structure of medieval temporality was more complicated than it might seem. Her analysis of dance and poetic form suggests that perceptual habits and cultural practices led medieval Europeans to experience time in more dynamic and multidimensional ways than superficial circularity might suggest: Seeta Chaganti, *Strange Footing: Poetic Form and Dance in the Late Middle Ages* (Chicago: University of Chicago Press, 2018).

[20] Cohen, *Transformations of Time*, 49–52; Alfred W. Crosby, *The Measure of Reality: Quantification and Western Society, 1250–1600* (Cambridge: Cambridge University Press, 1997), 75–86; David S. Landes, *Revolution in Time: Clocks and the Making of the Modern World* (Cambridge, MA: Harvard University Press, 1983), 53–82; Jacques Le Goff, *Time, Work, and Culture in the Middle Ages* (Chicago: University of Chicago Press, 1980), 29–42. But see also Steven A. Epstein, "Business Cycles and the Sense of Time in Medieval Genoa," *The Business History Review* 62, no. 2 (1988), who argues that this

reducing the importance of eternity, however, the mechanization of time, by converting the hours to the steady tick-tick of the hand, just made its fleeting nature more visible, more immediate, and more pressing. As time assumed a regular, quantifiable form, the need not to waste it but to live each moment as if it were one's final chance to secure salvation assumed a daily urgency in the message of preachers.[21] Dante's invocation of the working and chiming of a clock to describe of the first circle of the sun in Paradise – where the Pilgrim encounters Saint Thomas Aquinas and other leading theologians – was not a casual simile. The striking of the hours echoed in eternity.[22]

By the late fourteenth century, Italians inhabited a world of increasing temporal multiplicity, but one in which eternity still triumphed time as the ultimate concern for humanity. Francesco Petrarch's most popular Latin work, *De remediis utriusque fortunae* (*Remedies for Fortune Fair and Foul*) (ca. 1354–66), provides an illustrative example of the complexity of conceptions of time in the early Renaissance.[23] In the preface to the dialogues – written in the form of an address to Azzo da Correggio, *condottiere* and sometime lord of Parma – Petrarch identified humanity's perception of the passage of time as the source of all human misery. While all other living creatures live only in the present, humans alone, he wrote, possess "memory, intellect, and foresight – God-given and remarkable endowments of the mind, which we turn to our ruin and suffering." As a result, humanity lives constantly "beset by fretful cares, which are not merely trivial and useless, but harmful and noisome, we are racked by the present, and tormented by the past and the future."[24]

---

process of abstraction actually began prior to the introduction of mechanical clocks, pointing to changes in the canonical hours in the thirteenth century. This would suggest that Europeans adopted the mechanical clock to meet a preexisting need.

[21] Buttay-Jutier, *Fortuna*, 130–38; Stefan Hanß, "The Fetish of Accuracy: Perspectives on Early Modern Time(s)," *Past and Present*, no. 243 (2019): 278.

[22] Dante Alighieri, *Paradiso*, canto 10: 139–48.

[23] On the work's popularity, see George W. McClure, *Sorrow and Consolation in Italian Humanism* (Princeton, NJ: Princeton University Press, 1990), 52; James Hankins, *Virtue Politics: Soulcraft and Statecraft in Renaissance Italy* (Cambridge, MA: Belknap Press of Harvard University Press, 2019), 18.

[24] Francesco Petrarca, *Petrarch's Remedies for Fortune Fair and Foul*, ed. Conrad H. Rawski, 5 vols. (Bloomington: Indiana University Press, 1991), 1: 1. In the *Confessions* Augustine identified time as something that existed only in the perception of humanity. Past, present, and future, he wrote, "do somehow exist in the soul and I do not perceive them anywhere else: for the present of things past is memory; the present of things present is paying attention; and the present of things future is expectation" (Augustine, *Confessions*, book 11, chapter 20, 230). Augustine, in turn, possibly borrowed the idea from Cicero's definition of prudence in *De inventione*; see Cohen, *Transformations of Time*, 220. George McClure has interpreted *De remediis* as a handbook for earthly existence in which Petrarch presents the philosopher as the physician of the soul,

A focus on time instead of eternity was the cause of every human grief. Petrarch structured the dialogues that constitute *De remediis* around this perception of the passage of time. They occur as a mental conflict between Reason and the emotions provoked by Prosperity and Adversity, the two types of *fortuna* alluded to in the title. Joy and Sorrow initiate debate on remembered events and the perception of the past, while Hope and Fear appear as Reason's interlocutors on anticipated events and the perception of the future.[25]

Central to the conflict, and to Reason's inexorable dismissal and countering of the passions, is the triviality and uselessness of the things that inspire joy, hope, sorrow, and fear as time passes. To avoid the torments of these passions, Reason consistently counsels moderation, stoic endurance, and keeping one's eyes fixed on eternity. The specifics of Reason's advice in the individual dialogues is not always consistent and is occasionally contradictory due to the disputational format used by Petrarch, but the underlying religious and philosophical messages of the work remain coherent throughout. Indeed, in the very first dialogue, on being in the prime of life, Reason adjures Joy: "Life is short. Time is fleeting.... Awake from your slumber, it is time; and open your bleary eyes, get used to thinking of eternal things, to love them, to desire them, and, at the same time, to disdain what is transitory." The first book of *De remediis* concludes with Reason conceding that hope for eternal life "is the only hope for everyone. If you understand it properly, it will make you happy and, in fact, has made you happy already." In Book Two, when Sorrow laments wasting time, Reason observes that anything beyond care for one's soul and God's will represents a loss: "Man, surely, was born to this end and was given the benefit of time, to worship his Creator, to love Him, to think of Him! And whatever is done beyond this, doubtless, represents a loss of time."[26]

The imagery of time's fleeting passage and of Fortuna's wheel, inexorably turning, recur throughout the dialogues that constitute *De remediis*. When Joy revels in the possession of wealth, a great house, or a lordship, when Sorrow bewails financial losses, dearth and penury, or a fall in status, Reason evokes the relentless rise and fall of all earthly things and every human life.[27] Material possessions and worldly success, Petrarch

offering remedies and consolation for "the affect-ridden world of temporal existence": McClure, *Sorrow and Consolation*, chapter 3. The quoted phrase is at 53.
[25] Petrarca, *Petrarch's Remedies*, 1: xxiii–xxiv; and 3: 12.   [26] Ibid., 1: 15, 324; and 3: 59.
[27] See, for example, ibid., 1: 46, 50, 104–5, 109, 174, 243, 245, 264, 290; and 3: 25–26, 36, 48, 181. The imbalance reflects Petrarch's opinion that prosperity was more problematic than adversity. He describes the fleeting passage of time, and its destructive force, in the *Triumphus temporalis* also: Petrarca, *Rime*, 548–53.

points out, never truly belong to a person and so should be neither celebrated nor lamented. "And even if you insist on calling them goods – which many great men deny," Reason chides Sorrow, "you will have to call them not your goods but, whether you like it or not, the goods of Fortune. Thus you have not lost anything that is yours, nor she anything that is hers. She just has given it to someone else."[28] Prosperity, therefore, posed greater dangers than adversity. The latter required Christian suffering and patience, but the former subjected a person to Fortuna's whims and, more seriously, posed a distraction from the contemplation of impending death and eternity.

Petrarch's attitude toward time was complex and conflicted. Unlike Augustine, he clearly conceived of the passage of time as something that exists outside human perception. The language used in De remediis and the Triumph of Time and the Triumph of Eternity is material rather abstract, even as it remains metaphorical. In the latter text, in fact, Petrarch described the past and the future as hills "that used to dominate the view," now leveled in the present of eternity.[29] This imagery captures the heart of the early Renaissance hesitancy regarding the future. It might be conceivable and a source of anxiety, but ultimately it was a distraction, an obstacle to seeing what really mattered and so something that should not concern humanity. When Hope asserts its beneficial nature for mortal existence, Reason responds: "For those who think of the future, the presence melts away. When you look far into the distance, you do not see what is right under your eyes; and those who concentrate on living tomorrow do not live today."[30]

Rather than concerning oneself with hope or fear for the future, Petrarch (through Reason) counsels trust in Providence. In response to Joy's satisfaction with the tranquil nature of a secure and comfortable life brought about by hard work, Reason retorts: "Though much concerned with initial efforts, human curiosity is blind when it comes to gauging end results. Thick fog shrouds things to come from mortal gaze, and this discussion amounts to second-guessing Fortune. To say it in a better way: It is up to God, in Whose hands are the lots of all mankind."[31] When Sorrow admits being full of doubt, Reason comforts: "But God has no doubts. Let that satisfy you. Believe, trusting in Him, and say: My lots are in thy hands.... He is your faithful, your most loving pilot, steering you to salvation."[32]

---

[28] Petrarca, Petrarch's Remedies, 3: 48.   [29] Petrarca, Rime, 556, lines 70–71.
[30] Petrarca, Petrarch's Remedies, 1: 295.   [31] Ibid., 1: 241.
[32] Ibid., 3: 173. Emphasis in the original. The biblical verse cited here and alluded to in the previous quotation is Psalm 30:16 in the Douay-Rheims translation of the Vulgate Bible; Psalm 31 in the Jerusalem and King James Bibles.

The central elements of the Boethian moral allegory of *fortuna* as they appear in Petrarch's *De remediis* – the fleeting, transitory nature of human life and so of earthly possessions, and the greater danger that prosperity, rather than adversity, posed for humanity – recurred in other early Renaissance considerations of its role in human life. In 1402–3, Christine de Pizan (da Pizzano), an Italian transplant in war-torn France, composed a lengthy poem blending personal and universal history in a meditation on human existence and the roles of *fortuna* and Providence in it. Her individual experience of adversity and the miserable state of the French kingdom following the deaths of her husband and King Charles V framed and shaped the narrative. In the 1430s and 1440s, two leading members of the second generation of Renaissance humanists, Leon Battista Alberti and Poggio Bracciolini, subjected the passage of time and the problem of the unknown, unexpected nature of the future to a critical gaze. The impetus for both men, perhaps, lay in the uncertainty of opportunity and income that they endured working in the papal chancery.[33]

While the neoclassical mode favored by Alberti and Bracciolini provided little space – for rhetorical and aesthetic reasons – for the operation of Providence or the contemplation of eternity, the underlying themes and motifs in their treatment of *fortuna* align with those of Petrarch and Pizan. The figure of *fortuna* served as a moral allegory that dissuaded against the vanities of human existence, by dwelling on the instability and mutability of earthly possessions and rewards, or counseling forbearance and patience in the face of adversity. The implicit orientation of their work remained the eternal, which Petrarch and Pizan discussed explicitly.

Despite living most of her life in France – following an appointment as physician and astrologer to Charles V, her father moved his family from Venice to Paris around 1369, when she was four or five years old – Christine de Pizan remained proud of her heritage and identified herself in writing as "une femme ytalienne." In addition to the classics, her reading and education also included more recent, prominent Italian authors, such as Dante, Boccaccio, and Petrarch, whose influence imprints her work.[34] The figure of *fortuna* featured prominently in

[33] On this point, see Elizabeth McCahill, *Reviving the Eternal City: Rome and the Papal Court, 1420–1447* (Cambridge, MA: Harvard University Press, 2013), chapters 2 and 3. See also Hankins, *Virtue Politics*, 319–20, on the distinctive genre of curial literature produced in the 1430s and 1440s.
[34] On Pizan's biography, reading, and self-identification as Italian, see Carole Ann Buchanan, "The Theme of Fortune in the Works of Christine de Pizan" (PhD dissertation, University of Glasgow, 1994), 3–24, 49–54; Christine de Pizan, *The Book*

Pizan's works throughout her writing career, which began in the wake of the sudden death of her husband. Her first important historical work, *Le livre de la mutacion de Fortune* (*The Book of the Mutability of Fortune*) situated the Boethian moral allegory in a contemporary, fifteenth-century setting and traced its role in human experience.[35]

After an allegorized autobiography, casting herself as the ward and servant of Fortuna, Pizan presented a universal history from Creation to present-day France encountered in a series of paintings decorating the castle of the eponymous figure. In the poem, Fortuna appears embodied and described in a manner analogous to the medieval iconography: a "great crowned queen" with two faces – one white and beautiful, the other dark and hideous – who presides over a wheel turned by her brothers Luck (Eür) and Mischance (Meseür).[36] As the title of the work signposts, the narrative emphasizes the inconstancy of Fortuna and, more importantly, the transitory nature of her gifts and favors. She is presented as the supreme arbiter of human existence in earthly and physical matters: "she has the power to govern all that goes on in the world ... and she has infinite power over finite things."[37]

The relationship between Providence and Fortuna remains uncertain in Pizan's presentation. At times in the poem, she states that God bestowed on Fortuna her authority in human life, but elsewhere the poet attributes a diabolical origin to her: "I believe that the devil made her, so that she would undo all good and put man in servitude."[38] Pizan showed no doubt, however, as to the ultimate vanity and deceptiveness of Fortuna's gifts, especially in comparison with the promise of eternity. In contrast to the transitory nature of wealth, status, or power, the divine promise of Christian theology endures. "There is only one perfect asset: eternal heaven. May God lead us there in the end!" she declaims;

---

of the Mutability of Fortune, ed. Geri L. Smith (Toronto: Iter Press; Tempe: Arizona Center for Medieval and Renaissance Studies, 2017), 3–10; Ross, *The Birth of Feminism*, 19–30. De Pizan (da Pizzano) is a loconym and so recent scholarship tends to use Christine's first name alone. I have chosen to use it as a surname for consistency regarding the male authors discussed here.

[35] On the influence of Boethius on Christine, see Kevin Brownlee, "The Image of History in Christine de Pizan's *Livre de la Mutacion de Fortune*," *Yale French Studies* Special Issue: Contexts: Style and Values in Medieval Art and Literature (1991): 48; Buchanan, "The Theme of Fortune"; Miranda Griffin, "Transforming Fortune: Reading and Chance in Christine de Pizan's *Mutacion de Fortune* and *Chemin de long estude*," *The Modern Language Review* 104, no. 1 (2009): 58; Pizan, *Mutability of Fortune*, 4–5.
[36] Pizan, *Mutability of Fortune*, 1.II 30, 2.VI 55. The quotation is at 30. Note that Smith's translation is prose rather than verse, a choice explained at 25.
[37] Ibid., 1.II 30. On Fortuna's inconstancy, see also 2.I 50, and 3.XIX 104. On her supreme power on earth, see also 4.I 110, and 4.XVIII 120.
[38] Ibid., 4.XVIII 119. On the contrary position of Fortuna as a divine servant, see 3.XIX 105 and 4.XVIII 121. The latter refers specifically to the travails of the Jewish people as described in the Old Testament.

"There is no security in any other outcome, nor is there any other happiness."[39] The poem ends with Pizan adjuring study, solitude, and stoic endurance in the face of adversity, and quoting Saint Paul's second epistle to the Corinthians to warn the ruling princes of France to prize their eternal souls over their earthly estates.

Leon Battista Alberti, who keenly felt his own social and political exclusion as the illegitimate son born to a Florentine father in exile, had some personal experience of adversity like Pizan. He addressed the issue of the role of chance in human existence in several of the pieces that make up the *Intercenales* as well as in his comic masterwork, *Momus*. For Alberti, *fortuna* presented a moral problem in human existence by distributing earthly vanities – wealth, honor, power, and influence – often to the undeserving. So the true test of character, as it had been for Petrarch, lay in submitting to the course of events and this unfair distribution, rather than struggling for worldly gains. He illustrated the point most succinctly in "Pertinacia (Stubbornness)," the briefest tale in the *Intercenales*, a miscellany of stories, fables, and dialogues. In it a mighty oak tree felled by the south wind expresses admiration for the fact that the nearby reeds had withstood the storm. "Why do you stare?" the latter respond, "You lie prostrate because of your unbending stubbornness. We humble ones evade the assault of hostile *fortuna* with patience and yielding."[40]

The counsel to endure adversity with patience and bend in the wind like the reeds presumed, but never articulated, an orientation toward eternity. Life is fleeting and earthly success or possessions are, therefore, transient and not worthy of human hope or sorrow. Like Petrarch, Alberti dwells frequently on the theme of the pernicious nature of good fortune, often to satirical or ironic effect but still always with an underlying current of stoic acceptance and forbearance. Several of the pieces that constitute the *Intercenales* conclude with the observation that apparently adverse fortune generally brings greater reward and a better outcome than an apparently better or kinder fate.[41] The elaborate but oddly heavy-handed allegory "Fatum et Fortuna (Fate and Fortune)" develops

---

[39] Ibid., 2.VIII 57.

[40] Leon Battista Alberti, *Intercenales*, ed. Franco Bacchelli and Luca D'Ascia (Bologna: Edizioni Pendragon, 2003), 628; Leon Battista Alberti, *Dinner Pieces: A Translation of the Intercenales*, trans. David Marsh (Binghamton, NY: Center for Medieval and Early Renaissance Studies, 1987), 171. For references to the *Intercenales*, I have worked from, but sometimes altered, the translation of David Marsh in ibid. Where I have made changes, I have cited both the translation and the 2003 Latin edition, as in this case.

[41] On this *topos* in Petrarch and Alberti, and for some analysis of its classical roots, see Francesco Tateo, "L'Alberti fra il Petrarca e il Pontano: La metafora della fortuna," *Albertiana* 10 (2007): esp. 47–59.

the point with great deliberation. Through it, Alberti argued that those who have to struggle and make their own way in life enjoy "a better lot," succeeding by their own industry, than those seemingly more fortunate individuals who rely on others or the perilous supports of vice.[42] In "Felicitas (Happiness)," he made the same point with a sharply satirical edge. A group of enslaved people, brought to Italy by merchants, debate whom among them is least unfortunate, finally concluding it is the children: "Only you infants and children are fortunate in this worst of fortunes, for you will learn to endure without defiance whatever must be borne. No recollection of lost joys will arouse your grief. No change of *fortuna* will bring any lot but a better one."[43]

Adversity should teach patience, humility, acceptance of one's lot in life, and the vanity of material possessions and worldly influence. Alberti used this moral allegory of *fortuna* to highlight the hubris of human beings. The result is often both darkly humorous and pessimistic at one and the same moment, as he suggests that humanity usually learns this lesson too late. The dialogue "Defunctus (Deceased)," for example, which takes places in the underworld, presents a comical excoriation of human foolishness, vanity, and immorality. The recently deceased Neophronus ("newly wise") explains to Polytropus ("wordly wise") all that he has learned about the duplicity and treachery of his friends and relations since his death as well as the evil and immorality dominant in the world, even as he continues to cling stubbornly to his earthly attachments after his death.

In *Momus*, Alberti instead derided the hubris and pretensions of the wealthy and powerful by casting them in the guise of the gods of Olympus.[44] The entire world is reduced to chaos and brought to brink of destruction before Jupiter even considers wisdom. The catalyst for the events, and the eponymous anti-hero of the piece, is Momus (Blame), the god of grievances, mockery, and criticism, who wreaks havoc both in the heavens and on earth. At the denouement of the tale, however, in a

---

[42] Alberti, *Dinner Pieces*, 23–27, the quoted text is at 24. Compare *Intercenales*, 42–57.

[43] Alberti, *Dinner Pieces*, 31–33. The quoted text is at 33. Compare *Intercenales*, 72–79.

[44] *Momus* is a complicated text with no generally agreed-on interpretation. It clearly operates as a critique of courtly life, very probably of curial life in mid-fifteenth-century Rome, and is often read in this politico-civil context: for recent references, see Hankins, *Virtue Politics*, 318–25; McCahill, *Reviving the Eternal City*, 92–96; and Christine Smith, "The Apocalypse Sent Up: A Parody of the Papacy by Leon Battista Alberti," *MLN* 119, no. 1 (2004). George W. McClure, *Doubting the Divine in Early Modern Europe: The Revival of Momus, the Agnostic God* (Cambridge: Cambridge University Press, 2018), chapter 2, argues that in addition to this, however, the work conceals a more radical, dangerous subtext that critiques the institutions of religion and even flirts with unbelief.

characteristic Albertian twist, he is revealed as a source of authority. In Book Three, while the gods debate destroying the world, Momus offers Jupiter a series of notebooks containing philosophical wisdom, which the former had compiled during a period of terrestrial exile. The king of the gods ignores the gift until the very end of the story in the wake of the near catastrophe unleashed by the trickster's plotting.

Of course, Jupiter finds the books full of valuable, if somewhat obvious, advice on the art of governing, which – had he read them earlier – might have prevented the destruction that occurred. Among the recommendations, Momus advised that the divine monarch divide all earthly resources into three piles: the good, the evil, and those neither good nor evil in themselves. This last portion would include "riches, honors, and such things desired by mortals." Whereas Momus counseled Jupiter to distribute good and evil things to whomever desired them, the things that are neither good nor evil "should all be left to Fortuna's judgment. She should fill her hands with them and decide who should receive them and how much to give each one, as the fancy took her."[45] This passage presents a subtler vision of Fortuna's role in human life than that depicted by Petrarch and Christine de Pizan. The worldly goods delivered by the goddess are morally neutral, in themselves. However, Alberti's language clearly suggests their transitory and so ultimately worthless nature: they are "things desired by mortals." The distinction between these and those earthly resources identified as good just as obviously suggests that they are not actually beneficial despite their attractiveness. The unspoken implication is that the real problem with such things resides in human nature for desiring them in the first place.

The weakness and avarice of human nature appears as central to Poggio Bracciolini's De variatate fortunae (On the Fluctuating of Fortune). Written piecemeal over the central decades of the fifteenth century – between the early 1430s and the reign of Pope Nicholas V in 1447–55 – the work purports to record a discussion between Bracciolini and Antonio Loschi set shortly before the death of Pope Martin V, in February 1431.[46] Their dialogue begins on the Capitoline Hill, where the two men have paused to rest as they make their way through the ruins of ancient city. After discussing the extant traces of the classical metropolis, they turn to discussing the operation of Fortuna in human lives and

---

[45] Leon Battista Alberti, *Momus*, ed. James Hankins, trans. Sarah Knight (Cambridge, MA: Harvard University Press, 2003), 4.102, 354–55. I have slightly altered Knight's English translation.

[46] On the chronology of *De variatate*'s composition, see Iiro Kajanto, *Poggio Bracciolini and Classicism: A Study in Early Italian Humanism* (Helsinki: Suomalainen Tiedeakatemia, 1987), 36–38.

affairs, in response to the obvious collapse of the power and glory that was imperial Rome.

In the course of the first two books, Bracciolini appears to move away from the moral allegory of *fortuna* as a prompt toward eternity. Through the dialogue he identifies *fortuna* as a powerful agent operating in human life but never articulates clearly what it is or what relationship it has to Providence and divine will.[47] In this respect, he seems to consider the way that *fortuna* can work rhetorically to capture the unknowable nature of the future on a more human scale than Petrarch, Pizan, or Alberti. However, the moral force of the Boethian allegory remains an implicit and powerful undercurrent in *De variatate*. Fortuna appears in the work essentially as impersonal, amoral, and capricious. The fleeting transitory nature of life, and so the foolishness and futility of humanity in pursuing the material rewards offered by Fortuna, constitutes the central theme of the dialogue: "nearly all desire what seem to be the great and beautiful gifts of Fortuna, and in obtaining them they dedicate so much zeal and labor that they follow her like blind men."[48]

In pursuing these gifts, Bracciolini observes, humanity subjects itself to Fortuna's power. Like Petrarch and Alberti, Bracciolini asserts that prosperity is more perilous than adversity: "unfairness and perverse judgment and also constant change are the essence of Fortuna ... he whom she had raised to the highest, most prominent position, with a change of face she placed in the lowest with conspicuous dishonor."[49] While his language and characterization cast Fortuna as fickle and even malicious, neither of the protagonists of the dialogue – unlike Petrarch's Sorrow, Pizan's alter-ego in the *Mutacion*, or Neophronus in Alberti's "Defunctus," for example – accuses her of malice or lack of faith. Bracciolini clearly attributed the blame for any suffering to humanity itself. Fortuna appears as predictable in her unpredictability and so is absolved of guilt. Humanity's weakness, stupidity, and greed – in desiring and pursuing Fortuna's gifts – are the cause of all human misery. "We foolishly complain about her too much, since she deceives no one, does nothing secretly, but plainly exercises her dominion," observes Loschi at the conclusion of Book Two; "she does not deceive us as she is so notorious. Rather we are fools and mad men, who are supplicants wearying her with prayers to the point of provocation."[50] While never

---

[47] For analysis, see Iiro Kajanto, "Fortuna in the Works of Poggio Bracciolini," *Arctos: Acta philologica fennica* 20 (1986).
[48] Poggio Bracciolini, *De varietate fortvnae: Edizione critica con introduzione e commento*, ed. Outi Merisalo (Helsinki: Suomalainen Tiedeakatemia, 1993), 89. I am grateful to Davide Baldi for his assistance in translating Bracciolini's Latin.
[49] Ibid., 106.   [50] Ibid., 131.

expressing it explicitly, the work remains oriented toward eternity in its underlying moral message. The fleeting, transitory nature of life means that pursuing worldly goods instead of focusing on eternity reveals humanity's vanity and hubris.

The Christian allegory of *fortuna*, created by Boethius in the sixth century, enjoyed an enduring afterlife in the early Renaissance. The first and second generations of humanists used the figure as a powerful, rhetorical device to discuss the passage of time in a way that condemned human hubris and greed. The neoclassical conceits and prose of these authors subtly loosened the profound linkage between *fortuna* and Providence in their imagination and texts. Yet the allegorical force of *fortuna* in the mid-fifteenth century continued to serve as a prompt to orient humanity toward eternity and away from the transitory nature of time experienced on a human scale.

6 The Emerging of a New Allegory in Mercantile Culture

While early Renaissance humanist considerations of the passage of time and the tension between time and eternity roundly condemned the pursuit of worldly goods, merchants like Buonaccorso Pitti, unsurprisingly, demonstrated more acceptance in this regard. Pitti left behind a boastful, but also candid, chronicle of his rise to wealth and prominence in Florence at the turn of the fifteenth century, for the benefit of his heirs and descendants. Between 1375 and the end of the century, he amassed a considerable fortune. In the winter of 1390/91, while residing in Paris, he accounted his net worth at 10,000 gold francs "in wool, and in the house and furnishings, and in horses and equipment, and cash" as well as being the creditor to various people, including Amadeus VII, count of Savoy, for half that sum again.[1] Pitti engaged in speculative, often long-distance, commerce and until 1399 also gambled with aplomb, making little distinction between the two activities. In England in 1390, for example, he casually recorded: "I did not gamble, but gave 2,500 gold francs to Mariotto Ferratini and Giovanni Guerrieri de' Rossi, requesting that they purchase wool on my behalf and send it to me in Florence."[2] The merchant's lapidary note indicates that he made only a typological distinction between different types of investment, each with its own inherent risks and potential rewards, rather than considering commerce and gambling as exclusive activities.

The common element, of course, was the financial risk taken on a future outcome, either the roll of dice or the safe passage of wool from England to the Italian peninsula. Commerce and games of chance readily intertwined in premodern Europe.[3] As examined in the first four chapters, sixteenth-century merchants and gamblers presented

---

[1] Buonaccorso Pitti, *Cronica di Buonaccorso Pitti con annotazioni* (Bologna: Romagnoli dell'Acqua, 1905), 75.

[2] Ibid.

[3] Nicholas Scott Baker, "Deep Play in Renaissance Italy," in *Rituals of Politics and Culture in Early Modern Europe: Essays in Honour of Edward Muir*, ed. Mark Jurdjevic and Rolf Strøm-Olsen (Toronto: Centre for Reformation and Renaissance Studies, 2016); David

themselves as experts in futurity on the basis of their long professional experience and the deep familiarity with uncertainty and the unexpected that their métiers provided. Unsurprisingly, then, the bonds between Providence and *fortuna* began demonstrably to unravel in the mercantile imagination earlier than in other modes of expression.

This chapter examines the wider mercantile culture in which the humanists discussed in Chapter 5 lived and worked, through the writings of three fifteenth-century merchants from Florence, who all left behind considered reflections on the roles of God and *fortuna* in their commercial successes and failures. It reveals a growing tension between the Boethian moral allegory of *fortuna* and an emerging articulation of the figure as the personification of the unknown yet accessible future. By the last decades of the century, in the mercantile imagination at least, time had become increasingly concrete, something that could be measured, grasped, and priced, providing the foundation for the sixteenth-century experiences discussed earlier. The future, in particular, had begun to take shape as unknown yet accessible. As a result, a new allegory of *fortuna* began to emerge, expressing the need to seize an opportunity to profit from the unknowable time-yet-to-come before it passed.

Buonaccorso Pitti's attitude toward speculative investment reflected the self-assurance of European merchants in the mature, late medieval economy. By the last quarter of the fourteenth century, theologians had developed a range of arguments that supported and endorsed the role of merchants and the social value of commerce in Europe. Scholastic thinkers about economics based their arguments on Aristotle. As a result, like the Greek philosopher, they considered it a subfield of law and ethics. At the heart of the Aristotelian and scholastic models was the concept of just exchange. Aristotle discussed the subject in terms of both distributive justice and corrective or directive justice. While the former operated according to a notion of geometrically proportional exchange, in which each participant received a share according to their contribution, the latter followed arithmetically proportional exchange, each participant receiving an equal share.[4]

C. Itzkowitz, "Fair Enterprise or Extravagant Speculation: Investment, Speculation, and Gambling in Victorian England," *Victorian Studies* 45, no. 1 (2002). On the disentangling of gambling from other financial risk taking over the course of the eighteenth century, see Lorraine Daston, *Classical Probability in the Enlightenment* (Princeton, NJ: Princeton University Press, 1988), chapter 3.

[4] Aristotle discusses and defines distributive and corrective justice in Aristotle, *The Nicomachean Ethics*, ed. Jeffrey Henderson, trans. H. Rackham, revised ed. (Cambridge, MA: Harvard University Press, 1934; reprint, 2014), book 5, chapters 3, 4, 267–79.

Although they accepted Aristotle's ideas about the social utility of commerce, the earliest scholastic commentators on his economic thought resisted the relativity of geometric exchange and its implication that value was not essential but variable. Christian theology, initially, preferred a notion of equal exchange for a just price based on the objective value of the good. This value derived not from the natural worth of something – otherwise, Aquinas observed, a mouse (which is sentient) would be more valuable than a pearl (which is not) – but from its usefulness for meeting human needs and wants.[5]

In the thirteenth century, however, as Europe's medieval economy flourished, thinking about value became correspondingly complex. Two significant developments occurred, both of which appeared first in the thinking of Franciscans, particularly in the work of Peter John Olivi. The centrality of poverty to the Friars Minors' existence provided fertile ground for the development of thinking that favored relativity and elasticity in notions of value and exchange. They had to think in specific, concrete realities rather than in abstract concepts, for example, about the different meaning of necessity for a brother living through a northern European winter compared with one living in a milder Mediterranean climate. Wearing fur could be justified by the former, but would be a superfluous and sinful luxury for the latter.

The first shift came via the decoupling of profit from the sin of avarice. While the justification for commerce remained the provision of socially useful and necessary goods, with mercantile profits being incidental rather than central, scholastic thought increasingly recognized that merchants deserved compensation for their labor and risk in providing commodities, over and above a price based on utility alone. Second, when it came to determining prices, Olivi developed a more thorough and nuanced theory of value, identifying three specific components: usefulness, scarcity, and desirability. The first factor was simply the traditional element of objective utility (the inherent value of a good or product for satisfying a human need). The second element had been acknowledged by earlier thinkers also, as the explanation for why utility alone did not determine prices (explaining why gold, for instance, was

---

[5] On scholastic economic thought, see Joel Kaye, *Economy and Nature in the Fourteenth Century: Money, Market Exchange, and the Emergence of Scientific Thought* (Cambridge: Cambridge University Press, 1998); Germano Maifreda, *From Oikonomia to Political Economy: Constructing Economic Knowledge from the Renaissance to the Scientific Revolution*, trans. Loretta Valtz Mannucci (Farnham: Ashgate, 2012), 43–72; Raymond de Roover, *San Bernardino of Siena and Sant'Antonino of Florence: The Two Great Economic Thinkers of the Middle Ages* (Boston: Baker Library, Harvard Graduate School of Business Administration, 1967).

more valuable than water). With the third component, however, Olivi made an innovative addition by admitting the existence of subjectivity in the process, recognizing that the preferences and mood of a consumer affected the perception of value and utility. The admittance of this element, in combination with the rest of the Franciscan's more complex model, introduced qualitative notions into what had previously been considered only a quantitative exchange, permitting the reintroduction of distributive justice and geometrically proportional exchange into scholastic economic thought.[6]

The most significant implication of the introduction of elements of variability and qualitative elements for mercantile practices, and so for the career of Buonaccorso Pitti and other merchants, consisted in the increasing theological recognition of speculation as licit and of risk as deserving a price itself. Canon law defined usury very narrowly and precisely as the exaction of any sum above the principle of a loan, demanded only for the reason of the loan itself. The concept was limited only to a loan of fungible goods, such as money or foodstuffs, which are consumed in use and so have to be repaid with an equal but different quantity of the same sort. With the development of increasingly complex ideas about the relativity of value, scholastic thinkers began to permit a range of practices that allowed bankers to claim financial compensation for matters not inherent in a loan itself, such as potential damages suffered should a debtor not pay or because the goods or cash had been loaned and so were not available to the lender for immediate use. Most significantly, theologians started to recognize the validity of *lucrum cessans*, the loss of potential profits from an alternative investment rather than a loan.[7] The risks taken by merchants in the provision of goods and services now had a price expressed in the value of probable profits, considered as real as actual profits. Pitti's confident discussion of his commercial and gaming successes and failures reflected the penetration of such theological arguments into the practice of the early Renaissance marketplace.

Speculative risk taking on probable profits fueled Pitti's rise to wealth and commercial success. In one, particularly representative example, in March 1395, he made a deal to purchase 110 barrels of wine from Burgundy for 1,000 francs. He funded the investment with 400 francs

---

[6] On Franciscan economic thought and the importance of Olivi, see Giovanni Ceccarelli, *Il gioco e il peccato: Economia e rischio nel Tardo Medioevo* (Bologna: Il Mulino, 2003), 181–255; Kaye, *Economy and Nature*, 79–162; Maifreda, *From Oikonomia*, chapter 2; Roover, *San Bernardino of Siena*, 16–23; and Giacomo Todeschini, *Ricchezza francescana: Dalla povertà volontaria alla società di mercato* (Bologna: Il Mulino, 2004).

[7] Kaye, *Economy and Nature*, 79–115; Roover, *San Bernardino of Siena*, 27–33.

in cash and the remainder by a letter of credit from Philip the Bold, duke of Burgundy, for an unpaid debt from the purchase of three horses. The Florentine initially failed to find a buyer for the wine. In late April, however, a bitter frost struck vineyards in the region creating a dearth. As a result, Pitti managed to sell 100 of the barrels at a markup of fourteen francs each – earning a profit of 400 francs on the enterprise as well as keeping ten barrels for his own use. Pitti concluded his record of this transaction with a self-congratulatory note: "Thus, I did well from two of the riskiest [le più pericholose] commodities that exist, horses and wine."[8]

The taking of risks – whether successful or not – represented an important part of Pitti's self-presentation in the *Chronica*. He represented himself in the text as a man of action – willing to undertake acts that were consequential (having outcomes beyond the moment of acting) and problematic (having an undetermined result at the time of acting) in both material and immaterial terms, freely and consciously.[9] However, Pitti's commercial transactions – at least as he presented them in the *Chronica* – resembled his gambling, in the way that both involved little conscious calculation about the future. His commercial arithmetic, such as it was, remained simple and focused on ex post facto assessment and calculation of profit or lost. Pitti did not commodify the passage of time but simply gambled on eventually making a profit.

This absence of the commodification of time helps to disentangle the apparent contrast between Pitti's confident self-presentation in the text of the *Chronica* and the meditative self of the poem on Fortuna that opened Chapter 5. In verse, Pitti depicted himself, and other mortals, within the purview of eternity, in which fleeting successes such as that with the wine in 1395 matter only for the way they reflect on human choices. Pitti confessed that previously he had grieved over the action of "the holy and just lady, / who whips the world / with her justice because of our fault." But now, finding himself near the end of his life, he had come to realize that Fortuna always acted with reason and with right. Reflecting on adversity in his life, he admitted, "Of those true tests I can say a great deal, / because I have tasted them both on land and sea, / and I confess every time / that they ensued from my fault." Anyone who finds himself beaten by Fortuna, Pitti observed, knows that "he has not held to the

---

[8] Pitti, *Cronica*, 58. Compare Pitti's vocabulary with that of the sixteenth-century merchants discussed in Chapter 4.
[9] Erving Goffman, *Interaction Ritual: Essays on Face-to-Face Behavior* (Harmondsworth: Penguin, 1967), esp. 185: "By the term *action* I mean activities that are consequential, problematic, and undertaken for what is felt to be their own sake." See Chapter 2 above on gambling and action (in Goffman's sense) in sixteenth-century Italy.

most secure way." By contrast, the "wise, sincere, and diligent" man can "with divinely endowed judgment / take the good path / which will lead him where he seeks his salvation."[10] Like Petrarch, Christine de Pizan, Leon Battista Alberti, and Poggio Bracciolini, Pitti – for all his embrace of the speculative potential of the medieval marketplace – still thought about the future on an eternal and soteriological scale. Hence the simple, arithmetical nature of his calculations of profit and the absence of any sense of time or the future as a commodity in the *Chronica*. Fortuna, operating as the embodiment of the unknown future, still served as a moral allegory, guiding humanity toward the only future that actually mattered.

Pitti would have seen no contradiction between his pursuit of both profit and eternal salvation. Nor, indeed, would he have conceived of a tension between the way he presented himself in the *Chronica* and the more reflective self of the poem on Fortuna. As revealed in the analysis of the scholastic economic thought above as well as in the mercantile correspondence examined in Chapters 3 and 4, theological thought and religious impulses structured the mercantile culture of Renaissance Italy in fundamental ways. The correct and appropriate Christian attitude toward wealth lay in the ability to distinguish the necessary from the superfluous. Scholastic concerns about value reflect this. The ability to identify and pay the just price for goods, avoiding both luxury and avarice, lay at the heart of Christian Europe's medieval marketplace. In this understanding, merchants such as Pitti played a crucial role as professional evaluators: the ability to quantify goods and calculate prices provided a fundamental social service. Merchants provided useful and necessary goods at just prices, and so earned profit for their skill and labor.[11]

Several decades later, in the mid-fifteenth century, another Florentine merchant expressed the intertwining of religious faith and commerce with great clarity and self-reflection. Giovanni Rucellai did not chronicle his own life but rather compiled a *zibaldone*: a miscellany of personal observations, memoranda, and copied texts. He also achieved great personal wealth through his mercantile career. In 1458, according to his tax declaration, he was the third wealthiest man in Florence. Reflecting the changing nature of Italian commerce, Rucellai was a

---

[10] Antonio Lanza, ed. *Lirici toscani del Quattrocento*, 2 vols. (Rome: Bulzoni, 1975), 277–78.
[11] See Maifreda, *From Oikonomia*, 43–72, and Giacomo Todeschini, "Theological Roots of the Medieval/Modern Merchants' Self-Representation," in *The Self-Perception of Early Modern Capitalists*, ed. Margaret C. Jacob and Catherine Secretan (New York: Palgrave Macmillan, 2008).

sedentary merchant banker, investing from afar and operating through agents, factors, and managers across of range of enterprises, rather than traveling extensively as the peripatetic medieval merchants, such as Pitti, had done. By 1473, he recorded that in addition to a bank and investments in seven wool-working businesses in Florence with various partners, he "had companies and held houses" in Venice, Genoa, Naples, and Pisa.[12]

Rucellai ascribed his success to his appetite for speculation, his reputation, and divine favor. In a memoir dated 1464, he recorded "the many and infinite graces given to me by messer God." Together with his good birth and a marital connection forged between his family and the Medici, Rucellai included the "good *fortuna* conceded me in my business affairs, so that from the little wealth left me ... today I find myself beautifully wealthy with fine circumstance and with great credit and good faith."[13] A decade later, he observed, "In the arts of commerce and banking I speculated greatly [*sono stato molto aventurato*], through the grace of God.... In these arts I acquired the greatest credit and the greatest faith."[14] In a virtuous circle, Rucellai's faith and belief in God provided him with faith and credit in the commercial world; the success of his enterprises testified to the divine grace he had received, which in turn provided evidence of his faith.

While Rucellai ascribed his success to God, he displayed a fascination with the unpredictability of the future that demonstrated a subtle shift away from the Boethian moral allegory, which had shaped the earlier Renaissance conceptions of the figure of *fortuna* discussed in Chapter 5. He expressed a more abstract, less soteriological, and so more human idea of the unknowability of the future. In his *zibaldone*, Rucellai assembled a number of opinions on the subject of *fortuna*. Addressing his sons, Bernardo and Pandolfo, the intended audience of the miscellany, he noted: "it will be very useful to give you some sense of what *fortuna* is and what chance is ... so that you might understand if courage, prudence, and the good government of man can resist the occasions of *fortuna* or not, either in whole or in part."[15] Over the next several pages,

---

[12] Giovanni Rucellai, *Giovanni Rucellai ed il suo Zibaldone*, ed. Alessandro Perosa (London: Warburg Institute, 1960), 120–21. On Rucellai's commercial career, see also F. W. Kent, "The Making of a Renaissance Patron of the Arts," in F. W. Kent et al., *Giovanni Rucellai ed il suo Zibaldone, vol. 2: A Florentine Patrician and His Palace* (London: Warburg Institute, 1981), 33–36.

[13] Rucellai, *Zibaldone*, 117. Rucellai's son, Bernardo, married Lucrezia (called Nannina) di Piero di Cosimo de' Medici, in the early 1460s.

[14] Ibid., 120. As with Pitti, compare Rucellai's vocabulary with that of the sixteenth-century merchants discussed in Chapter 4.

[15] Ibid., 103.

Rucellai copied out various opinions and verses on the subject organized into three subgroups. The first, including Boethius, Petrarch, and Aristotle, asserted that *fortuna* had no real existence outside the will of Providence. The second, including Dante, Sallust, and Seneca, described humanity's inability to resist *fortuna*. The last, including Lucan, Cicero, Seneca, and Sallust, discussed humanity's ability to overcome the power of *fortuna*.

Most famously, Rucellai transcribed in full a letter written to him by the neo-Platonic philosopher Marsilio Ficino, which although undated was probably written in the early 1460s. According to Ficino's response, Rucellai had asked "if mankind can prevent or in another way remediate future events, especially those called fortuitous."[16] This suggests that the merchant banker thought of *fortuna* less as a moral allegory about the passage of time in general and more as a specific allegory about the unknowability of the future. Rucellai was beginning to think beyond the Augustinian eternal present that had underwritten the conceptions of Boethius and Petrarch and the image of Fortuna's relentlessly turning wheel. For him the future had begun to take on the quality of unknown time-yet-to-come.

The shifting conception of the future and speculation on unknown outcomes that lie behind Rucellai's thinking can be traced with particular clarity in the reiteration of a collection of ideas about money and wealth management that appeared first in Leon Battista Alberti's *Libri della famiglia* (*Book of the Family*) and eventually featured in Rucellai *zibaldone*. In the third book of Alberti's treatise, written before 1434, the figure of the elderly Gennozzo presents a cautious, conservative approach to finances. He argues strongly in favor of the superiority of real property over liquid wealth. His younger antagonist, Adovardo, prefers the readiness of cash over possessions, observing that "money is the center of all the arts, because he who possesses a copious quantity of money can easily flee from every necessity and fully satisfy a great number of his desires."[17] Gennozzo counters that "there is nothing less stable, less sure than money," and it requires great labor to conserve, "full of suspicions, full of dangers, and most full of misfortunes."[18] A prudent father protects against such risks by spreading his wealth, keeping some in cash, some in property, and in diverse locations. Alberti's text was copied, freely but largely intact, in the following decade by Agnolo Pandolfini in his *Trattato del governo della famiglia* (*Treatise on the Government of*

[16] Ibid., 114.
[17] Leon Battista Alberti, *Opere Volgari*, ed. Cecil Grayson (Bari: Laterza, 1960), 246.
[18] Ibid., 248.

Families). The condemnation of the riskiness of liquid wealth remained largely unchanged in this iteration.[19]

By 1457, however, when Rucellai copied and adapted portions of Pandolfini into his *zibaldone*, a noticeable shift had occurred. Rucellai appeared far less concerned to condemn the riskiness of wealth and far more open to the speculative opportunities available in the mid-fifteenth-century European marketplace. He reversed the order presented by Alberti and Pandolfini, addressing the question of money first, before then discussing the need for careful management of family possessions and wealth. He also began with some original thoughts that offer a striking insight into a commercial, risk-taking mentality: "In truth, money is very difficult to deal in and preserve and it is very much in the hands of *fortuna*, and there are few who know how to manage it," he cautioned his sons, before affirming more positively, "But he who possesses copious amounts of money and knows how to deal in it, is said to be lord of the artisans, because it is the center of all the professions." Money, Rucellai observed, offers protection against the buffets of "adverse *fortuna*."[20]

The image of money being "in the hands of *fortuna*" recalls, with some immediacy, the tradition of the Boethian moral allegory, which identified wealth, power, fame, and other worldly goods as being the particular purview of the goddess Fortuna. In Petrarch's *De remediis*, for example, Reason consoles Sorrow for financial loss, by observing, "You did not lose what is yours, and *you* could not possibly lose what is not yours in the first place. No matter how you look at it, the money is not yours ... but, as I have said, Fortune's, who lends it to be used by whom she selects for a short while and at high interest."[21] In Rucellai's usage, the meaning of *fortuna* had clearly shifted. The problem with money identified by the merchant banker is not that it is a fleeting, ultimately worthless object that no individual can claim ownership of, but rather that "it is difficult to deal in and preserve." For Rucellai, the figure of *fortuna* here – as in his query to Ficino – carried a sense of the unknown and unknowable time-yet-to-come.

---

[19] See Agnolo Pandolfini, *Trattato del governo della famiglia* (Milan: Giovanni Silvestri, 1822), 115–20.

[20] Rucellai, *Zibaldone*, 8.

[21] Francesco Petrarca, *Petrarch's Remedies for Fortune Fair and Foul*, ed. Conrad H. Rawski, 5 vols. (Bloomington: Indiana University Press, 1991), 3: 48. Compare the similar sentiment expressed in Christine de Pizan, *The Book of the Mutability of Fortune*, ed. Geri L. Smith (Toronto: Iter Press; Tempe: Arizona Center for Medieval and Renaissance Studies, 2017), 1.VIII, 57: "Thus Luck is but a game of chance, because the person who happens to have pursued him all his life will be chased far from him, yet Luck and all wordly goods will soon come to one who does not remember him. But that is not rightful wealth, to tell the truth, because there is much to reproach about it, and it is quickly made and unmade."

Money is difficult to manage and perilous to speculate in – and so increase or preserve – because future events remain beyond human perception and cognition. Money is in *fortuna*'s hands because financial investments involve staking on an unknowable future outcome. In the sixteenth century, Italian artists would, in fact, sometimes depict Fortuna carrying a cornucopia filled with wealth or scattering coins and riches.[22] Rucellai is clearly talking about investment and speculation, when he writes of dealing and managing money. Whoever knows how to take risks and amass credit and faith, like Rucellai himself, would find themself at the pinnacle of commercial achievement. Successful speculation on future financial outcomes, because of its difficulty, demonstrates the worth and *virtus* of the merchant. Moreover, adversity is now mitigated not by stoic submission but by the possession of wealth. Prosperity, rather than problematic, is a shield against unexpected, future misfortunes.

Around the time that he was writing this section of the *zibaldone*, in the late 1450s, Rucellai adopted a full, belled sail as a personal badge. It features in the relief decoration of the palace and loggia that he built, and runs proudly across the façade of the nearby basilica of Santa Maria Novella, which the merchant banker commissioned (Figures 6.1–6.3).[23] The sail also appears in a more complex and detailed device in an internal courtyard of the palace, grasped by the figure of a naked, young woman who stands in the place of the mast on ship, which is the crest of helmet, which, in turn, surmounts the Rucellai coat of arms (Figure 6.4). It seems likely that Rucellai adopted the badge of the wind-filled sail from, or had it bestowed by, the Este family, who ruled Ferrara, together with the diamond ring device that also adorns the façades of both the loggia and the palace. Both were emblems used by the marquises of Ferrara, who had counted the merchant banker as a supporter since 1446. Instances of foreign rulers granting the use of personal badges to Florentines occur regularly in the fifteenth century.[24]

---

[22] See Chapter 7 below.

[23] Much of the scholarly literature refers to this as an *impresa*, but Rucellai's use of the sail emblem is always purely visual and never has an accompanying text. An *impresa*, by contrast, consists of both image and text. The palace and loggia complex were completed between the late 1440s and the mid-1460s: Brenda Preyer, "The Rucellai Palace," in F. W. Kent et al., *Giovanni Rucellai ed il suo Zibaldone, vol. 2: A Florentine Patrician and His Palace*, 153–225; Charles Randall Mack, "The Rucellai Palace: Some New Proposals," *The Art Bulletin* 56, no. 4 (1974); Brenda Preyer, "The Rucellai Loggia," *Mitteilungen des Kunsthistorischen Institutes in Florenz* 21, no. 2 (1977). The façade of the basilica was begun in late 1462 and was largely completed in 1510: Rab Hatfield, "The Funding of the Façade of Santa Maria Novella," *Journal of the Warburg and Courtauld Institutes* 67 (2004).

[24] Preyer "Rucellai Palace," 198–201. The Pazzi family, for example, also used the sail device, after it was bestowed on them by René d'Anjou, titular king of Naples and Jerusalem and pretender to the throne of Hungary; Florence Buttay-Jutier, *Fortuna:*

Figure 6.1 Leon Battista Alberti (attr.), detail of the
façade of Palazzo Rucellai (1460s), Florence: Palazzo
Rucellai.
Credit: Palazzo Rucellai, Florence © 2020. Photo Scala,
Florence.

The combination of the sail with the other elements in the blazon
decorating the palace courtyard poses a more complicated problem.
The exact identity of the female figure and the meaning of the armorial
device carved by Bernardo Rossellino has remained a subject of scholarly
debate for over a century.[25] She stands dynamically *contrapposto*: her left

---

Usages politiques d'une allégorie morale à la Renaissance (Paris: Presses de l'Université
Paris-Sorbonne, 2008), 105–9; Volker Herzner, "Die Segel-Imprese der Familie
Pazzi," *Mitteilungen des Kunsthistorischen Institutes in Florenz* 20, no. 1 (1976).
[25] The founding work of analysis and exegesis was undertaken by Aby Warburg in his
1907 essay on Francesco Sassetti: *The Renewal of Pagan Antiquity: Contributions to the
Cultural History of the European Renaissance*, ed. Julia Bloomfield et al., trans. Caroline
Beamish, David Britt, and Carol Lanha (Los Angeles: Getty Research Institute for the
History of Art and the Humanities, 1999), esp. 240–42. Later contributions broadly
followed Warburg's identification of the figure as Fortuna: see especially Felix Gilbert,
"Bernardo Rucellai and Orti Oricellari: A Study on the Origin of Modern Political
Thought," *Journal of the Warburg and Courtauld Institutes* 12 (1949); Frederick Kiefer,

Figure 6.2 Leon Battista Alberti (attr.), Rucellai loggia
(1460s), Florence.
Credit: Loggia Rucellai, Florence © 2020. Photo Scala, Florence.

leg crossed over the right giving a sense of forward momentum; her head
turns toward the prow of the ship on which she stands, while her body
faces the viewer more directly. Her right hand grasps the gathered sail at
her hip while the left holds the mainyard, to which it attaches, above her
head. The front locks of her hair blow freely in the same wind that fills the
sail, extending before her. At its stern, the ship on which she stands
carries a banner depicting the lily of the Florentine commune.

"The Conflation of Fortuna and Occasio in Renaissance Thought and Iconography,"
The Journal of Medieval and Renaissance Studies 9, no. 1 (1979): 3–7; Edgar Wind,
"Platonic Tyranny and the Renaissance Fortuna: On Ficino's Reading of Laws IV,
709 A-712A," in *De artibus opuscula XL: Essays in Honour of Erwin Panofsky*, ed.
Millard Meiss (New York: New York University Press, 1961), 492; or disagreed only
with Warburg's assertion of Rucellai's individuality and originality in the use of the sail
device: see Herzner, "Die Segel-Imprese"; Preyer, "Rucelli Palace," 198–201. Most
recently, Florence Buttay-Jutier has rejected Warburg's identification in a detailed
analysis, but her counterproposal that the figure represents Occasio or Buona Ventura
represents more a refinement than a complete reconsideration of the interpretation:
Buttay-Jutier, *Fortuna*, 102–24.

Figure 6.3 Leon Battista Alberti, façade of Santa Maria Novella
(1458–70), Florence: Basilica Santa Maria Novella.
Credit: Santa Maria Novella, Florence, ItalyPhoto © Raffaello Bencini/
Bridgeman Images.

The image is problematic because its iconography is largely unpreced-
ented and also never repeated by Rucellai. It does, however, bear a
striking resemblance to what would become a widespread visual depiction of Fortuna in the sixteenth century: a young, alluring, naked woman,
often carrying a sail and sporting a prominent forelock. The 1525 frontispiece to Antonio Fregoso's *Dialogo de Fortuna* presents a fully developed,
representative example of this iconography (Figure 7.1).[26] For this
reason, scholars have tended to identify the Rucellai device as Fortuna,
reading the iconography back from later representations, even specifying
it as the initial model for the fashion.

It seems more likely, however, that the Rucellai badge represents just one
moment in the evolution of the iconography of Fortuna in Renaissance
Italy. It accords with the increasingly complex relationship between *fortuna*

[26] This sixteenth-century iconography is analyzed in detail in Chapter 7 below.

Figure 6.4 Bernardo Rossellino and workshop, Rucellai blazon
(1460s), Florence: Palazzo Rucellai.
Credit: Archivi Alinari, Firenze.

and the future legible in Giovanni Rucellai's *zibaldone*, but still looks back to
the older, moral, allegorical meaning. At first glance, the female figure is
clearly Occasio (Opportunity, the Roman cognate of Kairos), the embodiment of time imagined as a series of fleeting moments.[27] The distinguishing
features are her nudity, dynamism, and the flying forelock of hair that
indicates she must be seized on the instant or she will pass by. However,
several elements commonly associated with the figure from antiquity –
wings, a razor, scales – are conspicuously absent and neither the sail nor
the ship features in Occasio's traditional iconography.

These maritime associations were probably influenced by a tradition
dating back to antiquity, which associated *fortuna* with the action of

[27] This is identification is given by Buttay-Jutier, *Fortuna*, esp. 122–24, and my analysis
here is indebted to her own. But I think, as will become clear, that the identification is
less clear-cut than she argues and that it is closer to Warburg's initial interpretation than
she allows. On the iconography of Occasio and its evolution from the Greek, male
Kairos, see Simona Cohen, *Transformations of Time and Temporality in Medieval and
Renaissance Art* (Leiden: Brill, 2014), 199–243. Compare with the mercantile use of
occasione discussed in Chapter 4.

maritime storms on ships, as well as by the ephemeral art created by the Florentine merchant community in Naples to celebrate the triumphal entry of Alfonso V of Aragon on 26 February 1443, which was commemorated in a pair of *cassone* panels created for a member of the Ridolfi family.[28] While these elements point toward an interpretation of the device as an assertion of a risk-taking mercantile culture, other aspects of the composition suggest a more complex meaning closer to the Boethian moral allegory.[29]

The naked female figure clearly borrows from contemporary imagining of the figure of Venus, as windblown and sailing across the waves, which would later be manifested in engravings attributed to the workshop of Baccio Baldini (Figures 6.5 and 6.6) as well as Sandro Botticelli's better-known *Birth of Venus* (Figure 6.7).[30] In Neoplatonic literature, the beauty and allure of the classical goddess of love led the human soul to consider the beauty of the divine, raising the viewer's mind from profane to sacred love.[31] The banner flying on the stern clearly identifies the vessel as the ship of state, or more precisely the ship of the commonwealth.[32] However, the image of the ship also evoked the ark of the

[28] On literary connections between *fortuna* and the sea, see Kiefer, "The Conflation of Fortuna and Occasio," 4, and Wind, "Platonic Tyranny," 491–92. On *fortuna* meaning a storm at sea in mercantile correspondence, see Chapter 4 above. On the Neapolitan triumph and the *cassone* panels, see Ellen Callmann, "The Triumphal Entry into Naples of Alfonso I," *Apollo* 109, no. 1 (1979); Philine Helas, *Lebende Bilder in der italienischen Festkultur des 15. Jahrhunderts* (Berlin: Akademie Verlag, 1999), 61–86; and Chapter 7 below.

[29] This, of course, is the traditional interpretation, first articulated in Warburg, *The Renewal of Pagan Antiquity*, 240–42.

[30] On these engravings, which form part of the so-called Otto Prints, see Arthur M. Hind, *Early Italian Engraving: A Critical Catalogue with Complete Reproduction of the Prints Described. Part I: Florentine Engravings and Anonymous Prints of Other Schools, vol. 1: Catalogue* (London: Bernard Qaritch, 1938; reprint, 1970), 85–87. On the identification of the figures as Venus and not Fortuna, as they are commonly identified, see Buttay-Jutier, *Fortuna*, 109–14. Hind rejects this interpretation. On the classical and Renaissance connection between Venus and imagery of the wind, see Charles Dempsey, *The Portrayal of Love: Botticelli's Primavera and Humanist Culture at the Time of Lorenzo the Magnificent* (Princeton, NJ: Princeton University Press, 1992), 44–49. More broadly on the appeal of the figure of the nymph – "nubile young women in animated movement as expressed through the accessory forms of windblown hair and garments" – in both classical and vernacular contexts in later fifteenth-century Florentine art and literature, see Charles Dempsey, "Love and the Figure of the Nymph in Botticelli's Art," in *Botticelli: From Lorenzo the Magnificent to Savonarola* (Milan: Skira, 2004).

[31] Jane C. Long, "Botticelli's *Birth of Venus* as Wedding Painting," *Aurora: The Journal of the History of Art* 9 (2009): 4.

[32] Buttay-Jutier, *Fortuna*, 102–3; at 107, Buttay-Jutier points out – for the first time in the scholarship – the presence of the Florentine lily in the assemblage. See Gilbert, "Bernardo Rucellai," 103–5, who also places the device in the political context of mid-fifteenth-century Florence.

Figure 6.5 Baccio Baldini and workshop (attr.), *Venus* (ca. 1470), engraving, 6.5 cm diameter, Florence: Biblioteca Nazionale Centrale. Credit: Florence, BNC, Banco Rari 345, tav. 1 with permission of the Ministero per i beni e le attività culturali e per il turismo/Biblioteca Nazionale Centrale di Firenze.

Church and salvation, another connection with divinity. Florentine political mythology imagined the city as possessing a providential mission. The idea of Florence as the heir of Rome infused not only political ideas about civic republicanism but also eschatological notions about the city's role in the renewal of Christianity, and even the ushering of Christ's return and the establishment of a New Jerusalem.[33]

In its complex unity, then, the Rucellai device expressed ideas about the ship of the Florentine commune, imbued with its providential destiny, riding the winds of Prosperity – the opportune moment offered by

[33] Donald Weinstein, *Savonarola and Florence: Prophecy and Patriotism in the Renaissance* (Princeton, NJ: Princeton University Press, 1970), 35–56. Florence was not unique in the way in which its myths combined the political and the religious. The sacred played a central role in legitimizing communal government in late medieval Italy: Edward Muir, "The Sources of Civil Society in Italy," *Journal of Interdisciplinary History* 29, no. 3 (1999): 383–92; Hans Conrad Peyer, *Città e santi patroni nell'Italia medievale*, trans. Claudia Carduff (Florence: Le Lettere, 1998); Augustine Thompson, *Cities of God: The Religion of the Italian Communes, 1125–1325* (University Park: Pennsylvania State University Press, 2005), esp. 15–44, 103–40.

Figure 6.6 Baccio Baldini and workshop (attr.), *Venus* (ca. 1470), engraving, 6.7 cm diameter, Florence: Biblioteca Nazionale Centrale. Credit: Florence, BNC, Banco Rari 345, tav. 2 with permission of the Ministero per i beni e le attività culturali e per il turismo/Biblioteca Nazionale Centrale di Firenze.

Figure 6.7 Botticelli, *The Birth of Venus* (ca. 1485), tempera on canvas, 172.5 x 278.5 cm, Florence: Galleria degli Uffizi. Credit: Galleria degli Uffizi, Florence, Tuscany, Italy/Bridgeman Images.

Occasio – toward the safe harbor of good, Christian government and salvation. It oriented toward eternity. The positive nature of prosperity and *fortuna* expressed in the *zibaldone* recurs here but is directed toward heavenly rather than worldly returns. The forelock of Occasio reminds the viewer to seize and make use of every moment to ensure personal salvation as the collective security of the commune, both earthly and eternal, has been seized and ensured by the rule of the office-holding class. The simpler, more frequently repeated, badge of the wind-filled sail should be understood to bear the same richness of meaning for a fifteenth-century viewer.

While the blazon oriented toward eternity, some of the same maritime imagery permeated Rucellai's reflections on his own personal experience of commercial risk taking. In a *ricordo* dated 1473, having discussed his financial and social success, the merchant banker implied his achievements were particularly admirable because "I managed them in a time of adversity." Due to a close and continuing connection with his exiled father-in-law, Palla di Nofri Strozzi, Rucellai suffered political exclusion and suspicion between 1434 and 1461. So much so, he recorded, "that I needed to navigate very precisely and without error, and so much more marvelous is it that I arrived where I am."[34] In recalling his own life, he invoked the very image of the blazon: the harnessing of the winds of chance and piloting successfully to a safe harbor. Rucellai was possibly influenced in his choice of words and meaning by Ficino, who elaborated on Plato's nautical imagery in discussing the balance between chance, skill, and providence in his commentary on the *Laws*.[35]

In a twist of historical irony, the very next year the merchant banker's hubris foundered. In 1474, Ridolfo Paganelli, the manager of Rucellai's Pisan enterprise, defrauded the business of some 20,000 florins. The banker faced a spiraling circle of debt, which forced him to liquidate much of his real property – most famously selling an estate at Poggio a Caiano to Lorenzo and Giuliano de' Medici – along with his shares in government debt.[36] In his 1480 tax declaration, Rucellai confessed: "I used to run a bank in the Mercato Nuovo," but his latest venture, he continued, "has been beaten by *fortuna* and all the capital is consumed, I remain with debts and I was obliged to put an end to the company."[37]

---

[34] Rucellai, *Zibaldone*, 122.   [35] Wind, "Platonic Tyranny," 491–92.
[36] Rucellai, *Zibaldone*, 122; Kent "Making of a Renaissance Patron," 87–95.
[37] ASF, Catasto 1011: 344v: "Solevo fare bancho in merchato nuovo.... Et per esser stato perchosso dalla fortuna e chonsumato quello vi missa per il chorpo Sono rimasto chon debito e dammi chonvenuto fine ala chonpagnia."

The word Rucellai uses here – "beaten (*percosso*)," from the Italian verb *percuotere* (to strike, beat physically, wound) – reveals the continuing complexity and lack of any simple progression in thought about the figure of *fortuna* and the future. Earlier in the century, another merchant of humbler background, Gregorio Dati, had used precisely the same term to describe his own encounter with commercial adversity: "Now [ca. 1406], *fortuna* began to beat me [*percuotermi*] fiercely."[38] The physical language and tone recall the lamentations of Sorrow in Petrarch's *De remediis*. The deployment of this muscular image at moments of financial crisis – Rucellai declaring bankruptcy and Dati confronting the prospect of it – also invoked the Boethian moral allegory that envisioned Fortuna as the embodiment of providential will, guiding humanity away from the transient temptations of worldly success through its abrupt removal. Its appearance in an actual moment of adversity, in Rucellai's tax declaration, also bears some resemblance to his earlier reference to money as offering protection against "adverse *fortuna*," that is, against unexpected, unforeseen future events. A tension exists, then, between two senses of the future in Rucellai's use of the figure of *fortuna*, in both word and image: a tension between the emergent comprehension of the future on a human scale, as unknown time-yet-to-come, and the future as eternity, opposed to time and comprehended on a universal, soteriological scale.

The presence of this tension was not isolated. It appeared shortly after in the writing of another Florentine merchant, Francesco di Tommaso Sassetti. The general manager of the Medici bank, Sassetti penned a memorandum addressed to his eldest, surviving sons, Galeazzo and Cosimo, on Good Friday, 4 April 1488, in which he observed: "I do not know where *fortuna* will bring us to land, as you see from the upheavals and dangers in which we find ourselves (may it please God to concede us the grace to reach a safe port)."[39] Sassetti's choice of words was both literal, in the sense that he was departing Florence to journey to France, and more profound: the voyage was forced on him by an unexpected financial crisis in the Lyon branch of the Medici bank (which operated under Sassetti's name) that threatened his family's wealth and status.[40] The imagery of the language forcefully recalls the Rucellai

---

[38] Gregorio Dati, *Il libro segreto di Gregorio Dati*, ed. Carlo Gargiolli (Bologna: Gaetano Romagnoli, 1869), 116.
[39] Francesco Sassetti, "Memoria della mia ultima volontà" (1488), printed in Warburg, *The Renewal of Pagan Antiquity*, 233–36; the quoted text is at 235. Francesco was the great-great grandfather of the Filippo Sassetti discussed in Chapters 3 and 4.
[40] On the causes of the crisis, and Sassetti's share of responsibility for it, see Jacob Soll, *The Reckoning: Financial Accountability and the Rise and Fall of Nations* (New York: Basic Books, 2014), 42–47, and Florence Edler de Roover, "Francesco Sassetti and the

blazon. Sassetti imagined his future cast adrift on a sea of troubles but hoped for divine aid to pilot the bark of his family's fortunes to a secure harbor. A providential vision of the future unfolds in these brief sentences, containing the microcosm of the banker's immediate anxiety about the journey and the crisis awaiting him at its end within the macrocosm of more significant concerns about life, death, and the eternity of the afterlife. The "safe port" of Sassetti's prayer is at once an actual end point to his voyage, a successful conclusion to matters in France, and salvation for himself and his family.

In all of this, Sassetti's choice of the word *fortuna* seems almost a passing, rhetorical flourish or perhaps an invocation of the Platonic conjunction of chance, skill, and Providence that had entered Florentine discourse in the writings of Marsilio Ficino.[41] Yet it also appears charged with a meaning and significance that coincides with the sense of Giovanni Rucellai's *zibaldone*: the unknown and unknowable time-yet-to-come. It refers to a time pregnant with potential, the dimension in which money is made or lost. The figure of *fortuna* connected time with notions of value. In the memorandum Sassetti ordered his eldest sons not to decline their inheritance, regardless of the outcome of the crisis in the Medici bank: "do not refuse my legacy for any reason, even if it were to leave you with more debts than possessions, I want you to live and die in that same *fortuna*, for it seems to me that this is what your duty demands."[42]

For Sassetti, as it had done partially for Rucellai, the figure of *fortuna* expressed recognition of the future as unknowable. It articulated an awareness of the inescapable variability and instability of human experience, of the multiple potentials of tomorrow, both good and ill. It remained a moral allegory, but in the mercantile culture of mid- to late fifteenth-century Florence, as demonstrated in the evidence here, it increasingly bore the weight of lessons about opportunity to be seized or missed for financial, as much as soteriological, reasons. The abstraction of time into quantifiable units, into a series of discrete instants, which had begun with the introduction of mechanical clocks in the fourteenth century, was developing in new directions. Time's passing could have real economic value. As a result, *fortuna* could express the unknown yet accessible future as the time when profits would be realized or lost. Hence, a little later in the same document, Sassetti mandated that the Palazzo di Montui – "which has given great renown and reputation to my name and our family and is much celebrated throughout

Downfall of the Medici Banking House," *Bulletin of the Business Historical Society* 17, no. 4 (1943).
[41] See note 35 above.   [42] Warburg, *The Renewal of Pagan Antiquity*, 235.

Italy" – should be kept within the family patrimony if possible. But he adjured, "nevertheless, should *fortuna* turn against you, you will need to be content to sell it and let it go in order not to make things worse, especially as it is an excessive luxury and produces little."[43]

With this injunction, Sassetti more explicitly connected the uncertainty of the future with issues of financial risk and questions of value. Owning the palace represented a risk, because it was expensive to maintain and produced little by way of economic return, but the payoff – Sassetti suggested – was in social status and prestige. However, Sassetti placed the potential economic cost of owning the *palazzo* above the prestige. Its lack of financial value would outweigh its prestige-giving status should the risk of ownership turn sour at some future date.

The figure of *fortuna* had always been connected to ideas about value. In the Boethian moral allegory, it had taught humanity the real value of transient earthly goods when compared with spiritual wealth. In the late fifteenth century in the writings of Florentine merchants, however, the value associated with *fortuna* was no longer only boundless and eternal; it had also become fixed, defined, and human: the price of speculation in these same earthly goods, the social prestige of wealth. In these texts, an outline of the vision of the unknown future as something to be measured and priced, expressed by sixteenth-century merchants, starts to emerge.

Yet the overarching framework in which Sassetti deployed this language, as the beginning of his memorandum made explicit, remained providential. This emergent new conception of the future as unknown time-yet-to-come did not supersede or replace the older orders of time and the Christian ideal of eternity. Rather, the Florentine merchants considered in this chapter expressed the growing resolution of the opposition between time and eternity, the disentanglement of *fortuna* from Providence. Their changing conception of *fortuna* reflected the layering of yet another temporality over those that had already existed at the beginning of the fifteenth century. Human time, measured mechanically and valued according to human needs and wants, was beginning to take existence as distinct from, but not in opposition to or as contradiction of, the eternal present of God and salvation. The foundation of the multicausal futurity expressed by sixteenth-century merchants in Chapters 3 and 4 clearly existed in the complexity of the sense of time-yet-to-come demonstrated in the thoughts of their fifteenth-century forebears.

---

[43] Ibid., 236.

7   The Shifting Image of *Fortuna*

In 1525, a new edition of the *Dialogo de Fortuna*, written by the Genoese courtier and *litterato* Antonio Fregoso, appeared in Venice. Originally published in 1507, the text contained many elements of the traditional, Boethian moral allegory of *fortuna*, but also reflected the mature development of the new conception of the future, which had begun to emerge in the fifteenth century. Moreover, the frontispiece of this edition featured a representative example of the significant transformation in the iconography of *fortuna* that accompanied and, in many ways, anticipated the shifting meanings attached to the word (Figure 7.1). As discussed briefly in Chapter 6, elements of this new imagery had begun to emerge in the last decades of the fifteenth century, creating a hybrid figure that blended the iconography of *fortuna* – a sphere or wheel, a rudder, a cornucopia – with the iconography of *kairos* or *occasio* (opportunity) – youthfulness, dynamism, a distinctive forelock of hair – while also borrowing from the imagery of Venus, principally the image of wind-blown, naked woman riding on the sea. No fixed imagery developed analogous to the relentlessly turning wheel of medieval imagination. Instead, the development of the new image appeared to spin off into multiple new forms and shapes. The frontispiece to the 1525 edition of Fregoso's dialogue, however, captured many of the elements that had become standard in the new, hybrid iconography.

Fortuna appears in the frontispiece as a youthful, naked woman who stands, confidently facing the viewer, riding the waves astride a sphere atop a stand, which has toppled over. She grasps a belled sail behind her, holding the spar in her right hand above her head and gathering the bottom of the canvas in her left hand at her hip. The wind that fills the sail, personified in the clouds behind her left shoulder, also blows the woman's hair forward in billowing tresses that mimic the kairotic fore-lock. The back of her head, meanwhile, seems shorn or bald as no hair is blown across her face. A dolphin – a final remnant of venereal imagery, perhaps – emerges from the waves beside the base of the stand. Behind the figure a variegated landscape of mountains, forests, and buildings is

Figure 7.1 Frontispiece to Antonio Fregoso, *Dialogo de Fortuna*
(Venice: Niccolò Zoppino, 1525), Munich:
Bayerische Staatsbibliothek.
Credit: Bayerische Staatsbibliothek München, Res/P.o.it. 400, title page.

visible. The toppled sphere-and-stand represents an odd visual choice by the unknown artist. It serves, however, as a further reminder of the instability and mutability of time and human existence: no longer upright, fixed, and secure, the sphere-and-stand are now at mercy of winds, waves, and currents. In its entirety, the image clearly presents Fortuna as an alluring and attractive figure who promises opportunity, if only the viewer can seize her forelock and so benefit from the energy and dynamism of the sail. The future, the image suggests, is there for the taking, if one is only prudent and courageous enough to seize it.

This chapter traces how the new concept of the future crystallized in the Renaissance Italian visual imagination from the late fifteenth century. It does so by analyzing the ways in which the imagery of *fortuna* came to express an idea of the future as unknown, unknowable, yet accessible time-yet-to-come; the ways in which this new iconography articulated an awareness of the inescapable variability and instability of human experience, of the multiple potentials of tomorrow, both good and ill. The figure of *fortuna* remained a moral allegory in the sixteenth century, but it increasingly bore the weight of lessons about opportunity to be seized or missed. As a result, it expressed a conception of time as compartmentalized and connected to human ambitions: the uncertain future was the time when plans succeeded or failed, when profits were made or lost, when humanity could determine its own destiny. This new futurity and the new temporality that accompanied it did not erase or replace the older, providential, and Christian sense of the future. It was layered with existing temporalities, producing an increasingly multiplex conception of the passing of time in the sixteenth-century visual imagination.

As in the previous chapters, I do not offer a comprehensive genealogy of the new concept of the future expressed by *fortuna*. Instead, I deploy a similar methodology: presenting a series of complementary analyses of works, some well known, others more obscure, principally from Florentine and Venetian contexts. Cumulatively, these images demonstrate how the new concept of the future cohered and manifested visually, and also underline the complexity of ideas about temporality and the absence of any simple, linear progression from a medieval to a more modern sense of time's passing. In comparison with the texts examined in the previous chapters and in Chapter 8 below, the analysis presented here suggests that the new concept of the future began to mature and cohere in iconography prior to its articulation in writing. However, visual culture in Renaissance Italy existed in a complex, reciprocal relationship with texts, so simple notions of causality are difficult to trace. The artistic process of *inventio*, in the rhetorical sense of creating a new idea, invoked cultural memory: a rich, synthetic heritage of the classical world and

Christianity. Images could efficiently activate this memory by presenting a figure, to which ideas and concepts already adhered.[1]

Changes in the imagery associated with Fortuna began to emerge around the middle of the fifteenth century. The earliest visual conflation of the figures of *fortuna* and *kairos* seems to have occurred in the triumphal entry of Alfonso V of Aragon at Naples on 23 February 1443. As part of the festivities, the Catalan and Florentine merchant communities in the city staged lavish displays to welcome the new ruler. Several eyewitnesses left written accounts of the event, including the humanist scholar Antonio Beccadelli (known as Panormita), a Catalan resident (Antonio Vinyes), and an anonymous Sicilian. Almost a decade after the triumph, an unidentified artist depicted it on a pair of *cassoni* panels, possibly produced for the marriage of Alessandra di Antonio Serristori and Jacopo di Pagnozzo Ridolfi in Florence.[2] The early emergence of the *fortuna–kairos* hybrid in the mercantile imagination draws further connections between the risk-taking culture of Renaissance commerce and the crystallization of the new concept of the future around the turn of the sixteenth century. While elusive, a connection between the emergence of the *fortuna–kairos* figure as the embodiment of Opportunity and the use of *occasione* in mercantile correspondence seems too likely to dismiss.

The triumph produced by the Florentine merchants in Naples presented personifications of the seven cardinal virtues – Justice, Fortitude, Temperance, Faith, Hope, Charity, and Prudence – together with another female figure, which Panormita identified as Fortuna, balanced on a sphere and sporting a distinctive forelock. Following this procession of embodied allegories, came the person of Caesar carrying an orb and scepter. The artist of the *cassoni* panels compressed this into three key figures: those of Justice, Caesar, and Fortuna. While the image depicts

---

[1] Lina Bolzoni, *The Gallery of Memory: Literary and Iconographic Models in the Age of the Printing Press*, trans. Jeremy Parzen (Toronto: University of Toronto Press, 2001), esp. 179–235. For another example of how visual culture could precede and shape the textual in the invention of a new figure in fifteenth- and sixteenth-century Europe, see Charles Zika, *The Appearance of Witchcraft: Print and Visual Culture in Sixteenth-Century Europe* (London: Routledge, 2007).

[2] On the entry, see Ellen Callmann, "The Triumphal Entry into Naples of Alfonso I," *Apollo* 109, no. 1 (1979); Philine Helas, *Lebende Bilder in der italienischen Festkultur des 15. Jahrhunderts* (Berlin: Akademie Verlag, 1999), 61–88; and Hanno-Walter Kruft and Magne Malmanger, "Der Triumphbogen Alfonsos in Neapel: Das Monument und seine politische Bedeutung," *Acta ad Archaeologiam et Artium Historiae Pertinentia Institutum Romanum Norvegiae* 6 (1975): 214–19. Helas reproduces extracts from the contemporary texts at 209–212 and Kruft reproduces more complete versions at 289–98. Callman hypothesizes that the *cassoni* were produced for the Ridolfi–Serristori wedding based on the clear presence of the Ridolfi arms on the panels and a less certain identification of the arms of the Serristori.

the latter standing on an urn rather than a sphere, it clearly shows her hair arranged in a prominent forelock. The most recent historical analysis of the entry has concluded that the conflation of *fortuna* and *kairos* in the display at Naples represented a singular innovation with no visual precedent and only three textual antecedents with which it had no clear connection, the closest chronologically being an early fourteenth-century sonnet that introduced Ventura (an analogue of Fortuna) as "Bald behind and with a little lock on high."[3]

Notably, while the imagery of Fortuna in the Neapolitan triumph broke new ground, its meaning remained firmly connected with the Boethian moral allegory. She appeared as a warning to Alfonso, not as an incitement to seize a fleeting opportunity. The verses recited by the figure of Caesar, who addressed the new king directly, made this intention clear. After promising the monarch military victories so long as he kept the seven virtues in his heart, Caesar cautioned: "As for Ventura, who offers you her forelock, do not give yourself / completely to her, since she is false, / such that I, who triumphed, she placed in decline. / You see how the world changes! / Accept this as your destiny, that it is inconstant."[4] While not suggesting that Alfonso stoically endure adversity – the poem concluded by wishing him prosperity, and unambiguously urging him to leave Florence alone – the verses avowedly connected earthly success with God's grace and conventional morality, and recommended that Fortuna's blandishments be avoided. The forelock here is a lure, not an opportunity. Seizing it, the verse implies, will not give any power over her, but instead will bind one to her fickle will. Caesar's invocation of his own triumph and fall evokes the earlier imagery of the relentless turning of Fortuna's wheel.

A figure generally identified as Fortuna, also sporting a kairotic forelock, next made its appearance in the blazon decorating the courtyard of the Rucellai palace during the 1460s, on this occasion paired with a wind-filled sail (Figure 6.4). Here too, as I argued in Chapter 6, while

---

[3] Helas, *Lebende Bilder*, 79–80. The sonnet was written by Matteo di Dino Frescobaldi (d. 1348). It can be found in full in Francesco Trucchi, *Poesie italiane inedite di dugento autori all'origine della lingua infino al secolo decimosettimo*, vol. 2 (Prato: Ranieri Guasti, 1846), 76.

[4] Helas, *Lebende Bilder*, 71–72. I am grateful to Nerida Newbigin for her suggestions regarding the translation of this poem. The verse, attributed to Piero de' Ricci, is preserved in several manuscript copies in Florence, one of which is reproduced at 210. The anonymous Sicilian correspondent recorded the poem in full and Antonio Vinyes paraphrased it in two sentences, the second of which emphasized the caution against Fortuna's inconstancy: Kruft and Malmanger, "Der Triumphbogen Alfonsos," 289, 292. The identification of the figure as "Ventura" in the verses suggests a possible connection with Frescobaldi's sonnet from the previous century.

Figure 7.2 Antico, reverse of portrait medal of Gianfrancesco Gonzaga
(ca. 1490), bronze, 4.06 cm diameter, Washington, DC: National
Gallery of Art.
Credit: National Gallery of Art, Washington, DC.

the iconography of the figure was new, its essential meaning remained
more conservative and oriented toward the moral imperatives of the
Boethian allegory. By the last decades of the fifteenth century, however,
as the new hybrid image began to take on defined characteristics and a
developed form, it started to appear in contexts that no longer seemed to
direct the viewer toward eternity, but instead recommended seizing the
opportunity she offered.

To give some sense of the multiplicity of forms that the figure took,
I first consider two manifestations of the emerging image that contain
some but not all of the elements. The evolution of the emergent visual
allegory meandered like a stream rather than running smooth or straight
like the proverbial Roman road. Yet even in their iconographical variety,
these images shared a unity in the sense of fluidity and movement that
they expressed. The static nature of the relentlessly revolving wheel of
earlier centuries had disappeared.

Sometime between 1485 and 1490, the goldsmith and sculptor Pier
Jacopo di Antonio Alari Buonacolsi, known as Antico, created a medal
for the lord of Sabbioneta, Gianfrancesco Gonzaga di Rodigo, the reverse
of which featured a female figure identified as Fortuna (Figure 7.2). She
appears standing on a sphere, her gown seemingly blown by the wind so
that she is forced to grasp it with her left hand around hip height. Her
right hand is raised above her shoulder, in a gesture reminiscent of the
grasping of the spar in one of Baldini's Venus woodcuts (Figure 6.6),

although in Antico's medal the sail is missing. Notably, Fortuna's hair is neat and controlled. The kairotic forelock is completely absent. She is flanked on the right by a clothed female figure holding a spear (variously identified as Minerva or Diana) and on the left by a naked male (possibly Mars), his hands bound behind his back, both of whom appear with arms and armor. The shield accompanying the female figure may bear the *aegis*, suggesting she is Minerva.[5] Above the figures the medal is inscribed FOR[TUNA]-VIC[T]RICI (To conquering Fortuna), implying that Gonzaga possessed the necessary wisdom, fortitude, and *virtus* to seize Fortuna and control his own destiny. Possibly, then, the figure lacks the forelock because she has already been taken and controlled.

The Fortuna of Antico's medal appears in many ways as something of an intermediate figure. She possesses the instability and sense of movement of the new iconography but is not particularly accessible – being accompanied by gods and so confined to an Olympian realm – and is less deliberately alluring than later manifestations. Shortly after, however, something more closely resembling the developed figure of *fortuna–kairos* appeared in both word and image in the first edition of Francesco Colonna's *Hypnerotomachia Poliphili* (*Poliphilus's Strife of Love in a Dream*), printed in Venice in 1499. Although never mentioned by name, the female figure who Poliphilius describes surmounting an obelisk that he encounters early in the first dream clearly depicts the emergent hybrid image of Fortuna. The accompanying woodcut by an unknown artist (the design is attributed to Benedetto Bordone) matches the text (Figure 7.3). It depicts a winged, female figure balancing atop the obelisk on her left foot. Her legs are bare from the thighs. Her left hand is clutched to her breast, while her right holds a cornucopia upside-down, as if to empty its contents. Her head is strikingly bare except for a luxuriant forelock that billows in front of her face. In the text the entire figure is described as a weather vane, turning in the wind in a manner that underlined the inconstancy and variability of *fortuna*.[6] In stark contrast to the contained Fortuna of Antico's medal, the woodcut presents her seizure as an

[5] On the medal, see George Francis Hill, *A Corpus of Italian Medals of the Renaissance before Cellini*, 2 vols. (London: British Museum, 1930), 1: 51, 2: plate 38, no. 206; Eleonora Luciano, ed., *Antico: The Golden Age of Renaissance Bronzes* (Washington, DC: National Gallery of Art; London: Paul Holberton Publishing, 2011), esp. 45–58; Stephen K. Scher, ed., *The Currency of Fame: Portrait Medals of the Renaissance* (London: Thames & Hudson/Frick Collection, 1994), 77–80; Filippo Trevisani, ed., *Andrea Mantegna e i Gonzaga: Rinascimento nel Castello di San Giorgio* (Verona: Electa, 2006), 146, cat. I.16; and Filippo Trevisani and Davide Gasparotto, eds., *Bonacolsi l'Antico: Uno scultore nella Mantova di Andrea Mantegna e di Isabella d'Este* (Verona: Electa, 2008), 129, cat. I.7.

[6] Francesco Colonna, *Hypnerotomachia Poliphili* (Venice: Aldus Manutius, 1499), b recto.

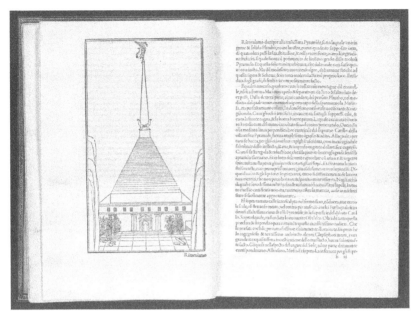

Figure 7.3 Benedetto Bordone (attr.), image of Fortuna atop an obelisk from Francesco Colonna, *Hypnerotomachia Poliphili* (1499), woodcut in printed book, 29.5 x 22 x 4 cm, New York: Metropolitan Museum of Art.
Credit: Metropolitan Museum of Art, New York.

impossible task: surmounting an obelisk, which stands atop a pyramid that dwarfs human scale. The future here remains out of reach and beyond human ambition.

Of these fifteenth-century depictions, only the Rucellai blazon presented the figure as nude, but full or partial nakedness became a central element of the fully developed hybrid *fortuna–kairos* visual allegory. The depiction of Fortuna as an alluring, young woman, either completely or partly disrobed, whose prominent forelock appeared to invite seizure, introduced a powerful gendered, and sometimes sexualized, current into the iconography, which some artists developed and made explicit in their rendering. A particularly confronting engraving, attributed to Marcantonio Raimondi, depicts the naked figure of Fortuna seized and beaten by an equally nude Herculean man (Figure 7.4). A battle between Hercules and Fortuna had featured in a pageant staged at the papal palace in 1501, to celebrate the wedding of Lucrezia Borgia, daughter of Pope Alexander VI, and Alfonso d'Este, the future duke of

Figure 7.4 Marcantonio Raimondi (attr.), *Virtus Beating Fortuna* (ca. 1510), engraving, 14.3 x 13.1 cm, New York: Metropolitan Museum of Art.
Credit: Metropolitan Museum of Art, New York.

Ferrara. This celebration may have provided some context for Raimondi's engraving, although it predated the image by several years and there is nothing to identify the male figure in the print specifically with Hercules.[7]

Fortuna balances precariously on two small spheres, one under each foot, suggestive of profound instability. Her right hand grasps a rudder, while the left hangs freely in the image's rear ground. She is bent over at the hips, her head and upper body forced brutally downward by the male

---

[7] On the Borgia–D'Este pageant, see Ernst Cassirer, *The Individual and the Cosmos in Renaissance Philosophy*, trans. Mario Domandi (Oxford: Basil Blackwell, 1963), 73, and Rudolf Wittkower, "Chance, Time and Virtue," *Journal of the Warburg Institute* 1, no. 4 (1938): 319–20. Wittkower connects the pageant and Raimondi's image. On the engraving and attribution, see Henri Delaborde, *Marc-Antoine Raimondi: Étude historique et critique suivie d'un catalogue raisonné des oeuvres du maître* (Paris: Librarie de l'Art, 1887), 200; Adam Bartsch, *Le peintre graveur*, vol. 14 (Vienne: J. V. Degen, 1813), 278–79, who attributes the design to Raimondi's teacher, Francesco Francia. See also Konrad Oberhuber, ed., *The Illustrated Bartsch*, vol. 27: *The Works of Marcantonio Raimondi and of His School* (New York: Abaris Books, 1978), 67.

figure's grasp of the kairotic forelock, here apparently formed by an elaborate gathering and shaping of the hair, rather than by the shaving of the back of the head. The male figure, hirsute and bearded, pulls sharply on this forelock with his left hand, while his right hand wields a whip or strap above his head. He appears in the act of flogging Fortuna across the buttocks and lower back. The image dates from around 1510 and immediately draws to mind Niccolò Machiavelli's slightly later declaration that "Fortuna is a woman and it is necessary, if you wish to keep her down, to beat and strike her."[8]

The male figure here clearly embodies the concept of *virtus* – manly self-control, a combination of moral and physical courage with force and vigor. The dynamic between the two figures is hierarchical and brutally physical, highlighting the implicit gendered underpinnings of the emergent conception of the future as unknown time-yet-to-come. The seizure of the opportunity and potential of the future was a manly act: an operation of self-assertion on the world, of confidence in one's skill and abilities, of *virtus*. That future, by contrast, was femininized – variable and mutable, capricious, passionate, and irrational – in need of the controlling and taming hand of masculinity.[9]

Analysis of the image, however, should resist too simple or straightforward a conflation between the sex of its figures and social norms and practices, notwithstanding the very real gender inequalities and prevalence of sexual violence in Renaissance Italy.[10] The projection of masculinity in sixteenth-century Italy may have been virile and assertive, but in most texts this ideal remained profoundly unstable rather than normative.[11] As noted at the beginning of this chapter, a visual allegorical figure served as an efficient vehicle for activating cultural memory and conveying a complex, multi-layered heritage of ideas and concepts. The depiction of Fortuna as female and the association of this with instability provided no comfort or positivity for women in Renaissance Italy, but the gender binary of *fortuna–virtus* reveals less about actual social relations between the sexes than it does about how Italians of the period were beginning to reconceive problems of human

---

[8] Niccoló Machiavelli, *Il principe*, ed. Mario Martelli (Rome: Salerno, 2006), 310.

[9] While not discussing the future explicitly, or the *fortuna–virtus* binary, several of the essays in Merry E. Wiesner-Hanks, ed., *Gendered Temporalities in the Early Modern World* (Amsterdam: Amsterdam University Press, 2018), note that when the early modern imaginary conceived of time as feminine, it was generally understood as unstable or fleeting.

[10] For a well-known and very relevant example of such conflation, see Hanna Fenichel Pitkin, *Fortune Is a Woman: Gender and Politics in the Thought of Niccolò Machiavelli* (Berkeley: University of California Press, 1984), esp. chapters 5 and 6.

[11] Valeria Finucci, *The Manly Masquerade: Masculinity, Paternity, and Castration in the Italian Renaissance* (Durham, NC: Duke University Press, 2003).

agency and power in the face of time's passing.[12] As also discussed in Chapters 1 and 2, the experience of the future embodied in the *fortuna–kairos* figure was not necessarily gendered itself nor exclusively male. Moreover, in line with the fluidity of much sixteenth-century thought, the gendering of the allegory did not occur along one simple binary. In Greek mythology, Kairos (Opportunity) had been male. The extant ancient relief fragments and descriptions show or describe a dynamic, young, male figure, winged and carrying a razor, the back of his head shorn, leaving only the distinctive forelock. The shift in gender appears to have occurred by the third or fourth century CE, perhaps to accommodate *occasio*, Latin's female cognate of the Greek *kairos*.[13]

At least some artists and intellectuals in Renaissance Italy knew that the classical *kairos* had been male. The Medici family collection in the fifteenth and sixteenth centuries apparently included a relief fragment of a male Kairos, which was probably the source for Francesco Salviati's mid-1540s fresco in the Sala dell'Udienza in the Palazzo Vecchio of Florence (Figure 7.5).[14] In Salviati's painting a mature, bearded, and winged male figure balances a set of scales on the blade of a knife held in his right hand. With the forefinger of his left hand he stills the movement of the balance, indicating that the opportune moment has been seized. The figure is distinctly bald on the crown and back of his head, but a thick forelock curls and billows free toward the scales. In the hybrid figure of *fortuna–kairos* that emerged around the turn of the sixteenth century, however, the female identity dominated the visual and literary imagination. Indeed, the confusion and hostility that colored the reception of Salviati's fresco in Florence suggests that the idea that the embodiment of opportunity could be imagined as male remained a limited and foreign one to the Renaissance imagination.[15]

---

[12] See, of course, Joan Wallach Scott, *Gender and the Politics of History*, revised ed. (New York: Columbia University Press, 1999), esp. 40–46.

[13] On the classical iconography and changing gender of *Kairos*, see Simona Cohen, *Transformations of Time and Temporality in Medieval and Renaissance Art* (Leiden: Brill, 2014), 199–217.

[14] On the so-called Medici *kairos* and Salviati's fresco, see ibid., 206–17; Beatrice Paolozzi Strozzi and Erkinger Schwarzenburg, "Un Kairos mediceo," *Mitteilungen des Kunsthistorischen Institutes in Florenz* 35, nos. 2–3 (1991). As with *fortuna*/Fortuna, when analyzing texts and images, I distinguish the concepts of *kairos* and *occasio* from their respective, classical embodiments, Kairos and Occasio. On the fresco, see Ettore Allegri and Alessandro Cecchi, *Palazzo Vecchio e i Medici* (Florence: Studio per edizioni scelte, 1980), 43; Luisa Mortari, *Francesco Salviati* (Rome: Leonardo – De Luca, 1992), 26–32, 110–12.

[15] On the reception of Salviati's Kairos, see Strozzi and Schwarzenburg, "Un Kairos mediceo," 307–8. Vasari, describing Salviati's frescos, did not identify the male figure as Kairos but simply as a personification of time: Giorgio Vasari, *Le opere di Giorgio Vasari con nuove annotazioni e commenti di Gaetano Milanesi*, facsimile ed., 9 vols. (Florence: Casa Editrice le Lettere, 1998), 7: 24. Alessandro Cecchi, "Francesco

Figure 7.5 Francesco Salviati, *Kairos* (1543–45), fresco, Florence: Sala dell'Udienza, Palazzo Vecchio.
Credit: Raffaello Bencini/Alinari Archives, Florence.

The gendered complexity of the visual allegory, however, extended beyond the sex of *fortuna*. *Virtus* was a masculine trait but did not belong exclusively to men.[16] Similarly, in the imagination of the new allegory the active figure was not always male. In the summer of 1548, Giorgio Vasari

Salviati et les Médicis (1543–1548)," in *Francesco Salviati (1510–1563) ou la Bella Maniera*, ed. Catherine Monbeig Goguel (Milan: Electa; Paris: Editions de la Réunion des musées nationaux, 1998), and David Franklin, *Painting in Renaissance Florence* (New Haven, CT: Yale University Press, 2001), esp. 216–18, provide a broader context for the hostility with which Salviati's work was received in Florence.
[16] See, for example, Nicholas Scott Baker, "Dux ludens: Eleonora de Toledo, Cosimo I de' Medici, and Games of Chance in the Ducal Household of Mid-Sixteenth-Century Florence," *European History Quarterly* 46, no. 4 (2016).

decorated the ceiling of the Sala del Camino in his house in Arezzo with an image of *Virtù Seizing Fortuna and Trampling Envy under Foot* (Figure 7.6) in which all the protagonists were female. The three figures tumble through an undefined cloudscape.[17] Virtù (the Italian cognate of *virtus*), winged and crowned with laurel, her clothing in disarray exposing her breasts, has seized Fortuna by the forelock with her right hand. In her upraised left hand she wields a short, wooden baton or club to beat her opponent into submission. Fortuna appears in a similar state of semi-undress, suggestive perhaps of the violence and urgency of the struggle between the two combatants. Her right hand grasps the familiar belled sail by its spar above her head, while her left hand flails in front of her body as if to ward off Virtù's blows or in an attempt to grab the weapon for herself. Fortuna's hair is arranged into the now defining forelock, which her opponent has seized. While these two figures are both youthful, blonde, and fair skinned, Envy, who sprawls beneath the struggle, is older. Her almost completely naked body is much darker and her hair is white. Virtù's right foot stands assertively on Envy's neck, and two snakes – emblematic of her deceits and venom, and alluding to envy's tendency to consume itself like a serpent devouring its own tail – accompany her free-falling figure.

The addition of Envy to the visual allegory is a choice that would recur in later paintings also (Figures 7.13 and 7.16, below). Her inclusion helps to underline the idea of time as compartmentalized into discrete moments, as something accessible on a human scale. In the new concept of the future as unknown time-yet-to-come, the figure of *fortuna* offered an opportunity to be taken or missed, manifest visually in the kairotic forelock. If the figure of Virtù represented the fortitude, prudence, and courage to seize this occasion, Envy expressed the bitterness of one who had failed to recognize and take advantage of it, as well as resentment at the success of her more fortunate companion.

The word *virtù* in Italian is female, which may explain Vasari's visual choices. But the image also underlines the complexity of gender in the imagining and construction of the new concept of the future. The female figure of Virtù embodies the quintessence of Renaissance manliness: the ability to impose oneself on the world, to seize the opportunities offered, and control both oneself and one's own destiny. Vasari's imagining calls

---

[17] On the decoration of the Casa Vasari, see Alessandra Baroni, *Casa Vasari* (Montepulciano: Editrice le Balze, 1999), 66–69; Liana de Girolami Cheney, *Giorgio Vasari: Artistic and Emblematic Manifestations* (Washington, DC: New Academia Publishing, 2012), 11–27; and A. Paolucci and A. M. Maetzke, *La casa del Vasari in Arezzo* (Florence: Cassa di Risparmio di Firenze, 1988), 45–88. Vasari himself left a vivid description of the painting in his account of his own works: Vasari, *Le opere*, 7: 686.

Figure 7.6 Giorgio Vasari, *Virtù Seizing Fortuna and Trampling Envy Underfoot* (1542–48), oil on panel, Arezzo: Museo di Casa Vasari.
Credit: Museo di Casa Vasari, Arezzo © 2020. Photo Scala, Florence.

Figure 7.7 Francesco Salviati, *Prudence Seizing Occasio* (1543–45),
fresco, Florence: Sala dell'Udienza, Palazzo Vecchio.
Credit: Raffaello Bencini/Alinari Archives, Florence.

attention to the complex and subtle ways in which this imagery worked
and its irreducibility to simple categories of male oppression and female
subordination.

Vasari's choice was not unique. Francesco Salviati paired his Kairos
with an image of Prudence seizing Occasio, in which both protagonists
were female (Figure 7.7).[18] In this image – in contrast to Vasari's – the
relationship between the two figures appears less agonistic; indeed, they
seem almost to collaborate. Occasio stumbles or steps forward off a
sphere. Her left foot remains on the globe, but her right is now firmly
planted on the trompe l'oeil pediment. Her upper body twists awkwardly

---

[18] On the fresco, see Allegri and Cecchi, *Palazzo Vecchio*, 41, and Mortari, *Francesco
Salviati*, 26–32, 110–12. Allegri and Cecchi identify the subject as Time seizing
Occasio, which not only seems a puzzling combination (why would Time need to take
hold of Opportunity?) but also does not seem to fit the iconography of the image.

away from the movement of her hips and legs. The right arm is contorted, almost painfully, from the shoulder across her torso. With the forefinger of her upraised left hand she seems to indicate her forelock, offering it for seizure. Prudence, who has two faces and is girt by a snake, appears as much to cradle Occasio as to tackle her. Prudence's right foot remains on the pediment, raised on her toes in a dynamic motion. Her left leg is swept under and behind Occasio, the lower leg and foot appear to sweep toward the latter's left leg (still placed on the sphere) as if to knock it off balance, while the thigh must rest beneath Occasio's buttocks, almost supporting part of her weight. Prudence's right arm is tucked firmly under the right arm of Occasio, again seeming as much to support the latter as seize hold of her. With her left hand, Prudence takes hold, apparently quite gently, of Occasio's proffered forelock. The overall impression is a stumbling, tumbling embrace, in which Occasio, knocked off balance by Prudence, surrenders to the latter's advances. Salviati's frescos formed part of the decorative program of what had recently become the home of Florence's new prince, providing a clear political context to allegory. Like its paired male Kairos, the image suggests the peaceful and triumphant taking of the opportune moment, a visual endorsement of the rule of Cosimo I de' Medici in Florence.[19]

However, most images of the new hybrid *fortuna–kairos* figure presented Fortuna alone, a construction that emphasized both her power and her allure. A much copied – in both paint and pen – image from the mid-sixteenth century, at one time attributed to Michelangelo but now thought instead to have originated with Alessandro Allori, can stand as representative (Figure 7.8).[20] Winged and naked, Fortuna sits astride a wheel, in a reversion to the older iconography, her wind-blown hair, while apparently neither shaped nor shaven, features a clear and distinct forelock. From her right hand she lets fall the worldly goods associated with her: a victory wreath, a crown, and a scepter. Her left hand instead scatters what appear to caltrops, traps for the unwary and imprudent. In such a configuration, Fortuna is clearly an object of desire and male gaze, but the ungrasped forelock also suggests freedom and foiled ambition for the subject who seeks to seize and master her. This was the most common and pervasive image of Fortuna in visual sources through the sixteenth century: alluring yet distant, uncontrolled yet potentially accessible, an image of the future as unknown yet laden with promise and possibility.

[19] For an analysis of the full context of the Sala d'Udienza decoration, see Cohen, *Transformations of Time*, 269–85.
[20] See Baroni, *Casa Vasari*, 33, and Luciano Berti, *La casa del Vasari in Arezzo e il suo museo* (Florence: Tipografia Giuntina, 1955), 31.

Figure 7.8 Unknown artist, after Alessandro Allori (?), *Fortuna* (mid-sixteenth century), oil on panel, 75 x 58 cm, Vienna: Kunsthistorisches Museum.
Credit: Kunsthistorisches Museum, Vienna, Austria/Bridgeman Images.

While this hybrid *fortuna–kairos* figure became the most prevalent image in the sixteenth century, the visual imagination of the unknown future did not remain static but continued to evolve in new and complex ways. Three notable works from Florence and the Veneto during the second half of the sixteenth century – executed by Giuseppe Porta (also known as Giuseppe Salviati), Paolo Veronese, and Alessandro Allori – blended elements of the new iconography with the older visual language of the wheel and the Boethian moral allegory. In this regard, they appear as visual analogues to the complex temporality of the sixteenth century and underline the need to resist notions of a simple, linear progression from a medieval to a modern sense of the time.

The earliest of these paintings, Porta's *Virtus between Fortuna and Fortitude* (Figure 7.9), was produced in 1556 as part of the program of decoration for the salone of the Biblioteca Marciana, the first public

Figure 7.9 Giuseppe Porta, *Virtus between Fortuna and Fortitude* (1556),
oil on canvas, 230 cm diameter, Venice: Biblioteca Marciana.
Credit: Biblioteca Marciana, Venice © 2020. Photo Scala, Florence.

library of Venice. It was one of several roundels painted by various artists
to decorate the ceiling of the chamber.[21] Fortuna sits naked and blindfolded on a sphere. Her back faces the viewer in a manner reminiscent of
foremost of the Graces in Raphael's *Cupid and the Three Graces*
(Figure 7.10), painted for Agostino Chigi in Rome in 1517–18 and which
Porta possibly saw in the 1530s.[22] The blindfold that she wears billows to

---

[21] See Nicola Ivanoff, "La Libreria Marciana: Arte e iconologia," *Saggi e Memorie di Storia
dell'Arte*, no. 6 (1968): esp. 71–72. On Porta's image, see also David McTavish, *Giuseppe
Porta Called Giuseppe Salviati* (New York: Garland Publishing, 1981), 240–41;
Wittkower, "Chance, Time and Virtue," 316–18.
[22] Porta was in Rome from 1535 to 1539, when he departed with his master, Francesco
Salviati, whose journey north to Florence and eventually Venice Porta shared: Iris
H. Cheney, "Francesco Salviati's North Italian Journey," *The Art Bulletin* 45, no. 4

Figure 7.10 Raphael, *Cupid and the Three Graces* (1517–18), fresco,
Rome: Villa Farnesina.
Credit: Villa Farnesina, Rome, ItalyGhigo Roli/Bridgeman Images.

the left of the image in an echo of the belled sail of the *fortuna–kairos*
imagery. With her extended right hand Fortuna proffers a crown in the
direction of the figure of Virtus, while her left hand conceals a chain and a
noose behind her back.

These latter two attributes appear to be a particularly northern Italian,
even Venetian, element of the iconography. While the crown clearly
represents the earthly rewards associated with Fortuna, the implements
of punishment provide an effective visual manifestation of the adversity
she could also visit upon the unwary. Some connection may also exist
between these elements and the figure of Nemesis, who is connected
mythologically with the goddess of luck, and brings retributive justice
that may correct the latter's irrational favors. Albrecht Dürer's so-called

Great Fortune (ca. 1501–2) actually depicts Nemesis and dates soon after his first visit to Venice.[23] More immediately, Porta's assemblage probably borrows from the woodcut images of Sorte (Figure 7.11) and Fortuna (Figure 7.12) designed for Francesco Marcolini's *Le ingeniose sorti*, a fortune book published in 1550. The artist designed the frontispiece for the volume and was involved in the design of the 100 woodcuts of allegorical figures and philosophers that formed steps in the game. He was probably responsible for the Fortuna image, while Sorte has most recently been attributed to Lambert Sustris.[24] The woodcut of Sorte depicts a woman, clothed *all'antica*, standing in a rural landscape with both arms upheld to head height. In her right hand she holds a crown, while her left grasps a noose, which is looped around the arm. The woodcut of Fortuna shows its subject seated, blindfolded on a sphere. She is clothed, but has her right breast exposed, and her hair blows forward in the distinctive, kairotic forelock. Without copying either woodcut, Porta blends elements of the two into his striking image.

The figure of Virtus in Figure 7.9, who resembles Minerva in some aspects – wearing armor and a Greek-style helm but possessing none of the other attributes of the goddess – turns away from Fortuna, while still gesturing toward her with her right hand. Virtus's right foot tramples a crown that has fallen to the ground, in an explicit rejection of worldly rewards. She turns her attention, instead, toward a cluster of three figures to her left. Sitting at her feet and looking up in a mixture of hope and surprise is Prudence, a mirror grasped in her right hand. Behind Prudence stands Fortitude, holding together the two portions of a broken column, and a third unidentifiable figure, whose head and shoulders appear at the far-right side of the image. As a whole, the image presents the traditional moral allegorical message of the rejection of easy success

---

[23] Jessen Kelly, "Renaissance Futures: Chance, Prediction, and Play in Northern European Visual Culture" (PhD dissertation, University of California, Berkeley, 2011), 35–41.

[24] McTavish, *Giuseppe Porta*, 64–122; Enrico Parlato, "Le allegorie nel giardino delle 'Sorti,'" in *Studi per le "Sorti": Gioco, immagini, poesia oracolare a Venezia nel Cinquecento*, ed. Paolo Procaccioli (Treviso: Edizioni Fondazione Benetton Studi Ricerche; Rome: Viella, 2007). On the long history of bibliomancy in Eurasian societies and the development of manuscript and later printed fortune or lottery books in medieval and early modern Europe, Johannes Bolte, "Zur Geschichte der Lösbucher," in *Georg Wickrams Werke*, ed. Johannes Bolte (Tübingen: Litterarischen Vereins, 1903), remains the most comprehensive survey. More recently, on early modern fortune books, see Bolzoni, *The Gallery of Memory*, 110–19; Kelly, "Renaissance Futures," chapter 2; Ottavia Niccoli, "Gioco, divinazione, livelli di cultura: *Il Triompho di Fortuna* di Sigismondo Fanti," *Rivista storica italiana* 96, no. 2 (1984); and Suzanne Karr Schmidt, *Interactive and Sculptural Printmaking in the Renaissance* (Leiden: Brill, 2018), chapter 11. Bolzoni and Kelly both emphasize the centrality of illustrations and visual culture to the functioning of such books.

Figure 7.11 After Lambert Sustris, *Sorte* from Francesco Marcolini, *Le ingeniose sorti* (Venice: Francesco Marcolini, 1550), woodcut in printed book, Los Angeles: Getty Research Institute.
Credit: Getty Research Institute, Los Angeles (3013-935).

Figure 7.12 After Giuseppe Porta (?), *Fortuna* from Francesco Marcolini, *Le ingeniose sorti* (Venice: Francesco Marcolini, 1550), woodcut in printed book, Los Angeles: Getty Research Institute. Credit: Getty Research Institute, Los Angeles (3013-935).

in favor of the harder road of virtue. The viewer should follow the guidance of Virtus and rely on Prudence and Fortitude to overcome adversity rather than accepting the easy gifts of Fortuna. This adheres to the overall thematic unity of the decoration of the Salone, which celebrates the benefits of education and study for the success of the Venetian nobility.[25]

The specific imagery of the figure of Fortuna in Porta's painting, however, presents a fascinating composite of elements. The sphere on which she sits, her nudity and alluring depiction, and the billowing, sail-like fabric of her blindfold all recall the hybrid *fortuna–kairos* figure and the conception of time as compartmentalized into moments of opportunity to be seized or missed. But the blindfold itself and the visualization of her gifts as a crown or a noose, as good or bad fortune, echo the Boethian moral allegory. In so doing, the painting also engages with the older conception of the passage of time as cyclical and the future as a distraction from eternity. While the allegorical and classical imagery of the roundel contains no obvious, direct allusions to Christian soteriology, the religious aspect of the message would not have been lost on contemporary viewers. Time, in Porta's painting, unfolds toward eternity rather than existing on a human scale, although it does not completely discount the possibility of seizing moments.

A similar visual complexity of time and the future appears in Paolo Veronese's frescos in the Sala del Cane in the Villa Barbaro at Maser, completed around 1561 and clearly influenced in some elements by Porta's *Virtus between Fortuna and Fortitude*, which Veronese had seen and admired. The subtle and erudite iconographic program for the Villa, most likely designed by its co-owner Daniele Barbaro, the patriarch-elect of Aquileia and a leading intellectual figure of the mid-sixteenth century in Venice, is no longer extant. As a result, scholars remain divided and uncertain as to its underlying theme and message. The most persuasive interpretation of the whole, which appears in the work of various scholars, suggests that the schema revolves around the key concept of Harmony as the law governing human existence and underlying the peace and serenity of family life at the villa.[26] In this exegesis, the frescos

---

[25] Ivanoff, "La Libreria Marciana," 71–72.
[26] See the contribution of Alba Medea in Bernard Berenson, ed., *Palladio, Veronese e Vittoria a Maser* (Milan: Aldo Martello, 1960), esp. 86; Richard Cocke, "Veronese and Daniele Barbaro: The Decoration of Villa Maser," *Journal of the Warburg and Courtauld Institutes* 35 (1972); and Remigio Marini and Guido Piovene, *L'opera completa del Veronese* (Milan: Rizzoli, 1968), 98–101. On the frescos and the role of Daniele Barbaro more generally, see also Richard Cocke, *Paolo Veronese: Piety and Display in an Age of Religious Reform* (Aldershot: Ashgate, 2001), 8–14; Luciana Larcher Crosato,

in the Sala del Cane evoke the passage of time in worldly existence and the transitory and ultimately fallible nature of earthly goods, a message counterbalanced by the frescos celebrating the force of the spirit in the Sala della Lucerna and products of the earth in the Sala di Bacco elsewhere in the villa.

Veronese decorated the south wall of the Sala del Cane, which features the illusionistic dog that gives the room its name, with a *sacra conversazione* in the lunette of the ceiling vault. It features the Holy Family with an infant John the Baptist and Saint Catherine of Alexandria, the patron saints of the Barbaro lineage.[27] This image provides the anchor for the remainder of the frescoed ceiling. The entire visual complex needs to be read as a whole oriented toward this sacred encounter.

The central image of the sala (Figure 7.13) is one of most disputed and obscure in the entire villa program. It depicts a group of three female figures arranged at various heights, increasing from lower left to upper right. At lower left, a woman sits, swathed in a gown of blue and gold, holding a knife in her right hand, which she conceals with her left arm. She looks over her left shoulder at the other two figures. In the center of the image, a crowned woman stands, richly wreathed in layers of pink, gold, and white fabric, with a belt of green cloth that billows sail-like behind her. A lion accompanies, or at least flanks, her, facing away from the viewer. With her right hand she seizes hold of the cornucopia held by the third figure. This last woman sits, naked, atop a pillow-like mass of golden cloth that crowns a globe. Her back is to the viewer, and the positioning clearly follows that of Porta and so, in turn, of Raphael. She cradles the cornucopia in her right arm, while her left hand has seized the right forearm of the standing woman, attempting to push her away. The three figures have been variously identified: the leftmost as Discord, Fraud, or Envy; that in the center as Fortitude, Ambition, Fortuna, or Munificence; the rightmost as Abundance, Providence, or Fortuna.

The naked figure on the globe is clearly Fortuna, not only because of the appropriation of Porta's pose but also because the cornucopia she cradles contains jewels rather than the produce associated with Abundance.[28] The presence of the lion beside the central figure struggling to seize these riches

---

"Cosiderazioni sul programma iconografico di Maser," *Mitteilungen des Kunsthistorischen Institutes in Florenz* 26, no. 2 (1982); Rodolfo Pallucchini, *Gli affreschi di Paolo Veronese a Maser*, 2nd ed. (Bergamo: Istituto italiano d'arti grafiche, 1943); Terisio Pignatti and Filippo Pedrocco, *Veronese*, 2 vols. (Milan: Electa, 1995), 1: 174–228; and Xavier F. Salomon, *Veronese* (London: National Gallery, 2014), 190–91.

[27] See Marini and Piovene, *L'opera completa*, 102–3.
[28] Here I agree with Crosato, "Cosiderazioni," 233–35.

Figure 7.13 Paolo Veronese, *Allegorical Image of Fortuna* (1560–61), fresco, Maser: Villa Barbaro.
Credit: Villa Barbaro, Maser, Veneto, ItalyGhigo Roli/Bridgeman Images.

indicates that she is Fortitude, and I would suggest the third, seated figure could be Envy, in light of Vasari's earlier combination. The precise identity of the figures, however, would seem to be less significant than the fresco's readily apparent overall message. The image presents a moral-allegorical warning against the transitory nature of the worldly goods in Fortuna's keeping: the seated figure with the knife is clearly biding her time, waiting to seize the cornucopia from the central figure by violence should she succeed in wresting it from Fortuna. While the fresco repeats the traditional Boethian moral allegory, it also suggests elements of more recent, sixteenth-century ideas. Fortuna appears – as in Porta's imagining – naked and alluring, in a guise more reminiscent of the *fortuna–kairos* hybrid than the relentless, imperious queen of the medieval iconography. Moreover, the central figure of Fortitude appears in the very act of

Figure 7.14 Paolo Veronese, *Chance Crowns a Sleeping Man* (1560–61),
fresco, Maser: Villa Barbaro.
Credit: Villa Barbaro, Maser, Veneto, ItalyGhigo Roli/Bridgeman Images.

attempting to seize the moment. The fresco suggests, in fact, that the
future does exist on a human scale, unknown yet accessible, while warning
against paying too much attention to this. Like Caravaggio's *Cardsharps*
(Figure 2.2), the denouement of the scene depicted remains uncertain and
unpredictable. In this way, the fresco materially manifests the unknowability of this new conception of time-yet-to-come.

This interpretation fits with, and is bolstered by, the other frescos in
the room. Images of two allegorical pairs, painted onto the base of the
barrel vault above the wall cornices, flank the ceiling grouping: on one
side, *Chance (Sorte) Crowns a Sleeping Man* (Figure 7.14), while to the
other sits *Time and History* (Figure 7.15). The figure of Chance appears
naked except for a girdle of green cloth bound beneath her breasts and
trailing across her right thigh. She has placed aside a chain and noose,
elements probably borrowed from Porta and the Marcolini woodcut, in
order to crown the elderly man at her side. Gray-haired and bearded,
richly dressed in gold-trimmed fabric of a deep reddish purple, this figure
sleeps with his head resting on his left hand. His right hand holds a
scepter. The pair warn against the fickle nature of earthly rewards and
power. Chance could as easily bind the man as crown him. Indeed, the

Figure 7.15 Paolo Veronese, *Time and History* (1560–61), fresco,
Maser: Villa Barbaro.
Credit: Villa Barbaro, Maser, Veneto, ItalyGhigo Roli/Bridgeman Images.

image almost appears as a visual analogue of the condemnations of the
unworthy nature of so many of the recipients of Fortuna's beneficence
that appeared in the work of authors such as Giovanni Pontano and
Niccolò Machiavelli earlier in the century.[29] The sleeping figure has
done nothing to earn the status given to him by Chance but is rather
merely subject to her whim.

On the opposite side of the vault, Time appears as an old, bearded
man, wearing a loose tunic of brownish red fabric, cradling a scythe in the
crook of his left arm. His right hand raises a bundle of fresh papyrus,
symbolizing ancient origin, toward his face.[30] His gaze is elusive, his head
turns to his right, but he appears to watch the viewer out of the corner of
his left eye. By contrast, History, seated at his side, looks directly at the
viewer. Wearing a gown of blue and gold, her head and shoulders

[29] See Chapter 8 below.
[30] Crosato, "Cosiderazioni," 231, with reference to Horapollo's *Hieroglyphica*, which
enjoyed great popularity in the sixteenth century following a first printed edition in
1505. See Karl Giehlow, *The Humanist Interpretation of Hieroglyphs in the Allegorical
Studies of the Renaissance*, ed. Andrew C. Fix, trans. Robin Raybould (Leiden: Brill,
2015), 312.

swathed in a blue-striped white scarf, she holds a folio bound in green
leather in her right hand. Three similarly large volumes are stacked at her
feet, the annals of the past. With her left hand she directs the viewer
toward the *sacra conversazione* on the south wall. This pairing reminds the
viewer of the passage of time – the relentless, inexorable turning of the
years that fall beneath Saturn's scythe to become ink and dust on the
pages of History – while guiding the viewer's attention toward eternity,
manifest in the Christ child.

In its totality, then, the fresco cycle of the Sala del Cane presents time
in a complex, dual manner. The images orient, metaphorically and
visually, toward eternity, toward the figures of the Holy Family on the
south wall, and away from the fleeting, mutable earthly existence. Yet
they also acknowledge the perception of time on a human scale of
moments and opportunities, in the central ceiling fresco and the pair of
Chance and the sleeping man. The future, in Veronese's frescos, exists in
a similar duality: as the unknown time-yet-to-come that possesses reality
but which also distracts from the time-yet-to-come that truly matters, the
life eternal promised by Christian soteriology.

Alessandro Allori's fresco of *Hercules and Fortuna in the Garden of the
Hesperides* (Figure 7.16), by contrast, contains elements of both the
Boethian moral allegorical conception of time with more recent changes
in temporality in a manner that embraces the immortality of fame and the
earthly rewards of *fortuna*. Painted between 1578 and 1582 as a counter-
point to Pontormo's *Vertumnus and Pomona*, which decorates the opposite
lunette, Allori's image finally completed the decoration of the salone at the
Medici villa of Poggio a Caiano, begun some sixty years earlier in the early
1520s.[31] Although the fresco depicts the eleventh labor of Hercules – to
steal the fruit of the garden of the Hesperides – it shows a symbolic and
allegorical scene rather than a narrative one. In the left-hand corner,
Hercules sits, his work complete, his arms crossed and resting on his club,
atop the vanquished body of Ladon, the dragon who had guarded the tree
and its golden bounty. Around the central oculus window, the four
Hesperides display six of these fruits, which here appear as citrons, deliberately numbered to match the *palle* of the Medici arms, among the boughs of
the tree. In the right-hand corner, Fortuna stands triumphant over Envy –

[31] On the decoration of the salone and Allori's contributions, see Janet Cox-Rearick,
Dynasty and Destiny in Medici Art: Pontormo, Leo X and the Two Cosimos (Princeton,
NJ: Princeton University Press), 87–97, 143–52; Simona Lecchini Giovannoni,
Alessandro Allori (Turin: Umberto Allemandi, 1991), 248–50; and Christina Strunck,
"Pontormo und Pontano: Zu Paolo Giovios Programm für die beiden Lünettenfresken
in Poggio a Caiano," *Marburger Jahrbuch für Kunstwissenschaft* 26 (1999). This is the villa
sold to the Medici by Giovanni Rucellai in the 1470s; see Chapter 6.

Figure 7.16 Alessandro Allori, *Hercules and Fortuna in the Garden of the Hesperides* (1578–82), fresco, Poggio a Caiano: Villa Medici.
Credit: Medici Villa, Poggio a Caiano © 2020. Photo Scala, Florence – courtesy of the Ministero Beni e Att. Culturali e del Turismo.

an old, semi-naked woman devouring a snake – and Vice – a similarly semi-naked, chained, weeping man (Figure 7.17). Fortuna appears in the guise of the *fortuna–kairos* hybrid, naked except for a white and gold cloth swathed across her loins. Her hair is short at the back but a luxuriant forelock curls and tangles around the branches of the tree of immortality. A patterned orange cloth billows behind her right shoulder, echoing the wind-filled sail of the earlier iconography. Her left hand, aloft above her head, holds the crown and scepter of the grand dukes of Tuscany. Her right hand drives a nail into the wheel at her side, stilling its movement.

Allori and Vincenzo Borghini, who designed the program for the fresco, took care to harmonize this lunette with that completed by Pontormo earlier in the century. In combination, the two present a coherent celebration of the resilience and success of the Medici dynasty. The two scenes both present hortological images of the revival of a Medicean golden age, encapsulated in the playful neologism GLOVIS, which appears on Pontormo's fresco. This reversal of *si volg[e]* (it turns) – also an acrostic of Gloria, Laude, Onor, Virtus, Iustitia, Salus (Glory, Praise, Honor, Virtue, Justice, Health) – used first by Pope Leo X (Giovanni de' Medici) before being adopted by his younger brother Giuliano,

Figure 7.17 Alessandro Allori, *Fortuna*, detail of Figure 7.16.
Credit: Elena Calvillo.

pronounces that the fortunes of the family had turned (and would always turn) from adverse to beneficial following their return from exile in 1512.[32] While Pontormo's image of *Vertumnus and Pomona* is more aspirational and hopeful, being designed and executed in the 1520s when the continuation of the dynasty was far from clear, Allori's is clearly triumphal. The legend in the painted cartouche that surmounts the oculus – VIRTVTEM FORTVNA SEQVETVR (Fortuna follows Virtus) – indicates that it should be interpreted as an image of the victory of *virtus* (embodied by Hercules, a long-term avatar for the Florentine state, and alluding to the ruling Grand Duke Francesco I de' Medici) over adversity and the vicissitudes of *fortuna*. Yet the figure of Fortuna in the fresco appears as conquering rather than conquered and as a willing

---

[32] On the origins and meanings of the word, see Erkinger Schwarzenburg, "Glovis, impresa di Giuliano de' Medici," *Mitteilungen des Kunsthistorischen Institutes in Florenz* 39, no. 1 (1995). On "glovis" as the key concept for the decoration of the salone, see Strunck, "Pontormo und Pontano."

participant in the immortalizing of Medici power and glory. Fortuna follows the *virtus* of the grand duke freely. While the gender binary remains the same, the violent dynamic of Raimondi's engraving (Figure 7.4) and Machiavelli's language is nowhere to be seen. The *fortuna–kairos* figure of Allori's fresco is not seized by her forelock but lets it entwine around a bough of the tree of the Hesperides, securing immortality for the Medici. Rather like Occasio in Salviati's fresco for the family in the Palazzo Vecchio (Figure 7.7), she is an equal participant in Hercules/Francesco seizing the opportunity that she offers. Similarly, she stills the turning of her own wheel, nailing it to a halt.[33]

The figure of Fortuna in Allori's fresco presents a fascinating juxtaposition of two conceptions of time and the future. The kairotic forelock, alluring nudity, and billowing, sail-like cloth evoke the newer imagining of time as compartmentalized into moments and opportunities to be seized or missed, of the future as unknown time-yet-to-come that promised profit or loss. The much older iconography of the wheel, however, recalls the medieval imagining of the relentless turning of the eternal present, now stilled in the Medicean golden age of the garden of the Hesperides. In this aspect, the fresco does not so much orient the viewer toward eternity, as Veronese's imagery at the Villa Barbaro does, as suggest that it had been achieved in the sense of secular fame and immortality. The future, in this regard, was not a distraction but irrelevant, as it had already arrived. The opportunity had been seized and the passage of time had been stilled.

In the sixteenth century, Renaissance Italians began to imagine the future as unknown and unknowable time-yet-to-come. As this chapter has shown, however, this invention did not proceed via a simple, linear revelation. The older, moral allegories of time did not disappear entirely but continued to color and influence ideas about the instability of human existence and the unknown time-yet-to-come. At the same time, a new moral allegory of the future, expressed by the figure of *fortuna*, clearly emerged. The future had become something conceivable on a human scale and graspable for human ends. The impenetrable nature of time-yet-to-come, its unknown contours and outline, meant that the allegorical force of the imagery of *fortuna* now warned against opportunities missed, against the failure to recognize and act upon occasions that presented themselves. A new temporality had taken shape, which coexisted with the older, providential, Christian sense of time. Time no longer consisted only as a relentless cycle, an eternal present, but also as a series of compartmentalized moments, unique, discrete, and unrepeatable.

[33] The image of Fortuna's wheel stayed developed around the same time as the Glovis wordplay and contributes to tying the two lunettes together; see Schwarzenburg, "Glovis," 155–56.

8   The Separation of *Fortuna* and Providence

Sometime between 1495 and his death in 1503, an Umbrian humanist who had made his name at the Neapolitan court, Giovanni Pontano, wrote a comprehensive treatise on the unexpected in human life, entitled *De fortuna* (*On Fortuna*). In this work he expressed several innovative ideas. Among them, that the gifts of Fortuna, far from being sources of temptation, were actually essential to human happiness, and also that with prudence and reason humanity could exercise free will and avoid the adversity that earlier authors had suggested was inevitable. By the later fifteenth century, as the previous chapters have demonstrated, Italians across a wide variety of contexts had begun to think about futurity in new ways. The evolution of a new allegory of *fortuna* as an opportunity to be seized or missed and the equally innovative idea of the future as unknown yet accessible time-yet-to-come crystallized around the turn of the six-teenth century. The mature visual figure of the *fortuna-kairos* hybrid appeared in the decades either side of 1500, as Chapter 7 has shown. As this chapter demonstrates, its textual counterpart also took shape in these years. In Pontano's thought, as in the work of other early sixteenth-century authors considered here, the working of *fortuna* had become largely disconnected from the will of Providence. The future was unknown and open to human action.

The coincidence between this development, the unfolding European encounter with the Americas, and the onset of the Italian Wars appears more than incidental. As discussed in Chapter 3, the existence of the New World profoundly disrupted European assumptions about temporality, throwing into doubt their understandings of the past and Christian soteriological beliefs about the future. The impact of the Americas on the Italian consciousness occurred gradually. The disrup-tion caused by the Italian Wars, however, was far more sudden. The expedition of the French king, Charles VIII, to conquer the kingdom of Naples in 1494 provoked over a half-century of endemic warfare on the Italian peninsula, which overturned the fragile geopolitical equilibrium of the city-states, revealed the hollowness of many of certainties and conceits of the previous century, and rewrote the map of Italy. In the first twenty years or so of the conflict, in particular, instability, impermanence, and the unexpected appeared the rule. The impact of the age of encounters and the French expedition on the society and culture of the Italian peninsula has been an object of keen historical analysis.[1] Recently, two scholars have also highlighted the role of the rediscovery of Epicurean philosophy – in particular its ideas about chance, evolution, and the fallibility of religion – through the Roman poet Lucretius's *De rerum natura* (*On the Nature of Things*) as a contributing factor to the transformation of Italy in this period. More precisely, changes in the way that humanists read Lucretius, paying more attention to the content and meaning of his words rather than to his language and form, introduced new, unsettling, and potentially dangerous ideas into the intellectual discourse of the peninsula.[2] In this chapter, I trace the impact of these two currents – the Epicurean ideas introduced through Lucretius and the devastation brought by the Italian Wars – set against the backdrop of the growing awareness of the Americas, on the articulation of the new allegory of *fortuna* and the correspondingly innovative idea of the future

[1] On the Americas, see, for example, Anthony Grafton, April Shelford, and Nancy G. Sirasi, *New Worlds, Ancient Texts: The Power of Tradition and the Shock of Discovery* (Cambridge, MA: Belknap Press, 1992); Elizabeth Horodowich, "Italy and the New World," in *The New World in Early Modern Italy*, ed. Elizabeth Horodowich and Lia Markey (Cambridge: Cambridge University Press, 2017); Margherita Azzari and Leonardo Rombai, eds., *Amerigo Vespucci e i mercanti viaggiatori fiorentini del Cinquecento* (Florence: Firenze University Press, 2013); and Lia Markey, *Imagining the Americas in Medici Florence* (University Park: Pennsylvania State University Press, 2016). On the Italian Wars, see, for example, David Abulafia, ed., *The French Descent into Renaissance Italy, 1494–1495: Antecedents and Effects* (Aldershot: Variorum, 1995); Stephen D. Bowd, *Renaissance Mass Murder: Civilians and Soldiers during the Italian Wars* (Oxford: Oxford University Press, 2018); Alison Brown, "Rethinking the Renaissance in the Aftermath of Italy's Crisis," in *Italy in the Age of the Renaissance, 1300–1500*, ed. John M. Najemy (Oxford: Oxford University Press, 2004); Jane Everson and Diego Zancani, eds., *Italy in Crisis, 1494* (Oxford: European Humanities Research Centre, 2000); Michael Mallett and Christine Shaw, *The Italian Wars, 1494–1559*, (Harlow: Pearson, 2012); Mario Santoro, *Fortuna, ragione e prudenza nella civiltà letteraria del Cinquecento*, 2nd ed. (Naples: Liguori, 1978).

[2] See Alison Brown, *The Return of Lucretius to Renaissance Florence* (Cambridge, MA: Harvard University Press, 2010); Alison Brown, "Rethinking the Renaissance in the Aftermath of Italy's Crisis"; Alison Brown, "Reinterpreting Renaissance Humanism: Marcello Adriani and the Recovery of Lucretius," in *Interpretations of Renaissance Humanism*, ed. Angelo Mazzocco (Leiden: Brill, 2006); Alison Brown, "Lucretius and the Epicureans in the Social and Political Context of Renaissance Florence," *I Tatti Studies: Essays in the Renaissance* 9 (2001); Alison Brown, "Philosophy and Religion in Machiavelli," in *The Cambridge Companion to Machiavelli*, ed. John M. Najemy (Cambridge: Cambridge University Press, 2010); Ada Palmer, "Reading Lucretius in the Renaissance," *Journal of the History of Ideas* 73, no. 3 (2012); and Ada Palmer, *Reading Lucretius in the Renaissance* (Cambridge, MA: Harvard University Press, 2014).

that it conveyed. As the previous chapters have shown, the early development of these concepts predated the 1490s, so their evolution did not
simply respond to events. Rather, I suggest that the French invasion had
a catalyzing effect. The conflagration of the following decades forged
preexisting needs and ideas into a more coherent and defined shape.

Several scholarly studies on the increasing proliferation of the figure of
fortuna in sixteenth-century Italian and European thought already exist.
The analysis in this chapter builds on these works but breaks with them
by emphasizing the essentially temporal nature of the allegory.[3] As in
previous chapters, I do not offer a comprehensive genealogy of the new
concept of the future expressed by *fortuna*. Indeed, earlier studies have
demonstrated that the number of texts that would be required for such a
project is impossibly large. Instead, I deploy what I hope has become a
familiar methodology: presenting a series of complementary analyses of
works, some well known, others more obscure, in order trace how the
new allegory of *fortuna* and the new concept of the future cohered and
took shape across the culture of early sixteenth-century Italy. The chapter examines texts from Florentine, Venetian, and Milanese contexts,
together with one key work produced in Naples, Pontano's *De fortuna*.
Cumulatively, these texts demonstrate how the new concept of the future
cohered and manifested, as well as underlining the continuing complexity of ideas about temporality and the absence of any simple, linear
progression from a medieval to a more modern sense of time's passing.
As with the images examined in Chapter 7, the new future – unknown
and unknowable – did not replace the eschatological time of the Church,
but rather coexisted with it through the sixteenth century.

The story of the rediscovery of Lucretius's Epicurean poem *De rerum
natura* by Poggio Bracciolini in 1417 in the library of a German monastery is a familiar one.[4] Once recovered, the single manuscript was reproduced, first by hand and then in print, and so spread across fifteenth-

---

[3] See, principally, Florence Buttay-Jutier, *Fortuna: Usages politiques d'une allégorie morale à
la Renaissance* (Paris: Presses de l'Université Paris-Sorbonne, 2008); Giuliano Procacci,
"La 'fortuna' nella realtà politica e sociale del primo Cinquecento," *Belfagor* 6 (1951); and
Santoro, *Fortuna*. As well as the less ambitious studies by Thomas Flanagan, "The
Concept of Fortuna in Machiavelli," in *The Political Calculus: Essays on Machiavelli's
Philosophy*, ed. Anthony Parel (Toronto: University of Toronto Press, 1972); and
Frederick Kiefer, "The Conflation of Fortuna and Occasio in Renaissance Thought
and Iconography," *The Journal of Medieval and Renaissance Studies* 9, no. 1 (1979).
Buttay-Jutier and Kiefer both consider the relevance of time to the shifting conception
of *fortuna*, the former seeing it as causative, the latter as reactive, but neither recognize the
way that the concept is used to convey ideas about futurity and temporality.
[4] Most recently, it has been recounted engagingly but controversially in Stephen
Greenblatt, *The Swerve: How the World Became Modern* (New York: W. W.
Norton, 2011).

century Italy. Florence and Naples constituted the two most important centers for the discussion and dissemination of the Roman poet's work. In hexameter verse, *De rerum natura* expounded, in particular, on Epicurean physics: an infinite universe that existed only through a random agglomeration of atoms, the product of a chance swerve (*clinamen*). However, it also detailed elements of Epicurus's ethical beliefs and views on morality – most dangerously in fifteenth-century Italy, the conviction that because the soul was mortal, death should hold no fear since no one would ever experience the absence of life.

At the very end of the century, the influence of Epicurus and Lucretius on ideas about *fortuna* appeared in the work of two significant male humanists whose professional lives were directly impacted by the onset of the Italian Wars and the dramatic changes that they wrought: Bartolomeo Scala and Giovanni Pontano. Elements and hints of Epicurean ideas also manifested in the writing of one of the most influential and important female humanists of the period, Laura Cereta, just prior to the conflict. Scala rose from provincial birth to become the Chancellor of Florence on the back of his literary talent and support from the Medici. Pontano, the scion of a minor noble family in Umbria, abandoned a legal career in Perugia to attach himself to the court of Alfonso of Aragon and Naples. He eventually achieved the position of first secretary and chancellor to Ferrante I, becoming a dominant intellectual figure in the royal capital. Of Venetian *cittadino* status and born in Brescia, Cereta achieved distinction as an intellectual and scholar through her unpublished *Epistolae familiares* (*Familiar Letters*), which circulated in manuscript from at least 1488.

Cereta wrote a defense of Epicurus and also explicitly discussed the figure of *fortuna* and the role of the unexpected in human life in three separate letters. In the earliest composed, a nuptial congratulation addressed to Barbara Alberti in November 1486, the Brescian humanist reflected on the sudden death of her own husband less than two years after their wedding. While an odd choice of subject given the intent and recipient, this permitted Cereta to console her own sorrow with a fairly standard recitation of the instability of human life the fleeting nature of earthly pleasures, as well as to lament the animosity of Fortuna. "Fortune always threatens us more when our happiness is most perfect," she warned the new bride. "From this it follows that no one lives secure in his possession of this life, nor does anyone enjoy good things in life for long."[5] Nothing unexpected or unusual presents itself in this traditional

---

[5] Laura Cereta, *Collected Letters of a Renaissance Feminist*, ed. Diana Robin (Chicago: University of Chicago Press, 1997), 134–35.

invocation of the perils of prosperity, familiar from the Boethian moral allegory. However, Cereta's bitterness and grief at the passing of Pietro Serina, only a few months earlier, refreshes the theme and endows it with particular poignancy.

Cereta returned to this theme – the hostile fickleness of *fortuna* and the transitory nature of human experiences – in a defense of Epicurus addressed to suor Deodata di Leno, dated 12 December 1487. The Brescian humanist framed an examination of the nature of pleasure within an account of her ascent of Montisola (a mountainous island in the Lago Iseo midway between Bergamo and Brecia) with friends. She articulates an apologetic for Epicurean ethics, emphasizing the philosopher's advocacy of a life that avoids extremes in preference for the peace of mind brought on by maximizing happiness. The letter describes the natural beauty of the island, the simple pleasures of climbing its eponymous mountain, of eating grapes by the handful, of bathing aching feet in a stream, and quenching thirst with fresh milk. Cereta presents her endorsement of Epicurus, against the objection of suor Deodata, as an affirmation of a life of Christian contemplation and worldly abnegation.

Cereta skirted the philosopher's dangerous ideas about the mortality of the soul, instead highlighting the more culturally resonant aspects of his thought: the rejection of "the painted enticements that Epicurus was accustomed to scorn as ephemeral and transitory pleasures." The "inquity of Fortune carries us and all other things away, and all grounds for arrogance fly upwards when the spirit has fled the body," she adjured, echoing the traditional moral allegory of the fleeting nature of fame, wealth, or power. "A pleasure that lives and endures is a thing not generally known," she continued, "for disdaining that which belongs to this world, it purchases that which is immortal with the currency of virtue."[6] The end point of human existence is the promise of eternity. Cereta implies that this should be the orienting point of life.

Finally, Cereta composed an undated epistolary lecture, which she may or may not have actually delivered, condemning belief in *fortuna*. The essay briefly considers the historic Roman cult of Fortuna, before reciting the triumphant successes and inevitable deaths of a familiar cast of generals and rulers from antiquity, in order to demonstrate the credulity of believing such events to be the outcome of anything other than the constant variability of life. The Brescian humanist unmasks Fortuna as simply a label for the unexpected and inexplicable: "Fortune is, after all, nothing whatsoever and there cannot be anything more worthless than

---

[6] Ibid., 120–21.

nothing." The rhetorical repetition of *nothing* drives home the point. As in the letter to suor Deodata, Cereta argues for a reliance on Providence and belief in the eternity promised by Christian theology, rather than what she derides as pagan superstition. In an intriguing moment, however, she raises but then dismisses Epicurus for teaching "that all things happen by chance or by some sort of contingency."[7] Although she condemns this as an enormous error, the aside is notable because it is unnecessary. Cereta presents her knowledge of Epicurean physics, then swiftly and safely disavows it. This effective rhetorical technique of plausible deniability would also be used by Bartolomeo Scala.

The essay on *fortuna* represents Cereta's most intriguing discussion of temporality and the unexpected, not least for its hint of atomistic thought, but it shares a core idea with the letter to suor Deodata about the nature of the future and time. Both pieces emphasize Christian soteriology, placing eternity as the ultimate end point of every life. Within this framework, however, people experience time on a human scale. It is "uncertain and aimless" yet "speeding onward" as the recitation of the fall of great men from past demonstrates, hence the futility of pursuing vain earthly pleasures and successes.[8] In identifying *fortuna* as a hollow convenience that people use to cover the unpredictability of the future, Cereta underlines this perception of time on a human scale. Cereta did not advise turning this knowledge toward anything other than the contemplation of eternity, but her forceful discussion of it (and brief acknowledgment of Epicurean atomism) demonstrate her willingness to think about the unknowability of the future in less conventional ways than orthodoxy demanded.

Bartolomeo Scala addressed the question of chance and the unknowability of the future as part of the *Apologia contra vituperatores civitatis Florentinae (Defense against the Detractors of Florence)*. Written in 1496, during the moral ascendancy of the millennarian Dominican preacher and prophet Fra Girolamo Savonarola and two years after the collapse of the Medicean regime precipitated by Charles VIII's expedition to Naples, the text counters those "who denounce, not only our misfortune ... but also the wisdom by which our republic is governed."[9] The detail of Scala's argument clearly demonstrates that "misfortune" indicated the loss of Pisa and Montepulciano from the Florentine dominion, in the wake of the French intrusion onto the Italian peninsula. The text

---

[7] Ibid., 157.   [8] Ibid., 121.
[9] Bartolomeo Scala, *Essays and Dialogues*, ed. James Hankins, trans. Renée Neu Watkins (Cambridge, MA: Harvard University Press, 2008), 234–37. I have slightly altered Watkins's translation.

defends republican government, the place of religion in a well-managed city, and the propriety of prophecy.

Before reaching the heart of the *Apologia*, however, Scala expounded a subtle discussion on the nature and role of chance and the unexpected in human life. The impulse for this apparent digression appears to be the question of Florence's recent misfortune, for which the chancellor noted "it is hard to blame us."[10] He implied that the loss of Pisa and Montepulciano, while now in the past, could have been neither anticipated nor expected. This short aside indicates a conviction that human events cannot be foreseen but remain in the unknown, unknowable realm of the future. Chains of causation, the chancellor observed, remain obscure from their midpoint. As so many had done before him, Scala cast the whole question in the figure of *fortuna*. However, he began in an innovative manner by invoking the name of Lucretius and the Epicurean concept of atomism, the attribution of creation to "a fortuitous conjunction of tiny atoms."[11] Like Cereta, he swiftly denied this proposition as unconvincing. Its appearance here, however, points to important currents emerging in late fifteenth-century Florentine intellectual circles. Under the influence of Marsilio Ficino (who would abandon interest in Epicureanism following his ordination), Scala, and Marcello Adriani, the city became the first place to engage with the ideas proposed in *De rerum natura*, rather than treating the poem simply as a valuable source for first-century BCE Latin style and lexicon.[12] Scala's denial of Epicurean physics in the *Apologia* is, therefore, less than convincing, not least because traces of the philosopher's ideas appear in other works.

Lucretius's ideas about death and humanity's fear of dying, particularly his condemnation of such anxiety as foolish and akin to children fearing the dark, as well as his descriptions of natural evolution and humanity's initial primitive state appear to have especially interested Scala. While always careful to veil his personal beliefs by situating discussion of these ideas in dialogues and fables, presenting them in an ironic or playful fashion, the Florentine chancellor framed them with relative admiration. In his *Dialogue on Consolation*, written for Cosimo il Vecchio de' Medici in 1463 on the death of his younger son, Giovanni, and in several fables, Scala tackled Lucretian attitudes toward death. In

---

[10] Ibid., 236–37.   [11] Ibid.
[12] See Brown, "Lucretius and the Epicureans"; Brown, "Reinterpreting Renaissance Humanism"; Brown, *The Return of Lucretius*, esp. 16–67; Palmer, "Reading Lucretius"; and Palmer, *Reading Lucretius*, 79–81. Franceso Sassetti (see Chapter 6) was one of those apparently influenced by the revival of Epicurean moral philosophy, marking several keys ideas about death, the afterlife, creation, and evolution in his personal copy of *De rerum natura*: Brown, "Lucretius and the Epicureans," 20.

the former, the protagonist Cosimo adopts a more favorable view of Epicurean pleasure on learning that it regards grief as the worst of evils. The dialogue still notes the dangers to civil society of the absence of an afterlife but quotes Lucretius on the futility of living in fear and also on the inability of wealth or status to provide a prophylactic against negative emotions, a particularly pointed observation given its recipient. In two fables written for All Souls' Day in 1492, Scala suggested that fear of death is manufactured by religion and equates it with fear of material loss, implying that it is better to live without material wealth than to live in fear of death. In the fable *Mores*, an Epicurean equates living a life of pain, labor, and worry instead of one of pleasure, tranquility, and leisure as ridiculous as horses riding men, deer pursuing wolves, and flocks of sheep keeping watch over dogs.[13]

Although philosophically opposed to the stoicism espoused by Petrarch in *De remediis*, obvious affinities appear between it and Scala's Lucretian musings. Both authors rejected the enslavement of humanity to emotions in response to the passage of time. Both criticized an attitude of fear toward the future, in favor of focusing on the present. Both also condemned humanity's obsession with material possessions. While Petrarch used these ideas to promote an orthodox, Christian attitude toward eternity – framing the role of chance and the unexpected in the Boethian moral allegory of *fortuna* – the influence of Lucretian ideas about natural evolution led Scala to consider the problem of the unknowability of the future in rather more heterodox ways. Having rejected Epicurean atomism in the *Apologia*, the chancellor offered instead a naturalist interpretation of the operation of chance that considers the future on a human, rather than a universal, scale. Scala rejected the notion of Fortuna as an omnipotent and omnipresent force in affairs but equally refuted the idea that chance is nonexistent and, therefore, that humanity can use prudence to avoid the unexpected entirely. He condemned such an idea as implausible because of the obvious obscurity of time-yet-to-come, with the resulting conclusion that "we cannot rely on will or reason but must await the course of nature and the outcome of unknown causes." In such moments, humans perceived the operation of *fortuna*.[14] The idea shares an affinity with Cereta's unmasking of the figure as nothing real.

---

[13] Brown, "Lucretius and the Epicureans," 28–33; David Marsh, *Renaissance Fables: Aesopic Prose by Leon Battista Alberti, Bartolomeo Scala, Leonardo da Vinci, Bernardino Baldi* (Tempe: Arizona Center for Medieval and Renaissance Studies, 2004); Brown, *Return of Lucretius*.

[14] Scala, *Essays and Dialogues*, 238–39.

Scala used the figure of *fortuna* in an attempt to unpick and explain how apparently random events occurred daily, if nothing happens in nature by chance but only according to divine will. The Florentine chancellor suggested that while the actual cause of these apparently random occurrences is natural, it is not inappropriate for humans to identify them with Fortuna because they "seem to happen by her beneficence rather than through any effort of our own."[15] While denying Fortuna any real existence or power, then, Scala did acknowledge the utility of the figure of *fortuna*. It made explicable what humans could neither see nor understand: "something that doubtless in itself is nothing."[16] For the Florentine chancellor, the figure served to explain why events seemingly occur with neither cause nor human intent. As these occurrences are actually natural, however, Scala observed that people can avoid most suffering and adversity with recourse to "reason and prudence." The extent to which humanity's perception of how Fortuna influences worldly affairs, therefore, "varies as men vary in their ability to be wise." Pain and difficulty in life, however, remain unavoidable entirely without divine assistance, "so that one may see beyond mortal vision and avoid Fortuna's assaults."[17]

In the *Apologia*, at least, the future appeared to have taken on very real existence for Scala as time-yet-to-come that was part of the tangible natural world and subject to the same laws as the present. Because of its reality and its naturalness, it remained unknowable, subject to chains of causation beyond human recognition and so possibly unavoidable. If *fortuna* had a moral force in Scala's usage, it was not in the Boethian sense of guiding humanity toward eternal preoccupations; rather, it spoke to the limits of human comprehension and knowledge and so warned against hubris. As with Sassetti's reflections, discussed in Chapter 6, as well as Cereta's considered above, Scala's perception of the future on a very human scale nested within a larger, universal scale of providential time. Ultimately, the only recourse humanity had against the unknowability of the future was God.

This framework took on particular significance in the *Apologia*, as Savonarola's divinatory claims and moral guidance are two of the subjects on which Scala felt obliged to defend Florence. He turned to the subject of those who could foretell the future at the end of the text. After presenting a roll call of respectable prophets from antiquity, the Old Testament, and the Christian past, the chancellor confronted the operation of revelation in contemporary society. Here, Providence and

[15] Ibid.   [16] Ibid.   [17] Ibid., 238–41.

eternity took precedence over time and human perceptions of the natural world. God sends warnings to humanity via a variety of messengers, human and angelic, "for our salvation," Scala wrote. Without such divine assistance, given the role of chance and the unexpected in human affairs, he continued, a real danger exists that "we will never emerge from the stormy waves of life, nor find solid ground on which to stand, nor any harbor and refuge from our afflictions."[18] The maritime imagery recalls Ficino's commentary on Plato, and the Rucellai blazon, in a striking way: a dynamic vision of divine guidance as necessary for successful navigation toward eternity.

The future existed for Scala and he considered time as something perceptible on a human scale, but – in his public role as chancellor, at least – eternity and the universal future ultimately trumped any earthly concerns. His fables, while mocking fear of that particular future beyond death, considered the pursuit of worldly goods just as risible. The *Apologia* grants humanity the prudence to plan for the future and avoid the unexpected to a certain extent and denies *fortuna* any actual existence. Scala's text does not reflect a vision of Fortuna as humanity's moral educator. But at the same time, the discourse framed the accessible future within eternity and a providential vision of time-yet-to-come. Time on a human scale, ultimately, did not matter in the face of the need for salvation. Knowing where Scala's personal beliefs fell in this spectrum of meaning is impossible. The ironic and mocking tone of the fables deliberately prevents alignment between their contents and authorial convictions. Similarly, the formal and public rhetorical purpose of the *Apologia* reflected Scala's professional concerns and position, as spokesperson for the Florentine commune, and cannot be read as a personal reflection. However, elements of his self and opinion surely exist in both. What matters more, perhaps, is the multivalent way in which the chancellor discussed and considered the future, the way in which time and eternity coexisted distinctly in his writing, the way in which *fortuna* and Providence had similarly become largely separated.

Cereta and Scala scattered traces of their thought about *fortuna* and the future piecemeal across numerous texts in which the influence of Epicurus and Lucretius remained carefully shrouded in plausible deniability. Shortly after the Florentine chancellor completed the *Apologia*, however, Giovanni Pontano wrote a comprehensive treatise on the unexpected in human life, titled *De fortuna*. The work was one of several he wrote between 1495 and his death in September 1503, during the chaotic

---

[18] Ibid., 276–77.

final years of the Aragonese dynasty following the death of Ferrante I and the military expedition launched by Charles VIII of France to claim the Regno in 1494. Through three books, Pontano explored the interconnections and contradictions between Providence, fate, chance, nature, and free will. The predominant naturalism of much of the treatise probably owed its inspiration to Lucretius, as the humanist circle in Naples presided over by Panormita and then Pontano himself was the second most significant center of interest in the Roman poet in the later fifteenth century after Florence; but the text also reveals a significant influence from Aristotelian philosophy.[19] In the treatise, Pontano developed a complex, but clear and definite, separation between Providence and *fortuna* as vehicles for explaining the unknowability of the future, and so the role of chance and the unexpected in life. He did so, fundamentally, by distinguishing the figure of *fortuna* solely as an explanatory device for occurrences on a human scale. Pontano invested the figure with a moral allegorical purpose; one, however, that differed markedly from the traditional, Boethian vision.

On an initial reading, *De fortuna* appears to lack a cumulative argument, to the point of seeming almost contradictory in places. However, closer consideration of the threads of the text reveals a careful internal consistency and coherence. Pontano explained that he hoped to discern the reasons for the apparently inexplicable distribution of worldly goods and the irrational nature of success in human affairs. Following in the tradition established by Boethius, and restated by Dante, Petrarch, and Christine de Pizan, among many others, the Umbrian humanist identified such goods – "those called external" – as within the remit of *fortuna*. He explained that they are clearly distinct from both goods concerning the soul and those concerning the body.[20]

While the traditional moral allegory of *fortuna* had considered possessions, wealth, and status as worthless distractions from eternity and the achievement of salvation, Pontano, in a significant shift, instead identified them as central to happiness. This transformed the figure of *fortuna* into the arbiter of human felicity, by dealing out external goods, such as wealth, clients, resources, friendship, public offices, even family. While conceding that a certain amount of happiness resided in matters relating to the soul – honesty, valor, virtue – Pontano suggested that

[19] On Lucretius in Naples, see Brown, "Lucretius and the Epicureans," 17–18. On Pontano and the writing of *De fortuna*, see also Jerry H. Bentley, *Politics and Culture in Renaissance Naples* (Princeton, NJ: Princeton University Press, 1987), 127–34; Giovanni Pontano, *La fortuna*, ed. Francesco Tateo (Naples: La scuola di Pitagora, 2012), 72–73.
[20] Pontanto, *La fortuna*, 1.1, 80–81.

possession of such traits is meaningless, useless, and without real joy in the absence of worldly trappings of success: "nevertheless, the ornament and, as it were, the seasoning of happiness itself derive from external goods and *fortuna*."[21]

The moral problem of *fortuna*, according to Pontano, was not that the pursuit of earthly success and rewards distracted one from the achievement of salvation and the spiritual goods that really mattered. Rather, it lay in the apparent unworthiness of so many of those who achieved worldly success. He laid out the issue in the opening chapter by observing that "actions conducted with prudence and carried forward in the right manner rarely have a happy result." By contrast, he continued, "frequently, for those who conduct themselves idly and incompetently and without reason things turn our most happily, beyond thought and purpose."[22] The disruption of European certainties that began in 1492 and the sudden inexplicable success of bold gambles like Columbus's or Charles VIII's imbued this problem with immediacy and materiality. Far from pursuing philosophical speculation, Pontano confronted a defining issue of the late fifteenth century. Explaining this conundrum is the work of the treatise, and Pontano presaged his eventual answer in the distinction that he made at the very beginning between goods of the soul, goods of the body, and external goods. This tripartite division finds its echo in the separation that he made between Providence, fate, and *fortuna*, and between spiritual and human realms of action.[23]

In Book One, Pontano argued that *fortuna* is neither natural nor divine as it operates contrary to reason, order, and prudence. Its action, therefore, is distinct from both fate, which operates in the natural world and on human bodies, and Providence, which deals with divine matters and human intellect.[24] Humanity, however, also possesses free will (*voluntatis*), with which it can mitigate against, or even evade, the necessities of fate. In the proem to Book Three, he offered a more precise explanation for the operation of free will. God leaves human affairs uncertain and variable, Pontano argued, so that while he could know the outcome of human lives, he chose not to do so. Knowledge of something, Pontano implies, does not make that thing inevitable, and human lives are infinitely variable.[25]

[21] Ibid., 1.25, 152–55. The quoted text is at 154. See also 1.1, 80–81.
[22] Ibid., 1.1, 82–83. As I suggested in Chapter 7, Veronese's *Chance Crowning a Sleeping Man* appears to work as a visual analogue to this idea (Figure 7.14).
[23] See Francesco Tateo, "La prefazione originaria e le ragioni del *De fortuna* di Giovanni Pontano," *Rinascimento* series 2, no. 47 (2007).
[24] Pontano, *La fortuna*, 1.2–4, 82–89; Tateo, "La prefazione originaria."
[25] Pontano, *La fortuna*, 3, Proem, 282-96.

Pontano thus argued that *fortuna* operated in the realm of "human will, of choices, decisions, intentions."[26] Indeed, he suggested that in the absence of humanity, *fortuna* would remain inactive but immanent in the world.[27] In Pontano's thought, the figure and its associations had become almost completely severed from Providence and the action of divine foresight, transforming instead into something explicable on a human scale and in terms of human interaction. For Pontano, the figure of *fortuna* described the operation of a sort of impetus in humanity that acts contrary to reason, prudence, or intellect. Those who respond to this impulse act without deliberation or consideration of future outcomes.[28] Its existence provides, then, the efficient cause that explains the unequal distribution of external goods in the world.

Although this impulse is present in everybody, Pontano explained that the apparently inexplicable and irrational distribution of material wealth and worldly success – "riches, resources, honors, clients, lordships, magistracies, sovereignties, and other things of this sort"[29] – occurs because only a few act on it. He identified these, using the figure of the *homo fortunatus*: a person who appears blessed by *fortuna*. Such individuals lie at the heart of the moral problem for Pontano because they frequently appear unworthy of the station and success that they have achieved in life: "very few are the merits that render them worthy of such advantages, neither assiduous and prudent thoughts or plans, nor valuable force of ingenuity nor yet the greatest and rarest ability."[30]

Pontano devoted Book Two of the treatise to elaborating on this problem, making it clear that he considered the *homo fortunatus* a negative, even pitiable, figure. He identified acting unhesitatingly, almost as a reflex, without reference to reason or prudence as the defining sign of the *fortunatus*. Indeed, Pontano argued not only that the working of the impulse described in Book One is hampered in non-*fortunati* because they continually revert to rational action, but also that any *fortunatus* who attempts to use reason is doomed to failure. In a particularly vivid metaphor, he suggested that the *homo fortunatus* resembles a defective and poorly made ship steered by an expert helmsman rather than a well-made ship with a poor helmsman.[31] The impulse of *fortuna* is responsible for the avoidance of grief, not anything inherent in the vehicle. By any objective measure, the defects of character and vices that such a person possesses should prevent their worldly success, but that person

---

[26] Ibid., 1.21, 140–41.   [27] Ibid., 1.23, 150–53.   [28] Ibid., 1.35–37, 172–81.
[29] Ibid., 1.11–12, 112–15. The quoted text is at 118. See also 1.8, 100–103 for a similar description of external goods.
[30] Ibid., 1.32, 166.   [31] Ibid., 2.19, 234.

overcomes lack of significant skill, intelligence, courage, and *virtus* by following the impetus of *fortuna* and acting heedlessly and without consideration.

In Book Three, however, Pontano suggested that the inequitable distribution of worldly success and wealth does not have to be inevitable. At this stage, the categories of fate, *fortuna*, and Providence, so clearly distinct in earlier sections of the treatise, start to collapse on themselves. The first two become increasingly intertwined, although operating in different ways – the former dealing with necessity, the latter with chance – as Pontano assigns predominance in the natural world to the stars and celestial forces.[32] However, he maintained the rigid distinction between mind and body, between spiritual and physical realms. The stars, Pontano argued, acting through fate and *fortuna*, exert influence only over the body, not the mind. Therefore, while the heavens have predetermined wealth and worldly success, humans can resist and even overcome both fate and *fortuna* through prudence and reason. At this point in the text, Pontano also returned to a more traditional moral argument by suggesting that the best prescription would be to ignore the irrationality of earthly success. A wise man with a good soul should instead submit to Providence, thus finding greater happiness in the good and making the bad more tolerable.[33]

In the end, then, Pontano hesitated to sever completely the bonds between *fortuna* and Providence, which remained nested together in the treatise, even if they no longer worked in tandem. He did distinguish submission to God from submission to *fortuna*, whereas Petrarch had suggested that these were one and the same. While he counseled acceding to divine prescription, Pontano followed up with the final parting thought that although the stars, fate, and *fortuna* cannot always be overcome, one can win only by struggling, suggesting that the act of resistance is more important than the outcome. Moreover, for Pontano, quite explicitly, time was not the eternal present described by Augustine. Time on a human scale, measured by the passage of a human life, mattered. Success in the world was important and central to human happiness. Within this framework, although Pontano did not discuss it explicitly, the future for any individual is immediate, tangible, and has real existence. It is also open to the operation of free will, of human choices and actions.

---

[32] Ibid., 3.1–6, 296–315. See also the Proem to Book 3 at 282–95. On Pontano's interest in astrology and earlier attempts to make sense of the relationship between Providence, chance, and free will, see Charles Trinkaus, "The Astrological Cosmos and Rhetorical Culture of Giovanni Gioviano Pontano," *Renaissance Quarterly* 38, no. 3 (1985).
[33] Pontano, *La fortuna*, 3.7–8, 314–43.

Pontano's ideas naturally influenced a younger generation of Neapolitan writers, such as Tristano Carraciolo, but the impact of Umbrian humanist's thought reached well beyond the Regno.[34] In the decades between 1490 and 1520, Florentine intellectual culture experienced a particularly fertile conjunction between Pontano's theories and Epicurean philosophy encountered through *De rerum natura*. Study and discussion of the latter received promotion, in particular, by Marcello Adriani, who became professor of poetry and oratory at the Florentine studio in 1494.[35] Four years later, following the death of Bartolomeo Scala, Adriani also received the post of First Chancellor in the city's bureaucracy. These two positions placed him at the heart of the city's intellectual life and gave him unparalleled influence over a generation of thinkers and writers. As a result, concepts about the unknowability of the future began to cohere around consistent themes in the work of several Florentine authors in the first half of the sixteenth century: the variability and instability of human existence, the necessity of seizing opportunities for future success, and the role of free will in explaining and permitting both of these former characteristics. Despite the variety and multiplicity of language and meanings, all of these authors expressed in one way or another a conception of the future as the unknown time-yet-to-come that had real existence.

In the 1490s, Adriani used his dual role to challenge the fear-mongering, penitential preaching of Savonarola as well as the Neoplatonic philosophical culture of the previous Medici regime by drawing on Epicurean ideas. As part of his professorial duties, he gave an annual prolusion to commence the academic year at the studio. In these lectures, Adriani discussed – not always explicitly naming Lucretius – three themes in particular that drew on the Roman poet's interpretation of Epicurus: the rejection of fear-driven religious superstition, the promotion of naturalism as an explanatory device, and physics based on atomism.

The prolusion, delivered in November 1497 and titled *Nil admirari* (*Wonder at Nothing*) possessed a particular significance, encapsulating the essence of Adriani's philosophy and demonstrating his intellectual courage. The topic of the oration was the utility of studying the humanities for civic life and a defense of reading classical authors against the preaching of Savonarola. The Dominican had mocked ancient

---

[34] On Carracciolo, see Bentley, *Politics and Culture*, 276–83; Santoro, *Fortuna*, 103–40.
[35] On Adriani's importance, see Brown, "Lucretius and the Epicureans"; Brown, "Reinterpreting Renaissance Humanism"; Brown, *Return of Lucretius*, esp. 42–67; Palmer, "Reading Lucretius," esp. 411–13; and Palmer, *Reading Lucretius*, 79–81.

philosophers in his 1496 Lenten sermons, specifically encouraging his audience to laugh at atomistic ideas. In response, Adriani argued that the fear-mongering of current religious practices in Florence possessed less morality and more superstition than classical philosophy. Instead of approaching the world in fear and trembling, he argued that humanity needed to comprehend the constant changeability of life and prepare itself to adapt to shifting circumstances. To achieve this, people needed to recognize the three authors of all events, which Adriani identified, in order, as *fortuna*, nature, and God. Through the study of history and philosophy, through the writings of ancient authors, the professor argued, humanity learned to fear neither the strange and the unexpected in nature nor the adversity of *fortuna*.[36] As with Pontano, Adriani's ideas belong squarely in a society and culture confronting significant, unanticipated disruptions.

The thought of Giovanni Pontano entered Florence in a less pronounced manner through the person of Bernardo Rucellai, son of the ill-fated merchant banker Giovanni discussed in Chapter 6. Rucellai did not follow in his father's commercial footsteps. Instead, he made a name for himself in late fifteenth-century Florence as a man of learning and political ambition. He served as resident ambassador in Naples from 1486 to 1487, and returned there in 1495 to intercede with King Charles VIII of France for the restoration of Pisa to Florentine control.[37] Rucellai encountered Pontano during these two visits, and subsequently brokered the Umbrian humanist's influence on Tuscan thinkers and writers.[38] Following his return from the second Neapolitan mission, Rucellai retired from active political life in protest against what he perceived as the weakening of the oligarchy's hold over the city. Between

[36] On Adriani's understanding and use of Lucretius, see Brown, "Reinterpreting Renaissance Humanism," and Brown, *The Return of Lucretius to Renaissance Florence*. For the 1497 prolusion, see particularly pp. 274–77 in the former, pp. 51–55 in the latter, as well as Brown, "Lucretius and the Epicureans," 47–50; Peter Godman, *From Poliziano to Machiavelli: Florentine Humanism in the High Renaissance* (Princeton, NJ: Princeton University Press, 1998), 162–67; Armando F. Verde, *Lo Studio fiorentino, 1473–1503: Ricerche e documenti, vol. 4: La vita universitaria Tomo III: Anni scolastici 1491/2–1502/3* (Florence: Olschki, 1985), 1309–18.

[37] On Rucellai's political, diplomatic, and literary careers, see Felix Gilbert, *History: Choice and Commitment* (Cambridge, MA: Belknap Press, 1977), 218–28; Brian Maxson, *The Humanist World of Renaissance Florence* (New York: Cambridge University Press, 2014), 114.

[38] See Gilbert, *History*, 220; Santoro, *Fortuna*, 141–85. In an undated letter to Roberto Acciaiuoli, Rucellai describes a meeting and conversation with Pontano in Naples: Pieter Burman, ed., *Sylloges epistolarum a viris illustribus scriptarum, vol. 2: Quo Justi Lipsii et aliorum virorum eruditorum multae etiam mutuae epistolae continentur* (Leiden: Samuel Luchtmans, 1727), 200–202.

1502 and 1506 he hosted regular scholarly conversations in an urban garden, the famed Orti Oricellari, which in its second incarnation the following decade would nourish several leading intellectual lights of the city, including Niccolò Machiavelli. Here, along with Lucretian and Ficinian Neoplatonic ideas, the influence of Pontano took root in Florence, not least in the writings of Rucellai himself, who began planning his *De bello italico* (*The Italian War*) in these years, although he probably wrote it largely between 1506 and 1512 in Marseille and Venice.[39]

Rucellai and other younger, better-known authors – such as Machiavelli – who experienced the intellectual confluence of Epicurus and Pontano in Florence found themselves in the position of participant observers to the grim helter-skelter of the Italian Wars. Less immediately, but constantly in the background, they lived through the unfolding recognition that the Americas constituted a new world, completely unanticipated in European thought. Epicurean physics with its emphasis on chance as a key determinant for the nature of the world, and Pontano's explanation for the irrational nature of success and the unworthiness of so many of life's winners, provided a framework from which to interpret these events and others. In the figure of *fortuna*, these Florentine politico-historical writers found an allegory that gave shape and form to this framework. They deployed it to make sense of a world that seemed to slide, too easily, toward chaos and dissolution and to understand the irruption of the unanticipated and unexpected in their lifetime. In so doing they helped to crystallize it an as allegory about time's passing and the unknowability of the future.

In *De bello italico*, Rucellai narrated Charles VIII's invasion of the Italian peninsula, his capture of Naples, and subsequent retreat from the city. The Florentine scholar-statesman knew the subject matter not only from observation but also from personal involvement, as ambassador to the French king in 1495. Perhaps counterintuitively, the ultramontane invaders do not appear as the villains of the account. Rucellai instead cast Piero de' Medici and Alfonso II of Naples in that role, accusing them (with the complicity of Pope Alexander VI) of destroying the peace and stability established by their respective fathers, Lorenzo il Magnifico and Ferrante I. According to Rucellai, the scheming of these

---

[39] Rudolf von Albertini, *Firenze dalla repubblica al principato: Storia e coscienza politica*, trans. Cesare Cristofolini (Turin: Giulio Einaudi, 1970), 67–69; Brown, *Return of Lucretius*, 88–109; Gilbert, *History*, 226–27; Bernardo Rucellai, *De bello italico/La guerra d'Italia*, ed. Donatella Coppini (Florence: Firenze University Press, 2011), 3–27; Santoro, *Fortuna*, 141–85.

two young heirs left Ludovico Sforza, duke of Milan, cornered, prompting him to summon Charles into Italy. In so doing, Medici and Alfonso proved the executors of their own downfall: "Thus it happened, that they, who had been great and powerful, soon made themselves a miserable spectacle among smaller examples of hardship, once *fortuna*, with the arts of power, changed."[40]

At the core of Rucellai's narrative, and underlying the way he used the figure of *fortuna* in the text, lay a contrast between those actors who possessed the prudence and judgment to act assertively and decisively at the opportune moment and those who were weak and vacillating, who judged poorly and missed opportunities. The future, *De bello italico* suggested, was unpredictable – unknown and unknowable. Chance and luck contributed to the course of events and so to the success or failure of human plans and intentions. Having identified Piero de' Medici and Alfonso of Naples as culpable for the catastrophe that befell Italy, Rucellai stated: "the initial motor of events is within the grasp of whomever you please, even the useless; but truly Fortuna herself, who cannot stay still in the one place, laid claim to the situation and the outcome."[41]

Probably influenced by Pontano, Rucellai assigned *fortuna* to the realm of human action and intentions. The figure provided an allegory for the futility of plans in the face of the inevitable variability of existence. Piero de' Medici and Alfonso II unleashed the chain of events that began the Wars. However, lacking foresight and understanding, they could not control the outcome of their scheming. The key to success in the dizzying chaos, Rucellai suggested, was to avoid indecision, to be prudent but also prompt, and so seize any opportunity that arose. The principal example of such strength of character in *De bello italico* is Ludovico Sforza. In contrast to his characterization of the fearfulness of Piero de' Medici, the terror of the Romans, and the vacillation of the Neapolitans, Rucellai depicted the Milanese duke as decisive. Alone of the Italian rulers, Sforza attempted to forestall the French advance by acting boldly and proposing a common alliance with Florence and Alfonso II against Charles VIII after the Neapolitan defeat at Rapallo: "truly that was an example to him not to trust *fortuna* blindy; convincing him rather that it was the most opportune time for bringing about peace and friendship; ... certainly peace, even if not attractive, was preferable to the uncertain hopes of war."[42] The Milanese duke failed in this initial attempt. However, according to Rucellai, he then proposed the formation of the League of

---

[40] Rucellai, *De bello italico*, 46.   [41] Ibid., 54.

[42] Ibid., 68. On the Neapolitan attempt to delay or disrupt the French advance at Genoa and the resulting battle at Rapallo, see Mallett and Shaw, *The Italian Wars*, 18–19.

Venice, which eventually united the eponymous republic with Ferdinand of Aragon, Emperor Maximilian I, the papacy, and Milan to harry the French from Italy. Rucellai did not pass uncritically over Sforza's faults – "[he] did not shrink from those arts that become a prince, except that *fortuna* had nourished an innate vanity in his soul with success in politics and worldly affairs" – but he contrasted the duke's decisiveness with the pusillanimity of the other Italian rulers and even of Charles VIII.[43] Rucellai argued that the French monarch's failure to depose Pope Alexander VI – which the Florentine claims Charles considered, on the basis of overheard conversations during his embassy – doomed the expedition to Naples. The king had the opportunity to ensure his mastery of Italy but permitted himself to be persuaded by self-interested counsel: "as usually happens in the majority of affairs, *fortuna* and bad advice won, so that each one, looking out for himself rather than for the king, preferred the soft living of France to worthy ways."[44]

As this condemnation indicates, the Boethian moral allegory of *fortuna* was not completely absent from Rucellai's narrative, but its intent and action differed from that of the previous century. For Rucellai the pursuit of worldly goods was not problematic in itself. Rather, avarice too easily led actors into poor decision making, which led to missed opportunities. The Italian polities, he suggested, had become indolent and vacillating due to the extended blessings of peace and wealth they had enjoyed in the decades preceding the French invasion.[45] As Charles VIII planned his conquest, Rucellai claimed that Louis Malet de Graville, the admiral of France, cautioned the king against "being dragged into a grave and dangerous war, whose victory would be hazardous and fickle." Despite the esteem the old nobleman enjoyed, "the opinion of those who vomited themselves forth to plunder the cities, goods, and riches of Italy" overruled his caution.[46] Later, during the French retreat from Naples in 1495, the Florentine historian would blame greed for the failure of the forces of the League of Venice to press home their advantage at the battle of Fornovo. When the Milanese nobleman Giangiacomo Trivulzio, fighting for Charles VIII, sacrificed the French baggage train, the Italians fell

---

[43] Rucellai, *De bello italico*, 130. On the League of Venice, see Mallett and Shaw, *The Italian Wars*, 27–32.
[44] Rucellai, *De bello italico*, 132.
[45] Rucellai describes Rome, for example, as "luxuriantis diuturna atque indulgentia fortunae": ibid., 116. See also the description of the vacillation of the Neapolitan commanders at page 122.
[46] Ibid., 60.

to looting rather than fighting and the Valois monarch escaped.[47] Humanity, Rucellai suggested, too easily trusted in the illusive promise of future gains, without considering the requisite prudence and wisdom needed to plan for the unexpected, and to recognize real opportunities when they arose.

The necessity of planning for the future and of identifying opportune moments emerged as central themes in the writing of another Florentine author, who displayed a notable interest in the unexpected in human experience, Niccolò Machiavelli. In particular, he shared with Rucellai an understanding that the variable nature of human life required both prudence and decisiveness for success. Despite their political differences, they drew on many of the same intellectual currents. Machiavelli was certainly familiar with Pontano's *De fortuna*, discussing it in correspondence with his close friend Francesco Vettori, in December 1514.[48] He also fell under the intellectual influence of Marcello Adriani. While Machiavelli may not have been a student of Adriani's at the studio, their contemporaneous employment at the chancery offered ample opportunity for the sharing of ideas.

Epicurean atomism exercised a special influence on Machiavelli's thought. He made his own copy of *De rerum natura*, probably prior to 1500, in which he annotated only those sections of the text addressing the functioning of an atomistic universe. These notes focus on Book Two and, principally, on the technical explanations of Epicurean physics that the poem supplied to describe the world as functioning without divine governance, so leaving space for free will. Machiavelli made a specific annotation at the discussion of the swerve (*clinamen*), by which Lucretius postulated a minimal degree of randomness in the movement of atoms to prevent nature operating as an automaton. Here the Florentine bureaucrat wrote: "that motion is variable, and from this we have free will."[49]

Belief that random variability existed in the universe, which both enabled and necessitated the exercise of free will by humanity, became a constant thread in Machiavelli's thinking about the passage of time. It

---

[47] Ibid., 140. On the battle of Fornovo, 6 July 1495, see Mallett and Shaw, *The Italian Wars*, 28–31.

[48] Niccolò Machiavelli, *Opere*, ed. Franco Gaeta (Turin: Unione Tipografico-Editrice Torinese, 1984; reprint, 2000), 478–80, 484–85: letter 242: Francesco Vettori, in Rome, to Machiavelli, in Florence, 15 December 1514; and letter 244: Machiavelli, in Florence, to Francesco Vettori, in Rome, 20 December 1514.

[49] Brown, "Philosophy and Religion"; Palmer, *Reading Lucretius in the Renaissance*, 81–88; Brown, *Return of Lucretius*. The translation is Palmer's. Palmer notes that Machiavelli's focus on atomism is almost unique in extant manuscripts of *De rerum natura*. The only other example is MS Laurenziana 35-32, which both Palmer and Brown identify as having been annotated by a student of Adriani.

provided a unifying concept that drew together his otherwise contrasting, even contradictory, exhortations to boldness and more fatalistic pronouncements. Both of these themes resolved themselves in the Lucretian emphasis on adaptability and mental flexibility.[50] Machiavelli first articulated these ideas in a letter to Giovanbattista Soderini, written at Perugia in the autumn of 1506. As Florentine legate to Pope Julius II, during his campaign to reassert authority over the papal states, Machiavelli witnessed the pontiff's precipitous actions firsthand, prompting the Florentine to speculate on human deeds and intentions.

The letter, known now as the *ghiribizzi* (fancies), addressed the problem of how the same action could have different outcomes and, conversely, how different acts could lead to the same end. After a brief reflection on Hannibal and Scipio, Machiavelli observed that Julius's impetuosity seemed to have brought him greater rewards than careful planning did for others. Machiavelli continued that the evidence of history showed many other examples in which kingdoms were won or lost more by chance than intention. From this he drew the obvious conclusion that the same action can lead to different outcomes at different times, as a result of which people "do not find fault with any one thing in particular, but blame heaven or the disposition of the fates." The problem he suggested is that different men possess "different skills and different imaginations" and that in order to be happy a man needs to "adapt his means of proceeding according to the time." However, Machiavelli concluded, very few people accommodate themselves with the spirit of their times and therefore *fortuna* reigns supreme in human affairs. A wise man, he stated, would recognize the constant variability of events and would accommodate himself to "the times and the order of things … But, because such wise men do not exist, humans being shortsighted and unable to control their nature, it follows that Fortuna changes and rules humanity, holding them under her yoke."[51] Because the future remains unknowable, due to the variability of human existence, Machiavelli reasoned that humanity needs to remain adaptable. However, he suggested that the majority of people are too myopic to plan for future contingencies and so are defeated by unexpected and unanticipated turns of events.

Similar themes appear in the tercet rhyme poem *De fortuna*, which Machiavelli probably penned around the same time and which he also dedicated to Soderini. The verse expressed the emergent, new moral

---

[50] On Lucretius as the "missing link" in Machaivelli's thought, see Brown, "Philosophy and Religion."

[51] Machiavelli, *Opere*, 242–44.

allegory of *fortuna*: the need to act decisively, yet prudently, in order to seize opportunities before they were lost. In the *capitolo* Machiavelli depicted Fortuna as amoral, capricious, and cruel. In particular, he emphasized her inconstancy and arbitrariness as well as her tendency to reward the unworthy. However, Machiavelli also acknowledged human potential to resist. He articulated this idea in the vivid image of a man nimbly ascending from wheel to wheel in Fortuna's palace. If one could understand Fortuna's inconstancy, "he would be always happy and blessed / who could rise from wheel to wheel," leaping from the point of ascendancy on one to the next. Machiavelli noted that daring and youth will succeed against the variability of human life more often than hesitancy and caution, observing that the successes of men such as Alexander the Great and Julius Caesar demonstrate that "one sees clearly how pleasing to her is / one who strikes her, who shoves her and who pushes her around."[52] Here Machiavelli first articulates an image that he would infamously restate in *The Prince* and which, as considered in Chapter 7, also became a prominent theme in the iconography of *fortuna* in the sixteenth century: a gendered vision of forceful, masculine assertiveness in the face of the inconstancy of human existence and the unknowability of the future.[53]

The inconstancy and variability of human affairs became an underlining idea in all Machiavelli's historical and political writings. Throughout his works he deployed the figure of *fortuna* to invoke and to express this theme vividly and efficiently. In *The Prince*, the figure usually appears in conjunction with a caution about the need to be prepared for instability in life. In chapter 14, for example, Machiavelli wrote that "a wise prince" will labor during times of peace to prepare for adversity "so that, when she changes, Fortuna finds him ready to resist her." Later, in chapter 24, he condemned the rulers of Italy in the years prior to 1494 "for never having thought in those quiet times that they could change, which is the common defect of men."[54]

The inevitability of change in human affairs also underlay the *Istorie fiorentine* (*Florentine Histories*). Here, however, Machiavelli at times used what seems like archaic imagery, such as when he described the arrest

---

[52] Niccolò Machiavelli, *Scritti in poesia e in prosa*, ed. A. Corsaro et al. (Rome: Salerno, 2012), 75–90. The quoted text is at pp. 84 and 87, respectively.
[53] While, as a rule, I have identified texts by their original Italian or Latin titles, I prefer to use *The Prince* because the work is so well known by this title that to refer to it by its original title *De principatibus* (*On Principalities*) seems both needlessly pedantic and potentially confusing. As noted in Chapter 7, historians need to take care not to conflate allegorical figures and images with social practices.
[54] Niccoló Machiavelli, *Il principe*, ed. Mario Martelli (Rome: Salerno, 2006), 215, 299.

and execution of Piero degli Albizzi in 1379, for conspiring against the *ciompi* regime: "Fortuna having conducted him to the summit of that [wheel] it was impossible that, if she continued turning it, he would not be dragged to the bottom." Or the comparable description of the execution of Jacopo de' Pazzi and the degradation of his corpse, following the failure of his conspiracy against the Medici in 1478: "Truly the greatest example of *fortuna*, to see a man of such wealth and the happiest estate fall into such misery, with such ruin and such vituperation!"[55]

In *The Prince* and later works, Machiavelli began to use the concept of *virtù* (the Italian cognate of *virtus*), usually in combination with prudence, to identify those qualities required for success in the face of the unknowability of the future. In so doing, he revived the contrariety between *fortuna* and *virtus* that had its origins in Roman literature and had also appeared in the writings of earlier humanists such as Petrarch and Bracciolini. Chapter 7 of *The Prince* presents, perhaps, the clearest articulation of this contrariety. Here Machiavelli discussed the rise to power of private individuals, comparing the contrasting fates of Cesare Borgia and Francesco Sforza.[56] The former is the archetype of the failed prince in Machiavelli's analysis: one who soars easily to the summit of power but then encounters great difficulties holding "that which Fortuna has placed in their lap." Borgia, he observed, "acquired the state with the *fortuna* of his father and he lost it with the same." By contrast, Francesco Sforza, who became duke of Milan "with a thousand labors," then held the state "with little effort" because his rule depended not on the caprice of *fortuna* but on his own *virtus* and fortitude.[57] Similarly, in the *Discorsi sopra la prima deca di Tito Livio* (*Discourses on the First Decade of Livy*), Machiavelli contrasted the strength of the Roman republic with the vulnerabilities of the contemporary regimes in Florence and Venice. Because of the difference between ancient and modern republics, Machiavelli observed, "One sees ... miraculous losses and miraculous acquisitions every day. Because where men have little *virtù*, Fortuna freely demonstrates her power and because she is variable, republics and states vary often."[58]

[55] Niccolò Machiavelli, *Opere storiche*, ed. Alessandro Montevecchi and Carlo Varotti, 2 vols. (Rome: Salerno, 2010), 1: 3.19, 347; and 2: 8.9, 718.
[56] On the centrality of this chapter to the themes of *The Prince*, see John M. Najemy, "Machiavelli and Cesare Borgia: A Reconsideration of Chapter 7 of *The Prince*," *The Review of Politics* 75 (2013).
[57] Machiavelli, *Il principe*, 126–27.
[58] Niccolò Machiavelli, *Discorsi sopra la prima deca di Tito Livio*, ed. Francesco Bausi (Rome: Salerno, 2001), book 2, chapter 30, 508–9.

For Machiavelli, *virtù* expressed an ability to prepare for the future and to have the will to act when the opportune moment required. With readiness and forethought, with sufficient prudence, courage, and fortitude, humanity could thrive in the face of the unexpected and the unknowability of the future. "Fortuna," he stated in the oft-quoted opening to chapter 25 of *The Prince*, "is the arbiter of half of our actions, but even she leaves the governing of the other half, or thereabouts, to us." Echoing Pontano and Rucellai, Machiavelli continued by evoking the metaphor of *fortuna* as a destructive river in flood and so emphasized the necessity to make appropriate plans and preparations during times of peace and quiet, just as embankments and dikes can be used to divert and control such a torrent. Because, he wrote, Fortuna "demonstrates her potency where *virtù* is not organized to resist her."[59]

In Machiavelli's thought, therefore, *fortuna* and *virtus* are not simply antithetical forces in human life. Rather, a central thread throughout his political and historical works is the necessity for a combination of both *fortuna* and *virtus* – luck and skill – for success in an inconstant and variable world. This is one of the key arguments of *The Prince*, a theme that threads through several chapters as the identifying attribute of successful princes. Specifically, such rulers succeed because they recognize and seize the opportunities offered by Fortuna. Concerning Moses, Cyrus, Theseus, and Romulus – historical examples of private citizens who founded new principalities – Machiavelli wrote: "one sees only that they had nothing from Fortuna except opportunity … without that opportunity the *virtù* of their spirit would have been spent, and without that *virtù* the opportunity would have arrived in vain."[60]

In the *Discorsi* he makes a similar claim with regard to the Roman republic. The Romans were able to surpass even the achievements of Philip of Macedon and his son, Alexander the Great, because the non-hereditary office of the consuls permitted the continual election of "the most excellent men" to government, "from whom, Rome enjoying both *fortuna* and *virtù*, could rise, within time, to that her ultimate greatness."[61] This emphasis on opportunity echoed Machiavelli's observation in the poem dedicated to Giovanbattista Soderini that daring and youth could succeed more frequently than cautious prudence, as well as the gendered image of *fortuna* as requiring masculine control. Such

---

[59] Machiavelli, *Il principe*, 302–3. See Rucellai, *De bello italico*, 68: "altissima quaeque flumina parva primo aggeris strue contineri alveo, qua dilapsa quantamvis postea molem obiectam facile exuperare."
[60] Machiavelli, *Il principe*, 115.   [61] Machiavelli, *Discorsi*, book 1, chapter 20, 123.

sentiment received its most memorable appearance in chapter 25 of *The Prince*, where Machiavelli argues that "it is better to be impulsive than cautious, because Fortuna is a woman and it is necessary, wishing to keep her down, to beat her and strike her."[62]

Significantly, *fortuna* expressed no prompt toward eternity in Machiavelli's works. Instead, it suggested forward-looking action in this life. He deployed the allegorical force of the figure to emphasize the necessity of seizing opportunities and planning for the unexpected future, rather than to remind humanity of the vanity of worldly possessions and the promise of eternal rewards. Time, for Machiavelli, was not the eternal present but a series of moments measured by human metrics of intent and action, of success and failure.

A clear affinity exists between this moral allegory of *fortuna* and the iconography of the *fortuna–kairos* hybrid, whose forelock offered opportunity to those quick and perceptive enough to seize it as she sped past. Both this visual figure and Machiavelli's language of opportunity (*occasione*) also shared an intellectual habitat – as well as a lexicon – with the merchants, whose correspondence I analyzed in Chapter 4. Successfully navigating the passage of time required awareness of inconstancy in the course of events, as well as the mental flexibility to change with it, just as commercial success necessitated constant calculation of changing variables and adaptability to markets and conditions. A good prince, Machiavelli wrote in chapter 18 of *The Prince*, needs to possess "a spirit disposed to turn itself according to that which the winds of *fortuna* and the variation of affairs command"[63] – a metaphor that calls to mind the prominent sail of the *fortuna–kairos* iconography, further highlighting the interaction between the visual and textual in the articulation of new ideas about the future.

Machiavelli's thought about the ability of humanity to seize the opportunities offered by *fortuna* varied and shifted throughout his oeuvre, although several key themes recur consistently. His thinking in *The Prince* remains fairly simple and straightforward. The structure and purpose of the text naturally shaped his discussion, emphasizing the need for a sufficiently prudent, skilled, and decisive ruler to take advantage of the passage of time and the unknowability of the future. By contrast, in the *Istorie fiorentine*, his most mature reflection on politics, history, and human affairs, Machiavelli appears far less sanguine about the possibility of human actors recognizing opportunities, or even adapting to the variability of existence. More often than leading to success, the narrative

---

[62] Ibid., 310.   [63] Machiavelli, *Il principe*, 240–41.

reveals the passage of time making fools of its protagonists, who stumble unworthily into rewards that they then easily lose.

The more pessimistic tone of Machiavelli's last major work resembles the outlook that pervades the writing of his younger friend, Francesco Guicciardini. Born into a politically prominent branch of an old patrician family in Florence, Guicciardini pursued a political career in the service of the Medici popes – Leo X and Clement VII – and played a leading role in the reorganization of the Florentine government in the 1530s, which transformed the city from a republic into an hereditary principality. Marginalized from influence and governance by the second Medici duke, Cosimo I, Guicciardini retired from public life to compose his magnum opus, the *Storia d'Italia* (*History of Italy*), which he left incomplete at his death on 22 May 1540. Guicciardini had begun the practice of composing political and historical works, as well as more personal reflective texts, in his twenties. Throughout his life, whenever he enjoyed (or endured) a lull in his career, he had turned to writing.

Guicciardini had attended the lectures of Marcello Adriani, and Epicurean ideas clearly influenced the perception and discussion of the passage of time in his later writings. In particular, a prominent theme that threads through his work was the need for individuals to prepare for the inevitable variability and instability of human existence. Indeed, in fitting with its pessimistic and dour tone, a sense pervades Guicciardini's thought that being prepared is the best that humanity can hope for, because it will inevitability fall victim to the course of events. The future had real form and existence for Guicciardini, as unknown time-yet-to-come that was measurable by human ambition and, especially, by human failing. If contemporary authors and artists increasingly used the figure of *fortuna* as an allegory for opportunity seized or lost, Guicciardini concluded that humanity would regularly and frequently fail to recognize the opportune moment. This stood in stark contrast to the assertions by Machiavelli and Rucellai that actors could, sometimes, seize *fortuna* by the forelock, and succeed in their endeavors. The moral allegorical force of *fortuna* in Guicciardini's use of the figure lay heavily on the hubris of humanity in thinking it could control its own destiny in the face of the unpredictability of events.

In the *Storia d'Italia*, Guicciardini attempted to write a new kind of history, one that rejected the still-predominant humanist tradition, which saw the past as a source of moral exemplars and guides for behavior.[64]

[64] Felix Gilbert, *Machiavelli and Guicciardini: Politics and History in Sixteenth-Century Florence* (New York: Norton, 1984), 236–301. See also Albertini, *Firenze dalla repubblica*, 240–44.

Instead, he wrote a form of future-oriented history: history as evidence of the need to prepare for the unknown time-yet-to-come. The only real lesson that could be drawn from the past, according to the *Storia d'Italia*, was the ultimate futility of human attempts to control events. Guicciardini took as his object history on a European scale, focusing not on a single city-state (as his humanist predecessors, and even his own earlier historical works, had done) but on the entire Italian peninsula. He sought to understand the causes of the Italian Wars, beginning with the expedition of Charles VIII of France in 1494, pursuing rational accounts and highly individualized studies of the motivations of the principal actors in events. Where rational explanation failed, Guicciardini turned to the figure of *fortuna*, in order to express the frustration and futility of most human plans in the face of the passage of time and the variability of events.

Guicciardini articulated his vision of the past, and the driving force of his historical narrative, in the opening chapter of the *Storia*. Invoking the memory of the chaos that had engulfed Italy since 1494, he asserted that "from innumerable examples will appear most clearly how much human affairs are subjected to instability, no less than a sea agitated by the wind." He continued, taking aim at the cupidity, vanity, and foolishness of Italian rulers, "who, failing to recall the constant variation of *fortuna*, and using the power given them for the common good to the harm of others, made themselves the authors of new perturbations, either through too little prudence or through too much ambition."[65] This image conveys no sense of the relentless wheel of *fortuna*, no sense of the Boethian moral allegory that worldly goods have no real value because they would be lost. The dizzying collapse of the Italian city-state system and the fall of so many Italian rulers was not inevitable, in Guicciardini's sense of time, history, and *fortuna*. Rather, these governments had doomed themselves through an unwillingness to prepare for the unknowability of the future. Lacking the foresight to make provisions for unexpected changes to come, they failed to account for contingencies and the unintended outcomes of any plans they made. The governors of Italy, prior to the descent of Charles VIII, willfully ignored the instability of human existence and the likelihood that the future would not accord with their hopes and intentions. The imprint of Lucretius's injunction that humanity be flexible and adaptable, so prominent in Machiavelli's writing, lay on that of Guicciardini too.[66]

---

[65] Francesco Guicciardini, *Storia d'Italia*, ed. Silvana Seidel Menchi (Turin: Einaudi, 1971), 1.1: 5.

[66] Although it does not address the Lucretian elements, the comparative analysis of the use of *fortuna* by Machiavelli and Guicciardini in Jean-Louis Fournel and Jean-Claude

In the final iteration of his *ricordi* – a collection of autobiographical fragments, aphoristic observations, and personal reflections – compiled around 1530, Guicciardini expressed a similar vision of instability as the only certainty in human life. In *ricordo* number 30, he observed: "Whoever considers clearly, cannot deny that in human affairs *fortuna* has the greatest power, because at every moment one sees they receive the greatest impetus from fortuitous accidents." The unknown and unknowable future – "fortuitous accidents" – was a principal driver of human experiences. In line with the function of these short observations – to provide guidance for his heirs and descendants – Guicciardini continued by providing some more practical advice. "Although human acuity and promptness can moderate many things," he wrote, "nevertheless, alone they do not suffice, for they also need good *fortuna*." Prudence and foresight, he observed, were insufficient to deal with time-yet-to-come; one also needed luck. In the following *ricordo*, number 31, he further observed that those who attribute success to *virtus* and prudence rather than *fortuna* can do so only because they had the good fortune to be born into a time which required their particular qualities.[67]

Machiavelli's great theme – the necessity of both skill and luck for human success – echoes here, as does the Lucretian emphasis on the need for mental flexibility. Like Machiavelli in the *ghiribizzi*, Guicciardini implied that most people lack this adaptability and so succeed only through a serendipitous conjunction of their particular talents with the needs of the time. He would return to this theme several times in the *Storia d'Italia* too. It received its most voluble manifestation in his characterization of Ferdinand of Aragon: "To the rare *virtù* of this king, the rarest, perpetual happiness attached itself." The monarch, Guicciardini continued, was "always superior and almost the dominator of all his enemies. And where *fortuna* appeared manifestly joined to industry, he covered all his cupidity under the guise of honest religious zeal and saintly pursuit of the common good."[68] The Florentine implied that Ferdinand owed his success to hard work and luck: the perfect conjunction of his ambitions with the instability of the early sixteenth century.

Zancarini, *La grammaire de la république: Lagages de la politique chez Francesco Guicciardini (1483–1540)* (Geneva: Librarie Droz, 2009), 447–68, examines the contrasts and similarities in their ideas.

[67] Francesco Guicciardini, *Ricordi: Edizione critica*, ed. Raffaele Spongano (Florence: Sansoni, 1951), 35–36.

[68] Guicciardini, *Storia d'Italia*, 12.9, 1267. See also pp. 362 (4.4), 578 (6.7), 749 (8.4), 1194 (12.6), 1429–30 (14.7), and 1511 (15.3).

For Guicciardini the future existed on a human rather than an eternal scale. Time-yet-to-come was unknown and unknowable because the unexpected and the unintended permeated human experiences. Life was unpredictable and endlessly unstable. The explanation for the calamities that had befallen the Italian city-states since 1494, according to the *Storia d'Italia*, was neither divine will nor the relentless turning of *fortuna*'s wheel, but rather the harm that humanity does to itself by failing to consider the constant variability of existence. Guicciardini suggested that the figure of *fortuna* provided a convenient cover for explaining the fallibility and foolishness of historical actors who had not considered the instability that accompanied the passage of time. Although he did not use the figure of *fortuna* in discussing the age of encounters, he similarly noted that the Portuguese circumnavigation of Africa and the Spanish crossing of the Atlantic had revealed that "the ancients deluded themselves in many things regarding knowledge of the world." Time's passing had made manifest their mistakes and, he added, provoked anxiety among theologians by casting doubt on the certainty of their interpretations of Scripture.[69]

Describing the advance of Charles VIII's army over the Apennines and into Florentine territory, Guicciardini observed that the fortifications of Serezanello should have provided a formidable obstacle, but that "either for the grace of *fortuna* or through the ordination of a higher power (if however the imprudence and faults of men merit these excuses), an immediate remedy to such an impediment unexpectedly arrived" in the person of Piero de' Medici, who rapidly surrendered not only this but all Florentine fortresses to the French monarch.[70] Elsewhere the text stressed that the defeats and frustrations ascribed to *fortuna* by observers can as easily be blamed on the poor judgment of human actors. For example, summing up the career of the *condottiere* Bartolomeo d'Alviano (whose impetuosity provoked the crushing Venetian defeat at Agnadello in 1509), Guicciardini observed that while courageous and decisive, "many times, due either to his ill *fortuna* or, as many have said, to being hasty in his counsel, he was overcome by his enemies."[71] While never explicitly stating that *fortuna* served as little more than a cipher for the inexplicable outcomes of human affairs – as Laura Cereta and Bartolomeo Scala had done – the Florentine historian envisaged and understood the future on a very human scale.

---

[69] Ibid., 6.9, 603.   [70] Ibid., 1.14, 96.
[71] Ibid., 12.19, 1267. See also pages 155–56 (2.3), 193 (2.9), 570 (6.6), 1271 (12.20), 1423 (14.6), and 1476 (14.14).

The emerging conception of the future as the unknown time-yet-to-come did not crystallize only in Florence, and only as a result of the influence of Epicurus and Pontano. An image of time on a human scale, distinct from the demands of eternity, appeared in the thought of writers far removed from the intellectual circles of the Tuscan city. While developments there appeared to follow a fairly clear trajectory of influence, from the local Lucretians (Scala and Adriani), on the one hand, and Pontano, on the other, they followed a more tangled path elsewhere in Italy. In works produced by the northern Italian authors considered here, Luigi da Porto, Girolamo Rorario, and Antonio Fregoso, the emphasis on opportunity and the instability of human existence appears far less pronounced that it does in the writing of Rucellai, Machiavelli, and Guicciardini. The northern Italian writers did not share in the rich mélange of Lucretius and Pontano. They did, however, have common experiences in the chaos of the Italian Wars and shock of the New World. Like Rucellai, Machiavelli, and Guicciardini, Da Porto, Rorario, and Fregoso were participant observers in the disruption unleashed by the French expedition to Naples in 1494. As with their Tuscan counterparts, the sense of living through a period of sudden and extreme dislocation to accepted norms and understandings shaped the way they thought about the passage of time and used the figure of *fortuna*.

These authors, while conceiving of the future as time-yet-to-come measurable by human actions and understandings, still continued to interweave more moralized and soteriological conceptions into their works. Their visions of the future were complex and multifaceted, blending ideas that appear uneasy bedfellows to twenty-first-century eyes. Like the paintings by Porta, Veronese, and Allori and the mercantile correspondence examined in earlier chapters, their work complicates the historical picture of apparent linear progression toward a more modern and secular temporality suggested in the preceding analysis of the Florentine authors. They testify to the ways that the new conception of future coexisted with older temporalities throughout the sixteenth century. They also demonstrate how these ideas cohered in texts other than histories, which axiomatically require a sense of temporality

Unlike Machiavelli and Guicciardini, the Vicentine nobleman and *litterato*, Luigi da Porto experienced and wrote about the Italian Wars from a military rather than a political perspective. As a Venetian loyalist, he enrolled as a commander in the republic's light cavalry in 1509, just prior to Venice's catastrophic defeat by the French at Agnadello. His battlefield experiences most famously provided the backdrop to the novella *Giulietta e Romeo*. Da Porto presented the story of the ill-fated lovers as having been told to him by a Veronese soldier under his command to pass the time on the road from Gradisca to Udine. More prosaically, Da Porto left a firsthand account of the war of the League of Cambrai in a series of letters written to a variety of recipients, including his maternal uncle, the influential Friulian nobleman Antonio Savorgnan, and his literary mentor, Pietro Bembo. They later appeared in print as the *Lettere storiche*.

The passage of time in Da Porto's letters bears a closer resemblance to the cyclical imaging of earlier authors such as Petrarch than to the compartmentalized vision of Machiavelli. A sense of inevitability and fatalism pervades the text. While the precise details of future events remain obscure, Da Porto invoked an image of certainty in their eventual arrival.[72] When he spoke of the future and the passage of time, using the figure of *fortuna* and the language of Providence, the relentlessly turning wheel of the medieval imagination underlay his vision. Worldly affairs, he wrote in an early letter dated 24 April 1509, are "placed under *fortuna*'s revolving, so that they continually leap from peace to war, and from war to peace." A little later, he observed, "heaven directs our affairs, as is usual, according to necessity, so that their implosion is close at hand."[73] On 10 July, recounting an unsuccessful Venetian attempt to suborn the imperial commander holding Padua into surrendering the city, Da Porto struck a more pessimistic note: "Certainly human counsel is worth nothing against the disposition of the heavens and the strange manner with which *fortuna* toys with us at times."[74] Three years later, in a letter dated 12 February 1512, he would muse on the shifting currents of the war, which saw imperial forces withdraw from Venetian territory and Venice join Julius II's Holy League: "But certainly this is a great revolution, which *fortuna* presently holds in our lands; because no sooner was the one army dissolved in one part, than the other in another part reformed greater, as at the present we see occurring."[75]

However, within this restless image, which emphasizes the inevitability of future events even if they remain obscure to humanity, elements that seem more in keeping with the contemporary shift toward a human conception of time emerged. Da Porto's allegorical use of *fortuna* was not directed toward the same moral ends as the Boethian tradition; rather, it adhered more clearly to the sense that pervades the work of Machiavelli and Guicciardini: humanity's freedom to act within the

---

[72] On the pervading fatalism of Da Porto's letters and the cyclical vision of history that they present, see also Achille Olivieri, "'Dio' e 'fortuna' nelle *Lettere storiche* di Luigi da Porto," *Studi veneziani* 13 (1971).
[73] Luigi Da Porto, *Lettere storiche*, ed. Bartolomeo Bressan (Florence: Felice le Monnier, 1857), 46–47.
[74] Ibid., 87.   [75] Ibid., 250.

course of events. Although he did not privilege opportunity as his Florentine contemporaries did, Da Porto implied that humanity needed to prepare for the future and to seize upon any occasion that presented itself. In the letter of 24 April 1509, in which he imagined the passage of time as the relentless turning of *fortuna*'s wheel from peace to war and back again, the Vicentine nobleman also suggested that Venice and its dominions had failed to prepare for this inevitable shift. "The long quietude, the long tranquility, the long peace," which the Veneto had enjoyed for many years, he wrote, left it attenuated and unable to cope with the travails of warfare. A month later, he recorded the fulfillment of his own prognostication. Lamenting the swift loss of Brescia, Cremona, and Bergamo to the advancing French, he observed that no provision had been made for adversity, and the Venetian government, in the form of magistrates and office-holders, appeared "fearful and lost." Many Venetian noblemen, Da Porto wrote, seemed to have already resigned themselves to surrendering the republic's Italian territories.[76] Even without the direct influence of Epicurus, a shared set of assumptions about instability and the need for foresight and prudence cohered across the culture of early sixteenth-century Italy. In the wake of the violent dislocation caused by the Italian Wars, these ideas began to adhere to the figure of *fortuna*.

Da Porto's understanding of the passage of time, in both his fictive and factual works, reveals the complexity of sixteenth-century conceptions of the future and the multiplicity of ideas that could operate at any given moment. He clearly identified, underlying all human affairs, the inexorable movement of time toward preordained fates, embodied in the *Lettere storiche* by *fortuna* and the force of the heavens. Da Porto's thought is not always clear on whether the latter indicates the working of Providence or of the stars. However, his interest in this momentum, which swept humanity along, directed not toward eternity and the end of time, but rather toward a concern on a purely human scale: the passage from peace to war and back again. This mundane and comprehensible scale left open a space for human action and free will.

While William Shakespeare would famously identify Da Porto's unhappy lovers as "star-crossed," the Vicentine nobleman's original telling of the tale of Romeo and Juliet has less of a sense of inevitability about it. Rather than resulting from the work of the stars, the course of events in *Giulietta e Romeo* unfolds under the impetus of human error, misunderstandings, and missed opportunities. The denouement of the

---

[76] Ibid., 46, 63.

tale unfolds with language redolent with bad luck and misfortune. "O my unfortunate [*sventurata*] life," Romeo exclaims when confronted with what he thinks is the corpse of his beloved. Then as he lies dying and Giulietta reveals the truth of her faked death to him, he laments, "my most miserable luck, o unfortunate [*sfortunato*] Romeo."[77]

Recounting the aftermath of a failed Venetian attempt to retake Brescia from French control by stealth, Da Porto described how one of the conspirators, the aptly named Ventura Fenaruolo, had taken refuge in a Carmelite monastery. Fenaruolo, Da Porto informed his correspondent, declared that he would rather take his own life than surrender to the French. The monks, naturally, forbade him to do so and enjoined him that: "Because man must be subject to death, he was required to wait until either nature or *fortuna* sent him there." Man, Da Porto has the monks observe, had received "the greatest gift of free will, so that he would in his freedom be able to ascend, through good works, to those above, the sort of the angels; but also fall to the level of the beasts, those below, through sin and vices."[78]

While the Epicurean-influenced Florentines emphasized the need to seize opportunities and prepare for the future because human life was unstable and time-yet-to-come was unknowable, Da Porto suggested that humanity needed to prepare for the unknown future because change was inevitable. The Vicentine recognized a space for human action and intention in shaping future outcomes, albeit within a larger framework of the predetermined unfolding of time, a nesting of temporalities similar to that expressed by Cereta and Scala in the late fifteenth century.

A similar complexity appears in the work of Girolamo Rorario, a nobleman from Pordenone who experienced the war of the League of Cambrai from the opposite side to Da Porto. As his family had been loyal vassals to the Habsburgs, Rorario – together with his brother Antonio and several other prominent nobles – went into exile in Vienna following the Venetian annexation of their hometown in 1508. While at the imperial court or in diplomatic service for the emperors Maximilian I and Charles V, from 1516 to 1522, he wrote a series of dialogues that rejected traditional courtly motifs in favor of a more satirical and polemical tone, modeled on Lucian and possibly the writings of Leon Battista Alberti.[79]

[77] Luigi Da Porto, *Giulietta e Romeo*, ed. Alessandro Torri (Pisa Fratelli Nistri, 1831), 39–40.
[78] Porto, *Lettere storiche*, 261.
[79] Aidée Scala, *Girolamo Rorario: Un umanista diplomatico del Cinquecento e i suoi Dialoghi* (Florence: Olschki, 2004), esp. 43–53.

Following the election of Pope Leo X in 1513, Rorario composed a pair of dialogues dedicated to, and in praise of, the new pontiff, whom he saw as the hope for peace in Italy. The first, *Medices sive Virtus* (*Medici or Virtus*) dwells on the problem of recognizing *virtus* in the turbulence and violence of contemporary Italy. It features Mercury traveling to recall Virtus, who has been hiding in the underworld, to human affairs now that Julius II is dead and Leo sits on the throne of Saint Peter.[80] In the second, and companion, piece, *Fortuna*, the eponymous subject laments her own misfortune now that Virtus is ascendant and triumphant in Rome. On one level, the dialogue presents the Boethian moral allegory of *fortuna*, albeit with a satirical twist. As the relentlessly unstable source of worldly goods, Fortuna mocks those who dedicate themselves solely to Virtus and so live in poverty and misery. She boasts: "How many ignoble men, how many useless and ignorant men have I embraced, who then have attained the name of noble, excellent, and wise!" Rorario shared the concern expressed by both Pontano and Machiavelli that *fortuna* favored the unworthy. A little later in the dialogue, Fortuna in fact laments that due to Virtus's ascendancy only the deserving have triumphed recently: "Did the king of gods and men in vain place me in command of human affairs, so that I revolve and change them according to my pleasure?"[81] In this sense, Rorario implied that the worldly goods associated with Fortuna were unstable and so less valuable than they might superficially appear. Further on he makes the point explicit, having Fortuna declare: "I make blind and insane those whom I embrace."[82]

On another level, however, the dialogue conforms to the increasingly human conception of time detectable in the sixteenth-century Florentine authors. Like Da Porto, Rorario gave no sense that the moral allegorical force of *fortuna* directs humanity toward eternity and a concern for salvation. Indeed, like Pontano he implied that the worldly goods associated with *fortuna* are a significant part of human happiness and, like Machiavelli, that both *virtus* and *fortuna* are necessary for true felicity and enduring success. The crux of Fortuna's lament, from the very beginning of the dialogue, is that Virtus threatens the natural order and the passage of time by isolating herself and attempting to govern human affairs in Italy on her own: "she will destroy the chain of events, sweep away the order of the fates, break the laws of nature."[83] Human affairs,

---

[80] Girolamo Rorario, *Le opere*, ed. Aidée Scala (Pordenone: Associazione Pordenone/ Accademia San Marco, 2004), 112–21; Scala, *Girolamo Rorario*, 59–63. The cast of protagonists in this dialogue recalls that of Alberti's fifteenth-century dialogue "Virtus": Leon Battista Alberti, *Dinner Pieces: A Translation of the Intercenales*, trans. David Marsh (Binghamton, NY: Center for Medieval and Early Renaissance Studies, 1987), 21–22.
[81] Rorario, *Le opere*, 123.   [82] Ibid., 124–25.   [83] Ibid., 123.

Rorario has Fortuna declaim, are constantly in flux and unstable. The only predictability in this vision is that everything should and will eventually change with the passing of time.

Recognition of the inevitable mutability of human existence led Rorario, like the Florentine authors discussed earlier, to emphasize the necessity of realizing every opportunity. When her handmaiden Adulation suggests that Fortuna take refuge in the "Adriatic swamp" (i.e., Venice), which is beyond the reach of Virtus, Fortuna responds with disgust. She dismisses the Venetians with contempt, noting that whenever she has previously dealt favorably with them, through hesitancy and indecision "they let slip the most beautiful opportunities." Fortuna continues, asserting that she never aids the cowardly but only the bold, "those who strike or flee according to the occasion ... who bear adversities with a steadfast soul, and scorn greatness with the same spirit."[84]

This statement captures the complexity of Rorario's thought about the passage of time in microcosm. On the one hand, Fortuna adjures stoic endurance and the type of suspicion of prosperity that had colored the Boethian moral allegory, which suggested that the trials and rewards of mortal life were of little consequence. On the other hand, she also clearly endorses adaptability, mental flexibility, and opportune action. The passage of time was something to be both endured and exploited. In either case it existed on a human scale, comprehensible and graspable. Rorario's dialogue largely skirted the question of the nature of the future, but his complex vision of the passage of time suggests that he saw time-yet-to-come both as unknown and open to human action as well as relentless in its sweep.

This complexity of vision, the holding of two apparently contradictory conceptions of time, appeared also in Antonio Fregoso's *Dialogo de fortuna*. As discussed at the beginning of Chapter 7, the second edition of the dialogue featured the hybrid *fortuna–kairos* on the frontispiece, a fitting acknowledgment of the complex image of the figure developed in the text. The illegitimate son of the lord of Carrara, Fregoso became a courtier in Milan, frequenting the cultural circles cultivated by Cecilia Gallerani, the famed mistress of Duke Ludovico Sforza. Fregoso survived the transition to French rule in 1499 but retired from court life to his villa at Colturano, to pursue a literary career. He initially explored the state of human existence in the paired *terza rima* poems: *Il riso di Democrito* (*The Laughter of Democritus*) and *Il pianto di Heraclito* (*The Tears of Heraclitus*), written between 1505 and 1507. In these verses, he

---

[84] Ibid., 124–25.

adopted the classical juxtaposition of Democritus's and Heraclitus's responses to the human condition in order to lament the foolishness and miserableness of life.[85] Fregoso contended that these conditions were the result of humanity's attachment to worldly goods instead of eternal rewards, the familiar refrain attached to the Boethian moral allegory of *fortuna*. When he turned to consider the concept directly and at length in the *Dialogo de fortuna*, however, the Genoese courtier moved beyond this tradition. The dialogue, written in verse, follows a Dantesque model with the author appearing as the protagonist of a metaphysical journey that reveals the true nature of *fortuna* through eighteen chapters.

The dialogue opens with Fregoso (as protagonist) entering a pleasant garden on a summer day and meeting two friends, Curzio Lancino and Bartolomeo Simonetta, on a lawn by a fountain. At Lancino's prompting, Fregoso begins, reluctantly, to discourse on the subject of *fortuna*. He laments his own personal history, stating that Fortuna has made "a game" of his life since birth and that he is scarred all over by her blows.[86] In the opening stanzas Fregoso offered a standard interpretation of Fortuna as all-powerful and capricious. However, he also engaged in a more profound consideration of the relationship between chance and Providence, as well as articulating a conflict between reason and experience in his comprehension of their role in human existence. He struggled to reconcile the apparent dominance of Fortuna – "whoever says Fortuna is omnipotent / has, according to me, sound judgment ... and whoever considers rightly the truth / with experience will find, in effect / every mortal thing under her command" – with belief in divine mercy and human reason. He cannot believe, he says, that God would be so "unjust and variable" as to permit Fortuna's complete dominance. Nor can he credit that humanity cannot use reason to avoid her caprices, despite the evidence of his senses to the contrary: "experience and reason war within me / the one saying that Fortuna rules / the world, all subject to her pronouncements, / the other then saying that to her unjust laws / the wise man cannot be subject."[87] In the opening gambit of the dialogue, then, Fregoso explored the tensions between the two competing visions of the future: as subject to the relentless turning of *fortuna* or as governed by the will of Providence. He also injected an important element of human

---

[85] On the origins and development of the tradition that paired Democritus and Heraclitus, see Cora E. Lutz, "Democritus and Heraclitus," *The Classical Journal* 49, no. 7 (1954). On Fregoso's poems, see Santoro, *Fortuna*, 187–233.

[86] Antonio Fileremo Fregoso, *Opere*, ed. Giorgio Dilemmi (Bologna: Commissione per i Testi di Lingua, 1976), 90.

[87] Ibid., 92–93.

ability into this vision, by suggesting that with foresight and prudence humanity can control its own future. The conversation between the friends is soon interrupted by Truth, who rises naked from the fountain where she had taken shelter from Ignorance. Having overheard their discussion, she offers to teach the three men who Fortuna really is by leading them to her home, so that she might understand why she holds such power over humanity. The description of the journey and its destination follows an easily anticipated trajectory that superficially conforms to the tradition of the moral allegory of Fortuna. The travelers leave the "short and expedient way" followed by others, to take the more arduous path to the "sacred hostel of Virtù [*virtus*]." From there they can see the abode of Fortuna, which a great mass of humanity struggles to reach. The travelers realize that this palace, initially seeming ornate and beautiful, is actually just mud and vapor. They notice also that some of the humans who enter it bear the features of animals and that these are soon cast out again. Truth explains these entered only though Fortuna's favor, rather than by any merit. The animal heads represent their true nature. Truth then observes that while those who are modest may keep their own visage, they are still subject to Fortuna and that only those who follow the path to *virtus*, as Fregoso and his companions did, need not fear her.[88] Although the two descriptions are quite distinct, the image of humanity struggling by several paths to ascend to the palace of Fortuna recalls Christine de Pizan's *Livre de la mutacion de Fortune*, and may have been inspired or modeled on it.[89]

In this description, Fregoso articulated elements of the Boethian moral allegory. The rewards of *fortuna* – the worldly goods of wealth, status, power – appear fleeting and worthless. While the dialogue imagined a mountain instead of a wheel, the inexorable passage of humanity rising and falling (each individual according to their own path) recalls earlier medieval conceptions of time's relentless turning. The future for each individual is obscure, but follows a predetermined course of ascent and inevitable fall. Only those who seek *virtus*, like the protagonists of the dialogue, avoid this outcome.

Fregoso's dialogue strayed from the traditional allegorical imagining of *fortuna*, however, and began to explore the passage of time on a more human scale. This occurs when Truth discusses the true identity of

---

[88] Ibid., 115–21.
[89] Pizan had some connection with Milan and several of her works were sent there in manuscript from France during the fifteenth century: Sarah Gwyneth Ross, *The Birth of Feminism: Woman as Intellect in Renaissance Italy and England* (Cambridge, MA: Harvard University Press, 2009), 326, n. 6.

Fortuna and the nature of the unknown future. While leading the three protagonists on their journey, she explains that Fortuna's father was Human Judgment – "which almost always is foolish and vain" – and her mother was Opinion. This pair, Truth continues, is also the source of all evils in the world, leading humanity to value wealth above all else, which results in "murders, banishments, and war, / which is the evil fortune of realms. / For this cities are thrown down, / and Charity is everywhere extinct, / and Probity dispersed through the world."[90] The depiction adds layers of complexity to this traditional moral allegorical image, however, because in the dialogue, Lancino challenges Truth, suggesting that without a desire for wealth all industry and creativity in the world would cease, while humans "would be like animals / brutish and indolent and lazy ever more, / leading life like irrational beings." Truth concedes the point but responds that too great a desire for wealth is poisonous and deleterious to human happiness. Like wine, she observes, profits must be enjoyed only in moderation. The heart of the problem is the relentless turning of time and the fleeting nature of Fortuna's gifts, which leave humanity ever desirous for more.

A more significant development occurs, when Simonetta objects that Fortuna cannot be the daughter of Opinion and Human Judgment because certain events happen simply by accident (*ventura*). Truth turns to an Aristotelian notion of causality to rebut him. She states that Fortuna is different to chance. The latter "is an accident / which proceeds solely from itself / and not from the stars or the intention of a human mind." Fortuna, however, is "an event / which proceeds from human intention." Here, amid the traditional moral envisioning, irrupts a startlingly clear conception of the unknown future on a human scale. The near time-yet-to-come is "an event" determined solely by human actions and aims. Truth points out that while someone might come upon a precious stone on the road purely by chance, the decision of what value to ascribe to it and so whether to pick it up is a matter of human judgment.[91] Although Fregoso does not use the language of opportunity, the example of the gem immediately suggests the need to recognize and act on opportunities when they occur. Rather like Cereta and Scala in the previous decade, Fregoso suggests that the figure of *fortuna* is, in fact, just a label used to make explicable the unknowability of future outcomes.

[90] Fregoso, *Opere*, 103.
[91] Ibid., 110. On the Aristotelian theory of unexpected events as caused not by chance but by the meeting of two chains of causation, see Jerold C. Frakes, *The Fate of Fortune in the Early Middle Ages: The Boethian Tradition*, ed. Albert Zimmerman (Leiden: Brill, 1988), 25–28.

The French expedition to Naples in 1494 unleashed chaos and dislocation on the Italian city states. The political map of the peninsula
shifted several times as Spanish and imperial ambitions collided with
those of the crown of France. The certainties of the late fifteenth century
collapsed. The wild merry-go-round of war saw dynasties driven out,
then return to power, only to flee into exile once more, while a shifting
kaleidoscope of alliances turned yesterday's allies into today's enemies,
leaving tomorrow's allegiances uncertain. All of this occurred as Italy also
received and attempted to comprehend the increasing tide of revelations
about the New World.

The apparent end of certainty provoked by the Italian Wars and the
age of encounters served as an impetus toward the crystallization of the
figure of *fortuna* into a new concept of the future as unknown time-yet-to-
come. As participant observers in these disruptions, the authors considered in this chapter struggled to make sense of the transformations
occurring around them. In doing so, they transformed the figure of
fortuna into a moral allegory of the need to prepare for the mutability of
existence and to seize opportunities when they arose because human life
was inevitably unstable, a textual analogue to *fortuna–kairos* figure with
her forelock, dynamism, and alluring presence. The reception of certain
Epicurean ideas transmitted via Lucretius – the role of chance in the
world, the ridiculousness of fearing death, in particular – in the same
period shaped the understanding of some of these authors. But with or
without the influence of the Roman poet, the conflagration of Italian
certainties forged the figure of *fortuna* into the service of a new concept of
the future, as unknown, unknowable, yet accessible to those prudent or
fast enough to make most of the chances offered by time's passing.

Beyond the realm of literature, history, and intellectual speculation,
the gamblers, hustlers, and merchants of sixteenth-century Italy recognized this new futurity as something familiar. Authors such as Gerolamo
Cardano, discussed in Chapter 1, saw an opportunity to offer their
expertise in guidance to the perplexed and bewildered. They sought to
explain this new concept of the unknown time-yet-to-come, to accultur-
ate their readers to it. As considered in Chapter 1, these authors carried
their vision much further than any of the authors or artists considered in
these last three chapters. They offered a much starker idea of the future,
one in which outcomes were governed more by chance than by
Providence – an idea that looks much more familiar to twenty-first-
century eyes – a future that began around 1500.

Conclusion
Time and the Renaissance

I have argued through this book that between the mid-fifteenth and mid-sixteenth centuries, a new concept of the future materialized and cohered in Renaissance Italian culture. In contrast to the eschatological vision of Christian theology, the claims of various divinatory techniques, and the everyday, prudential sense of the future with which Europeans had operated for centuries, this new conception held that time-yet-to-come was unknown and unknowable and that the world of tomorrow could potentially be very different to that of yesterday and today.

Central to this development was the transformation of the figure of *fortuna*, a textual and visual allegory about the passing of time that engaged a rich cultural heritage, both Christian and classical. In the fourteenth and early fifteenth centuries, authors and artists identified the figure of *fortuna* as a servant of Providence, an angelic power in the world that worked to educate humanity about the true value of possessions and success. The sudden, unforeseen triumphs or falls – political, social, economic – over which Fortuna presided, imagined in the form of the relentlessly turning wheel of medieval art, had a moral purpose. They reminded mortals of the vanity, fleeting nature, and ultimate worthlessness of worldly goods and status. The allegory of *fortuna* in this form asserted that the only future that mattered was the one promised by the teachings of the Church; it admonished humanity to endure adversity stoically on the promise of eternal rewards.

From around the mid-fifteenth century, the figure of *fortuna* began to undergo a transformation, in both images and texts. By the end of the century, the worldly goods over which she presided were longer considered inimical to human well-being but, rather, integral to happiness. The allegorical force of the figure became an enjoinment to prudence in order to prepare for, and so mitigate against, the inevitable mutability of human existence, and to the taking of risks in order to seize opportunities as they appeared because they would not recur. The future referred to by this reimagined figure of *fortuna* was unknown yet accessible, embodied in the alluring nudity and tempting forelock of the *fortuna–kairos* imagery.

At the end of the fifteenth century, the European encounter with the Americas, the onset of the Italian Wars, and the penetration of Epicurean physics and philosophy into Renaissance culture had crucial catalyzing effects on the emergence of this new conception of time-yet-to-come. The first two upended the certainties and conceits of the fifteenth century, ushering in a world in which it seemed that the old rules no longer applied and transforming the political map of the peninsula. The latter, less pervasively, introduced the dangerous and unsettling notion that perhaps the universe and all human existence was the result of a chance collision of atoms rather than divine Providence and ordination.

The crystallizing effect of these forces was significant not only for the role that it played in forging the new figure of *fortuna* and the new idea of the future, but also because it helps explain what changed in the Renaissance. The medieval European sense of the future was anticipatory. Time-yet-to-come might be obscure and contingent, but it was not unknowable. The rules, principles, and values that governed human existence today would continue to operate tomorrow. The impact of the New World, Epicurus, and the Italian Wars, in particular, engendered a realization of the potential randomness of existence, the disturbing recognition that pure chance played a role in events, and so the framework of tomorrow might be completely different to that of yesterday and today.

I have been careful throughout the preceding chapters to stress that the emergence of this new concept of the time-yet-to-come did not require the abandonment or replacement of preexisting ideas about the future. It did not transform Renaissance Italians into secular moderns. They did not cease to believe in divine foreknowledge and the biblical prevision of the end of time; neither did they abandon beliefs in prophecy, astrology, and other divinatory arts nor suddenly stop making provisions for the future on the assumption that tomorrow would be broadly similar to today. Instead, the new concept of the future, embodied in the transformed figure of *fortuna*, added yet another layer to the multiple temporalities existing in premodern Europe. I have avoided any suggestion of a sudden break between the medieval and the modern as part of the narrative of this book. But what then might be at stake in the transformation that I have traced across the preceding chapters? If the new concept of the future simply added to the heterochronicity of European culture, why does the emergence of an idea of time-yet-to-come as unknown yet accessible matter? I want to use this conclusion to essay an answer, by arguing that it is deeply implicated in the very idea of the Renaissance itself.

As a historical period, the centuries that historians label the Renaissance in Italy were ones when time mattered, when a remarkably wide range of historical actors displayed a particular sensitivity to temporality. The recognition that a new relationship between Europeans and the past lay at the heart of humanist culture is an accepted truism of historical scholarship. Philological practice and a sense of historical discontinuity demonstrated that the Europe of classical antiquity was a very different place to that of their own lifetime, a realization shared by a much larger portion of the population than was once understood.[1] Ideas about change over time, about decline and progress, eventually about the ability of contemporary knowledge to surpass that of the ancient world, constituted significant aspects of this process. As this book has demonstrated, the Renaissance also witnessed the emergence of a new relationship between Europeans and the future.

As a historiographical label, the Renaissance is also deeply entwined with notions of temporality and chronology. This Renaissance was the creation of nineteenth-century historians, most prominently Jules Michelet, who named it, and Jacob Burckhardt, who described it so vividly.[2] The Renaissance, indeed, was one of the first-born offspring of the academic discipline of history, as it took shape in universities on both sides of the Atlantic. It was also, therefore, one of the first-born offspring of European modernism, which imbued time with purpose and direction. Modernist time moved forward, in a single stream, toward the civilization of Europe's secular, industrial, national age. The Renaissance became a defining moment in this march of progress, the era when Europeans threw off the chains of superstition and faith that had bound their consciousness in the Middle Ages, when they recovered the inheritance of classical antiquity, when they discovered – as both Michelet and Burckhardt emphasized – the world and themselves. Despite his hostility to modernity, Burckhardt shared with Michelet a conception of the Renaissance as the progenitor to the nineteenth-century world. This idea and identity took root and flourished beyond the work of these two historians.[3]

---

[1] On the pervasiveness of humanist culture beyond the erudite sphere of scholars and literary practitioners, see Brian Maxson, *The Humanist World of Renaissance Florence* (New York: Cambridge University Press, 2014), and Sarah Gwyneth Ross, *Everyday Renaissances: The Quest for Cultural Legitimacy in Venice* (Cambridge, MA: Harvard University Press, 2016).

[2] On the idea of the Renaissance as both a historical period and a historiographical label, see, as a convenient and recent starting point, the effective summary in William Caferro, *Contesting the Renaissance* (Malden, MA: Wiley-Blackwell, 2011), chapter 1.

[3] On the imbrication of the Renaissance as a historiographical category, modernism, and modernity, see Anthony Molho, "The Italian Renaissance, Made in the USA," in

The conception of temporality defined by modernism, in which the Renaissance played so a prominent part, was universalist, linear, singular, and Eurocentric. The academic discipline of history as it developed in the nineteenth century aimed to arrange the past – the object of its analysis – in a single, chronological order. This order progressed only toward the modernity of contemporary Europe. As a measure of history, it axiomatically consigned the non-European world as backward, insufficiently advanced along this same chronology, and, so, out of time.[4] In the wake of the transformation of the discipline of history wrought since the middle of the twentieth century – the progressive decentering of the objects of its analysis – historians have rejected this modernist, linear chronology as Eurocentric and universalist, although it has retained a powerful grip on the historical imagination.[5] A principal flaw in the work of Reinhart Koselleck, who thought deeply and critically about time, is that it never entirely escaped the entanglement of European modernity and the discipline of history. If we are completely to provincialize Europe, to reconstruct the discipline along with the other social sciences in a manner that disconnects them from their modernist origins, if we are to develop new notions of time and temporality that are heterochronous, understanding the deep historical origins of this chronology is important. If we are to rewrite the stories that the West has told itself about itself, we need better to comprehend where and how these stories are wrong.[6]

The evidence in this book helps to explain how historical notions about the development of modernist time might be misconceived. The new idea of the future that emerged in sixteenth-century Italy looks so familiar to twenty-first-century eyes because it appears to anticipate the

Imagined Histories: American Historians Interpret the Past, ed. Anthony Molho and Gordon S. Wood (Princeton, NJ: Princeton University Press, 1998), esp. 264–70; Keith Moxey, *Visual Time: The Image in History* (Durham, NC: Duke University Press, 2013), esp. chapter 2; and Jo Tollebeek, "'Renaissance' and 'Fossilization': Michelet, Burckhardt, and Huizinga," *Renaissance Studies* 15, no. 3 (2001).

[4] Dipesh Chakrabarty, *Provincializing Europe: Postcolonial Thought and Historical Difference* (Princeton, NJ: Princeton University Press, 2000); Patricia Clavin, "Time, Manner, Place: Writing Modern European History in Global, Transnational, and International Contexts," *European History Quarterly* 40, no. 4 (2010): 625–26; Moxey, *Visual Time*, esp. 1–8.

[5] On the transformation of history as a process of decentering, see Natalie Zemon Davis, "Decentering History: Local Stories and Cultural Crossings in a Global World," *History and Theory* 50, no. 2 (2011).

[6] On the challenges of writing European history in the twenty-first century and the need to do so in a manner that recognizes this past as particular rather than universal, see the contributions to a special issue of *European History Quarterly* 40, no. 4 (2010). On the importance of rewriting the histories of modern European temporality, in particular, see also A. R. P. Fryxell, "Time and the Modern: Current Trends in the History of Modern Temporalities," *Past and Present*, no. 243 (2019): esp. 286–92.

modernist conception of the future that predominates today. However, as I have shown, the path toward this future was neither linear nor direct. Renaissance Italians inhabited a world of multiple temporalities and multiple futures. They experienced time not as a river but as a delta, diverging into many branches and channels.

Even as they articulated an idea of the future as unknown and unknowable, the authors, artists, merchants, and gamblers considered in the preceding chapters continued also to think about the future in terms of divine Providence and foreknowledge, and of time as unfolding toward a known, if obscure, end point. In precisely the same decades that the figure of *fortuna* was reconceived and the concept of the unknown time-yet-to-come took root, the Sistine Chapel in Rome was decorated with frescoes expressing confidence in the Christian conception of time. Other artists and authors presented complex visions in which the unknown time-yet-to-come nested within a broader vision of the eschatological future of the Church's doctrine. Merchants, as well as purchasers of lottery tickets, expressed a conviction that God would ultimately determine the outcome of their speculations, even as they sought to profit from the uncertainty of the future.

The evidence of this book suggests, however, that if the Renaissance did not witness the establishment of modernist temporality, it did provide the framework and outline to flatten, compress, and forget the multiple temporalities of premodern Europe, and so to arrange the history of the entire globe in a single, linear chronology. The new conceptions of the past and the future that developed in the Renaissance provided the pattern for the later construction of this chronology: a single narrative beginning in classical antiquity stretching to the now, which considers the future as unknown and assuredly distinct from the past. The new concept of time-yet-to-come that emerged in the sixteenth century looks familiar to twenty-first-century eyes – so much so that I could begin this book by stating that "the future began in Italy around 1500" – because it is the blueprint for the regime of futurity that predominates today.

In the wake of the emergence of this development, sixteenth-century merchants and gamblers – in different ways – presented themselves as experts in this new futurity, capable of navigating its uncharted waters and deriving benefits and material profits by seizing the opportunities offered by *fortuna*. They developed methods for thinking probabilistically about the chance of particular outcomes in the unknown future. Bankers and insurance brokers began to commodify risk itself as something that could be priced and speculated on. Cardano, and later mathematicians, started to identify and develop mathematical probability. A new regime of risk taking accompanied the emergence of the future as unknown yet accessible time-yet-to-come.

This book has traced the emergence of this new futurity by examining the tangled relationships between time, religion, morality, wealth, and commerce from the late fourteenth to the late sixteenth centuries across a wide variety of sources. It has explored the slow, complex, and never simple process by which Renaissance Italians developed new relationships with time-yet-to-come and new, less certain, expectations about what tomorrow might bring. I have not done so in order to claim that modern European temporality began in the sixteenth century, that the modern sense of the future and the regime of commercial risk taking that accompanies it emerged in the years immediately after 1500. To make that claim would deny the significant changes that occurred in the eighteenth and nineteenth centuries.

Instead, I hope I have demonstrated how the complex interactions examined in the preceding chapters complicate and problematize straightforward claims about the Renaissance, the origins of modernity, and the modernist sense of time. The Renaissance in Italy was a period in Europe's past in which time mattered, in which perceptions of time were altered, and sensitivity to time's passing was heightened. New ways of thinking about time – in particular, how the past was different and how the future might also be different – emerged. These transformations were crucial for developments in later centuries and still profoundly influence how historians think about time and chronology and how bankers, financiers, and and many others think about the taking of chances on unknown future outcomes.

Bibliography

Archival Sources

Archivio di Stato, Florence (ASF)
    Catasto 1011
    Lettere di commercio e famiglia (LCF) 711, 712, 713, 723, 742, 743,
    1053, 1089, 2927
    Mediceo del Principato (MDP) 1170A, 1171, 1175
    Mercanzia 11516, 11517
    Otto di Guardia e Balìa del Principato (OGBP) 2215, 2225
Archivio di Stato, Genoa (ASG)
    Archivio Secreto 1016
    Manoscritti, Leges 1528-1600
Archivio di Stato, Milan (ASM)
    Famiglie 1
    Governatore degli statuti, Gride e citazioni 78
    Governatore degli statuti, Registri di atti sovrani (Registri) 27, 28
Archivio di Stato, Venice (ASV)
    Esecutori contro la bestemmia (Esecutori) 54, 61
    Miscellanea di carte non appartenenti ad alcun Archivio (MCNA) 18/
    19, 20
    Miscellanea Gregolin (MiscGreg) 12 bis 1
Archivio Storico Civico, Genoa (ASCG)
    Archivio Brignole Sale (BS) 102, 103, 104
Archivio Storico Civico, Milan (ASCM)
    Registri lettere ducali (RLD) 15, 18, 21

Printed Sources

Abulafia, David, ed. *The French Descent into Renaissance Italy, 1494–1495: Antecedents and Effects*. Aldershot: Variorum, 1995.
Adelman, Howard E. "Leon Modena: The Autobiography and the Man." In *The Autobiography of a Seventeenth-Century Venetian Rabbi: Leon Modena's Life of Judah*, edited by Mark R. Cohen, 19–49. Princeton, NJ: Princeton University Press, 1989.

Alberti, Leon Battista. *Dinner Pieces: A Translation of the Intercenales*. Translated by David Marsh. Binghamton, NY: Center for Medieval and Early Renaissance Studies, 1987.

Intercenales. Edited by Franco Bacchelli and Luca D'Ascia. Bologna: Edizioni Pendragon, 2003.

Momus. Translated by Sarah Knight. Cambridge, MA: Harvard University Press, 2003.

Opere Volgari. Edited by Cecil Grayson. Bari: Laterza, 1960.

Albertini, Rudolf von. *Firenze dalla repubblica al principato: Storia e coscienza politica*. Translated by Cesare Cristofolini. Turin: Giulio Einaudi, 1970

Alighieri, Dante. *The Divine Comedy, vol. 1: Inferno*. Translated by Mark Musa. New York: Penguin, 2003.

The Divine Comedy, vol. 2: Purgatory. Translated by Mark Musa. New York: Penguin, 1985.

Allegri, Ettore, and Alessandro Cecchi. *Palazzo Vecchio e i Medici*. Florence: Studio per edizioni scelte, 1980.

Arcangeli, Alessandro. *Recreation in the Renaissance: Attitudes towards Leisure and Pastimes in European Culture, c. 1425–1675*. Basingstoke: Palgrave, 2003.

Aretino, Pietro. *Aretino: Selected Letters*. Translated by George Bull. Harmondsworth: Penguin, 1976.

Le carte parlanti. Edited by Giovanni Casalegno and Gabriella Giaccone. Palermo: Sellerio, 1992.

Del primo libro dele lettere di M. Pietro Aretino. Paris (?): Matteo il Maestro (?), 1609.

Aristotle. *The Nicomachean Ethics*. Revised ed. Translated by H. Rackham. Cambridge, MA: Harvard University Press, 2014.

Aslanian, Sebouh. "'The Salt in a Merchant's Letter': The Culture of Julfan Correspondence in the Indian Ocean and the Mediterranean." *Journal of World History* 19, no. 2 (2008): 127–88.

"Social Capital, 'Trust' and the Role of Networks in Julfan Trade: Informal and Semi-Formal Institutions at Work." *Journal of Global History* 1 (2006): 383–402.

Augustine. *Confessions*. Edited by Carolyn J.-B. Hammond. Cambridge, MA: Harvard University Press, 2016.

Azzari, Margherita, and Leonardo Rombai, eds. *Amerigo Vespucci e i mercanti viaggiatori fiorentini del Cinquecento*. Florence: Firenze University Press, 2013.

Baker, Nicholas Scott. "Deep Play in Renaissance Italy." In *Rituals of Politics and Culture in Early Modern Europe: Essays in Honour of Edward Muir*, edited by Mark Jurdjevic and Rolf Strøm-Olsen, 259–81. Toronto: Centre for Reformation and Renaissance Studies, 2016.

"Dux ludens: Eleonora de Toledo, Cosimo I de' Medici, and Games of Chance in the Ducal Household of Mid-Sixteenth-Century Florence." *European History Quarterly* 46, no. 4 (2016): 595–617.

"A Twenty-First Century Renaissance." *I Tatti Studies: Essays in the Renaissance* 22, no. 2 (2019): 273–78.

Bandera, Sandra, ed. *I tarocchi: il caso e la fortuna*. Milan: Electa/Ministero per i Beni e le Attività Culturale, 1999.

Barocchi, Paola. "Sulla collezione Botti." *Prospettiva*, nos. 93–94 (1999): 126–30.

Baroni, Alessandra. *Casa Vasari*. Montepulciano: Editrice le Balze, 1999.

Barret, J. K. *Untold Futures: Time and Literary Culture in Renaissance England.* Ithaca, NY: Cornell University Press, 2016.

Bartsch, Adam. *Le peintre graveur.* Vol. 14. Vienne: J. V. Degen, 1813.

Bec, Christian. "Au début du XVe siècle: Mentalité et vocabulaire des marchands florentins." *Annales. Histoire, Sciences Sociales* 22, no. 6 (1967): 1206–26.

"Fortuna, ratio et prudentia au début du Cinquecento." *Les Langues Neo-Latines*, no. 181 (1967): 93–102.

Bellhouse, David. "Decoding Cardano's *Liber de Ludo Aleae.*" *Historia Mathematica* 32 (2005): 180–202.

Bentley, Jerry H. *Politics and Culture in Renaissance Naples.* Princeton, NJ: Princeton University Press, 1987.

Berenson, Bernard, ed. *Palladio, Veronese e Vittoria a Maser.* Milan: Aldo Martello, 1960.

Berni, Francesco. *Rime.* Edited by Danilo Romei. Milan: Mursia, 1985.

Berti, Luciano. *La casa del Vasari in Arezzo e il suo museo.* Florence: Tipografia Giuntina, 1955.

Biorci, Grazia, and Ricardo Court. *Il registro di lettere di Giovanni Francesco di Negro (1563–1565): Regole e prospettive di un mondo non clamoroso.* Novi Ligure: Città di Silenzio, 2014.

Boethius. *The Consolation of Philosophy.* Translated by P. G. Walsh. Oxford: Oxford University Press, 1999.

Bolte, Johannes. "Zur Geschichte der Lösbucher." In *Georg Wickrams Werke,* edited by Johannes Bolte, 276–342. Tübingen: Litterarischen Vereins, 1903.

Bolzoni, Lina. *The Gallery of Memory: Literary and Iconographic Models in the Age of the Printing Press.* Translated by Jeremy Parzen. Toronto: University of Toronto Press, 2001.

Bowd, Stephen D. *Renaissance Mass Murder: Civilians and Soldiers during the Italian Wars.* Oxford: Oxford University Press, 2018.

Bracciolini, Poggio. *De varietate fortvnae: Edizione critica con introduzione e commento.* Edited by Outi Merisalo. Helsinki: Suomalainen Tiedeakatemia, 1993.

Brady, Andrea, and Emily Butterworth, eds. *The Uses of the Future in Early Modern Europe.* New York: Routledge, 2010.

Braudel, Fernand. *The Mediterranean and the Mediterranean World in the Age of Philip II.* Translated by Siân Reynolds. 2 vols. New York: Harper and Row, 1973.

Brogi, Alessandro. *Ludovico Carracci (1555–1619).* Vol. 1. Ozzano dell'Emilia: Tipoarte, 2001.

Brown, Alison. "Lucretius and the Epicureans in the Social and Political Context of Renaissance Florence." *I Tatti Studies: Essays in the Renaissance* 9 (2001): 11–62.

"Philosophy and Religion in Machiavelli." In *The Cambridge Companion to Machiavelli,* edited by John M. Najemy, 157–72. Cambridge: Cambridge University Press, 2010.

"Reinterpreting Renaissance Humanism: Marcello Adriani and the Recovery of Lucretius." In *Interpretations of Renaissance Humanism,* edited by Angelo Mazzocco, 267–91. Leiden: Brill, 2006.

"Rethinking the Renaissance in the Aftermath of Italy's Crisis." In *Italy in the Age of the Renaissance, 1300–1500*, edited by John M. Najemy, 246–65. Oxford: Oxford University Press, 2004.

The Return of Lucretius to Renaissance Florence. Cambridge, MA: Harvard University Press, 2010.

Brown, Judith C. "Economies." In *The Cambridge Companion to the Italian Renaissance*, edited by Michael Wyatt, 320–37. Cambridge: Cambridge University Press, 2014.

Brownlee, Kevin. "The Image of History in Christine de Pizan's *Livre de la mutacion de Fortune*." *Yale French Studies* Special Issue: Contexts: Style and Values in Medieval Art and Literature (1991): 44–56.

Buchanan, Carole Ann. "The Theme of Fortune in the Works of Christine de Pizan." PhD dissertation, University of Glasgow, 1994.

Burman, Pieter, ed. *Sylloges epistolarum a viris illustribus scriptarum, vol. 2: Quo Justi Lipsii et aliorum virorum eruditorum multae etiam mutuae epistolae continentur*. Leiden: Samuel Luchtmans, 1727.

Burrow, J. A., and Ian P. Wei, eds. *Medieval Futures: Attitudes to the Future in the Middle Ages*. Woodbridge: Boydell Press, 2000.

Buttay-Jutier, Florence. *Fortuna: Usages politiques d'une allégorie morale à la Renaissance*. Paris: Presses de l'Université Paris-Sorbonne, 2008.

Caferro, William. *Contesting the Renaissance*. Malden, MA: Wiley-Blackwell, 2011.

Cairns, Christopher. *Pietro Aretino and the Republic of Venice: Researches on Aretino and His Circle in Venice*. Florence: Olschki, 1985.

Callmann, Ellen. "The Triumphal Entry into Naples of Alfonso I." *Apollo* 109, no. 1 (1979): 24–31.

Cantini, Lorenzo, ed. *Legislazione Toscana*. 32 vols. Florence: Pietro Fantosini e Figlio, 1800–1808.

Cardano, Girolamo. *The Book of My Life*. Translated by Jean Stoner. New York: New York Review Books, 2002.

De propria vita liber. Paris: Iacobus Villery, 1643.

Liber de ludo aleae. Edited by Massimo Tamborini. Milan: FrancoAngeli, 2006.

Practica arithmetice et mensurandi singularis. Milan: Iohannes Antonins Castellioneus, 1539.

Casale, Giancarlo. "Did Alexander the Great Discover America? Debating Space and Time in Renaissance Istanbul." *Renaissance Quarterly* 72, no. 3 (2019): 863–909.

Cassirer, Ernst. *The Individual and the Cosmos in Renaissance Philosophy*. Translated by Mario Domandi. Oxford: Basil Blackwell, 1963.

Castiglione, Baldassare. *Il libro del Cortegiano*. Edited by Amedeo Quondam and Nicola Longo. Cernusco: Garzanti, 1998.

Cavallo, Sandra, and Tessa Storey. *Healthy Living in Late Renaissance Italy*. Oxford: Oxford University Press, 2013.

Ceccarelli, Giovanni. "Gambling and Economic Thought in the Late Middle Ages." *Ludica* 12 (2006): 54–63.

Il gioco e il peccato: Economia e rischio nel Tardo Medioevo. Bologna: Il Mulino, 2003.

Un mercato del rischio: Assicurare e farsi assicurare nella Firenze rinascimentale. Venice: Marsilio, 2012.

"The Price for Risk-Taking: Marine Insurance and Probability Calculus in the Late Middle Ages." *Journal Electronique d'Histoire des Probabilités et de la Statistique/ Electronic Journal for History of Probability and Statistics* 3, no. 1 (2007).

Cecchi, Alessandro. "Francesco Salviati et les Médicis (1543–1548)." In *Francesco Salviati (1510–1563) ou la Bella Maniera*, edited by Catherine Monbeig Goguel, 61–65. Milan: Electa; Paris: Editions de la Réunion des Musées Nationaux, 1998.

Cereta, Laura. *Collected Letters of a Renaissance Feminist.* Edited by Diana Robin. Chicago: University of Chicago Press, 1997.

Chaganti, Seeta. *Strange Footing: Poetic Form and Dance in the Late Middle Ages.* Chicago: University of Chicago Press, 2018.

Chakrabarty, Dipesh. *Provincializing Europe: Postcolonial Thought and Historical Difference.* Princeton, NJ: Princeton University Press, 2000.

Champion, Matthew. *The Fullness of Time: Temporalities in the Fifteenth-Century Low Countries.* Chicago: University of Chicago Press, 2017.

Cheney, Iris H. "Francesco Salviati's North Italian Journey." *The Art Bulletin* 45, no. 4 (1963): 337–49.

Cheney, Liana de Girolami. *Giorgio Vasari: Artistic and Emblematic Manifestations.* Washington, DC: New Academia Publishing, 2012.

Christian, David. "History and Time." *Australian Journal of History and Politics* 57, no. 3 (2011): 353–65.

Cioffari, Vincenzo. "The Function of Fortune in Dante, Boccaccio and Machiavelli." *Italica* 24, no. 1 (1947): 1–13.

Clavin, Patricia. "Time, Manner, Place: Writing Modern European History in Global, Transnational, and International Contexts." *European History Quarterly* 40, no. 4 (2010): 624–40.

Cocke, Richard. *Paolo Veronese: Piety and Display in an Age of Religious Reform.* Aldershot: Ashgate, 2001.

"Veronese and Daniele Barbaro: The Decoration of Villa Maser." *Journal of the Warburg and Courtauld Institutes* 35 (1972): 226–46.

Cohen, Elizabeth S. "Honor and Gender in the Streets of Early Modern Rome." *Journal of Interdisciplinary History* 22, no. 4 (1992): 597–625.

Cohen, Simona. "The Early Renaissance Personifications of Time and Changing Concepts of Temporality." *Renaissance Studies* 14, no. 3 (2000): 301–28.

Transformations of Time and Temporality in Medieval and Renaissance Art. Leiden: Brill, 2014.

Colonna, Francesco. *Hypnerotomachia Poliphili.* Venice: Aldus Manutius, 1499.

Connell, William J. "The Eternity of the World and Renaissance Historical Thought." *California Italian Studies* 2, no. 1 (2011).

Conti, Ginori, ed. *Il libro segreto della ragione di Piero Benini e comp.* Florence: Olschki, 1937.

Costantini, Claudio. *La Repubblica di Genova nell'età moderna.* Turin: Unione Tipografico-Editrice Torinese, 1978.

Court, Ricardo. "De fatigationibus: What a Merchant's Errant Son Can Teach Us about the Dynamics of Trust." In *Il registro di lettere di Giovanni Francesco di Negro (1563–1565): Regole e prospettive di un mondo non clamoroso,* edited by Grazia Biorci and Ricardo Court, 49–130. Novi Ligure: Città del silenzio, 2014.

"*Januensis ergo mercator:* Trust and Enforcement in the Business Correspondence of the Brignole Family." *The Sixteenth Century Journal* 35, no. 4 (2004): 987–1003.

"The Language of Trust: Sixteenth-Century Genoese Commercial Correspondence." *The UCLA Historical Journal* 20 (2004): 1–25.

Cox-Rearick, Janet. *Dynasty and Destiny in Medici Art: Pontormo, Leo X and the Two Cosimos.* Princeton, NJ: Princeton University Press, 1984.

Cropper, Elizabeth. "The Petrifying Art: Marino's Poetry and Caravaggio." *Metropolitan Museum Journal* 26 (1991): 193–212.

Crosato, Luciana Larcher. "Cosiderazioni sul programma iconografico di Maser." *Mitteilungen des Kunsthistorischen Institutes in Florenz* 26, no. 2 (1982): 211–56.

Crosby, Alfred W. *The Measure of Reality: Quantification and Western Society, 1250–1600.* Cambridge: Cambridge University Press, 1997.

Da Porto, Luigi. *Giulietta e Romeo.* Edited by Alessandro Torri. Pisa Fratelli Nistri, 1831.

Lettere storiche. Edited by Bartolomeo Bressan. Florence: Felice le Monnier, 1857.

Dal Prete, Ivano. "'Being the World Eternal …': The Age of the Earth in Renaissance Italy." *Isis* 105, no. 2 (2014): 292–317.

D'Amico, Stefano. *Spanish Milan: A City within the Empire, 1535–1706.* New York: Palgrave Macmillan, 2012.

Daston, Lorraine. *Classical Probability in the Enlightenment.* Princeton, NJ: Princeton University Press, 1988.

Dati, Gregorio. *Il libro segreto di Gregorio Dati.* Edited by Carlo Gargiolli. Bologna: Gaetano Romagnoli, 1869.

Davis, Natalie Zemon. "Decentering History: Local Stories and Cultural Crossings in a Global World." *History and Theory* 50, no. 2 (2011): 188–202.

De Giorgio, Nicola Antonio. "Un 'padovano' cartaro accusato di frode." In *Il giuoco al tempo di Caravaggio: Dipinti, giochi, testimonianze dalla fine del '500 ai primi del '700,* edited by Pierluigi Carofano, 78–86. Pontadera: Bandecchi & Vivaldi, 2013.

De Vivo, Filippo. *Information and Communication in Venice: Rethinking Early Modern Politics.* Oxford: Oxford University Press, 2007.

Delaborde, Henri. *Marc-Antoine Raimondi: Étude historique et critique suivie d'un catalogue raisonné des oeuvres du maître.* Paris: Librarie de l'Art, 1887.

Dempsey, Charles. "Love and the Figure of the Nymph in Botticelli's Art." In *Botticelli: From Lorenzo the Magnificent to Savonarola,* 25–37. Milan: Skira, 2004.

The Portrayal of Love: Botticelli's Primavera and Humanist Culture at the Time of Lorenzo the Magnificent. Princeton, NJ: Princeton University Press, 1992.

Di Giampaolo, Mario, and Elisabetta Fadda. *Parmigianino: Catalogo completo dei dipinti.* Santarcangelo di Romagna: Idea Libri, 2003.

Doria, Giorgio. "Conoscenza del mercato e sistema informativo: Il know-how dei mercanti-finanzieri genovesi nei secoli XVI–XVII." In *La repubblica internazionale del denaro tra XV e XVII secolo*, edited by Aldo de Maddalena and Hermann Kellenbenz, 57–121. Bologna: Il Mulino, 1986.

Dossena, Giampaolo, Gino Benzoni, Filippo Pedrocco, and Alberto Fiorin. *Fanti e denari: Sei secoli di giochi d'azzardo*. Venice: Arsenale, 1989.

Dunlop, Anne. "On the Origins of European Painting Materials, Real and Imagined." In *The Matter of Art: Materials, Practices, Cultural Logics, c. 1250–1750*, edited by Christy Anderson, Anne Dunlop, and Pamela H. Smith, 68–96. Manchester: Manchester University Press, 2014.

Edelstein, Bruce. "The Camera Verde: A Public Center for the Duchess of Florence in the Palazzo Vecchio." *Mélanges de l'Ecole Française de Rome: Italie et Méditerranée* 115, no. 1 (2003): 51–87.

Ekserdjian, David. *Parmigianino*. New Haven, CT: Yale University Press, 2006.

Elias, Norbert. *Time: An Essay*. Translated by Edmund Jephcott. Oxford: Blackwell, 1992.

Emiliani, Andrea, ed. *Ludovico Carracci*. Bologna: Nuova Alfa, 1993.

Epstein, Stephan R. "L'economia italiana nel quadro europeo." In *Commercio e cultura mercantile*, edited by Franco Franceschi, Richard A. Goldthwaite, and Reinhold C. Mueller, 3–47. Treviso: Fondazione Cassamarca/Angelo Colla Editore, 2007.

Epstein, Steven A. "Business Cycles and the Sense of Time in Medieval Genoa." *The Business History Review* 62, no. 2 (1988): 238–60.

"Secrecy and Genoese Commercial Practices." *Journal of Medieval History* 20 (1994): 313–25.

Esposito, Roberto. "Fortuna e politica all'origine della filosofia italiana." *California Italian Studies* 2, no. 1 (2011).

Everson, Jane, and Diego Zancani, eds. *Italy in Crisis, 1494*. Oxford: European Humanities Research Centre, 2000.

Ferente, Serena. "Parties, Quotas, and Elections in Late Medieval Genoa." In *Cultures of Voting in Pre-Modern Europe*, edited by Serena Ferente, Lovro Kunčević, and Miles Pattenden, 187–204. London: Routledge, 2018.

Finucci, Valeria. *The Manly Masquerade: Masculinity, Paternity, and Castration in the Italian Renaissance*. Durham, NC: Duke University Press, 2003.

Flanagan, Thomas. "The Concept of *Fortuna* in Machiavelli." In *The Political Calculus: Essays on Machiavelli's Philosophy*, edited by Anthony Parel, 127–56. Toronto: University of Toronto Press, 1972.

Fournel, Jean-Louis, and Jean-Claude Zancarini. *La grammaire de la république: Lagages de la politique chez Francesco Guicciardini (1483–1540)*. Geneva: Librarie Droz, 2009.

Frakes, Jerold C. *The Fate of Fortune in the Early Middle Ages: The Boethian Tradition*. Edited by Albert Zimmerman. Leiden: Brill, 1988.

Franklin, David. *Painting in Renaissance Florence*. New Haven, CT: Yale University Press, 2001.

Franklin, James. *The Science of Conjecture: Evidence and Probability before Pascal*. Baltimore, MD: Johns Hopkins University Press, 2001.

Freedberg, Sydney J. *Parmigianino: His Works in Painting*. Cambridge, MA: Harvard University Press, 1950.

Fregoso, Antonio Fileremo. *Opere*. Edited by Giorgio Dilemmi. Bologna: Commissione per i Testi di Lingua, 1976.

Fryxell, A. R. P. "Time and the Modern: Current Trends in the History of Modern Temporalities." *Past and Present*, no. 243 (2019): 285–98.

Gahtan, Maia Wellington. "Notions of Past and Future in Italian Renaissance Arts and Letters." In *Symbols of Time in the History of Art*, edited by Christian Heck and Kristen Lippencot, 69–83. Turnhout: Brepols, 2002.

Geertz, Clifford. *The Interpretation of Cultures: Selected Essays*. New York: Basic Books, 1973.

Giaccone, Gabriella. "Le *Carte parlanti* di Pietro Aretino." *Lettere Italiane* 61, no. 2 (1989): 225–39.

"La scrittura come gioco: Da Aretino a Calvino." *Critica Letteraria* 17, no. 65 (1989): 769–80.

Giehlow, Karl. *The Humanist Interpretation of Hieroglyphs in the Allegorical Studies of the Renaissance*. Translated by Robin Raybould. Leiden: Brill, 2015.

Gilbert, Felix. "Bernardo Rucellai and Orti Oricellari: A Study on the Origin of Modern Political Thought." *Journal of the Warburg and Courtauld Institutes* 12 (1949): 101–31.

History: Choice and Commitment. Cambridge, MA: Belknap Press, 1977.

Machiavelli and Guicciardini: Politics and History in Sixteenth-Century Florence. New York: Norton, 1984.

Giovannoni, Simona Lecchini. *Alessandro Allori*. Turin: Umberto Allemandi, 1991.

Godman, Peter. *From Poliziano to Machiavelli: Florentine Humanism in the High Renaissance*. Princeton, NJ: Princeton University Press, 1998.

Goffman, Erving. *Interaction Ritual: Essays on Face-to-Face Behavior*. Harmondsworth: Penguin, 1967.

Goldthwaite, Richard A. *The Economy of Renaissance Florence*. Baltimore, MD: Johns Hopkins University Press, 2009.

Goldthwaite, Richard A. "Il sistema monetario fino al 1600: Pratica, politica, problematica." In *Studi sulla moneta fiorentina (Secoli XIII–XVI)*, 9–106. Florence: Olschki, 1994.

Grafton, Anthony, April Shelford, and Nancy G. Sirasi. *New Worlds, Ancient Texts: The Power of Tradition and the Shock of Discovery*. Cambridge, MA: Belknap Press, 1992.

Greenblatt, Stephen. *The Swerve: How the World Became Modern*. New York: W. W. Norton, 2011.

Greif, Avner. "The Maghribi Traders: A Reappraisal." *The Economic History Review* 65, no. 2 (2012): 445–69.

"Reputation and Coalitions in Medieval Trade: Evidence on the Maghribi Traders." *The Journal of Economic History* 49, no. 4 (1989): 857–82.

Griffin, Miranda. "Transforming Fortune: Reading and Chance in Christine de Pizan's *Mutacion de Fortune* and *Chemin de long estude*." *The Modern Language Review* 104, no. 1 (2009): 55–70.

Guerzoni, Guido. "The Social World of Price Formation: Prices and Consumption in Sixteenth-Century Ferrara." In *The Material Renaissance*, edited by Michelle O'Malley and Evelyn Welch, 85–105. Manchester: Manchester University Press, 2007.

Guicciardini, Francesco. *Ricordi: Edizione critica*. Edited by Raffaele Spongano. Florence: Sansoni, 1951.

Storia d'Italia. Edited by Silvana Seidel Menchi. Turin: Einaudi, 1971.

Hacking, Ian. *The Emergence of Probability: A Philosophical Study of Early Ideas about Probability Induction and Statistical Inference*, 2nd ed. New York: Cambridge University Press, 2006.

Hatfield, Rab. "The Funding of the Façade of Santa Maria Novella." *Journal of the Warburg and Courtauld Institutes* 67 (2004): 81–128.

Hankins, James. *Virtue Politics: Soulcraft and Statecraft in Renaissance Italy*. Cambridge, MA: Belknap Press of Harvard University Press, 2019.

Hanß, Stefan. "The Fetish of Accuracy: Perspectives on Early Modern Time(s)." *Past and Present*, no. 243 (2019): 267–84.

Helas, Philine. *Lebende Bilder in der italienischen Festkultur des 15. Jahrhunderts*. Berlin: Akademie Verlag, 1999.

Herlihy, David, and Christiane Klapisch-Zuber. *Tuscans and Their Families: A Study of the Florentine Catasto of 1427*. Translated by David Herlihy and Christiane Klapisch-Zuber. New Haven, CT: Yale University Press, 1985.

Herzner, Volker. "Die Segel-Imprese der Familie Pazzi." *Mitteilungen des Kunsthistorischen Institutes in Florenz* 20, no. 1 (1976): 13–32.

Hill, George Francis. *A Corpus of Italian Medals of the Renaissance before Cellini*. 2 vols. London: British Museum, 1930.

Hind, Arthur M. *Early Italian Engraving: A Critical Catalogue with Complete Reproduction of the Prints Described. Part I: Florentine Engravings and Anonymous Prints of Other Schools, vol. 1: Catalogue*. London: Bernard Qaritch, 1970.

Horodowich, Elizabeth. "Italy and the New World." In *The New World in Early Modern Italy*, edited by Elizabeth Horodowich and Lia Markey, 19–33. Cambridge: Cambridge University Press, 2017.

Horodowich, Elizabeth, and Lia Markey. "Italy's Virtual Discovery: An Introduction." In *The New World in Early Modern Italy*, edited by Elizabeth Horodowich and Lia Markey, 1–16. Cambridge: Cambridge University Press, 2017.

Huizinga, J. *Homo Ludens: A Study of the Play-Element in Culture*. Reprint. London: Routledge, 1999.

Husband, Timothy B. *The World in Play: Luxury Cards, 1430–1540*. New York: Metropolian Museum of Art, 2015.

Infelise, Mario. "La circolazione dell'informazione commerciale." In *Commercio e cultura mercantile*, edited by Franco Franceschi, Richard A. Goldthwaite, and Reinhold C. Mueller, 499–522. Treviso: Fondazione Cassamarca/Angelo Colla Editore, 2007.

Itzkowitz, David C. "Fair Enterprise or Extravagant Speculation: Investment, Speculation, and Gambling in Victorian England." *Victorian Studies* 45, no. 1 (2002): 121–47.

Ivanoff, Nicola. "La Libreria Marciana: Arte e iconologia." *Saggi e Memorie di Storia dell'Arte*, no. 6 (1968): 33, 35–78, 163–91.

Kajanto, Iiro. "Fortuna." In *Aufstieg und Niedergang der römischen Welt: Geschichte und Kultur Roms im Spiegel der neueren Forschung*, edited by Hildegard Temporini and Wolfgang Haase, 502–58. Berlin: Walter de Gruyter, 1981.

"Fortuna in the Works of Poggio Bracciolini." *Arctos: Acta philologica fennica* 20 (1986): 25–59.

Poggio Bracciolini and Classicism: A Study in Early Italian Humanism. Helsinki: Suomalainen Tiedeakatemia, 1987.

Kaye, Joel. *Economy and Nature in the Fourteenth Century: Money, Market Exchange, and the Emergence of Scientific Thought*. Cambridge: Cambridge University Press, 1998.

Keenan, Paul R. "Card-Playing and Gambling in Eighteenth-Century Russia." *European History Quarterly* 42, no. 3 (2012): 385–402.

Kellenbenz, Hermann. "I Borromeo e le grandi casate mercantili milanesi." In *San Carlo e il suo tempo: Atti del convegno internazionale*, 805–13. Rome: Edizioni di Sstoria e Letteratura, 1984.

Kelly, Jessen. "Renaissance Futures: Chance, Prediction, and Play in Northern European Visual Culture." PhD dissertation, University of California, Berkeley, 2011.

Kent, F. W. "The Making of a Renaissance Patron of the Arts." In *Giovanni Rucellai ed il suo Zibaldone*. 2 vols. *Vol. 2: A Florentine Patrician and His Palace*. London: Warburg Institute, 1981.

Kiefer, Frederick. "The Conflation of Fortuna and Occasio in Renaissance Thought and Iconography." *The Journal of Medieval and Renaissance Studies* 9, no. 1 (1979): 1–27.

Koselleck, Reinhart. *Futures Past: On the Semantics of Historical Time*. Translated by Keith Tribe. Cambridge, MA: MIT Press, 1985.

The Practice of Conceptual History: Timing History, Spacing Concepts. Translated by Todd Samuel Presner and Kerstin Behnke. Stanford, CA: Stanford University Press, 2002.

Koslofsky, Craig. *Evening's Empire: A History of the Night in Early Modern Europe*. Cambridge: Cambridge University Press, 2011.

Kroke, Antonella Fenech. "Ludic Intermingling/Ludic Discrimination: Women's Card Playing and Visual Proscriptions in Early Modern Europe." In *Playthings in Early Modernity: Party Games, Word Games, Mind Games*, edited by Allison Levy, 49–71. Kalamazoo: Medieval Institute Publications, Western Michigan University, 2017.

Kruft, Hanno-Walter, and Magne Malmanger. "Der Triumphbogen Alfonsos in Neapel: Das Monument und seine politische Bedeutung." *Acta ad Archaeologiam et Artium Historiae Pertinentia Institutum Romanum Norvegiae* 6 (1975): 213–305.

Landes, David S. *Revolution in Time: Clocks and the Making of the Modern World*. Cambridge, MA: Harvard University Press, 1983.

Lane, Frederic C. *Andrea Barbarigo, Merchant of Venice, 1418–1449*. New York: Octagon Books, 1967.

Lanza, Antonio, ed. *Lirici toscani del Quattrocento*. 2 vols. Rome: Bulzoni, 1975.

Lapina, Elizabeth. "Gambling and Gaming in the Holy Land: Chess, Dice and Other Games in the Sources of the Crusades." *Crusades* 12 (2013): 121–32.

Le Goff, Jacques. *Time, Work, and Culture in the Middle Ages.* Chicago: University of Chicago Press, 1980.

Leach, E. R. *Rethinking Anthropology.* London: Athlone Press, 1966.

Lemaître, Alain J. "Une nouvelle approche." In *Pour une histoire culturelle du risque: Genèse, évolution, actualité du concept dans les sociétés occidentales,* edited by Emmanuelle Collas-Heddeland, Marianne Coudry, Odile Kammerer, Alain J. Lemaître, and Brice Martin, 13–24. Strasbourg: Éditions Histoire et Anthropologie, 2004.

Long, Jane C. "Botticelli's *Birth of Venus* as Wedding Painting." *Aurora: The Journal of the History of Art* 9 (2009): 1–27.

Luciano, Eleonora, ed. *Antico: The Golden Age of Renaissance Bronzes.* Washington, DC: National Gallery of Art; London: Paul Holberton Publishing, 2011.

Lutz, Cora E. "Democritus and Heraclitus." *The Classical Journal* 49, no. 7 (1954): 309–14.

Machiavelli, Niccolò. *Discorsi sopra la prima deca di Tito Livio.* Edited by Francesco Bausi. Rome: Salerno, 2001.

  Opere. Edited by Franco Gaeta. Turin: Unione Tipografico-Editrice Torinese, 1984.

  Opere storiche. Edited by Alessandro Montevecchi and Carlo Varotti. Rome: Salerno, 2010.

  Il principe. Edited by Mario Martelli. Rome: Salerno, 2006.

  Scritti in poesia e in prosa. Edited by A. Corsaro, P. Cosentino, E. Cutinelli-Rèndina, F. Grazzini, and N. Marcelli. Rome: Salerno, 2012.

Mack, Charles Randall. "The Rucellai Palace: Some New Proposals." *The Art Bulletin* 56, no. 4 (1974): 517–29.

Maifreda, Germano. *From Oikonomia to Political Economy: Constructing Economic Knowledge from the Renaissance to the Scientific Revolution.* Translated by Loretta Valtz Mannucci. Farnham: Ashgate, 2012.

Mainoni, Patrizia. "L'attività mercantile e le casate milanesi nel secondo Quattrocento." In *Milano nell'età di Ludovico il Moro: Atti del convegno internazionale 28 febbraio–4 marzo 1983,* 575–84. Milan: Comune di Milano/ Archivio Storico Civico e Biblioteca Trivulziana, 1983.

Mallett, Michael, and Christine Shaw. *The Italian Wars, 1494–1559.* Harlow: Pearson, 2012.

Marini, Maurizio. *Caravaggio "pictor praestantissimus": L'iter artistico completo di uno dei massimi rivoluzionari dell'arte di tutti i tempi.* Rome: Newton and Compton, 2001.

Marini, Remigio, and Guido Piovene. *L'opera completa del Veronese.* Milan: Rizzoli, 1968.

Markey, Lia. *Imagining the Americas in Medici Florence.* University Park: Pennsylvania State University Press, 2016.

Marsh, David. *Renaissance Fables: Aesopic Prose by Leon Battista Alberti, Bartolomeo Scala, Leonardo da Vinci, Bernardino Baldi.* Tempe: Arizona Center for Medieval and Renaissance Studies, 2004.

Martelli, Ugolino di Niccolò. *Ricordanze dal 1433 al 1483*. Edited by Fulvio
   Pezzarossa. Rome: Edizioni di Storia e Letteratura, 1989.
Martin, John Jefferies. *Myths of Renaissance Individualism*. Houndmills: Palgrave
   Macmillan, 2004.
Maxson, Brian. *The Humanist World of Renaissance Florence*. New York:
   Cambridge University Press, 2014.
McCahill, Elizabeth. *Reviving the Eternal City: Rome and the Papal Court,
   1420–1447*. Cambridge, MA: Harvard University Press, 2013.
McClure, George W. *Doubting the Divine in Early Modern Europe: The Revival of
   Momus, the Agnostic God*. Cambridge: Cambridge University Press, 2018.
   Sorrow and Consolation in Italian Humanism. Princeton, NJ: Princeton
   University Press, 1990.
McTavish, David. *Giuseppe Porta Called Giuseppe Salviati*. New York: Garland
   Publishing, 1981.
Mellyn, Elizabeth W. *Mad Tuscans and Their Families: A History of Mental Disorder
   in Early Modern Italy*. Philadelphia: University of Pennsylvania Press, 2014.
Mews, Constant J., and Ibrahim Abraham. "Usury and Just Compensation:
   Religious and Financial Ethics in Historical Perspective." *Journal of
   Business Ethics* 72, no. 1 (2007): 1–15.
Milanesi, Marica. *Filippo Sassetti*. Florence: La Nuova Italia Editrice, 1973.
Modena, Leon. *The Autobiography of a Seventeenth-Century Venetian Rabbi: Leon
   Modena's Life of Judah*. Translated by Mark R. Cohen. Princeton, NJ:
   Princeton University Press, 1988.
Molho, Anthony. "The Italian Renaissance, Made in the USA." In *Imagined
   Histories: American Historians Interpret the Past*, edited by Anthony Molho and
   Gordon S. Wood, 263–94. Princeton, NJ: Princeton University Press, 1998.
Mortari, Luisa. *Francesco Salviati*. Rome: Leonardo – De Luca, 1992.
Moxey, Keith. *Visual Time: The Image in History*. Durham, NC: Duke University
   Press, 2013.
Muir, Edward. "The Double Binds of Manly Revenge in Renaissance Italy." In
   Gender Rhetorics: Postures of Dominance and Submission in History, edited by
   Richard C. Trexler, 65–82. Binghamton, NY: Center for Medieval and
   Early Renaissance Studies, 1994.
   "The Sources of Civil Society in Italy." *Journal of Interdisciplinary History* 29,
   no. 3 (1999): 379–406.
Nagel, Alexander. "Some Discoveries of 1492: Eastern Antiquities and
   Renaissance Europe." Groningen: Gerson Lectures Foundation, 2013.
Nagel, Alexander, and Christopher S. Wood. *Anachronic Renaissance*. New York:
   Zone Books, 2010.
Najemy, John M. "Machiavelli and Cesare Borgia: A Reconsideration of
   Chapter 7 of *The Prince*." *The Review of Politics* 75 (2013): 539–56.
Nederman, Cary J. "Amazing Grace: Fortune, God, and Free Will in Machiavelli's
   Thought." *Journal of the History of Ideas* 60, no. 4 (1999): 617–38.
Niccoli, Ottavia. "Gioco, divinazione, livelli di cultura: *Il Triompho di Fortuna* di
   Sigismondo Fanti." *Rivista storica italiana* 96, no. 2 (1984): 591–99.
   Prophecy and People in Renaissance Italy. Translated by Lydia G. Cochrane.
   Princeton, NJ: Princeton University Press, 1990.

Normore, Calvin. "Future Contingents." In *The Cambridge History of Later Medieval Philosophy: From the Rediscovery of Aristotle to the Disintegration of Scholasticism, 1100–1600*, edited by Norma Kretzmann, Anthony Kenny, Jan Pinborg, and Eleonore Stump, 358–81. Cambridge: Cambridge University Press, 1982.

Oberhuber, Konrad, ed. *The Illustrated Bartsch, vol. 27: The Works of Marcantonio Raimondi and of His School*. New York: Abaris Books, 1978.

Olivieri, Achille. "'Dio' e 'fortuna' nelle *Lettere storiche* di Luigi da Porto." *Studi veneziani* 13 (1971): 253–73.

"Giuoco, gerarchie e immaginario tra Quattro e Cinquecento." In *Rituale, cerimoniale, etichetta*, edited by Sergio Bertelli and Giuliano Crifò, 163–80. Milan: Bompiani, 1985.

"Jeu et capitalisme a Venise (1530–1560)." In *Les jeux à la Renaissance*, edited by Philippe Ariès and Jean-Claude Margolin, 151–62. Paris: Librarie Philosophique J. Vrin, 1982.

Ore, Oystein. *Cardano: The Gambling Scholar*. Princeton, NJ: Princeton University Press, 1953.

Orlandi, Angela. "Note su affari e devozione nei documenti di alcuni mercanti fiorentini (1450–1550)." *Storia economica* 13, no. 3 (2010): 319–44.

Ortalli, Gherado. "The Origins of the Gambler-State: Licenses and Excises for Gaming Activities in the XIII and XIV Centuries (and the Case of Vicenza)." *Ludica* 3 (1997): 108–31.

"Lo stato e il giocatore: Lunga storia di un rapporto difficile." In *Il gioco pubblico in Italia: Storia, cultura e mercato*, edited by Giuseppe Imbucci, 33–43. Venice: Marsilio, 1999.

Otte, Enrique. "Los Botti y los Lugos." *Coloquio de Historia Canario-Americana* III Coloquio, vol. 1 (1980): 48–85.

Padgett, John F., and Paul D. McLean. "Economic Credit in Renaissance Florence." *The Journal of Modern History* 83, no. 1 (2011): 1–47.

Pallavicino, Giulio. *Inventione di Giulio Pallavicino di scriver tutte le cose accadute alli tempi suoi (1583–1589)*. Edited by Edoardo Grendi. Genoa: Sagep Editore, 1975.

Pallucchini, Rodolfo. *Gli affreschi di Paolo Veronese a Maser*, 2nd ed. Bergamo: Istituto italiano d'arti grafiche, 1943.

Palmer, Ada. "Reading Lucretius in the Renaissance." *Journal of the History of Ideas* 73, no. 3 (2012): 395–416.

Reading Lucretius in the Renaissance. Cambridge, MA: Harvard University Press, 2014.

Pandolfini, Agnolo. *Trattato del governo della famiglia*. Milan: Giovanni Silvestri, 1822.

Paolucci, A., and A. M. Maetzke. *La casa del Vasari in Arezzo*. Florence: Cassa di Risparmio di Firenze, 1988.

Parlato, Enrico. "Le allegorie nel giardino delle 'Sorti.'" In *Studi per le "Sorti": Gioco, immagini, poesia oracolare a Venezia nel Cinquecento*, edited by Paolo Procaccioli, 113–37. Treviso: Edizioni Fondazione Benetton Studi Ricerche; Rome: Viella, 2007.

Parlett, David. *A History of Card Games*. Oxford: Oxford University Press, 1991.

Patch, Howard R. *The Goddess Fortuna in Mediaeval Literature*. London: Frank Cass, 1967.

Patton, Bernardette. *Preaching Friars and Civic Ethos: Siena, 1380–1480*. London: Centre for Medieval Studies, Queen Mary and Westfield College, University of London, 1992.

Pertile, Vincenzo. "Il convento dei Carceri e gli affreschi di Giuseppe Salviati." *Rivista d'Arte* 18 (1936): 195–211.

Petrarca, Francesco. *Petrarch's Remedies for Fortune Fair and Foul*. Edited by Conrad H. Rawski. 5 vols. Bloomington: Indiana University Press, 1991.

Rime, trionfi e poesie latine. Edited by F. Neri, G. Martellòtti, E. Bianchi, and N. Sapegno. Milan: Riccardo Ricciardi, 1951.

Petti Balbi, Giovanni. "Le *nationes* italiane all'estero." In *Commercio e cultura mercantile*, edited by Franco Franceschi, Richard A. Goldthwaite, and Reinhold C. Mueller, 397–423. Treviso: Fondazione Cassamarca/Angelo Colla Editore, 2007.

Peyer, Hans Conrad. *Città e santi patroni nell'Italia medievale*. Translated by Claudia Carduff. Florence: Le Lettere, 1998.

Pezzolo, Luciano. "The Venetian Economy." In *A Companion to Venetian History, 1400–1797*, edited by Eric R. Dursteler, 255–89. Leiden: Brill, 2013.

"The *via italiana* to Capitalism." In *The Cambridge History of Capitalism*, edited by Larry Neal and Jeffrey G. Williamson, 267–313. Cambridge: Cambridge University Press, 2014.

Pignatti, Terisio, and Filippo Pedrocco. *Veronese*. 2 vols. Vol. 1. Milan: Electa, 1995.

Piron, Sylvain. "L'apparition du resicum en Méditerranée occidentale aux XIIème–XIIIème siècles." In *Pour une histoire culturelle du risque: Genèse, évolution, actualité du concept dans les sociétés occidentales*, edited by Emmanuelle Collas-Heddeland, Marianne Coudry, Odile Kammerer, Alain J. Lemaître, and Brice Martin, 59–76. Strasbourg: Éditions Histoire et Anthropologie, 2004.

Pitkin, Hanna Fenichel. *Fortune Is a Woman: Gender and Politics in the Thought of Niccolò Machiavelli*. Berkeley: University of California Press, 1984.

Pitti, Buonaccorso. *Cronica di Buonaccorso Pitti con annotazioni*. Bologna: Romagnoli dell'Acqua, 1905.

Pizan, Christine de. *The Book of the Mutability of Fortune*. Edited by Geri L. Smith. Toronto: Iter Press; Tempe: Arizona Center for Medieval and Renaissance Studies, 2017.

Pocock, J. G. A. *Virtue, Commerce, and History: Essays on Political Thought and History, Chiefly in the Eighteenth Century*. Cambridge: Cambridge University Press, 2002.

Point-Waquet, Françoise. "Les Botti: Fortunes et culture d'une famille florentine (1550–1621)." *Mélanges de l'Ecole française de Rome: Moyen-Age, Temps Modernes* 90, no. 2 (1978): 689–713.

Pontano, Giovanni. *La fortuna*. Edited by Francesco Tateo. Naples: La Scuola di Pitagora, 2012.

Porzio, Francesco. *Caravaggio e il comico: Alle origini del naturalismo*. Milan: Skira, 2017.

Prange, Sebastian R. "'Trust in God, but tie your camel first': The Economic Organization of the Trans-Saharan Slave Trade between the Fourteenth and Nineteenth Centuries." *Journal of Global History* 1, no. 2 (2006): 219–39.

Preyer, Brenda. "The Rucellai Loggia." *Mitteilungen des Kunsthistorischen Institutes in Florenz* 21, no. 2 (1977): 183–98.

"The Rucellai Palace." In *Giovanni Rucellai ed il suo Zibaldone*. 2 vols. *Vol. 2: A Florentine Patrician and His Palace*. London: Warburg Institute, 1981.

Procacci, Giuliano. "La 'fortuna' nella realtà politica e sociale del primo Cinquecento." *Belfagor* 6 (1951): 407–21.

Purdie, Rhiannon. "Dice Games and the Blasphemy of Prediction." In *Medieval Futures: Attitudes to the Future in the Middle Ages*, edited by J. A. Burrow and Ian P. Wei, 167–84. Woodbridge: Boydell Press, 2000.

Puttevils, Jeroen. "Invoking *Fortuna* and Speculating on the Future: Lotteries in the Fifteenth- and Sixteenth-Century Low Countries." *Quaderni storici* 52, no. 3 (2017): 699–725.

Puttevils, Jeroen, and Marc Deloof. "Marketing and Pricing Risk in Marine Insurance in Sixteenth-Century Antwerp." *The Journal of Economic History* 77, no. 3 (2017): 796–837.

Quinones, Ricardo J. *North/South: The Great European Divide*. Toronto: University of Toronto Press, 2016.

The Renaissance Discovery of Time. Cambridge, MA: Harvard University Press, 1972.

Renucci, Paul. "Fille ou garçon? Un singulier jeu de hasard florentin du XVIe siècle." *Revue des études italiennes* 24 (1978): 164–73.

Rizzi, Alessandra. "Gioco, disciplinamento, predicazione." *Ludica* 7 (2001): 79–96.

"Il gioco fra norma laica e proibizione religiosa: L'azione dei predicatori fra Tre e Quattrocento." In *Gioco e giustizia nell'Italia di Comune*, edited by Gherado Ortalli, 149–82. Treviso: Fondazione Benetton; Rome: Viella, 1993.

Roberti, Giorgio. *I giochi a Roma di strada e d'osteria: Dalla "Passatella" alla "Morra," dalla "Ruzzica" alla "Zecchinetta," più di 400 modi per divertirsi ricostruiscono il vivace e popolare spaccato della Roma d'una volta*. Rome: Newton Compton, 1995.

Roberts, David A. "Mystery to Mathematics Flown: Time and Reality in the Renaissance." *The Centennial Review* 19, no. 3 (1975): 136–56.

Roover, Florence Edler de. "Early Examples of Marine Insurance." *The Journal of Economic History* 5, no. 2 (1945): 172–200.

"Francesco Sassetti and the Downfall of the Medici Banking House." *Bulletin of the Business Historical Society* 17, no. 4 (1943): 65–80.

Roover, Raymond de. *San Bernardino of Siena and Sant'Antonino of Florence: The Two Great Economic Thinkers of the Middle Ages*. Boston: Baker Library, Harvard Graduate School of Business Administration, 1967.

Rorario, Girolamo. *Le opere*. Edited by Aidée Scala. Pordenone: Associazione Pordenone/Accademia San Marco, 2004.

Rospocher, Massimo. "Beyond the Public Sphere: A Historiographical Transition." In *Beyond the Public Sphere: Opinions, Publics, Spaces in Early Modern Europe*, edited by Massimo Rospocher, 9–28. Bologna: Il Mulino; Berlin: Duncker & Humblot, 2012.

Ross, Sarah Gwyneth. *The Birth of Feminism: Woman as Intellect in Renaissance Italy and England*. Cambridge, MA: Harvard University Press, 2009.

Everyday Renaissances: The Quest for Cultural Legitimacy in Venice. Cambridge, MA: Harvard University Press, 2016.

Rucellai, Bernardo. *De bello italico/La guerra d'Italia*. Edited by Donatella Coppini. Florence: Firenze University Press, 2011.

Rucellai, Giovanni. *Giovanni Rucellai ed il suo Zibaldone*. Edited by Alessandro Perosa. London: Warburg Institute, 1960.

Ruggiero, Guido. "Getting a Head in the Renaissance: Mementos of Lost Love in Boccaccio and Beyond." *Renaissance Quarterly* 67, no. 4 (2014): 1165–90.

Salomon, Xavier F. *Veronese*. London: National Gallery, 2014.

Santoro, Mario. *Fortuna, ragione e prudenza nella civiltà letteraria del Cinquecento*, 2nd ed. Naples: Liguori, 1978.

Sanuto, Marino. *I diarii di Marino Sanuto*. 58 vols. Bologna: Forni, 1970. Venice, 1896.

Sassetti, Filippo. *Lettere edite e inedite di Filippo Sassetti*. Edited by Ettore Marcucci. Florence: Felice le Monnier, 1855.

Scala, Aidée. *Girolamo Rorario: Un umanista diplomatico del Cinquecento e i suoi Dialoghi*. Florence: Olschki, 2004.

Scala, Bartolomeo. *Essays and Dialogues*. Translated by Renée Neu Watkins. Cambridge, MA: Harvard University Press, 2008.

Scher, Stephen K., ed. *The Currency of Fame: Portrait Medals of the Renaissance*. London: Thames & Hudson/The Frick Collection, 1994.

Schmidt, Suzanne Karr. *Interactive and Sculptural Printmaking in the Renaissance*. Leiden: Brill, 2018.

Schmitt, Jean-Claude. "Appropriating the Future." In *Medieval Futures: Attitudes to the Future in the Middle Ages*, edited by J. A. Burrow and Ian P. Wei, 3–18. Woodbridge: Boydell Press, 2000.

Schneider, Ivo. "The Market Place and Games of Chance in the Fifteenth and Sixteenth Centuries." In *Mathematics from Manuscript to Print, 1300–1600*, edited by Cynthia Hay, 220–35. Oxford: Oxford University Press, 1988.

Schütze, Sebastian. *Caravaggio: The Complete Works*. Cologne: Taschen, 2009.

Schwarzenburg, Erkinger. "Glovis, impresa di Giuliano de' Medici." *Mitteilungen des Kunsthistorischen Institutes in Florenz* 39, no. 1 (1995): 140–66.

Scott, Joan Wallach. *Gender and the Politics of History*, revised ed. New York: Columbia University Press, 1999.

Shaw, James E. "Market Ethics and Credit Practices in Sixteenth-Century Tuscany." *Renaissance Studies* 27, no. 2 (2013): 236–52.

Sella, Domenico, and Carlo Capra. *Il Ducato di Milano dal 1535 al 1796*. Turin: Unione Tipografico-Editrice Torinese, 1984.

Sgarbi, Vittorio. *Parmigianino*. Milan: Rizzoli/Skira, 2003.

Shaw, Brent D. "Did Romans Have a Future?" *Journal of Roman Studies* 109 (2019): 1–26.

Smith, Christine. "The Apocalypse Sent Up: A Parody of the Papacy by Leon Battista Alberti." *MLN* 119, no. 1 (2004): S162–S177.

Soll, Jacob. *The Reckoning: Financial Accountability and the Rise and Fall of Nations*. New York: Basic Books, 2014.

Sood, Gagan D. S. "'Correspondence Is Equal to Half a Meeting': The Composition and Comprehension of Letters in Eighteenth-Century Islamic Eurasia." *Journal of the Economic and Social History of the Orient* 50, nos. 2–3 (2007): 172–214.

Spike, John T. *Caravaggio*, 2nd revised ed. New York: Abbeville Press Publishers, 2010.

Stelling-Michaud, Sven. "Quelques aspects du problème du temps au moyen âge." *Schweizer Beiträge zur allgemeinen Geschichte/Études suisses d'histoire générale/Studi svizzeri di storia generale* 17 (1959): 7–30.

Strozzi, Beatrice Paolozzi, and Erkinger Schwarzenburg. "Un Kairos mediceo." *Mitteilungen des Kunsthistorischen Institutes in Florenz* 35, nos. 2–3 (1991): 307–16.

Strunck, Christina. "Pontormo und Pontano: Zu Paolo Giovios Programm für die beiden Lünettenfresken in Poggio a Caiano." *Marburger Jahrbuch für Kunstwissenschaft* 26 (1999): 117–37.

Sylla, Edith Dudley. "Business Ethics, Commercial Mathematics, and the Origins of Mathematical Probability." *History of Political Economy* 35, Annual Supplement (2003): 309–37.

Taddei, Ilaria. "Gioco d'azzardo, ribaldi e baratteria nelle città della Toscana tardo-medievale." *Quaderni storici* n.s. 92/a. 31, no. 2 (1996): 335–62.

Tamalio, Raffaele. *Federico Gonzaga alla corte di Francesco I di Francia nel carteggio privato con Mantova (1515–1517)*. Paris: Honoré Champion, 1994.

Tasso, Torquato. *Dialoghi: Edizione critica*. Edited by Ezio Raimondi. Florence: Sansoni, 1958.

Tateo, Francesco. "L'Alberti fra il Petrarca e il Pontano: La metafora della fortuna." *Albertiana* 10 (2007): 45–67.

"La prefazione originaria e le ragioni del *De fortuna* di Giovanni Pontano." *Rinascimento* Series 2, no. 47 (2007): 125–63.

Thompson, Augustine. *Cities of God: The Religion of the Italian Communes, 1125–1325*. University Park: Pennsylvania State University Press, 2005.

Todeschini, Giacomo. *Ricchezza francescana: Dalla povertà volontaria alla società di mercato*. Bologna: Il Mulino, 2004.

"Theological Roots of the Medieval/Modern Merchants' Self-Representation." In *The Self-Perception of Early Modern Capitalists*, edited by Margaret C. Jacob and Catherine Secretan, 17–46. New York: Palgrave Macmillian, 2008.

Tollebeek, Jo. "'Renaissance' and 'Fossilization': Michelet, Burckhardt, and Huizinga." *Renaissance Studies* 15, no. 3 (2001): 354–66.

Tonelli, Giovanna. "The Economy in the 16th and 17th Centuries." In *A Companion to Late Medieval and Early Modern Milan: The Distinctive Features of an Italian State*, edited by Andrea Gamberini, 142–65. Leiden: Brill, 2015.

Tracy, James D. "Syria's Arab Traders as Seen by Andrea Berengo, 1555–1556." *Oriens* 37 (2009): 163–76.

Trevisani, Filippo, ed. *Andrea Mantegna e i Gonzaga: Rinascimento nel Castello di San Giorgio*. Verona: Electa, 2006.

Trevisani, Filippo, and Davide Gasparotto, eds. *Bonacolsi l'Antico: Uno scultore nella Mantova di Andrea Mantegna e di Isabella d'Este*. Verona: Electa, 2008.

Trinkaus, Charles. "The Astrological Cosmos and Rhetorical Culture of Giovanni Gioviano Pontano." *Renaissance Quarterly* 38, no. 3 (1985): 446–72.

Trivellato, Francesca. *The Familiarity of Strangers: The Sephardic Diaspora, Livorno, and Cross-Cultural Trade in the Early Modern Period.* New Haven, CT: Yale University Press, 2009.

Trucchi, Francesco. *Poesie italiane inedite di dugento autori all'origine della lingua infino al secolo decimosettimo.* Vol. 2. Prato: Ranieri Guasti, 1846.

Tucci, Ugo. "La formazione dell'uomo d'affari." In *Commercio e cultura mercantile*, edited by Franco Franceschi, Richard A. Goldthwaite, and Reinhold C. Mueller, 481–98. Treviso: Fondazione Cassamarca/Angelo Colla Editore, 2007.

"Monete e banche nel secolo del ducato d'oro." In *Storia di Venezia dalle origini alla caduta della Serenissima*, edited by Alberto Tenenti and Ugo Tucci, 753–805. Rome: Istituto della Enciclopedia Italiana Fondata da Giovanni Treccani, 1996.

Tucci, Ugo, ed. *Lettres d'un marchand vénitian Andrea Berengo (1553–1556).* Paris: S.E.V.P.E.N., 1957.

Vasari, Giorgio. *Le opere di Giorgio Vasari con nuove annotazioni e commenti di Gaetano Milanesi*, Facsimile ed. 9 vols. Florence: Casa Editrice le Lettere, 1998.

Verde, Armando F. *Lo Studio fiorentino, 1473–1503: Ricerche e documenti, vol. 4: La vita universitaria Tomo III: Anni scolastici 1491/2–1502/3.* Florence: Olschki, 1985.

Vettori, Francesco. *Viaggio in Alemagna.* Florence, 1837.

Walker, Jonathan. "Gambling and Venetian Noblemen, c. 1500–1700." *Past and Present*, no. 162 (1999): 28–69.

Wandel, Lee Palmer. *The Reformation: Towards a New History.* Cambridge: Cambridge University Press, 2011.

Warburg, Aby. *The Renewal of Pagan Antiquity: Contributions to the Cultural History of the European Renaissance.* Translated by Caroline Beamish, David Britt, and Carol Lanham. Los Angeles: Getty Research Institute for the History of Art and the Humanities, 1999.

Weinstein, Donald. *Savonarola and Florence: Prophecy and Patriotism in the Renaissance.* Princeton, NJ: Princeton University Press, 1970.

Weissman, Ronald F. "The Importance of Being Ambiguous: Social Relations, Individualism, and Identity in Renaissance Florence." In *Urban Life in the Renaissance*, edited by Susan Zimmerman and Ronald F. Weissman, 269–80. Newark: University of Delaware Press, 1989.

Welch, Evelyn. "Lotteries in Early Modern Italy." *Past and Present*, no. 199 (2008): 71–111.

"Making Money: Pricing and Payments in Renaissance Italy." In *The Material Renaissance*, edited by Michelle O'Malley and Evelyn Welch, 71–84. Manchester: Manchester University Press, 2007.

Wiesner-Hanks, Merry E., ed. *Gendered Temporalities in the Early Modern World.* Amsterdam: Amsterdam University Press, 2018.

Wilding, Nick. "Galileo and the Stain of Time." *California Italian Studies* 2, no. 1 (2011).

Wind, Edgar. "Platonic Tyranny and the Renaissance Fortuna: On Ficino's Reading of Laws IV, 709 A-712A." In *De artibus opuscula XL: Essays in Honour of Erwn Panofsky*, edited by Millard Meiss, 491–96. New York: New York University Press, 1961.

Wittkower, Rudolf. "Chance, Time and Virtue." *Journal of the Warburg Institute* 1, no. 4 (1938): 313–21.

Zdekauer, Ludovico. *Il gioco d'azzardo nel Medioevo italiano*. Florence: Salimbeni, 1993.

Zika, Charles. *The Appearance of Witchcraft: Print and Visual Culture in Sixteenth-Century Europe*. London: Routledge, 2007.

Zorzi, Andrea. "Battagliole e giochi d'azzardo a Firenze nel tardo Medioevo: Due pratiche sociali tra disciplinamento e repressione." In *Gioco e giustizia nell'Italia di Comune*, edited by Gherado Ortalli, 71–107. Treviso: Fondazione Benetton; Rome: Viella, 1993.

Index

9 781108 826945